**ADMINISTRATION
IN THE
PUBLIC SECTOR**

# ADMINISTRATION IN THE PUBLIC SECTOR

**HAROLD F. GORTNER**
School of Public and Environmental Affairs
Indiana University

**John Wiley & Sons**
New York    Santa Barbara    London    Sydney    Toronto

Cover art after Mordillo.

*Library of Congress Cataloging in Publication Data:*

Gortner, Harold F.          1940-
    Administration in the public sector.

    Includes bibliographical references and index.
    1. Public administration. I. Title.

JF1351.G67              350              76-40084
ISBN 0-471-31891-4

Printed in the United States of America

10 9 8 7 6 5 4 3 2

TO SYLVIA

# PREFACE

Two major factors have influenced the field of public administration during the last two decades. First, there has been a decided shift in the location of most public employees and those public programs that directly affect the citizens of the United States. The major growth in public administration has occurred at the state and local levels of government. The focus, in most classrooms and most textbooks, has tended to underplay the importance of the public administrator at the "more immediate" levels of government (more immediate in the sense that actions at these levels of government have a more direct effect on our daily lives and are more easily observed by interested citizens). This textbook attempts to give proper cognizance to the increasing role of state and local public administrators within the study and practice of the discipline.

Second, public administrators are increasingly recognized as actors playing a unique role in our democratic system. They must understand and use the functions of management in guiding the complex public organization; at the same time, they must understand and know how to operate within the political system and the public policy process, because the public agency exists in a political environment. This textbook was specifically prepared with this apparent dichotomy in mind, for these two opposing, yet intermingling, forces must be the focus of any realistic text on public administration. The first part of the book considers the political environment in which the organization exists and the public administrator works. Although the public administrator is a manager, he must work with and for politicians, and this means that it is essential to understand the way that politicians think about and react to the society around them. The second part of this textbook deals with the functions of management from the viewpoint of the public administrator. As the manager of the organization, he or she is responsible for the efficiency and effectiveness of the public agency as it spends the citizens' money. Each chapter focuses on a particular function of management and points out the impact of the political system on the decisions of the public administrator and the actions of the public agency.

A third aspect of the field of public administration must be considered, even though it is more specialized, because of its centrality to the entire field of study and operation; this aspect is the place of the two staff functions of personnel administration and financial administration. The third part of the text discusses the place of these two functions in the overall administrative operation, and it specifically deals with the recent political forces that are influencing these areas of public administration.

Many modern books on public administration have become so involved in describing public policy that the management of public affairs has been overlooked; this text attempts to restore a balanced perspective of the interacting processes. Such a balance is essential to an understanding of public administration.

There are several individuals whom I wish to recognize because of their assistance, at various times and in various ways, while this book was being written. During the formative stages of the manuscript, Roy Young and Ted Norton, two of my colleagues at San Jose State University, gave me a great deal of encouragement and reviewed some of the early material. The completed manuscript was reviewed by Tom Henderson, Kentucky State Government; Ronald Schmidt, California State University, Long Beach; and Dean Yarwood, University of Missouri. Their comments and suggestions were exceedingly useful and helped to strengthen the impact and the rationality of the text. John Hunger, my colleague within the School of Public and Environmental Affairs, has given me a great deal of encouragement, and he has reviewed several of the chapters during the final stages of the work. Three individuals, Richard Delong, city manager of Mountain View, California; Robert Farnquist, city of San Jose, California; and Ann McFarren, Planned Parenthood Association of Northwest Indiana, Inc. have cooperated in the preparation of the case studies included in the book. Kathie

Marlatt typed some of the original manuscript while I was at San Jose State University. I express my gratitude to each of these people. Above all, I thank my daughter, Maryanne, for her patience, and my wife, Sylvia, who has been typist, proofreader, and research assistant throughout the writing of this book.

HAROLD F. GORTNER

# CONTENTS

# ADMINISTRATION
# IN THE
# PUBLIC SECTOR

# THE SUBSTANCE OF PUBLIC ADMINISTRATION

*Energy in the Executive is a leading character in the definition of good government.*

*Alexander Hamilton*

The success of a government rests as much on the way the public bureaucracy functions as on any other part of the governmental system. George Washington recognized this fact immediately after becoming president when he began to set up the original national bureaucracy. When asking for nominees for the various positions that were to be filled, Washington used a strict rule of fitness, for he observed that

if injudicious or unpopular measures should be taken by the Executive under the New Government with regards to appointments, the Govern-

# CHAPTER 1

ment itself would be in the utmost danger of being subverted by those measures.[1]

During the hundred years following Washington's presidency, both politicians and scholars appeared to lose sight of the importance of the public bureaucracy, and it was not until the latter part of the nineteenth century that the role of the bureaucracy was again recognized. This recognition began with Woodrow Wilson; most scholars trace the birth of the study now called public administration to Wilson's pioneer article entitled "The Study of Administration" which appeared in 1887.[2] Since its origin, the field of public administration has been one of the most dynamic disciplines in the educational field, outstripped only by the changes and demands that have befallen the practitioners of the discipline. Dramatic changes have occurred in our perception of what comprises public administration and in what the role of the bureaucracy is within the government. During the last few decades, there has been a meteoric rise in the importance of the governmental bureaucracy; as public administration has become a more significant part of everyone's life, there has been a reciprocal increase in the attempt to understand the phenomenon. By defining the subject being discussed and by noting how that definition has changed during its century of existence, it is possible to comprehend the dynamic nature of the field of public administration.

## DEFINITION OF PUBLIC ADMINISTRATION

Administration has existed since humans first banded together in prehistoric times. Those who examine any of the physical monuments of history or study the governments of prior civilizations are really taking note of the successful results of the bureaucracy of that day. The pyramids of Egypt were built by an extensive public bureaucracy, as was the British Empire, although in each case it is likely that if the heroes of that period were questioned, they would claim that success came *in spite of* the bureaucracy. Public administrators have formed one of the most essential groups in society, but often they have not been given proper credit for their role in shaping the success of the other participants.

The role of the bureaucracy was no less important in the United States during the first century of its existence. The impact of George Washington and the Federalists was heightened by the type of individuals whom they chose to run the administration; the high quality of the civil servants undoubtedly helped to consolidate the opinion of the people behind the fledgling government. Also, it is true that the public's opinion of the civil service changed drastically when the spoils system developed during and after the administration of Andrew Jackson. Political economists, who were the forerunners of political scientists, did not

---

[1] Quoted in Leonard D. White, *The Federalists: A Study in Administrative History*, MacMillan, New York, 1956, p. 258.

[2] Woodrow Wilson, "The Study of Administration," *Political Science Quarterly, II* 197-222 (June 1887).

appear to recognize the importance of the bureaucracy, and little information can be found among the early literature on American politics that deals with the workings of the administrative branches of government.[3] During the latter part of the nineteenth century, a growing outcry against the spoils system led to an ·increasing interest in the public bureaucracy, and this growing interest was catalyzed by Woodrow Wilson's distinguished appeal to recognize public administration as worthy of scholarly study. In his article entitled "The Study of Administration," Wilson argued simply and directly that

. . . no practical science is ever studied where there is no need to know it. The very fact, therefore, that the eminently practical science of administration is finding its way into the college courses in this country would prove that this country needs to know more about administration, were such proof of the fact required to make out a case.[4]

Although most people agreed with Wilson as to the need of studying the "science of administration" within the government, the actual development of the discipline moved forward slowly. Nearly forty years passed before public administration, as a field of study, developed to a point where Leonard White wrote the first textbook for college use.[5] Since 1926, when White's text was published, public administration has been recognized as a legitimate field of study, with most of the major colleges and universities in the United States offering degrees to interested students and practitioners.

How can the field of public administration be defined? In actuality, this entire text deals with this question, for each segment of the book attempts to define in greater detail the complexities of what public administration is and what public administrators do. Any attempt to define public administration in a single sentence would be inadequate because of the complexity of the field. However, it is necessary to start with some common basis upon which it will be possible to continue the discussion. For this purpose, let us say that public administration involves *the coordination of all organized activity, having as its purpose the implementation of public policy.* Such a definition has two major parts. The first portion (the coordination of organized activity) is common to all administrative endeavors, whether in a private or public organization. The second segment of the definition (implementation of public policy) is the key factor within the phrase. The involvement of the public administrator with the political world creates a unique environment that is not shared in the same way by administrators in any other type of organization. A closer examination of these two

[3] Perhaps the best discussion of administration in the young United States was written by Alexis de Tocqueville in his work *Democracy in America*, of which several editions exist.

[4] Wilson, p. 197.

[5] Leonard D. White, *Introduction to the Study of Public Administration*, MacMillan, New York, 1926.

aspects of our definition will help to clarify the particular role of the public administrator in a democratic society.

## The Coordination of Organized Activity

Administration implies that there is an organization. There is no need for the skills used by an administrator unless a group of people have banded together. An organization is made up of two or more people who have combined their efforts in an attempt to achieve a commonly sought goal. Normally, the people will have combined their efforts because they could not separately achieve the goal being sought or they could achieve a greater level of satisfaction through cooperation. The complexity of the organizations in society varies dramatically from that of a husband and wife in the organization called a family to that of the modern hospital, police department, or military force. A family is an organization in which the individuals involved (husband and wife) have made a decision to combine many, perhaps most, of the activities in their lives in the hope that, together, they may attain certain goals that would be unreachable on an individual basis. The family is one of the most simple organizations, yet an intricate pattern of interactions is involved in this "simple" organization; everyone is aware of the high mortality rate among such enterprises. These facts point out two additional elements of organization. First, organizations are always open to numerous results (only a few of which were originally intended or recognized as possible). Unless some kind of leadership is present, an organization may end up far from its intended goal. Second, it is important to recognize that organizations have a life cycle similar to that of living organisms. Organizations are created, or born, they generally go through a period of growth, they may achieve a position of maturity, and, finally, they may die. Organizations may be temporary—established to accomplish a single goal or set of goals, after which the organization is disbanded—or they may be considered permanent, with no one foreseeing an end to their existence.

By examining simpler organizations, it is possible to get an overview of the factors that compose more complex organizations. However, by the time an administrator gets involved in coordinating activities, the structure and functions of the group may have changed dramatically. A simple grouping of individuals does not require much coordination, but as larger numbers of people get involved, the technological skills used in the organization usually increase in number and complexity. Thus, the manager finds that he or she is heading a "complex organization," which is *a formal, structured system of roles and functional relationships designed to accomplish preordained goals.* It is important to notice in the definition just given that nothing is said about people. Complex organizations are made up of *positions and roles attached to the positions.* Although people fill the positions, the modern organization is not attached to any particular individual. The organization has a continuity beyond any individual or group of individuals. This is not true of simple organizations, such as the family; however, a city government or the state revenue department can and does survive numerous changes in the individuals who fill the assigned roles of particular positions.[6] Most modern public administrators coordinate complex organizations and thus need the heightened skills required of leaders in such radically changing organizations. A major portion of this book deals with the role of the public administrator in his or her attempt to coordinate and direct the public bureaucracy.

The general administrative side of the public administrator does not vary greatly from the role played by the manager of an enterprise in the private sector of the economy. Most of the managerial theories that are currently accepted as valid may be used by public or private officials because the ideas are based on relatively universal concepts about human beings. This commonality between public and private administration has been recognized since the very beginning of the public administration movement. In fact, Wilson accepted the fact that "the field of administration is a field of business,"[7] and Leonard D. White, in his first text on the subject, commented that "public administration is . . . the execution of the public business."[8] Earlier, Frank Goodnow published a book entitled *Politics and Administration*, in which the central theme was that public administrators were not, and should not be, involved in politics; they were to manage the "business of government" according to the principles being applied to the successful businesses of the day.[9] Regardless of the way that public administration was defined or discussed during the years between Wilson's original call for study and the first text published by White, it was taken for granted that the bureaucrats were to be totally separated from politics. By the time White wrote his text, he was willing to recognize that his definition, "public administration is the management of men and materials in the accomplishment of the purposes of the state," did not deal with the political side of the question; he also recognized that public administration could not be totally separated from politics, for he conceded that

it (White's definition of public administration) leaves open the question to what extent the administration itself participates in formulating the purposes of the state, and avoids any controversy as to the precise nature of administrative action.[10]

---

[6] This does not mean that the individuals in the various positions do not affect the organization's success in meeting its goals. They do! But it is important here to point out the formal side of the organization. The interlocking characteristic of the formal and informal side of the organization will be discussed in the third part of this book.

[7] Wilson, p. 209. To quote him more completely: "The field of administration is a field of business. It is removed from the hurry and strife of politics . . . Administrative questions are not political questions" pp. 209-210.

[8] White, p. 4.

[9] Frank Goodnow, *Politics and Administration*, MacMillan, New York, 1900.

[10] White, p. 2.

It is now a commonly accepted idea that the public administrator's role is not only that of carrying out the policy mandated by the legislature but also that of being an active participant in making the policy in the first place.

### The Implementation of Public Policy

Although an argument can be made for the similarity of management tasks in both public and private organizations, there are also differences. These differences need to be emphasized just as the similarities must be acknowledged. Since most of the differences occur because of the role played by public policy in public administration, it is necessary to define what is meant by the term "public policy." It can be succinctly defined as *the desired goals that have been established by the polity,* which refers to the politically organized community. Each individual or organization has some specific situation, or state of being, that he, she, or it wishes to achieve, both now and at some point in the future. That situation is a goal, whether it is the personal situation of Jane Smith being the first woman president or a sociopolitical situation of every citizen being equal before the law without regard to race, creed, sex, economic station, or national origin. In the case of *public* policy, one is dealing specifically with those goals or objectives that have been established, *through the political process*, by *all or part of the citizens* in a particular governmental jurisdiction.[11] Thus, public policy answers the question of what the public administrator and the public bureaucracy are supposed to do. However, if the bureaucracy is going to serve the public in a manner that is acceptable to society, one more factor must be considered as implicit in the definition. Public policy often not only describes the *substance* of what is to be done but also describes the *process* by which it is to be done. In a democratic state where the political system is founded on the philosophy of the inherent value of each individual, not only must public policy take into consideration what the final objective of any action is but also how that action will affect each citizen as the object is being attained. It is this constant concern with the substance and process of citizen desires that creates a different environment for the public administrator.

## PUBLIC VERSUS PRIVATE ADMINISTRATION

There are several characteristics that make public administration unique when compared to business administration. It is important, however, to remember that in all of the cases discussed, the differences are a matter of degree; in no case are the differences of an absolute nature. Perhaps this point can best be described by the policy continuum shown in Figure 1. Most businesses and government agencies fall into the areas toward the center and away from the extreme ends of the

---

[11] This definition of public policy attempts to deal only with democratic states although the discussion may be applicable to all political systems. It is important to note that public policy is set through the interaction of the *politically* active citizens of a society.

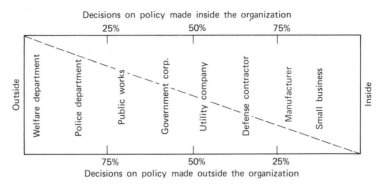

**Figure 1**

Policymaking continuum. The various organizations are placed on the continuum according to the amount of interference each receives from inside or
outside while attempting to make the major policy decisions that influence what
the organization does and how it carries out that service. No organization falls
at either extreme of the continuum. Welfare departments are highly political
agencies, with outside groups constantly watching every action taken. Small
neighborhood businesses that do not depend in any way on government contracts
or support are relatively independent, although the government reserves the
power of regulation in certain ways. There is a gray area toward the center. In
particular cases there may be some government corporations with a bit more
flexibility (internal control) than some utilities, but generally the position of the
organizations is as pictured.

continuum, with business tending to fall more toward the right end of the
spectrum.

One of the differences that exists between public and private administration,
and that sometimes creates intense frustration among government employees, is
caused by the fact that goals may be established for the bureaucracy by other
parts of the political system and then forced upon the administrative branch. In
most cases, these goals may create no problems, and all parties may be satisfied
with the results. However, if the goals of government are set outside the bureaucracy, occasionally the policies are going to be unrealistic or repugnant to the
bureaucracy. The public is going to expect something different from the bureaucracy than that which can be delivered, or they may set goals that are higher
than those that can be achieved. Since the goals are unattainable, the public may
be dissatisfied with the performance of the bureaucracy. At the same time, the
bureaucrats will probably become frustrated and bitter because of the lack of
understanding on the part of the public and other segments of the political
system. In a private organization, the policies are usually internally determined,
and they could be internally revoked or changed if they proved inappropriate.
This is not so in a public agency, which may have some control over the policies

it is administering but which always faces the possibility of having its policies adopted and maintained by outside parties.[12]

A second difference between public and private administration that must be noted involves the type of services generally delivered by the government. Most businesses operate in a relatively competitive market. Those that do not are usually controlled by government regulation; therefore, they are more like public agencies. If a business operates in a competitive market, its customers have a choice: they may refuse to accept the products or services of one organization and turn to another organization that more satisfactorily meets their needs. The element of choice forces the competing businesses to maintain the efficiency and quality of their operations in order to survive. Most operations carried out by governmental organizations, however, are monopolistic in nature. The government is the only organization offering the service, and the people generally *cannot refuse to use the service.* In other words, they have no choice.[13]

The fact that the public has no choice is not necessarily bad. There are many services that should be delivered by the government as the only acceptable body to control those services. For instance, the delivery of police service should be handled by the government. In spite of the complaints that are continuously registered against the police, no thoughtful citizen would prefer to place complete trust in a police force that was controlled by a private organization, one that offered its services to the highest bidder, or one that had to operate at a profit in order to continue in existence. Each of these particular situations presents grave problems for equity and honesty in service. The best answer appears to be that of allowing the government to deliver the service. The problem that is created when the government is delivering a monopoly service is that pressure for efficiency and quality may not exist in the same way that it does in business. This does not mean that there is no pressure for quality of service. The pressure does not come from a fear for survival; rather, it comes from public demands, com-

---

[12]The comments in this section are couched in extreme language in order to point out the differences between public and private administration. Of course, the public bureaucracy has a tremendous impact upon the public policy that it administers, both in the policy formulation stage and its implementation stage; still, the problem that is dealt with in this particular paragraph does exist and has caused serious rifts between different segments of the government and other parts of the political system (such as the political parties) in the past.

[13]This discussion does not attempt to examine the problems of which level of government should deliver the service, what the size of the area served by a particular department should be, or how much "citizen participation" should exist. Those are questions that are secondary to the major issue at hand. It can be argued that an individual citizen *can* refuse a public service. For example, a citizen may refuse to have his garbage picked up by the city's scavenger service and dispose of the garbage himself, or a citizen may refuse to call for the police department's help when his house is ransacked; however, these citizens *cannot* refuse to pay for such services although they may not use them. In many other cases, it is impossible to refuse to accept public services even if they are not desired by the recipient. For example, a citizen, when he receives a ticket for speeding or illegal parking, cannot refuse to accept the "service" of a traffic policeman.

petition with other public agencies that are fulfilling other needs for society, and internal commitment to the goals of the organization.

Third, the problem of measuring efficiency and success in operation is further complicated by the fact that the public agencies do not possess the one yardstick of achievement that is common to all businesses—*profits*. Regardless of the goals that a business may have, and they are numerous, the ultimate goal of a business is to make money—to show a profit, or return, on investment. In fact, if this is not the reason for an organization's existence, it should not be classified as a business but should fall into some other category of organization. On the other hand, public agencies do not have profit as a primary goal. Usually, profit is not a criteria used in measuring the success or failure of a public agency because profit is irrelevant to the goals of the organization.[14] Many activities are carried out by governmental agencies primarily because there is no chance to make a profit while delivering that particular service. If the service is profitable, private industry will raise the question as to whether or not the government is invading the realm of private enterprise.

Fourth, since the public bureaucracy is involved in implementing public policy, usually through monopolistic means, and since it is difficult to measure the success or failure of the enterprise, public administrators generally find themselves in a visible and vulnerable position. The technical problems of the TFX airplane bring about a flurry of public and congressional discussion, while the failure of the Edsel is shrugged off as a "poor business decision" with no public discussion of the millions of dollars lost on this business venture. Citizens, as taxpayers and recipients of the services, tend to watch the public bureaucracy more carefully than they observe private enterprise (although the amount of surveillance of private enterprise seems to be increasing rapidly).

Fifth, the closer scrutiny of public administrative actions by the public and by other governmental organs leads to another difference between public and private bureaucrats. Public administrators must be able to justify their actions if at any time those actions are challenged by clients, the public, or other governmental agencies or branches. In order to protect themselves, public administrators tend to view the available alternatives from a perspective similar to that held in the Roman legal system—it is only possible to do something if the law specifically grants that privilege. Administrators in the private sector, on the other hand, can usually operate under the common law perception that any action is legal unless specifically forbidden by law. The difference in freedom of action will become apparent after short consideration. This does not mean that public administrators cannot choose to operate and make decisions under the broader interpretation of the law, but if they choose to interpret the guidelines more loosely, there is a distinct chance that the failure of a decision may bring public displeasure to bear without any legal support for the decision that was made. It takes a brave or foolish person to act in such a manner. Such people do

---

[14] Government corporations may consider profits when making policy decisions, but they are *quasi-public* in their essence.

exist in the public bureaucracy, but the point is that all the pressure tends toward caution and legal justification for action.

Finally, such close scrutiny of public administrative action means that the public administrator must always be prepared to defend any action that is taken and be able to trace the action from its beginning to its end. The need for justification and accountability is one of the major causes of "red tape" in the public bureaucracy. Red tape is a phenomenon that is inherent to any bureaucracy, but the added weight of the public scrutiny that exists for the government organization leads to the emphasis on triplicate copies and voluminous paperwork that often exists in government. We often decry red tape, but there appears to be no way to escape it if the goals of objectivity in service and accountability. for actions are to remain central to the public bureaucracy.

## THE PUBLIC BUREAUCRACY IN A DEMOCRACY

If bureaucracy is inefficient, and if public bureaucracies are even more inefficient than private bureaucracies, then why not do away with them and set up a different structure to carry out the public's services and needs? To paraphrase Winston Churchill, the answer must be that "Bureaucracy is the most inefficient system for organizing people known to man except for *all* of the other systems." With all of its faults (many of which will be discussed in this book), it is still the most efficient structure that has yet been discovered when attempting to coordinate the actions of large groups of people toward a specific goal. In fact, Peter Blau argues that antagonism toward bureaucracy usually results from the ruthless efficiency of bureaucracy, not its inefficiency.[15] The reason that people become antagonistic is because the bureaucracy is efficient in carrying out its task *as defined by the bureaucracy*; when people rebel, they are upset by the bureaucracy's impersonal objectivity and efficiency, for it tends not to recognize human and individual characteristics.

When the efficiency of bureaucracy is attached to the public sphere and the goal of the bureaucracy is to carry out public policy, it is doubly important that accountability be built into the system. Max Weber points out that bureaucracy is a power instrument of the first order *for the one who controls the bureaucratic apparatus.*[16] In a democracy, "the people" must have some way of controlling the bureaucracy or it is very likely that the bureaucracy will end up

---

[15] Peter M. Blau and Marshall W. Meyer, *Bureaucracy in Modern Society*, Second Edition, Random House, New York, 1971, pp. 148-151.

[16] Max Weber, *The Theory of Social and Economic Organization*, trans. and eds., A. M. Henderson and Talcott Parsons, Oxford, New York, 1947.

holding the reins of power in its own hands.[17] Thus, one of the major questions that must be faced when studying public administration is, "In a democracy how can the public bureaucracy be controlled so that it serves the people?"[18] This question must remain in the forefront of any deliberation regardless of the aspect of public administration that is being examined. If there is to be public control of public administration, it is probable that some of the inefficiency and red tape that citizens complain about will have to be accepted as inevitable. It is essential to examine all of the practices carried out by the public bureaucracy for both efficiency and accountability. Both questions must be given equal consideration, for the public bureaucracy is one of the most central and vital parts of the political system.

## SUMMARY

One of the major factors that determines the success of any government is the way in which the public bureaucracy functions; however, this view was not widely accepted during the first century of our country's existence. Widespread acceptance of public administration as a field of study, and as a profession, has occurred only during the last fifty years. If *public* administration is to be studied with understanding, it is essential to define the field and to compare it to *private* administration.

Public administration involves the coordination of all organized activity and has as its purpose the implementation of public policy. Thus, a public manager heads a "complex organization" which is a formal, structured system of roles and functional relationships designed to accomplish preordained goals. The goals, in this case, are public policy, which is the set of desired goals that has been established by the polity.

Public administration and private administration overlap in many respects; however, among the several important differences that do exist are the following: (1) goals are often established by other parts of the political system that are outside the control of the administrators; (2) the services delivered by government usually are established as monopolies; therefore, citizens cannot refuse to use the services; (3) profit is not an important measurement of success in government organizations; (4) public agencies tend to be more closely scrutinized by society than are private businesses; (5) public administrators tend to interpret their legal foundation for existence, and for operation, more narrowly than do

---

[17] For a pointed commentary on the power of the public bureaucracy when it is uncontrolled, see: Milovan Djilas, *The New Class: An Analysis of the Communist System*, Praeger, New York, 1957.

[18] Charles Hyneman, *Bureaucracy in a Democracy*, Harper and Row, New York, 1950.

private administrators; and (6) all of these lead to "bureaucratic red tape." These differences must be understood if the functioning of the public bureaucracy is to be studied and influenced toward serving the citizens of the democracy.

# BIBLIOGRAPHY

Caiden, Gerald E., *The Dynamics of Public Administration: Guidelines to Current Transformations in Theory and Practice,* Holt, Rinehart and Winston, New York, 1971.

Caldwell, Lynton K., *The Administrative Theories of Hamilton and Jefferson,* University of Chicago, Chicago, 1944.

Charlesworth, James C., ed., *Theory and Scope of Public Administration: Scope, Objectives and Methods,* Monograph 8, American Academy of Political and Social Sciences, Philadelphia, 1968.

Davy, Thomas J., "Public Administration as a Field of Study in the United States," *International Review of Administrative Sciences, LXIV,* 63-78 (June 1962).

Dimock, Marshall E., "The Study of Public Administration," *American Political Science Review, XXXI,* 28-40 (February 1937).

Gaus, John M., Leonard D. White, and Marshall E. Dimock, *The Frontiers of Public Administration,* University of Chicago, Chicago, 1936.

Goodnow, Frank, *Politics and Administration,* MacMillan, New York, 1900.

Herring, E. Pendleton, *Public Administration and the Public Interest,* Russell and Russell, New York, 1936.

Marini, Frank, ed., *Toward a New Public Administration: The Minnowbrook Perspective,* Chandler, Scranton, Penn., 1971.

Martin, Roscoe C., ed., *Public Administration and Democracy,* Syracuse University, Syracuse, N.Y., 1965.

McCurdy, Howard E., *Public Administration: A Bibliography,* College of Public Affairs, The American University, Washington, D.C., 1972.

Murray, Michael A., "Comparing Public and Private Management: An Exploratory Essay," *Public Administration Review, XXXV,* 364-371 (July-August, 1975).

Redford, Emmette S., *Ideal and Practice in Public Administration,* University of Alabama, University, 1958.

Simon, Herbert A., Donald W. Smithburg, and Victor A. Thompson, *Public Administration,* Knopf, New York, 1950.

Stein, Harold, ed., *Public Administration and Policy Development, A Casebook,* Harcourt Brace Jovanovich, New York, 1952.

Stillman, Richard J. II, "Woodrow Wilson and the Study of Administration: A

New Look at an Old Essay," *American Political Science Review, LXVII,* 582-588 (June 1973).

Waldo, Dwight, *The Administrative State,* Ronald Press, New York, 1948.

Waldo, Dwight, *The Study of Public Administration,* Random House, New York, 1955.

Waldo, Dwight, *Public Administration in a Time of Turbulence,* Chandler, Scranton, Penn., 1971.

White, Leonard D., *Introduction to the Study of Public Administration,* MacMillan, New York, 1926.

White, Leonard D., *The Federalists,* MacMillan, New York, 1948.

White, Leonard D., *The Jeffersonians,* MacMillan, New York, 1951.

White, Leonard D., *The Jacksonians,* MacMillan, New York, 1954.

White, Leonard D., *The Republican Era,* MacMillan, New York, 1958.

Wilson, Woodrow, "The Study of Administration," *Political Science Quarterly, II,* 197-222 (June 1887).

Yarwood, Dean L., *The National Administrative System: Selected Readings,* Wiley, New York, 1971.

# COMPETING TO EXIST

*Nothing is so permanent as a temporary government bureau.*
*Nothing is so permanent as a temporary tax.*
*Nothing is so permanent as a temporary university building.*

*Variations on a Theme*

Government organizations have great similarities in structure, program emphasis, staffing, and procedures; yet each organization is quite unique when it is examined more closely. Even when two organizations appear to be identical upon first consideration—for example, police departments in contiguous middle-class suburbs—closer scrutiny points out contrasts that not only lead to different

# CHAPTER 2

procedures but also indicate quite divergent departmental goals. In order to understand the peculiarities of each organization, it is essential to examine the "life history" of that bureau or agency and to note the crucial or formative occurrences that have led to the particular adaptation that is currently observable; in the case of each organization, just as is true with individuals, the resulting entity is unprecedented and unduplicatable.

Although there may still be controversy in some quarters of society about Darwin's theory of evolution as it applies to biological entities, when it is applied to governmental organizations there is little debate. Agencies of government go through a life cycle, and in their political world, the law is "survival of the fittest." The debate in public affairs primarily centers around the elements that constitute "fitness" in a public agency and the way to measure fitness in a system that does not have the measurement devices that are available in the private sphere of society. The life cycle of public organizations closely resembles that of biological entities; therefore, in this chapter, we shall examine the four major phases of organizational life: bureaucratic genesis; bureaucratic growth; bureaucratic maturity; and bureaucratic death.

## BUREAUCRATIC GENESIS

Public organizations come into being because someone in the society believes that a problem exists and that it should be handled by a public agency. This individual or group serves as a promoter for the development of a new public program to take care of the problem; however, such a procedure is almost certain to generate counterpressures, for the essence of politics is the fact that at least two sides exist on almost every issue. Such a situation guarantees a battle, which will occur simultaneously at several levels of political debate and action. First, there will almost certainly be a debate as to whether or not the problem actually exists. Second, the philosophical question of the government's rightful role in handling particular issues will usually be invoked within the overall debate. Third, a vigorous controversy will undoubtedly occur in reference to the structures, processes, and controls that should be established as the program is brought into existence. Each of these issues is intertwined with the other two, but it is necessary to consider them separately.

Most problems are initially recognized by only a few persons. They begin to write and talk about those problems with varied levels of success. Senator George Norris advocated the development of the Tennessee Valley Authority, with its concept of total development of the resources of a geographic area, for years before the idea became acceptable or interesting to a very large segment of Congress.[1] On the other hand, Ralph Nader published his book, *Unsafe at Any Speed*, and immediately saw a groundswell of public reaction that led to the development of automobile safety standards.[2] Problems may be recognized, and

---

[1] Bertram Gross, *The Legislative Struggle*, McGraw-Hill, New York, 1953, p. 196.

[2] Ralph Nader, *Unsafe at Any Speed*, Grossman, New York, 1965.

solutions proposed, from either inside or outside of the government; in the cases just mentioned, it is interesting to note that the issue raised outside of the government received the greater immediate attention and quicker action. The initial recognition of problems usually occurs among individuals who are close to the problems because of their professional interest, their close proximity while carrying out their job, or their personal involvement. Many programs are suggested by public bureaucrats who recognize new difficulties or problems that have not been solved by current efforts. Social workers have been instrumental in initiating numerous welfare reforms and programs; likewise, corrections officials are often the leading proponents of new rehabilitation programs for criminals.

The most difficult part of this educational process may be convincing the public that a problem exists. On any particular issue, the public tends to be largely uninformed; usually the issue is of no interest to most people unless they are personally affected by it. The battle between the United Farm Workers and the Teamsters Union for the right to represent the farm laborers of California is the most important issue in the world to those who are involved in the struggle. To the average Californian in a major metropolitan area, the issue is a peripheral item that is brought to his or her attention by pickets outside a grocery store or through the latest pronouncements on the news or in a newspaper editorial. It is doubtful that the average citizen, who does not live in California, wishes to know about the conflict. The resolution of the conflict through a state labor relations law for farm workers is hardly noticed by most of the citizens of the United States.[3]

Therefore, the battle over the validity and scope of any problem is usually carried out by a relatively small group of interested parties. While the proponents try to make the strongest case possible for the importance of the problem, the opponents will be just as diligently attempting to show that the problem, as defined by the proponents, is not a problem at all, or that the problem is of such a narrow scope that it should not be dealt with by the government. Even now there are opponents to the automobile safety standards that have been established in response to Ralph Nader's criticism of the automobile industry. These opponents point to the continuing rise in deaths and injuries on the highways, the cost of the safety systems, and the practice by many drivers of subverting and bypassing these devices as evidence that the American public is not interested in Nader's charges of negligence and danger. Similar debates center around most public programs, especially during the period when the programs are being considered but have not yet been established.

The second level of debate involves philosophical questions that have been the center of controversy since the founding of our nation. Alexander Hamilton

---

[3] Edward J. Walsh, "Milestone in California: Farmworkers and Their Elections," *Commonweal, CII,* 325-326, (August 15, 1975). See also: "California Compromise," *Time, CV,* 18 (May 19, 1975).

wished to involve the national government in economic matters so that manufacturers would be encouraged to develop the industrial potential of the new country; Thomas Jefferson believed that the "backbone" of the democracy was the landowner and the agrarian citizen. He opposed governmental intervention and supported instead a strong individualistic tradition. These two traditions have continued down through the 200 years of our nation's existence, with every major governmental program being sworn to, or sworn at, under the banner of these two philosophies. Economic regulation was opposed on the grounds that government regulation would destroy competition; it was supported on the grounds that regulation would maintain and increase competition by protecting the small, independent business. In a similar manner, the debate over the welfare programs has focused around these two philosophies. Proponents of welfare programs argue that the government has accepted the responsibility of maintaining citizens at a minimum level of subsistence; in addition, citizens have the individual right to demand financial aid from the government when they are unable, for any reason, to earn an adequate income. Opponents of welfare programs argue that the government is not the guarantor of a minimum level of subsistence for all citizens; rather, the government establishes the rules within which individuals can compete for the resources of society. Opponents also maintain that the growth of welfare programs and the rise in benefits kill individual initiative, both among the recipients who find it easier to remain on welfare than to find work and among the working taxpayers who find ever larger portions of their earnings going into taxes to pay for the welfare programs. Thus, the two philosophies of governmental responsibility and individual rights are enjoined on almost every issue that leads to new government programs and agencies.

During the debate over the importance of the problem, several proposals for solution may be presented. Some of these will include government action. In the meantime, if an issue does not fade away, it is likely that some organized groups will develop an interest in the problem. At the local level, it is common for advocates of a special project to approach the service clubs, such as the Kiwanis or Rotary clubs, or to present the idea to church groups, the Parents and Teachers Association, or the Chamber of Commerce, in an effort to gain support. This activity will narrow the alternatives under consideration to a relatively small number of proposals that fall within the acceptable limits of the political system.

At this point, the issue begins to receive legislative consideration; it also enters into the third phase where structures, processes, and controls are debated. When the legislature begins to consider the proposal, the style of debate shifts, with the shift often causing difficulties for the interested groups. As Simon, Smithburg, and Thompson point out,

The evolution of concrete proposals will . . . usually reveal that the various groups interested in the problem and agreed that action is needed are not agreed as to the precise form of action. Hence, an intricate process of compromise will generally follow, designed to discover a proposal that will retain the interest of diverse groups and that will receive the support of enough of them to give it a chance of legislative success.[4]

New programs are generally proposed and supported by individuals who Anthony Downs refers to as "zealots," people who are such ardent supporters of the program that they become rigid in their approach to the problem and its solution.[5] To these people, any revision of the proposal that they support is unacceptable because they are convinced that their proposal is logically and technically complete; therefore, any compromises or changes will render the program less effective. In the political world, however, compromise is often a necessary ingredient for legislative success; most major legislation—legislation establishing new programs or bureaus—seldom passes in its original form; in fact, it may bear little resemblance to the original proposal in either purpose or structure.

Advocates of new programs who are wise in the ways of politics recognize the necessity of bargaining and compromise; consequently, they attempt to prepare for exactly such a process. Again quoting Simon, Smithburg, and Thompson, they suggest that

it is important for the initiators to recognize in advance the areas from which opposition is likely to arise and to develop means for coping with such opposition. It is also necessary to have clear objectives so that compromises can be accepted gracefully when they do not endanger the major objectives envisaged. It is often possible after an agency has become established to strengthen by amendment provisions in its basic legislation that had to be compromised when it was first set up . . .[6]

As the necessity for labor relations organizations became obvious, several states established boards to hold representation elections and to carry out fact-finding, mediation, or arbitration when negotiations were deadlocked. In almost every case, the structure, processes, and powers of these state boards were established through a series of compromises, resulting in agencies that totally satisfied none of the interested parties—including those within the new agencies. However, the organizations exist and are able to go about their tasks, and it is possible to amend the structure, processes, and powers of these agencies as the need becomes apparent.

The fate of the new program, and the organization that will carry out that program, ultimately rests in the legislature; it is there that the law that estab-

---

[4] Herbert A. Simon, Donald W. Smithburg, and Victor A. Thompson, *Public Administration*, Knopf, New York, 1950, p. 36.

[5] Anthony Downs, *Inside Bureaucracy*, Little, Brown, Boston, 1967, pp. 5-7.

[6] Simon, Smithburg, and Thompson, p. 36.

lishes the structure, processes, and powers of the agency is hammered out. The battle between advocates and opponents of a program may lead to the development of a monster, a normal, healthy organization, or a stillborn agency (one that fails to operate properly from the time it comes into existence). Proponents of a new program often try to protect the agency by building into the law an extended description of the new organization's structure; at the same time, opponents may attempt to build structures that they believe will be detrimental to the program in hope that the program will fail or that the necessity of amendments to the enabling legislation will allow renewed attacks on the program. In either case, most legislators are amateurs at developing and administering government bureaucracies; therefore, the results of overspecific legislation can be horrendous if the legislators get carried away in their law-making duties. Ideally, new organizations are created through enabling acts that specifically spell out the goals of the program and the powers mandated to the agency. On the other hand, public administrators generally prefer that the legislation leaves as much flexibility as possible in the areas of organizational structure and processes, so that the organization can adapt to changing environmental pressures.

## BUREAUCRATIC GROWTH

In this chapter, we are examining the dynamics of public agency growth and demise; we shall focus on the internal variables and circumstances that lead to change in the fortunes of the organization. Included as an "internal" factor is the relationship of an agency with the chief executive, because this is a natural and necessary relationship for every public agency.

The period of rapid growth in bureaucracy usually occurs immediately after the organization is established. It is during this period that the most frantic activity takes place and the final debates about structure and powers are settled. First, a final determination must be made as to the amount of autonomy the organization will be allowed. Second, whatever the result of the debate over autonomy, the members of the organization will attempt to prove that its services are valuable to society and that the new organization is the most effective body for delivering those services.

The chief executive must have some way of mounting a united attack on problems in society, and this is impossible if all the executive agencies are independent. In a similar way, it is necessary for the chief executive to be responsible for the efficiency and effectiveness of public programs; however, the mayor, governor, or president can be held accountable for the results of programs only when there is a concomitant power to control the agency. These factors add up to a conclusion that every new agency must have its autonomy limited.

At the same time, any organization that hopes to survive must have some autonomy; this statement applies at all levels of government as well as to nongovernmental public agencies. In relation to this issue, Douglas Fox argues that state administrators are quite aware of the need for autonomy; nor does the demand come only from political or patronage administrators, because

employees of professionalized agencies today are in fact the chief supporters of structural bureau autonomy. Attempts to consolidate all line agencies under his [the governor's] control are met by criticism from bureaus and their interest group allies, who accuse him of treating their programs in a "political" manner, and who may launch campaigns to enlist opposition. . . . According to the bureaucrats, the only safeguard against political interference is a guarantee of structural autonomy.[7]

However, autonomy for an organization may refer to more than the formal structure. Clark and Wilson point out that autonomy is essential for survival; however, they define autonomy in relatively broad terms, because

the proliferation of associations and the division of labor in society has meant that there is almost no way for an organization to preserve itself by simply seeking ends for which there are no other advocates. Thus, the maintenance of organizational autonomy is a critical problem. By *autonomy* we refer to the extent to which an organization possesses a distinctive area of competence, a clearly demarcated clientele or membership, and undisputed jurisdiction over a function, service, goal, issue, or cause. Organizations seek to make their environment stable and certain and to remove threats to their identities. Autonomy gives an organization a reasonably stable claim to resources and thus places it in a more favorable position from which to compete for those resources. *Resources* include issues and causes as well as money, time, effort, and means.[8]

Every organization, and this is especially true of public bureaucracy, has enemies who wish to see the organization disbanded or rivals who are competing for the same scarce resources. The key period for any new bureau occurs during the first short interval of time before the bureau arrives at what Anthony Downs calls its "initial survival threshold"—the point at which the organization "has become large enough to render useful services, and old enough to have established routinized relationships with its major clients."[9] During this incubation period, a fledgling bureau needs isolation so that it can develop its own character, after which the bureau should be able to compete with the rest of the political world. Moreover, according to Phillip Selznick,

[7] Douglas M. Fox, *The Politics of City and State Bureaucracy*, Goodyear, Pacific Palisades, Calif., 1974, p. 13.

[8] Peter B. Clark and James Q. Wilson, "Incentive Systems: A Theory of Organization," *Administrative Science Quarterly, VI,* 157 (September 1961).

[9] Downs, p. 9.

. . . the more readily subject to outside pressure a given value is, the more necessary is this isolation. (Roughly, this means that the more technical a function is, the more dispensable is organizational isolation. In highly technical fields, a large degree of isolation is won simply by the use of esoteric techniques and language, and by evident importance of professional criteria as to appropriate methods of work.) . . . An approach to autonomy in these terms is a radical departure from the attempt to build organizations according to the logical association of functions. That principle—which will of course always be relevant—is often violated in practice, and for good reason. It must be violated whenever values are unequal in strength. Organization planning is unrealistic when it fails to take account of the differential capacity of subordinate units to defend the integrity of their functions.[10]

A new agency such as the Atomic Energy Commission, which fulfills a regulatory and developmental function dealing with a volatile and hazardous substance and technology, has little trouble in maintaining its autonomy. Few understand the technology involved in the peaceful application of atomic energy; on the other hand, even fewer want decisions on the use of, and placement of, atomic energy installations to be politically determined. However, a new community development agency in any metropolitan area will be instantly beset by numerous friends, foes, interested civic groups, politicians, benefactors, and beneficiaries with each one attempting to place its mark upon the agency. Such an organization must fight to maintain its independence long enough to determine what its goal is (as established through the political process), what procedures best help to meet this goal, and what structure the organization should adopt. Then the organization can attack the problem of developing support within the political system.

Each new agency is supposedly established to fulfill some social function. New agencies are usually dominated by employees who have a deep commitment to the mission of the bureau or who have a desire to see the agency grow and be successful for personal reasons. In either case, these employees can be expected to court, and to develop contacts with, supporters of the program. Support may come from several directions and for widely divergent reasons; however, the agency is dependent on supporters for its survival in the struggle for resources because resources are ultimately allocated through the political process. The U.S. Department of Defense has been able to use its unique position as the sole purchaser of certain supplies and services to create a vocal interest group, or lobby, for the department. Many "private" corporations are dependent upon the Department of Defense for their survival; therefore, it is in their interest to serve as a mouthpiece for the Army, Navy, or Air Force when new weapons systems are being considered by Congress. The Veteran's Administration can readily call upon the millions of veterans that it serves in an attempt

[10]Phillip Selznick, *Leadership in Administration,* Harper and Row, New York, 1957, pp. 119-130.

to develop new programs or to protect old ones. In this case, the recipients of the services recognize that it is to their benefit to support the desires of "their" agency. In numerous cities, the local Fraternal Order of Police organizations are establishing auxiliaries made up of local businessmen and other interested citizens, because the police departments are losing their traditional position of dominance in local budget deliberations. The police officers hope to use their newfound supporters as spokesmen before the city councils.

In those cases where new agencies have not been able to develop interest-group clientele, or where the clientele has little political influence, the agencies have quickly disappeared or have labored under a permanent condition of crisis and insufficiency in resources—insufficient to accomplish fully the publicly announced goals of the organization. The Office of Economic Opportunity was finally dissolved by the Nixon Administration in spite of the fact that a rearguard action was fought by supporters of the agency in the courts and in Congress. Had the OEO been able to tap a few more influential parts of society, the agency might have withstood the attacks of a president who was opposed to the program. Other programs, such as the Civil Defense Agency and the Job Corps, have suffered a similar fate. The Agency for International Development is a good example of an agency that has managed to maintain its existence without strong interest group support; however, the agency has gone through repeated reorganizations and suffered from consistent underfunding for the programs that it is managing. Correction agencies have also suffered from the fact that they have few supporters with political influence; it is doubtful if any correction system has adequate funding to carry out the goal of "correction" —which appears to mean rehabilitation—of criminal offenders. In this case, the classic issue of the contradiction between public pronouncements and actual practice appears to be paramount, but no organized group with political influence has shown enough interest in the issue to correct the disparity. Sayre and Kaufman describe the New York City Fire Department as an organization that cannot count on support from its clientele: the National Board of Fire Underwriters has recommended that the fire department force be reduced; taxpayers groups and other economy-minded factions are constantly attempting to hold down the fire department budget; and the businesses subject to inspection and licensing do not appreciate the department or support it in any way.[11] Nonsupport leads the fire fighters to the conclusion that they are losing money in the annual budget, and this opinion leads to generally lower morale among the people in the department.

If a new public agency does achieve an adequate level of autonomy, and if it develops sufficient ties with appropriate interest groups, the natural tendency is for the organization to experience rapid expansion for a brief period of time before the opposing forces become strong enough to slow the momentum. The

---

[11] Wallace S. Sayre and Herbert Kaufman, *Governing New York City,* Russell Sage, New York, 1960, pp. 279-285.

major causes of growth and decline are rooted in factors outside the organization, but, as Downs remarks,

> ... the interplay between external and internal developments tends to create certain cumulative effects of growth or decline. They occur because bureaus can experience significant changes in the character of their personnel in relatively short periods of time. In spite of the career nature of bureau employment, there is often a considerable turnover of personnel in specific bureaus. Also, growth that doubles or triples the size of a bureau in a short time can swiftly alter its whole structure and character.[12]

According to Downs, the most important internal element in growth is the makeup of the personnel in the agency. The key to the management style and to the culture of any public agency is the attitudes and habits of the top officials in that agency; those officials are able to dominate the decision-making process and to reward those bureaucrats who operate in the desired fashion. Downs further argues that new agencies are usually heavily endowed with advocates and zealots, and these people, whether they are in positions of authority or are regular employees, have a strong desire to see the agency gain size and power; with greater size and power comes the ability to meet the ends established for the organization. A third type of employee is also found in the new and expanding agency, however; this employee is identified as the "climber," or the individual who is attracted to the organization because of the opportunity to build a successful career. This individual will stay with the new organization, and help in the fight to see it grow, as long as the organization continues to offer the climber a chance for advancement.

All of these types of individuals will strive to strengthen the new public agency as long as they feel that they are receiving worthwhile compensation for their effort. Whether or not the compensation remains adequate depends on the maintenance of a position of *equilibrium* between *inducements and contributions.*[13] Each participant—and this includes both external and internal participants—must contribute something—be it time, money, moral support, or any other resource —for which the organization offers an inducement. For example, a professor contributes a variety of elements including knowledge, time, personal prestige, and research capabilities to a college; in return, the college induces the professor's continued contribution by offering a salary, the prestige of the institution, freedom to carry out research, and facilities that aid in the research. In this case, both the college and the professor may feel there are net benefits for continuing the interrelationship, since the equilibrium model is not necessarily based on the "zero-sum game" concept, where one partner in the process can win only if the other partner loses. Both the professor and the college can

---

[12] Downs, pp. 10-11. The discussion in the next few paragraphs is drawn from this source.

[13] Simon, Smithburg, and Thompson, pp. 381-383.

receive more benefits than are given in costs because the unique aspects of their relationship cannot be matched in any other way. As long as the organization can remain "solvent," the combination of contributions the organization receives is sufficient to provide inducements to the essential participants. The major inducements necessary to maintain the advocates' and zealots' contributions may be nonmaterial; the most important inducement to these people may be the fact that they are able to be part of an organization that is accomplishing what they see as a vital function in society. On the other hand, the climber is induced to remain inside the organization because of the opportunity for professional and career advancement.

Growth, therefore, has what Downs calls an "accelerator effect" whereby growth tends to create cumulative pressure for even more expansion. Once the expansion begins, whether it is taking place in a new organization or occurring in an organization that has remained stable for a period of time, several forces work toward accelerating or maintaining the growth. Innovators and opportunists will use the situation to increase their sphere of influence; at the same time, a growing organization attracts even more individuals of a similar inclination into its ranks. Society often looks to such organizations for answers to further questions that are facing the government; if the agency was successful in one area, the natural tendency is to let it try again in another area where there is a pressing problem.

In addition to the dynamic pressures for growth, which are related to the type of personnel that a new or expanding agency attracts, there are natural pressures which are present within all organizations. First, there are economies of scale through specialization and better utilization of employees and resources. Second, as organizations grow, they are able to impose some stability on the internal functions of the organization; the most vital parts of the organization can be shielded from the variations in resources and pressures that occur in the environment. Closely related to this idea is the fact that organizations can bargain with society from a stronger position as they grow, so the interaction between a large organization and its external environment is carried out on a more equal basis.[14] Third, as organizations grow larger, they are able to spend greater amounts of money on research and development; this gives them an even greater advantage in their battle with other organizations in society. Finally, growing organizations tend to have less internal conflict and higher morale because there are opportunities for individuals and groups to increase their rewards, power, or prestige without decreasing the share of other organizational participants. This factor creates an especially strong incentive for leaders to strive for bureau expansion, because the morale and effort of employees can be more easily maintained under these circumstances.

[14] James Thompson, *Organizations in Action*, McGraw-Hill, New York, 1967. See also: William H. Starbuck, "Organizational Growth and Development," in James G. March, ed., *Handbook of Organizations*, Rand McNally, Chicago, 1965, pp. 451-533.

## THE MATURE ORGANIZATION

Every public organization eventually runs into circumstances that restrict growth and require a new approach to carry on the functions of the agency. Several forces limiting growth will appear almost immediately, and other factors will increase in strength in a ratio equal to the growth experienced by the organization (therefore, the larger the bureau, the greater the force working against further expansion.)

The resources of society are limited. Every time resources are allocated to one public program, all other programs, bureaus, agencies, and departments are denied resources that they feel are needed to do an adequate job. Some functions are so basic to government that there is no argument about the need for expenditures in those areas; however, there certainly will be heated argument about the amount of total available resources to be allocated to the program. There is no question about the need for a defense system in our modern world, and this fact is constantly reiterated by the Defense Department as budgets are prepared, weapons systems approved, and manpower plans reviewed; the debatable questions are those concerning the kind of defense program we need considering the changes in the confrontation between the Communist bloc and the Western societies, the amount of resources to be allocated to this defense system, and therefore, the relative importance of defense in comparison to other social problems such as health research, urban redevelopment, education, housing, and welfare. Once the Defense Department achieves a certain size and technical proficiency, the balance of power shifts toward the other priorities in society; the total expenditure of resources on defense has not decreased, but the *ratio* of expenditures on defense, in comparison to other programs, has dropped steadily over the last decade. As any program grows larger, it encounters more and more resistance to further relative growth because it can only occur at the expense of other programs that have their own supporters.

Any program that is actively carrying out its function is going to make enemies as well as friends. First, as it delivers the specified service to one group of individuals, some other group will be disadvantaged, or lose ground, in relation to the agency's clientele. If a consumer protection agency functions effectively, it can expect to earn the wrath of many in the business community. Likewise, if a regulatory agency is sympathetic to the problems of the industry over which the agency is a watchdog, the members of society, who must use the regulated product or service, will grumble that the agency is a captive of those whom it is supposed to be regulating. Many local government officials have opposed citizen's organizations and legal aid offices that have been established through the War on Poverty because the most successful organizations have been able to challenge local officials and force them to change long-established policies that have been advantageous to the local governments at the expense of ghetto citizens; if the new agencies were not able to force changes in local government policy, the local officials would not care about the existence of the War on Poverty.

This example points to a second type of hostility that is generated by an active and expanding agency. Not only does the agency create enemies among the general public but it also generates opposition among the other public organizations that are threatened by the expansive nature of their competitor. More stable or smaller organizations fear that they will lose resources or that some of their functions will be pirated; therefore, they will actively oppose, within the executive branch, further growth in other agencies. Also, the more stable agencies will rally their friends and supporters outside of the executive branch in an effort to stop threatening programs if such a course of action seems to be necessary.

Not only does an organization have difficulty in its environment, such as gaining additional resources and creating hostile counterforces, but every organization also has internal difficulties as it continues to grow. One of these internal problems involves the communication, planning, and control processes of the bureau. As any program grows, an increasing amount of the time and effort of the personnel is used in maintaining coordination between the various segments of the total organization. Communication becomes essential both for planning (so the organization can make the necessary adjustments in structures and processes) and for control (so that the effort of all parts of the organization is properly coordinated). In addition, most officials recognize that their prestige within the organization is directly reflected by such factors as the number of employees they supervise and the types of communications they clear or control; therefore, there is a natural tendency for the number of employees and the volume of communications to increase unless an immense effort is expended to control this growth. In fact, C. Northcote Parkinson has argued that public administrative departments will invariably grow *even when the amount of work to be done remains constant.*[15]

At the same time that more of an agency's total effort is used in "nonproductive" effort—effort not directly involved in delivering the agency's service or product—the quality of the employee force is usually diluted. A small group of dedicated and efficient employees can produce astounding amounts of output per person; as more employees are added, it is difficult to maintain the level of dedication or proficiency. (It must be recognized, however, that these problems can be partially compensated for by economies of scale, which means that the larger size allows more efficient use of resources and employees' skills.) When these problems are combined, it becomes difficult for an organization to maintain its initial momentum and level of service. In addition, few organizations can hold the attention of the general public for very long. During the time immediately after an organization is created, the public may watch the program's progress, and the program may appear to perform miracles in the beginning because it can attack the most dramatic problems or those most easily solved. Later, any agency tends to be accepted as a part of the normal range of government services, and the level of public interest drops dramatically. At the

[15] C. Northcote Parkinson, *Parkinson's Law and Other Studies in Administration,* Houghton Mifflin, Boston, 1962, p. 12.

same time, the work of the agency becomes more routine, with fewer dramatic events occurring that might appear in the news media. Thus, both real per capita productivity and the appearance of productivity decrease at the same time; such a condition leads to a braking effect on organization growth.

At some point in the history of the public bureaucracy, the organization reaches maturity. At this time, the organization has passed the heady period of relatively unlimited growth; on the other hand, it has now developed a secure relationship with the interested segments of the public, and it has achieved a level of stability in its internal processes and structures. The rush, scurry, and excitement of constant reorganization and crises is past: the leaders and employees have developed a bureaucratic culture that controls internal relationships; a similar balance has been struck between the bureau and its environment; and the clientele has developed a regularized relationship with the bureau. *It is at this time that the agency faces its most serious, albeit insidious threat to the organization.* That threat is complacency and rigidity. Organizations can suffer from hardening of the arteries and calcification of the bones in a way quite similar to that experienced by human beings. Many organizations will resist shrinking, or losing ground, in total size and effort; some organizations allow themselves to lose ground in relation to other competing agencies and do not or cannot put up a struggle to reverse the trend; in a great many cases, however, organizations lose their ability to adapt to changes in their environment; therefore, they lose a part of their effectiveness.

The ultimate key to success for a mature public bureau is adaptability, which is defined as "the ability of a system to react to environmental (or internal) disturbances in a way that is favorable to the continued operation of the system."[16] Adaptation is essential because the demands of the public do change, and "the government agency must reflect to some degree the 'felt needs' of the time . . . (which) are expressed through political demands and political pressures."[17] As long as the agency continues to represent and serve the public, the organization will remain healthy. While discussing such a situation, however, it is necessary to avoid personifying the organization, for as Simon, Smithburg, and Thompson comment,

. . . we must be careful not to attribute to organizations any mythical "will to survive." If organizations do commonly adjust to their environments in order to survive, the explanation for the adjustment process must lie in the aims and motivations of their executives and other employees.[18]

---

[16] H. Randolph Bobbitt, Jr., Robert H. Breinholt, Robert H. Doktor, and James P. McNaul, *Organizational Behavior: Understanding and Prediction,* Prentice-Hall, Englewood Cliffs, N.J., 1974, p. 241.

[17] Samuel P. Huntington, "The Marasmus of the ICC," *Yale Law Journal, LXI, 470 (March, 1952).*

[18] Simon, Smithburg, and Thompson, p. 389.

The level of adaptability, compromise, and change that can occur depends on the level of attachment that individuals have to the goals of the organization, the organization as a social group, and their own personal advancement and aggrandizement.

To the extent that members are sincerely attached to the organizational goals, they will seek to preserve the organization as a vehicle for achieving those goals, or coming as close to this achievement as possible. To the extent they identify with the group, survival of the organization takes on direct value. In so far as they wish their advancement, they will work for the survival and especially the growth of the organization. All three motivations will prepare the members for compromise and opportunism when these are essential to survival.[19]

Those most likely to accept the need for adaptation are the members of the administrative hierarchy. The members of the bureaucracy who are specialists, or who are immersed in the day-to-day operation of the organization, are often not aware of fluctuations in the environment; on the other hand, those who constantly have some interaction with the outside world are more likely to recognize environmental shifts that require internal adjustment. Those who have risen to the top in the organization are likely to have a more receptive attitude toward organizational adaptation because: (1) they generally rose to the top by maintaining a flexible approach to problems as they appeared at the personal level; (2) they have been mobile in their rise to the top (top executives in most public organizations have held positions in several different organizations "on the way up"); (3) they have a much broader perception of the agency and its goals from their more lofty position in the hierarchy, and therefore they can better understand the overall implications of any particular change; and (4) they have a more direct source of information about the environment, and their organization's place in it, because they spend a large portion of the time mingling with individuals from the rest of society.

One of the most dramatic examples of this type of evolution in organizations was described by David L. Sills in his book, *The Volunteers*.[20] One of the voluntary organizations that he studied was the National Foundation for Infantile Paralysis, better known as the March of Dimes. The major goal of the foundation was to find a cure or control for polio; this goal—which was a highly visible goal and one that appeared achievable in a relatively short time—had helped to maintain a high level of motivation among those in the organization. The development of the Salk vaccine meant the achievement of the foundation's goal, and although there were many past victims of polio who would continue to need help throughout the coming years, the foundation could have celebrated its

[19] *Ibid.*

[20] David L. Sills, *The Volunteers,* Free Press, New York, 1958, pp. 153-270.

success and gone out of existence. Instead, Sills predicted that the foundation would choose to remain in existence and to use the experience it had gained in raising money to attack another health or welfare problem. Volunteers who were interviewed by Sills recognized the March of Dimes as a "pacesetting" organization, an organization that had accomplished many goals, and therefore one that should continue its activities in some new battle against disease. In summarizing his research, Sills said that

in the final analysis, . . . the most compelling reason for predicting that the foundation will in the future make a successful adjustment to the achievement of its major goal is that the organization has in fact *already* been transformed, in large part by its Volunteers, into something other than a special purpose association. For those Volunteers . . . have come to regard the organization as a "social movement" or a "pacesetter" [and] have altered not only the character of their own participation but the character of the Foundation as well. Implicit in these perceptions is the notion that the Foundation has an institutionalized status which transcends its current goals. Since the Foundation includes among its Volunteers so many who are able to conceptualize their involvement in terms of its ultimate implications (for themselves, or for society as a whole), rather than only in terms of a limited, pragmatic goal, it has already become an organization as deeply committed to its mode of operation as to its current purposes. In a word, it is an organization which is as committed to a means as it is to an end.[21]

Sills' prediction was accurate, for shortly after his research was published, the foundation announced that it had decided to continue in existence and that the new area of health science toward which it would direct its efforts was the problem of birth defects. This approach to the problem of the organization's *raison d'etre* was what Sills referred to as *the succession of goals,* the acceptance of new or sharply modified goals when the original purposes either were achieved or became irrelevant.[22] He also pointed out numerous other organizations, such as the American Legion, the Planned Parenthood Federation of America, the YMCA, and the American Red Cross, which have gone through a similar process of goal change.

Many organizations established at the local government level continue to exist through the completion of several goals. In these cases, the cities, counties, or special districts recognize that the expertise available in the particular organizations is worth retaining or else the organizations are able to find new goals toward which the bureaucracy can work. Many of the War on Poverty agencies

---

[21]*Ibid.,* p. 270.

[22]The term "succession of goals" was borrowed from: Peter M. Blau, *The Dynamics of Bureaucracy,* University of Chicago, Chicago, 1955. See also: Peter M. Blau and Marshall W. Meyer, *Bureaucracy in Modern Society,* Second Edition, Random House, New York, 1971.

are still in existence; some are still continuing their original functions, but most have either added new duties or changed their goals and functions. The same type of procedure has occurred among the numerous manpower programs that have come into existence during the last decade; however, in this case, the local agencies have often moved to the administration of a new federal or state manpower program as an older program was completed; therefore, the goal did not change although the funding, and the processes used by the agency, shifted on a regular basis.

## ORGANIZATIONAL DEATH

Public agencies are most susceptible to both evolution and dissolution during the first short period of their existence. Once organizations have managed to exist for a while in the political arena the chances of survival increase immensely. Often the services offered by public agencies cannot be received from any other source; therefore, those who are dependent on that service will demand that the agency continue regardless of the inefficiency, ineffectiveness, or unpopularity of the program. It is commonly reputed that government bureaus do not engage in all-out conflicts with one another, and this leads to an extremely low "death rate." Anthony Downs says that

in essence, bureaus resemble large oligopolistic firms. Like such firms, they try to avoid all-out wars because they are too costly to all involved. Second, if two or more bureaus engage in a "war" concerning control over certain social functions, they inevitably attract the attention of the government's central allocation agencies. . . . This is extremely hazardous because the bureau's opponents are sure to call attention to some of its major shortcomings. Moreover, top officials in every bureau fear any detailed investigation, since it is almost certain to uncover embarrassing actions.[23]

Thus, the demise of large bureaus has resembled that of oligopolistic firms. Hence, the most important factor determining the probability of dissolution, according to Downs, is size; the larger a government bureau, the less likely it is to die.

Nevertheless, public organizations do die occasionally, and when death occurs it can be attributed to failure in one of three ways: (1) the original functions have declined in relative importance, while, at the same time, the organization has failed to add new objectives or functions; (2) the functions of the organization have remained important, but the organization has proved incapable of performing them efficiently; or (3) the functions have remained important, but some other organization has proved more effective in delivering the service.

[23] Downs, p. 23.

In each of these three situations, the probable cause of failure is ultimately an inability to adapt, which can be traced to one or more of three problems: (1) the organization has been established without the support of major interest groups essential to its long-term well-being; therefore, it cannot hope to make the adjustments necessary to gain the external support essential to survival; (2) the members of the organization are so attached to the original goals that it is impossible for the organization to develop the flexibility necessary to adapt; (3) the organization may suffer from inertia and therefore find it impossible to adapt.

If an organization comes into existence without the support of its potential clientele, that support must be quickly gained; this is even more true if the potential clientele has "political clout," because the clients will almost certainly turn against an agency unless it appears useful to them. Grant McConnell, in his book, *The Decline of Agrarian Democracy*,[24] describes the relatively short history of the Farm Security Administration, an agency established in 1937 to deal with rural poverty. The FSA did not originate in the Department of Agriculture, where it was housed, nor was it favored by the external organization with which the Department of Agriculture was allied on matters of administrative organization and on points that seemed relatively trivial; however, the FSA had no support and was never able to win over the Farm Bureau (because none of the rural poor aided by the FSA belonged to the Farm Bureau). By 1943, the agency was decimated, and in 1946, approximately nine years after it was established, The Farm Security Administration was formally ended.

Even if an organization starts with the support of important external groups, it may lose that support if the organization cannot adapt to the changing desires and needs of those external groups. An affinity to the goals of the organization is important and can lead to healthy organizational adaptation; on the other hand, if affinity becomes fixation, it may lead to an intransigence on the part of organization members who reject any shift in goals or priorities as an attempt to subvert the original ends of the organization.

Adaptation may also be made difficult if the system develops a "culture" or set of norms and habits that emphasizes the processes used by the agency. This phenomenon also often appears in individuals within a bureaucracy. Robert Merton refers to this phenomenon as "displacement of goals," and in this situation the processes of the organization become as important as the original goals; the key phrase is "do it by the book." In this case, habits have become ritual, and it requires a great deal of effort to break out of the mold and learn new ways of doing jobs and thinking about situations; it may be even more painful to admit that the old ways were not the best ways, because many people take the change personally—believing that acceptance of the new is an admission of prior failure. Welfare agencies have struggled with this problem during the last fifteen

[24] Grant McConnell, *The Decline of Agrarian Democracy*, University of California, Berkeley, 1953, pp. 84-111.

years, as have most other public agencies. The frustration and resentment that can be built up under circumstances of forced change are poignantly stated in the lament of a county commissioner, who was recently faced with a federal court mandate for the development of an affirmative action plan. The mid-western state in which he resides and works has a strong tradition of patronage in local government employment, and the affirmative action program is seen as a threat to all that is "holy" in the traditional personnel practices. According to the commissioner, "Those procedures will completely upset the way we have done business for the last forty years. This affirmative action thing will cause chaos and halt our county government in its tracks. If we did everything wrong before how did we ever get the job done? It's like being asked when you stopped beating your wife. If you respond—if you establish the new procedures—you are admitting that you did everything wrong up till now." Occasionally, this attitude is so strong in an organization that change does not occur; when this is con-tinued for a very long time, the organization may suffer the ultimate consequence.

When an organization loses so much support that it can no longer maintain its viability, it must choose between two alternatives: it can simply disband, usually recognized formally by the executive and legislative branches, or it can transfer those important or viable functions that still exist into some other existing organization. Usually some form of the second alternative is chosen by everyone concerned.

Even though it appears that the problem of organizational demise does not appear to be of immediate concern to most public administrators, it is a prob-lem that will be faced at some time; therefore, it is a phenomenon that is of interest to students of public bureaucracy. Anthony Downs notes that

despite the low death rates of bureaus within their own cultures, very few bureaus—or organizations of any kind—have managed to survive for really long periods of time, that is, hundreds of years. Most government bureaus disappear when the particular government that created them is replaced, as did Roman bureaus. Similarly, private bureaus do not usually outlive the cultures that spawn them. Churches and universities seem to be the hardiest species, as the Roman Catholic Church and Oxford University illustrate.[25]

## SUMMARY

In phase one, the new organization comes into existence. A call for action from the public, or some part of it, generally precedes a new program. A battle, sometimes long and arduous, between proponents of action may be involved; however, new organizations are established. Phase two begins immediately after establishment. This period sees a public agency attempting to "make hay while

[25] Downs, p. 23.

the sun shines" by proving both its ability to serve *and* the necessity and popularity of its services. Phase two usually is the period when rapid growth takes place, so it can be referred to as the "youth" of the organization. Phase three begins as the successful organization ceases its rapid growth and becomes a mature, relatively efficient agency serving a satisfied clientele. The major emphasis of the organization then becomes that of maintaining its position in relation to the many other competing bureaus. Phase four involves those organizations that have not been successful in protecting their resources; they must adapt to meet changing conditions, reorganize, develop new goals, or face the possibility of extinction. In spite of the apparent indestructibility of public bureaucracies, some public agencies do complete the life cycle and die.

# BIBLIOGRAPHY

Blau, Peter M., and Marshall W. Meyer, *Bureaucracy in Modern Society,* Second Edition, Random House, New York, 1971.

Clark, Burton R., *Adult Education in Transition,* University of California, Berkeley, 1956.

Crozier, Michel, *The Bureaucratic Phenomenon,* University of Chicago, Chicago, 1964.

Downs, Anthony, *Inside Bureaucracy,* Little, Brown, Boston, 1967.

Gross, Bertram, *The Legislative Struggle,* McGraw-Hill, New York, 1953.

March, James G., and Herbert A. Simon, *Organizations,* Wiley, New York, 1958.

Parkinson, C. Northcote, *Parkinson's Law and Other Studies in Administration,* Houghton Mifflin, Boston, 1962.

Selznick, Philip, *TVA and the Grassroots: A Study in the Sociology of Formal Organization,* University of California, Berkeley, 1949.

Sills, David L., *The Volunteers,* Free Press, New York, 1958.

Simon, Herbert A., Donald W. Smithburg, and Victor A. Thompson, *Public Administration,* Knopf, New York, 1950.

Thompson, James D., *Organizations in Action,* McGraw-Hill, New York, 1967.

# THE BUREAUCRACY IN THE POLITICAL SYSTEM

*A faith in majorities does not eliminate the necessity for governance by individuals and small groups. Wherever there is organization, whether formally democratic or not, there is a split between the leader and the led, between the agent and the initiator.*

*Philip Selznick*

All the public organizations that survive in the political world do so for two reasons. First, they function efficiently enough to fulfill the purpose for which they were established. Second, they continue to fulfill a function that some part of society desires. The organization may not serve the interests or goals for

# CHAPTER 3

which it was originally established; nevertheless, it must be serving someone's goals, for the continued existence of the organization in the political world requires the support of politically powerful groups. For this reason, public organizations can be described as "expressions of the policy intent of a group or coalition of groups seeking to equate their interest(s) with the public interest."[1] Since this is true, both a department's policies and its structure can be expected to be allied closely to those groups served by, or represented by, the bureaucracy in question. The close connection between the public bureaucracy and those whom it serves also helps to explain why the public organization is centrally located in the political process. Therefore, it is important to emphasize the political environment and the interaction that occurs between the public bureaucracy and the rest of the political system.

In order to consider how the political environment interacts with the public bureaucracy, it is necessary to examine the total public policy process from beginning to end. Consideration of the process can best take place by using the systems approach. Therefore, within this chapter, the concept of the "political system" is described, the steps within the policy process are defined, and finally, the interaction of the public bureaucracy with these major segments of its environment (norms, external constituencies, and governmental constituencies) in the public policy process is discussed.

## THE POLITICAL SYSTEM

One way to examine public policy is to look at it as the result, or output, of a political "system" where a variety of forces interact in order to decide who will get what, when, where, why, and how (Figure 2). Public policy (a desired goal or value) is produced within the political structure of society (that group of institutions "which functions authoritatively to allocate values for a society");[2] but the political structure and therefore the policies are also affected by the demands and support that are inputs from the environment. At the same time, the demands and support that reach the political structure may be influenced by the form of the political structure and by the policies that are established. For example, at the local level, the types of ordinances passed by the city council will depend, in part, on the demands made by citizens; however, the structure of the local government may also have been established because of pressure from local citizens, who may have the right to choose between the mayor–council or council–manager forms of government. Along with reform of the governmental structure may go a change in the way that council members are selected (from districts or "at large") and the way that civil servants are

---

[1] William L. Morrow, *Public Administration: Politics and the Political System,* Random House, New York, 1975, p. 4.

[2] Thomas R. Dye, *Understanding Public Policy,* Second Edition, Prentice-Hall, Englewood Cliffs, N.J., 1975, p. 36.

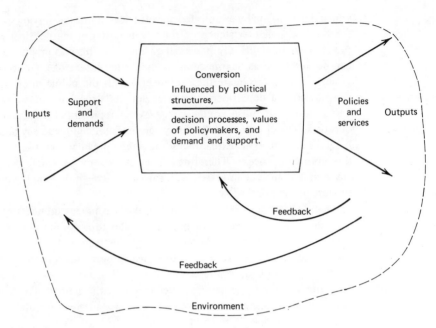

**Figure 2**

The political system. (The systems model is based on the theories of: David Easton, *A Framework for Political Analysis*, Prentice-Hall, Englewood Cliffs, New Jersey, 1965.)

chosen (patronage or merit). With each of these changes in structure, a concomitant change in policies may be expected, because the different selection processes create distinct patterns of influence and response on the part of the public officials and bureaucrats.[3] Patronage employees usually pay careful attention to the desires of party officials or the political officers to whom the employees owe their jobs; on the other hand, merit employees may not pay much attention to party officials, but they may look to other parts of the community for their cues to behavior in office. At the same time, the types of public policy that are produced by each system may vary in scope on a regular basis. When citizen groups find out who usually "wins" and who "loses," the result may be that some groups are encouraged to make greater demands on the political structure, because they think they can win, while other groups reduce their demands simply because they expect to lose. All of this implies that each element of the political system is interrelated and that each element will react to changes in any of the other elements.

[3] Robert Lineberry and Edmund Fowler, "Reformism and Public Policies in American Cities," in James Q. Wilson, ed., *City Politics and Public Policy*, Wiley, New York, 1968, pp. 97-123.

## STEPS OF THE PUBLIC POLICY PROCESS

Every society has some way of dealing with public problems and establishing societal goals and values; this procedure is referred to as the public policy process. While every society maintains such a process, it is doubtful that any other political system is more complex than that of the United States. It is possible, however, within the intricacies and varieties of the almost innumerable processes, to discover some similarities and to establish a common procedure. Whenever the public policy process is functioning, the following steps always seem to occur: (1) problem *identification* begins the process and ultimately leads to a demand for action to resolve the problem; (2) *formulation* of the proper course of action occurs after much competition between alternatives and the supporters of the various alternatives; (3) *legitimation* is given to the course of action that is finally developed when the action is adopted by the appropriate parts of the political system; (4) *application* of the legitimate policy then occurs, as some administrative organization implements the program or makes sure that the value involved is properly observed in society; and, finally, (5) *evaluation* of the policy is received from a variety of sources to see if it is accomplishing its goal, thus leading (if there is any dissatisfaction with the results of the policy or its application) to new demands because of the newly identified problems.[4]

This general procedure is followed whether the policy being considered is detente between the United States and the Soviet Union or a law to deal with motorists who are using a particular segment of a county road as a drag strip. In both cases, the problem may come to the attention of the policymakers from a variety of sources; numerous groups of private citizens may interact with a variety of governmental institutions while the appropriate policy is chosen and legitimized. It is a certainty that any policy established will be scrutinized by everyone who has an interest in it, and someone will be dissatisfied with the results and demand additions, deletions, or changes to the policy; at this point, the cycle will start again. In addition, it should be recognized that a logical conclusion to this cycle may be the decision not to change the current policy.

## THE PUBLIC AGENCY AND ITS ENVIRONMENT IN THE PUBLIC POLICY SYSTEM

The focus of this discussion is the interaction of the public bureaucracy with the other segments of the "political world" as public policy is formulated and implemented. In dealing with this subject, it is impossible to consider the full range of the political world or all the interactions that occur; therefore, we shall concentrate on "the public agency" (any single governmental department or agency) and those forces or groups with which it interacts. This interaction can

---

[4] This process is based on: Charles O. Jones, *An Introduction to the Study of Public Policy,* Duxbury Press, Belmont, Calif., 1970, pp. 12-14.

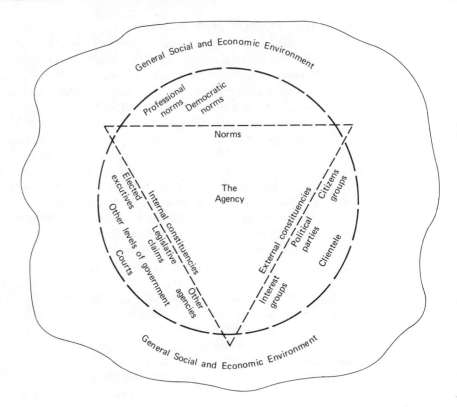

**Figure 3**

The public agency and its environment.

best be demonstrated by the model presented in Figure 3. In this model, each side of the triangle represents an area of interaction between the public agency and its environment. The largest number of transactions, and usually the most important, occurs between the agency and those parts of its environment represented by the three sides of the organization: norms, external constituencies, and governmental constituencies. While the norms that interact with the agency cannot be personified, there is definitely a lifelike quality about them, with the norms affecting, and being affected by, the agency. The most important norms are those of the democratic ethic, those of traditional administration, and those of the professions to which members of the agency belong or aspire to belong. Included among the "external constituencies" are political parties (which play an important role in the public policy process but are not sanctioned by the Constitution), the interest groups, and the clients that are served by the agency (not including the clients who are themselves other governmental agencies). The "governmental constituencies" include the elected executives (city managers must be included in this category even though they are "elected" by the city council), the legislature and individual legislators, the courts, other governmental agencies that are competing *and* cooperating with the agency being considered, and the governmental jurisdictions and agencies at other levels of the federal system.

Although most of the interactions between any particular agency and its environment can be placed within these three categories, there are other transactions that do not fit into any generalized pattern or that occur only occasionally and yet are of importance in the policy process and the life of the agency. This is represented by the points of the agency that extend into the "general, social and economic environment." Events outside the normal purview of an agency may suddenly have a tremendous impact on the way it operates; conversely, an agency may suddenly discover that its interpretation or implementation of policy may be having unanticipated consequences in an unexpected part of society. For example, the oil crisis of 1974 had a long-lasting impact on the way many government agencies operated. Not only did it create immediate problems but it also forced many programs that used a lot of energy to start thinking seriously about alternative sources of power; it forced the national government to reexamine its policies about energy production and dependence on foreign sources of energy.

In another example that involved the ecology, the U.S. Food and Drug Administration approved the use of fluorocarbon as a propellant in aerosol sprays. After careful examination, there did not appear to be any harmful effects on people using the sprays. Several years later, scientists suddenly began to worry about the effects of fluorocarbon, which appeared to have a deleterious impact on the ozone shield that protected humans from the sun's x-rays and thus increased the chances of skin cancer. The information and therefore the opposition to the FDA policy came from a part of the agency's political environment that it had not thought about when the original decision was made.

If we are to understand the interaction between the public bureaucracy and its environment, it is necessary to examine what occurs at each of the three major interfaces. Each interface generates special problems for the agency and for those dealing with the agency; therefore, we can learn additional facts about the policy process and the bureaucracy by looking at the transactions that take place at these points in the public agency's system. It must be remembered, however, that the different parts of the environment are interacting with each other as well as with the public agency; therefore, the following discussion, which deals primarily with each interface separately, is somewhat oversimplified for the sake of clarity. Even so, it is not possible to deal with each segment of the environment separately in all cases, for some overlapping between parts of the environment must be considered.

## Norms and the Public Bureaucracy

The most pervasive forces that affect the public agency are the norms that surround it. Norms, also referred to as "social rules" by many writers, may be defined as the authoritative standards or patterns against which attitudes and behavior can be measured. Although attitudes cannot be seen or directly measured, they are regularly attributed to an agency or an individual bureaucrat because of observed actions; correctly or incorrectly, behavior is regularly interpreted as having been caused by the understanding and attitudes of those who are being observed. Every action that takes place either meets or fails to meet the expectations of those who are involved with the members of the bureaucracy; of course, the individuals or groups who are interacting with the public agency are also measured against the norms established for them.

Austin Ranney specifically mentions three levels of social rules that exist and may serve as limitations on or supports for action.[5] The first level of norms is that of the law—the body of rules that is legitimated by the fact that they emanate from the part of the political system established to create these rules. If these rules are not followed, the state has the right to use its power to arrest the offender, and the courts will use these rules to judge the propriety of the offender's actions. The second level of rules is that of custom—rules of behavior directed by what others expect one to do. In this case, one's actions are determined by a desire to avoid being regarded as "peculiar." Customs are enforced primarily by the actions of one's peers, and these actions may vary from the registration of surprise at one's behavior to total ostracism if the breach of custom is considered unforgiveable. The third level of rules is that of moral precepts—rules that are obeyed because people "believe that it is good to do so regardless of what others may think."[6] When an individual firmly believes that a moral precept is involved, other types of force may be meaningless to that individual, and the threats of governmental force or social ostracism will not stop the "necessary action."

All three types of norms become involved in the interactions between a public agency and those with whom the agency must deal. To point out the difficulties of this situation, let us look at the police department and the community as both are faced with the opening of the first adult bookstore in the town. The owner of the store loudly proclaims his constitutional right to operate the shop, and he threatens the police department with all kinds of lawsuits if the store is closed or if he is harrassed by the officers. The owner can cite the criminal and civil codes pursuant to his business, and he may be able to gain the support of groups, such as the local civil liberties organization, that defend his right to do business because of their adamant belief in the concept of freedom of speech rather than their acceptance of the materials in the store. The new store is undoubtedly not the type of business normally established and considered "acceptable" in the community; therefore, the store and its proprietor will probably be shunned by most of the citizens in the town, and the owner will not

---

[5] Austin Ranney, *The Governing of Men,* Revised Edition, Holt, Rinehart and Winston, New York, 1966, pp. 32-34.

[6] *Ibid.,* p. 34.

be welcomed into membership in any of the commercial organizations. Indeed, the other commercial proprietors may be making polite inquiries of the police department as to whether or not the new establishment has met all licensing codes and other regulations of the town. The strong insinuation that the police department will be "doing what is right for the town if it can close the dirty bookstore" may even occur, and the insinuators may link their suggestions to comments about future cooperation with, and support for, the police department in other civic endeavors. Meanwhile, the city council may support the commercial proprietors who are opposed to the bookstore. In addition, the churches of the town may instigate a "holy war against the pornographic bookstore"; hence, the police department may find itself in the uncomfortable position of protecting the adult bookstore from the irate churchgoers who "are not willing to allow immorality to creep into their town." Until the issue is settled and a decision is reached as to which norms will triumph, the interactions between the police department and the other parts of the community will be frequent and frantic. Each group participating in the fray will have become involved because of its norms, and its actions will likewise be guided by what its members believe to be "appropriate behavior" in the situation. The actions of the police department will be judged by every participant in the situation; the result will lead not only to a new policy for the community but also to a fresh alignment of groups in the community as they make new demands on the police department or lend the department their support.

In such a situation, the three major types of norms that are present in public agency operation are involved. It is the job of the police department to see that the law is respected as the case is handled and a policy is established. Several other parts of the governmental structure must also be involved in this process. The police department must attempt to fulfill the traditional norms of administration. Even though a minicrisis is swirling around the issue of the adult bookstore, the department is expected to continue operating in an efficient and effective manner; the community must be patrolled in order to maintain the peace, traffic must be regulated, and emergencies must be answered; all duties must be performed with a minimum of expense and inconvenience to the members of the department. The success of the department will be measured, both internally and externally, by these standards. The members of the department will look toward other police agencies to see if any norms of behavior have been established for similar situations; they will try to follow "accepted police behavior" that has been established in law enforcement circles. Other individuals and groups will judge the results, and the means used to achieve those results, by their particular professional standards, whether that is the legal profession, the ministerial profession, or sociological profession (if an urban sociologist happens to be observing the action as an experiment in his urban laboratory.) Finally, the actions and their results will also be judged by the general norms of the community, including the community's understanding of the way democracy is supposed to work and the rights and duties it gives to each individual. Community norms, as well as the other norms being considered, are interpreted quite differently in other parts of our country or society. In relation to this idea, Philip Selznick has noted that there are

. . . significant differences in attitude and custom which are the elements of diversity within our general cultural and political unity. These differences cannot adequately be safeguarded when programs are formulated in national terms. Methods of approach . . . may well be homogeneous if we consider only the interests or convenience of the bureaucracy. But the people treasure their special folkways, and protect them as basic elements of welfare and security.[7]

If a public agency can align itself with important norms in the society, it can strengthen its position in the political world. Such a procedure allows the organization to develop a close relationship with those groups in society that agree with it. This relationship can be used to defend the agency or to help on the offensive if such a position is desirable. If the ideology and norms are accepted throughout the agency, it is likely that "rubrics of thought and decision" are similar; therefore, the different technical specialists will be bound together, and it may be possible to decentralize the administration of the organization.[8]

However, there is danger inherent in such close attachment to an ideal. Selznick notes that

. . . it is essential to remember how diverse and unstable are the sources and functions of any set of guiding ideas with which an organization becomes identified. Some organizations are born of ideological conflict, and administered by the victors with a view of furthering "the cause." . . . But there are other sources of ideas, sources close to the special problems of organization as such, which require some attention.[9]

If those "other sources of ideas" are not attended to because an agency has become too attached to a set ideal, the agency may find itself in serious trouble. Attachment to a particular norm means inflexibility, which leads to difficulty in coping with a changing political system. Close attachment to one norm means that the members of the organization may not clearly perceive environmental changes and new demands that must be dealt with if the agency is to continue. Any organization that is closely tied to groups that have strong attachments to a particular goal may find it impossible to broaden its support base without losing its current support, and any idea that garners the ardent advocacy of one group is likely to generate the ardent opposition of other groups. Finally,

[7] Philip Selznick, *TVA and the Grassroots: A Study in the Sociology of Formal Organization*, Harper and Row (Torchbooks), New York, 1966, p. 24. This book was originally published in 1949 by the University of California, Berkeley.

[8] *Ibid.*, pp. 50-51.

[9] *Ibid.*, p. 49.

when an agency is closely allied to a cause, it may find that it is affiliated with other groups that it may or may not wish to claim as allies, but who, for reasons of their own, are espousing the same ideal. In fact, Selznick notes that a new organization seeking support for survival and autonomy

... has to adapt itself not so much to the people in general as to the actually existing institutions which have the power to smooth or block its way. It therefore becomes ideologically convenient to fall in with the general practice in the area of identifying the existing agencies with the people, and permitting de facto leadership ... to be its own stamp of legitimacy.[10]

When a public agency is expected to fit smoothly into the ongoing social structure of a community, there is no problem with such an arrangement. However, when an agency is created to serve a new clientele or to deliver a radically new service that is supposed to change the balance of power in the community (e.g., a program to help low-income individuals gain more political power), identifying with the current leaders in the community is unacceptable.

The norms and ideals that are espoused by a public agency are very important, and any public official must know which norms are accepted by the important groups surrounding the agency. It is essential to maintain the proper balance between commitment and flexibility so that the public bureaucracy can maintain the support of those groups within the political system that give the agency a chance to succeed. At the same time, the public administrator must not become so involved in the norms of the organization that he forgets to deal with the other interfaces of the public agency.

## External Constituencies

The occurrence of interaction among groups is a central fact of politics, and to the extent that public agencies are involved in politics (the policy process), the involvement includes a number of external groups. *External groups* include clusters of people who have organized or united together for a common cause and who exist outside of the governmental structure. Public policy may be defined as the equilibrium reached in the group struggle, and in this struggle the public agency is just one of many groups that is involved in the policy process. The interaction between the public agency and external groups also continues as the agency implements policy through its programs. The public agency is dependent upon the support of various groups at all times and must consider the desires of the groups' members in order to maintain viability. The opposite is also true, however, because external groups depend on the public agency to serve them, to carry out programs that they favor, and to support them in the perennial battle for resources. Matthew Holden, Jr., argues that even "the most saintly idealist (if a saintly idealist ever could arise to such a high post) could

[10] *Ibid.*, p. 61.

not function if he abandoned the maxim of 'my agency, right or wrong'." This must be the approach of the "administrative politician" as he courts interest groups in an attempt to increase his agency's power "in an administrative habitat crowded with other agencies."[11] The way to gain power, according to Holden, is to have a favorable balance of constituencies. According to his definition,

Constituency means any group, body or interest to which the administrative politician looks for aid and guidance, or which seeks to establish itself as so important (in his judgement) that he "had better" take account of its preferences even if he finds himself averse to those preferences. The constituency of the agency . . . includes not only those with whom the politician has a stable *and friendly* relationship, but those who support his ends, those who oppose his ends, and those who wish to intervene for what he regards as "irrelevant" purposes.[12]

All these types of groups make up the *relevant external constituency* of the public agency. For purposes of this discussion, we shall look at four constituency groups (the clientele, interest groups, political parties, and citizen participation groups) and observe the way that they influence the decisions and actions of the public agency.

**Clientele**. The first and most obvious group that the public agency must worry about is the clientele that it serves. Many executive departments at the national level have been established to serve and to represent the views of a particular clientele. The clientele represented can usually be identified by the title of the department, for example: the Department of Agriculture, the Department of Commerce, the Department of Labor, and the Department of Health, Education, and Welfare. Concerning these departments, William Morrow notes that

their official mission is twofold—to oversee the implementation of policy, and to offer advice on substantive policies to political superiors. Unofficially, most of them constitute intrabureaucratic lobbies for certain biases. Their existence indicates that at one time the government endorsed the social purpose underlying their policies. Usually, influential interest groups have led crusades to achieve line agency status and representation of certain claims.[13]

[11]Matthew Holden, Jr., "'Imperialism' in Bureaucracy," *The American Political Science Review, LX,* 944 (December 1966).

[12]*Ibid.*

[13]Morrow, p. 63.

The same type of ties between state and local departments and interest groups occur. For example, Morrow points out that regional and demographic biases change the emphases in different parts of the country.

Conservation tends to be high priority in the Western and Plains states, agriculture in the Midwest, and urban matters in those states containing highly populated metropolitan areas. In these natural responses to claimant pressures, the administrative system incorporates the traits of political pluralism in the United States. Therefore, line agencies compete with each other for the right to guide public policy in directions favorable to those interests served by the agencies themselves.[14]

The clientele of a public agency has the most to gain from the agency's establishment and continuation; therefore, the potential clientele is usually the major group to demand the formulation of the policy and the agency, and it is the major source of support for the agency. During the agency's first stages, it is likely to benefit from the interest of the clientele because this group is inclined to think of any resistance as "old fogeyism" and, equally, having just gone through the process of creating the agency, will be much on the alert for possible external threats.[15] Such support from the clientele is clearly based on a concern for the protection of its own interests. Once the agency has matured and developed stability through a record of success in serving its clientele, a reciprocity develops in which each group has a strong dependency on the other; hence, close cooperation is the normal mode of operation.

The influence of the clientele, both as a support to the agency and as a pressure on agency action, is decided by the composition of that group. If the clientele of an agency is made up of people who have a recognized status or a position of esteem in society, that status gives the clientele a position of strength. Likewise, if an agency serves a large constituency (in numbers), the size may be used by the clientele (or by the agency) to develop political influence. Other factors, such as the level of interest the clientele shows in the services or the geographic dispersion of the group, are also important in deciding how closely the agency administrators must listen to those who they serve and how much the clientele can be used to help the agency in its political battles.

In many cases, it becomes difficult to know who is in control and who is served as the interaction between the public agency and its clientele continues over the years. This problem is most apparent when the independent regulatory commissions (Federal Communications Commission, Securities and Exchange

[14] *Ibid.*, p. 65.

[15] Holden, p. 945.

Commission, Interstate Commerce Commission, etc.) are concerned.[16] They are independent because they exist outside of the regular executive department hierarchy, they are governed by commissioners who are appointed for definite terms in office, and they possess a more comprehensive authority than that of an executive department. Each commission regulates activity in a particular segment of the economy, and as the regulatory agency, it has the power to issue rules governing that activity, to oversee the implementation of the rules, and to serve as the judge when disputes arise over the interpretation and application of the rules. The regulatory commission's reason for being, in every case, is to "protect the public interest." Of course, the regulatory commission becomes immersed in "the politics of administration" because of its unique position and power.

The interaction between a regulatory commission and its clientele is intense. All of the factors (size, status, geographic dispersion, and level of interest) mentioned in relation to the power of the clientele lead to an inordinate amount of influence on the part of those being regulated. It would appear that the regulated industries were aware of this fact, because the interests that were to be regulated by these commissions often supported the legislation that established the commissions; therefore, it would appear that the industries felt that they would have a strong impact on the thinking and actions of the commissions.[17] The industries were right; after an initial burst of aggressive policy on key issues, the commissions have succumbed to the pressures of the interests that they regulated. In time, the commissions have developed an "understanding" with the regulated industries, have accepted the status quo, and usually have become an advocate for industry policy and programs. Bernard Schwartz noted this tendency and commented that although the commissions were

set up to regulate in the public interest, they have more and more tended to equate that concept with the private interests of those being regulated. Designed to remove regulation from politics, they have failed to resist pressures from political branches. Conceived as quasi-judicial tribunals, they have acted in a manner grossly contrary to the cannons of judicial ethics. Intended to promote competition, they have fostered monopoly.[18]

---

[16] Most states have comparable commissions controlling intrastate industries.

[17] Anthony Lewis, "To Regulate the Regulators," in Samuel Krislov and Lloyd D. Musolf, eds., *The Politics of Regulation: A Reader*, Houghton Mifflin, Boston, 1964, pp. 7-13.

[18] Bernard Schwartz, "Crisis in the Commissions," in Samuel Krislov and Lloyd D. Musolf, eds., *The Politics of Regulation: A Reader*, Houghton Mifflin, Boston, 1964, p. 25.

The reason that such a distortion of agency goal and mission occurs is related to two major factors. First, in an attempt to staff the commissions with competent personnel (employees who have the technical expertise to deal with the regulated industries), most of the appointees have come from within the industries; therefore, the commission staffs bring with them a great deal of "intellectual baggage" that has been created by the staffs' backgrounds. They are cognizant of and sympathetic toward the problems and perceptions of the industries that they are supposed to regulate neutrally. (Such a problem is always easier to recognize and to criticize than it is to solve.) This bias is bound to have an effect on the decisions and actions of the regulators.

The second reason for the seemingly inevitable evolvement of regulatory agencies has to do with who makes up the "interested publics" of the commissions. The constituency of the regulatory agency is, officially, the entire citizenry; nevertheless, the natural tendency of any agency is to recognize as its real constituency that part of the public that takes an active interest in the policies and programs of the agency. The general public does not pay much attention to the procedures and rulings of the regulatory agencies; however, those industries that are directly affected by the actions of the commissions are constantly watching and reacting to the commissions. Since each commission serves a single industry or a group of related industries and since almost all of the demands, support, and feedback within their policymaking system comes from that industry, it should not be surprising that the commission's version of the public interest lacks breadth and scope.[19]

While it is fashionable to criticize the regulatory commissions because they tend to be biased in their operations, it must be remembered that they simply represent one end of a continuum; to some extent, all public agencies interact with their clientele in a similar way, and to that extent the same process of intermixing client and agency goals exists.

**Interest Groups.** Interest groups (often referred to as pressure groups) are made up of individuals who have banded together because they share a common characteristic or concern and wish to promote that issue. Many interest groups are the clientele of a particular public agency (veterans, farmers, etc.); however, the focus of this discussion is on the impact of nonclient interest groups on public agencies. Interest groups keep watch over a variety of issues in which the groups have only a secondary, or peripheral, involvement; in these issue areas the members of the group are not directly affected by the decisions on policy or the actions of the implementing agencies. Nevertheless, the issues are of sufficient

---

[19] Marver H. Bernstein, "The Life Cycle of Regulatory Commissions," in Samuel Krislov and Lloyd D. Musolf, eds., *The Politics of Regulation: A Reader,* Houghton Mifflin, Boston, 1964, pp. 80-87.

interest to the groups that they wish to become involved in the development of policy and its administration. In fact, there are situations where interest groups actively represent the concerns of unorganized citizens or groups who are not prepared to protect their own interests; consumers, convicted criminals, welfare recipients, and minority groups have had their causes represented by organizations such as Common Cause, the American Civil Liberties Union, and the consumer groups that have been inspired by Ralph Nader.

The major avenues of influence open to these groups are lobbying with the legislature or public agency, appealing to the courts, and educating the public. Interest groups are accepted as a legitimate part of the political system; therefore, they can usually gain some access to both the policymaking process and to the policy-implementation process, and they can influence the result of both processes. For instance, interest groups can influence the results of elections, so legislators are careful to show proper deference and attention to the ideas of such groups; after all, the legislator may be able not only to blunt the *opposition* of a group (the minimally desired result) but also to gain the *support* of that group (the maximally desired result). Public agencies are responding to interest groups for the same types of reasons. On the other hand, the amount of access—therefore, influence—does vary for the different groups; and, as Austin Ranney points out, unless a group gets a serious hearing it cannot expect much success in swaying the perceptions and actions of the policymakers and implementers.

The access of any particular group depends upon several factors, such as its general prestige and social position, and the reputation and skill of its lobbyists at dealing with public officials. Thus, for example, a Roman Catholic cardinal or archbishop is more likely to have access to committees of the Massachusetts legislature than is a representative of the Jehovah's Witnesses, and a lobbyist whom the legislators have long known as a reasonable, practical, well-informed, and friendly person is more likely to get a serious hearing than one with a reputation of being cantankerous or ignorant or merely a "do-gooder."[20]

If interest groups are not successful in gaining the cooperation of legislators or administrators, their next logical step is to appeal to the court for redress of their grievance. For example, since many of the state and local government legislatures and public health departments have refused to listen to the pro-abortion groups, these groups have appealed to the courts, and they have finally achieved their aims through a Supreme Court decision. At this point, the interest groups have been able to force their views on what has often been a recalcitrant bureaucracy—as well as the policymakers. Quite often, public agencies now find themselves working out compromise settlements with interest groups under the watchful eye of a judge.

[20] Ranney, p. 374.

Whether or not the first two tactics lead to meaningful cooperation between public agencies and interest groups, the interest group will usually attempt to have an indirect impact on the demands and supports that exist within the general environment for the public agency by carrying on a program of mass education (propaganda if one disagrees with the interest group, which is usually called a pressure group in that case.) Most major interest groups are active in the area of public relations and education in an attempt to change the attitudes and perceptions of the general public toward those issues of consequence to the groups. To the extent that an interest group changes the public's opinion toward any issue, policy, or program, the public agency has to react to those changes in order to continue its support; thus, the interest group is able indirectly to have an impact on agency policy and action.

Of course, it must be remembered that the interaction between an agency and its interest groups occurs in both directions. Public agencies depend on interest group support when dealing with the legislature; at the same time, the agency may choreograph the actions of several such groups as they go before the legislature to push for new or changed policies. Likewise, it is not uncommon for a public agency to encourage interest groups to take an issue to court, either to clarify the issue for everyone concerned or to overturn a policy that is mutually objectionable. Finally, it is common for public agencies to use interest groups as vehicles for educating the public, because interest groups have already established communications lines to a large number of people and they regularly have the skills needed for educational campaigns. Therefore, the interaction between public agencies and interest groups often proves to be mutually advantageous.

**Political Parties.** The main purpose of a political party is to nominate candidates and to contest elections in the hope of winning public elected offices. If the party places its candidates in office, it then gains control over the policies and, to a certain extent, the personnel of the government. Where the patronage system still exists, the connection between the party and the bureaucracy is direct; people usually must belong to the party in order to secure jobs, or they must prove their loyalty to a particular political official. In such a case the party can have a tremendous impact on the policies and activities of the public agency. However, even where the merit system exists, the parties still interact with the agencies, and each uses the other in an attempt to control the public policy process.

Under a merit system, the top managerial, policymaking positions are appointive rather than being included among the nonpolitical jobs; therefore, the policies and attitudes of the winning political party are well represented in the upper levels of bureaucracy. Since much of the organizational character and style of operation is established by the leadership of an organization, the philosophies and policies of the parties have an impact on the morale, efficiency, and effectiveness of the public bureaucracy.

Public agency managers and personnel maintain ties with both parties whenever possible, because bureaucrats recognize the political realities and know that control may shift between parties; therefore, it is best to maintain bipartisan relationships. In addition, the bureaucracy is able to gain support for its policies through party espousal; many of the new programs proposed by politicians and their parties are actually originated by the public agencies working in the relevant area. Even though the interaction between these two groups is quite cautious (because each distrusts the intentions of the other and because partisan activity within the public bureaucracy is generally frowned upon by society), the cooperation that takes place is usually considered valuable by both sides.

**Citizen Participation.** Since we live in a democracy, it is taken for granted that citizens may participate in their government if they so desire. Participation, however, has often been interpreted as working in and voting in elections. Only lately has the idea of citizen participation in the administrative process become a central issue. If one of the ideals of democracy is maximum participation by the citizens, why should not the citizens be involved in the administration of their own government? Would not such involvement help the bureaucracy deliver the kind of service that the citizens desire, and, at the same time, increase citizen control over the bureaucracy? Other advocates argue that greater citizen participation would increase overall satisfaction with the bureaucracy because of the increased public understanding of the problems faced by governmental employees in their attempt to deliver programs. Proponents of citizen participation argue that such programs are successful and should be expanded, while those opposed counter that when the citizens become involved in the administrative side of the government, it only makes matters worse for everybody.

Citizen participation has always existed to a limited extent. Many interested individuals and groups have always made their wishes and complaints known to the administrators at all levels of government, but proponents of greater citizen participation have felt that a systematized program, which would bring in larger numbers and a wider variety of citizens, would be beneficial to policymakers and implementers. Suggestions for ways to involve greater numbers of citizens have usually included either citizen advisory boards or neighborhood or geographic councils.

In response to the pressure for increased citizen participation, many city councils have recently established commissions of citizens that are expected to increase the input of information from the public to the council. In some cases, these commissions have been established for a particular length of time, and they are expected to present to the council a report containing what the wider citizen group sees as the goals of the community. In other cases, cities have established ongoing bodies to serve in an advisory capacity. In either case, these bodies often become involved in advising administrators and in reviewing administrative programs, as well as working with the council; however, such activities are usually in an unofficial and informal capacity.

It is not uncommon to find advisory commissions working directly with department heads. For example, the head of the local department of recreation may have groups of citizens who help to establish priorities for parkland purchase and development as well as helping to decide what kind of recreational and cultural activities should be established in neighborhood playgrounds and centers. Such advisory bodies are automatically involved in the administrative process because they are participating in the decisions that the bureaucracy is going to implement. At the same time, members of an advisory board of this kind will also have a chance to influence the actions of the employees of the department because the commission members have access to the supervisors of the employees. If people in the community become aware of the existence of such a board, other citizens are likely to come to the members with suggestions and complaints about the department and its programs and employees.

Sherry Arnstein indentifies eight rungs on a ladder of citizen participation, with three major levels appearing on the ladder. The first level is *nonparticipation* and includes (1) manipulation by the power structure and (2) therapy for the organization. The second level is composed of *token participation* and includes (3) communication with the groups, (4) consultation with the groups, and (5) placation of the groups. Finally, the third level includes three rungs of *real citizen power,* which are referred to as (6) partnership, (7) delegated power, and (8) citizen control.[21] Daniel Moynihan argues that the part of the Economic Opportunity Act that deals with citizen involvement was written by men who were passionately desirous of bringing about social change by arousing the poor. The goal of these men was to get the poor involved in all the stages of program development and implementation and to teach and encourage them to use all the democratic techniques, such as forums, discussions, electioneering, and similar activities.[22] In other words the policymakers wanted to see the poor and lower-class citizens become involved at steps 6, 7, and 8 of Arnstein's ladder.

The results show that, while there have been a few successful programs, "most programs 'manipulate' citizen groups, provide 'therapeutic' activities for citizens, or offer degrees of 'token participation'."[23] According to John Hutcheson, Jr., and Frank Steggert, although some involvement has been created,

for the most part, model cities staff members (where the greatest emphasis on citizen involvement occurred) reflect the same general views as government officials and community knowledgeables. Staff members see participation as an advisory input into program planning. They believe that citizens ought to be

[21] Sherry R. Arnstein, "A Ladder to Citizen Participation," *Journal of the American Institute of Planners, XXXV,* 216 (July 1969).

[22] Daniel P. Moynihan, *Maximum Feasible Misunderstanding,* Free Press, New York, 1969, pp. 90-97.

[23] John D. Hutcheson, Jr., and Frank X. Steggert, *Organized Citizen Participation in Urban Areas,* Center for Research in Social Change, Emory University, Atlanta, 1970, p. 119.

"consulted." And most see present problems of citizen involvement in terms of structural deficiencies. Citizen mobilization and community organization and control are not considered legitimate program objectives.[24]

As is true in all the cases mentioned previously, the interaction between the public agency and the external constituency—in this case the citizens' participation organizations—may be relatively intense and of great importance to both groups; however, the evidence points toward the use of the citizens by the agencies with a minimum of citizen impact. Even so, the process cannot take place without it having some impact on the agency. Citizens may have a greater chance to make demands upon the public agency because of the establishment of participatory programs, and the groups have certainly increased feedback through the political system to both the policymakers and the agencies implementing the policies.

## Governmental Constituencies

Just as a public agency must consider many external groups, it must also recognize the existence of a large number of groups inside government that are essential to successful, effective operation. Included among the governmental organizations or institutions that must be considered by a public agency are the elected executive, the legislature, the courts, other governmental agencies on the same level, and the governments at the other levels of the federal system. The first three institutions will be discussed very briefly here; a detailed discussion of their role as bureaucratic control agents appears in the next chapter; the last two factors, or groups, will be dealt with here in greater detail.

**The "Constitutional" Institutions.** The institutions of the chief executive, the legislature, and the courts are rooted in the Constitution with the idea that they are expected to balance and check each other, thereby protecting the interests of the citizens and guaranteeing that the duties of government will always be performed. The bureaucracy is directly responsible to the chief executive, except in the case of a few agencies such as the independent regulatory commissions and the General Accounting Office. Since there is an executive budget, and the president has the right to appoint the department heads, there is a close tie between the president and the public agencies. This tie is often even more apparent at the local government level where a mayor or city manager can interact directly with the various city departments. When there is close cooperation between the chief executive and the agencies, tremendous amounts of work can get done and progress can be made. When competition or a lack of trust and cooperation develops, the amount of work accomplished dwindles, and both the agencies and the chief executive must often defend their lack of output.

[24]*Ibid.*

When cooperation breaks down, the public agency usually turns to other parts of the government or to outside groups for support in the continuing battle with the chief executive.

Every public agency attempts to maintain excellent relationships with the legislative branch of government. Even though the agencies are directly responsible to the chief executive, they realize the importance of contented legislators; hence, there is a constant interaction between the two groups. Just as department structure generally follows the lines of the major interests in society, so does the committee structure of any large legislative body. Legislators ask for committee assignments according to their special interests; therefore, a strong affinity often develops between public bureaucrats in an agency and their counterpart legislators. The strength of this combination can overcome even the desires of the chief executive in many cases, and both the legislators and officials of the public agencies use this cooperation to establish their favorite policies and programs, or to continue and expand them, in spite of the opposition of other groups.

The third constitutional institution, the courts, functions within the policy system primarily as a check on the actions of public agencies. However, public agencies may join with or use the courts on occasion to accomplish their goals. In fact, many governmental agencies turn regularly to the courts to enforce their rules and regulations. For example, the Equal Employment Opportunity Commission can use the judicial process to enforce the Equal Employment Opportunity guidelines that have been established; the courts may accept employment discrimination cases brought to them from outside the government as well as cases brought by the commission. In cases where the commission and the organization being charged with discrimination cannot achieve a mutually acceptable resolution of the problem, it is possible that the organization may lose any federal funds that it would normally receive. The courts have ruled, in a few of these cases, that federal moneys are to be frozen! When this action takes place, the authority of the public agency is geometrically augmented because both the agency and the courts are apparently interpreting the agency's goal and legal basis for action in the same way. Of course, on occasion, the courts and the agency do not agree; when this happens, the agency must accomplish its goals in a new way, redefine its policies, go to the legislature for a rewriting of the law, or stop the function that has been ruled unconstitutional.

These three institutions are the major participants in the policymaking and policy-interpreting phases of the policy process. The demands that they make upon the public agency are primarily in the form of laws and constitutionally mandated interpretations of those laws. The support that these institutions give are in the form of (1) the legal basis for agency operation and (2) the physical resources needed to carry on the agency's program. Obviously, their impact on the public policy system is the most direct of any of the groups that have been mentioned.

**Competition and Cooperation between Governmental Agencies.** Every public agency finds itself in competition with other similar organizations. There is a limited amount of resources available, and there is also a limited amount of authority or power; at the same time, there are numerous agencies attempting to assure themselves of the power and resources necessary to fulfill their mission— and, if possible, to expand their mission. As appears to be true in most similar situations, there are more competitors and demands for power and resources than there are supplies of these resources; therefore, the agency administrators participate in an activity which Matthew Holden, Jr., calls "bureaucratic imperialism." According to Holden:

Bureaucratic imperialism seems pre-eminently a matter of inter-agency conflict in which two or more agencies try to assert permanent control over the same jurisdiction, or in which one agency actually seeks to take over another agency as well as the jurisdiction of that agency.[25]

The competitive mode of operation is created by the political system because the laws that establish the agencies have created overlapping jurisdictions and intermixed missions. It is common to find several agencies of the federal government involved in regulating, developing, and administering different parts of a single program, and it is not uncommon to find two agencies with directly overlapping jurisdictions (and sometimes working in contradictory directions). One can choose any major policy area at the federal level and name numerous agencies dealing with the problem. For instance, the area of transportation includes the Department of Transportation with its numerous bureaus and agencies, independent regulatory commissions (the Federal Aviation Administration), the Federal Energy Administration, and agencies from several other federal departments.

Given such an intermixture of missions, it is to be expected that a variety of constituency interests "shop" from one agency to the next looking for the best "deal" in return for their support. Such a situation provides an ambitious agency head with numerous opportunities to make deals in order to gain support and broaden the agency's jurisdiction; however, as Holden points out:

Each time the expanding agency acquires a new constituency, that constituency co-opts part of the agency's money, people, time, skill, and working doctrine. If the agency then seeks to shift those resources, it may find itself constrained by the demands of the co-opting constituency which has . . . now acquired a first mortgage on those resources.[26]

For this reason, ambitious public administrators prefer to make deals that are not absolutely firm. This does not mean that agency heads are constantly shift-

[25] Holden, p. 941.
[26] *Ibid.*, p. 945.

ing constituencies or that deals between agencies and constituencies are made only for a short time; instead, the agency head must have the ability to compromise and "beat other agencies to the punch," if he or she is aggressively seeking to "ward off new challenges or to respond to new opportunities provided by the incidence of constituency 'shopping'."

In a similar manner, it is possible for two agencies to cooperate with each other when it is to their advantage to do so. In this case, however, the cooperation is usually only temporary, and it is to be expected that the agencies will be "jockeying for position" constantly so that when the cooperation breaks down or ends each will be in a position to have gained from the prior collaboration. Such behavior is often frowned upon by people who only partially understand the intricacies of politics and administration; however, bureaucratic competition and imperialism

. . . may be deemed "irrational" or "pathological" if, but only if, one has assumed that there is at some point a central policy mechanism capable of articulating a single "public interest" and that those interests not so articulated ought not to be permitted avenues of realization. Those who advocate this may describe it as "rational planning," but gamblers have a more honest name: they call it stacking the deck.[27]

In reality, the world of the public agency is "a place of confusion and uncertainty, with false signals strewn about like dandelion seeds in an open meadow."[28] The competition helps to maintain an empathetic and responsive bureaucracy while, at the same time, it furnishes a process by which the decision makers in the public agency can clarify and better understand the "needs, preferences, ambitions, and hopes" of the public.

Cooperation can be expected to continue on a longer and more stable basis if the associated agencies are from different levels of government or from different jurisdictions at the same level, because there is a chance that an agreement might be reached that would give the agencies some benefits from the collaboration while they would not have to compete directly for jurisdiction and resources. Even here, however, the interaction between agencies is laden with danger; therefore, let us look at cooperative and competitive interaction between different governmental jurisdictions.

*Interaction between jurisdictions in the federal system.* When we discuss intergovernmental interaction, it is necessary to consider two different facets of the issue. First, there is a tremendous amount of interaction between levels of government (throughout the federal system), and second, there is an equal amount of interaction between agencies and jurisdictions of government at the same level. In order to comprehend how all of these fit together, let us look

[27] *Ibid.,* p. 950.

[28] *Ibid.*

at the interaction faced by an administrator in a local governmental unit that is relatively specialized, such as the superintendent of a local school district. This individual's major concern in the public service is the area of planning (a normal management function) for the educational needs of the community; however, planning for education requires the consideration of numerous other governments. First, no plan will be complete unless the other local governmental units in the area are asked to spell out their own plans for development during the time being considered by the superintendent. The local government plans will affect the projection of how many students will be incorporated into the school system, where they will attend those schools, and what levels of the system they will be using. Organizations such as transit authorities may be consulted so that transportation systems for the students can be arranged. Second, state organizations, especially the legislature and the state education department, must be considered. Between these two groups, many of the educational requirements and much of the funding is controlled; therefore, the local superintendent must keep in close contact with these groups if plans are to be adequate and reasonable. Third, the same type of analysis must be done concerning federal support and federal programs; through the U.S. Department of Health, Education, and Welfare, the school district may be receiving funds from a half-dozen special programs, with new ones always on the way; and there may be a connection with other departments, such as the Department of Agriculture, for school lunch programs.

All of this interaction between levels of government is very important because many of the missions of government cannot be accomplished without cooperation between all levels. Although the national government has targeted certain problem areas, it frequently must turn to state and local governments and their agencies to carry out the programs. In return, local governments, because of their limited resources, have increasingly had to turn to the national government for aid in attacking some of their most pressing problems. In fact, Victor Jones, who is a long-time student of the metropolitan scene, has commented that "the most startling and far-reaching change in American federalism is the emergence of the National Government as the focus for discussion of urban and metropolitan affairs."[29] The interaction and, indeed, the intermingling of governmental programs and agencies are often compared to the composition of a marble cake, with the various layers of government running throughout society in an amazing array of combinations. In another analogy, it may be said that— like the girl with the curl in the middle of her forehead—when they (the governmental cooperative programs) are good, they are very, very good, but when they are bad, they are horrid. The difference between success and failure for many public agencies depends on the cooperation, or lack thereof, that is gained from counterpart agencies at other levels of government.

The newest approach to coordinating the work of public agencies has occurred

[29] Victor Jones, "Representative Local Government: From Neighborhood to Region," *Public Affairs Report*, University of California, Berkeley, April 1970.

at the local government level. In an attempt to guarantee that services and programs are effectively delivered, there have been two attempts at coordination, or even uniting, of agencies and programs; the first approach might be called the move toward regionalism, while the second is the establishment of councils of governments. Let us examine each separately and consider how these types of intergovernmental cooperation affect public agencies within the involved local governments.

---

### METHODS OF LOCAL ADAPTATION TO AREA-WIDE PROBLEMS

1. Informal cooperation
2. The service contract
3. Parallel action
4. The conference approach
5. The compact
6. Transfer of functions
7. Extraterritorial jurisdiction
8. Incorporation
9. Annexation
10. City-county separation
11. Geographical consolidation
12. Functional consolidation
13. The special district
14. The authority
15. Metropolitan government
16. The regional agency

---

From Roscoe C. Martin, *Metropolis in Transition,* Housing and Home Finance Agency, Washington, D.C., 1963, pp. 1-11. See this source for further definition and explanation of terms.

As local governments, especially cities and counties, have faced population increases and a higher demand for services, they have tried to deal with the ensuing problems in a variety of ways. In fact, Roscoe Martin, in his report on the *Metropolis in Transition,* points out sixteen different methods of adaptation that he is able to identify.[30] In a similar vein, Paul Friesema, in a study encompassing ten cities in a Standard Metropolitan Statistical Area, found 252 interjurisdictional agreements covering many of the functional areas of local government.[31] One of the ideas that is common to all these actions is the concept of regionalism. The kinds of activities that seem to need this approach for resolution generally fall into three categories:

[30] Roscoe C. Martin, *Metropolis in Transition,* Housing and Home Finance Agency, Washington, D.C., 1963, pp. 1-11.

[31] H. Paul Friesema, "Interjurisdictional Agreements in Metropolitan Areas," *Administrative Science Quarterly, XV,* 246 (June 1970).

(1) Those which are supportive of the jurisdictional boundary crossings which people in metropolitan areas normally engage in in great numbers (e.g., highway planning, mass transit, open space planning, airport planning and operation, planning for the regional job market, etc.); (2) those where the negative (or non) actions of one jurisdiction may undercut the actions of another jurisdiction (e.g., air pollution, low cost housing, waste disposal); and (3) those where economies of scale may demand interjurisdictional planning and operation (e.g., water supply, specialized hospitals, etc.).[32]

The ultimate result of this effort has led, in a few cases, to the development of metropolitan governments, and where this has occurred, the state legislatures have played an important role in the creation of the new systems. In Indianapolis–Marion county, Indiana, the reorganization has resulted in "uni-Gov"; in Minneapolis–St. Paul there is a Metropolitan Council with real power to govern; variations of metropolitan reorganization have also occurred in such states as California, Florida, Oregon, and Tennessee. In other situations, a group of cities may band together and contract for all or a portion of their services through county-administered districts (called the Lakewood Plan).

In most areas, however, "the metropolitan voter seems largely satisfied with the fragmented character of metropolitan government,"[33] and it appears that the most that can be hoped for is that

in the years immediately ahead interlocal service agreements will continue to grow in number, mainly because of the rising pressure to deal with certain needs and problems and the lack of general appeal of more comprehensive methods. But it also appears likely that such agreements will remain ineffective for dealing with area-wide needs.[34]

Not only are the citizens satisfied but so are the elected officials and the bureaucrats. It must be remembered that

like other interest groups, and like government in the metropolis itself, local officialdom and its accompanying bureaucracy are highly pluralistic. Each unit, whether a school district, municipality, or county-wide sewer district, has its own entrenched officials and employees and its own fenced-in area of jurisdiction.[35]

---

[32] Melvin B. Mogulof, *Governing Metropolitan Areas*, The Urban Institute, Washington, D.C., 1971, p. 10. For a more specific breakdown of the criteria for determining areawide or local functions, see: Advisory Commission on Intergovernmental Relations, *Performance of Urban Functions: Local and Areawide*, Washington, D. C., 1963, pp. 41-60.

[33] *Ibid.*, p. 4.

[34] John C. Bollens and Henry J. Schmandt, *The Metropolis: Its People, Politics, and Economic Life*, Second Edition, Harper and Row, New York, 1970, p. 370.

[35] *Ibid.*, p. 135.

Public officials and the members of public agencies have an established rapport with their environment, and this includes an understanding of how to interact with all the other agencies and governmental units in the area. In most cases, a hierarchy is formed, with priorities established and resources distributed accordingly, and the prestige, power, and jurisdiction of each agency understood, however vaguely. Metropolitan or regional reorganization upsets all of these established behaviors; almost everyone is afraid of what will happen to their position, jurisdiction, and resources. Therefore, most public agency personnel are just as afraid of reorganization as are the politicians, especially those members of smaller or weaker jurisdictions.

In an attempt to increase cooperation between governments (and particularly between interrelated agencies) while overcoming the resistance to unification, many areas now have "councils of governments." The council of government usually receives its authority from the local governments that comprise its membership, and it serves primarily as a planning and coordination device in program areas that overlap and are common to all of these jurisdictions. This leads to utilization of these councils as review agencies for grant programs and other area-wide functions supported by the state and national governments. The council of government usually becomes a clearinghouse for information, and many programs of the U.S. Department of Transportation, Department of Housing and Urban Development, Office of Management and Budget, Environmental Protection Agency, and other similar agencies often seek to coordinate their programs through this body.[36]

Public agencies and local governments expect the council of governments to protect and to serve the member organizations, while the state and national governments expect the council "to make judgements and take actions which may be perceived as harmful by the council's member governments."[37] Thus, we find that the interactions between public agencies, at all levels of government, often become institutionalized, with a special agency being established to work out the appropriate balance between cooperation and competition. Through the intermediary organization, bargains can be struck as to how much local autonomy is given up by an agency in return for national government funds or, vice versa, how much of a particular national goal can be purchased for a price. Similarly, public agencies at the same level can decide exactly how much independence must be surrendered in order to deal adequately with regional problems. However, the council of governments simply establishes a formal arena for such activities to take place; this type of interaction between public agencies must occur on a regular basis whether or not a formal arena for such action exists.

The formulation, implementation, and evaluation of public policy depend on the interaction of the various public agencies. Each step of the policy process is

[36] Mogulof, p. 20.

[37] *Ibid., p. 15.*

directly influenced by the cooperation and competition that develops within the system of governmental jurisdictions and their bureaucratic agencies. No public agency stands and operates alone; the only path to success in the accomplishment of the agency's goal is through interaction with the rest of the political system.

## SUMMARY

Public agencies must attempt to accomplish their goals while operating within a complex political system. Numerous groups make demands and give support to the political institutions that convert these factors into political output, or public policy. Included in the political system is also a feedback loop, which allows the system to make necessary corrections in public policy and its implementation. The major role of the public bureaucracy is in the area of policy implementation; however, the bureaucracy becomes involved in all steps of the public policy process. (These steps include (1) problem identification, (2) policy formulation, (3) legitimation, (4) implementation, and (5) evaluation.)

The public agency, as it carries out its task, must interact with numerous segments of the political world. These other forces or groups can, for the sake of simplicity, be placed into three categories: (1) the norms of the social and political systems; (2) external constituencies; and (3) governmental constituencies. Among the more important norms are those surrounding the democratic ethic, the traditional administrative ideal, and the codes of ethics developed by professional organizations. Public agencies must consider all three types of norms in almost every aspect of "doing the public's business." The success of a public agency's existence is also closely related to the type of relationships maintained with external constituencies, such as agency clientele, interest groups, political parties, and citizen's participation organizations. Finally, almost every important public agency must interact with the "constitutional institutions" (the chief executive, legislature, and courts) as well as with other governmental agencies, both at the same level of government and at other levels of the federal system. Only when all these groups are considered can the public bureaucrat feel certain that most important elements in the political system have been taken into account; even then, the public agency's management must always be watching for important occurrences in the general social and economic environment that may have unanticipated consequences on the political system and the public bureaucracy.

# BIBLIOGRAPHY

Alford, Robert R., *Bureaucracy and Participation: Political Cultures in Four Wisconsin Cities,* Rand McNally, Chicago, 1969.

Banfield, Edward C., *The Unheavenly City Revisited,* Little, Brown, Boston, 1974.

Deutsch, Karl W., *The Nerves of Government,* Free Press, New York, 1963.

Devine, Donald J., *The Attentive Public: Polyarchal Democracy,* Rand McNally, Chicago, 1970.

Dror, Yehezkel, *Public Policymaking Reexamined,* Chandler, Scranton, Penn., 1968.

Dye, Thomas R., *Understanding Public Policy,* Second Edition, Prentice-Hall, Englewood Cliffs, N.J., 1975.

Easton, David, *A Framework for Political Analysis,* Prentice-Hall, Englewood Cliffs, N.J., 1965.

Easton, David, *A Systems Analysis of Political Life,* Wiley, New York, 1965.

Elazar, Daniel J., *American Federalism: A View from the States,* Crowell, New York, 1966.

Hilsman, Roger, *The Politics of Policy Making in Defense and Foreign Affairs,* Harper and Row, New York, 1971.

Hutcheson, John D., Jr., and Frank X. Steggert, *Organized Citizen Participation,* Center for Research in Social Change, Emory University, Atlanta, 1970.

Jones, Charles O., *An Introduction to the Study of Public Policy,* Duxbury Press, Belmont, Calif., 1970.

Krislov, Samuel, and Lloyd D. Musolf, eds., *The Politics of Regulation: A Reader,* Houghton Mifflin, Boston, 1964.

League of Women Voters Education Fund, *Supercity/Hometown U.S.A.: Prospects for Two-Tier Government,* Praeger, New York, 1974.

Lindblom, Charles E., *The Policy-Making Process,* Prentice-Hall, Englewood Cliffs, N.J., 1968.

Michael, James R., ed., *Working on the System: A Comprehensive Manual for Citizen Access to Federal Agencies,* Basic Books, New York, 1974.

Milbrath, Lester W., *The Washington Lobbyists,* Rand McNally, Chicago, 1963.

Mogulof, Melvin B., *Governing Metropolitan Areas,* Urban Institute, Washington, D.C., 1971.

Moynihan, Daniel P., *Maximum Feasible Misunderstanding,* Free Press, New York, 1969.

*Performance of Urban Functions: Local and Areawide,* Advisory Commission on Intergovernmental Relations, Washington, D.C.

Wade, Larry L., *The Elements of Public Policy,* Charles E. Merrill, Columbus, Ohio, 1972.

Wilson, James Q., ed., *City Politics and Public Policy,* Wiley, New York, 1968.

Zeigler, Harmon, and Michael Baer, *Lobbying: Interaction and Influence in American State Legislatures,* Wadsworth, Belmont, Calif., 1969.

# ACCOUNTABILITY AND RESPONSIBILITY

*If a democracy as a method of social action has any single problem, it is that of enforcing the responsibility of leadership or bureaucracy.*

*Philip Selznick*

In 1970, a task force on society goals reported to the membership of the American Society for Public Administration that

administrators find themselves having to make more and more policy in league with each other, and having to draft most of the legislation that is theoretically handed to them as a mandate . . . .

# CHAPTER 4

Public executives . . . are in charge. They are responsible for the operation of our society; they cannot wait around for somebody to tell them what to do.[1]

To a great extent, such a charge is true. At the national level, the deliberations of Congress are dominated by "agency bills"—legislation introduced by interested, sympathetic senators or congressmen after the bills have been prepared by the career bureaucrats and executive officers of the various departments and agencies.[2] Once the bills are passed, the administrators are charged with the responsibility of carrying out the policies "established by Congress." At the state and local levels, the administrators appear to be just as involved in politics as do administrators at the national level. Mayors and governors are expected to be policy promoters, but city managers are equally involved in policymaking. When David Booth surveyed 140 managers in towns of 2,500-10,000 population, he found that 83 percent felt that a city manager should play a leading role in policymaking in his city.[3] Analyses in various areas of the country always seem to produce the same type of results. Managers willingly admit that they are intimately involved in the policy process *and most mayors and council people admit they encourage the managers to initiate actions that result in policy decisions.*[4]

Although it is not surprising to find city managers involved in local policymaking activities, there may be more questioning of the role of local bureaucrats. It is obvious from our discussion in  the last three chapters that local bureaucrats are involved in policymaking activities. When Professor Edward Banfield examined the question of who wielded political influence in Chicago, he found that even though the career bureaucrats lacked power because of the strong influence of the party organization, the bureaucrats still were involved in proposing new policy measures as well as implementing policy. Therefore, Banfield argues that

being a civil servant is no impediment to . . . acting politically. . . . On the contrary, most of (the civil servants) are oriented not so much toward changing the distribution of power. . . . Each was quick to tell the politicians what they should and should not do. And each held—not very far out of sight—the possibility of giving trouble to any politician who acted contrary to (the bureaucrat's) advice on a matter crucial to the organization.[5]

[1] *News and Views*, American Society for Public Administration, *XX*, 5 (October 1970).

[2] Francis E. Rourke, *Bureaucracy, Politics, and Public Policy,* Little, Brown, Boston, 1969, p. 49.

[3] David A. Booth, *Council-Manager Government in Small Cities*, International City Management Association, Chicago, 1968, p. 105.

[4] Ronald O. Loveridge, *City Managers in Legislative Politics*, Bobbs-Merrill, Indianapolis, 1971. See also: James Kweder, *The Roles of Manager, Mayor and Councilmen in Policy Making: A Study of 21 North Carolina Cities*, University of North Carolina, Institute of Government, Chapel Hill, 1965.

[5] Edward Banfield, *Political Influence*, Free Press, Glencoe, Ill., 1961, p. 266.

Bureaucratic power in the present political process is a fact of life. Increased bureaucratic influence on policymaking and implementation is a reasonable projection for the future. If these two statements are correct, then the basic question becomes that of how bureaucratic involvement in the political arena will affect the political system, because bureaucratic participation in the process may have positive or negative effects on the responsiveness and success of the government. Of course, the negative effects are usually stressed by the citizenry, the press, and the politician, but the *independent power*, which is required to participate in the political arena of the bureaucracy has, on occasion, protected the citizen even as it has, at other times, allowed the bureaucracy to ignore the desires of the public. For instance, Peter Woll and Rochelle Jones argue that during the Watergate affair, the bureaucracy turned "into a vital although little noticed safeguard of the democratic system."[6] In a similar vein, Thomas Cronin, one of the leading students of the presidency, comments that in the Watergate situation, the bureaucracy became the preserver of the Constitution, civil rights, and due process.[7] Is it possible to guarantee that the bureaucracy will function in a way that will benefit the public, both in the area of policy initiation and policy implementation? What controls the bureaucracy and how is it controlled? These are vital questions that must be faced in our "bureaucratic society." After a brief resume of the bases of bureaucratic power, the problem of control of the bureaucracy will be the focus of this chapter.

## BUREAUCRATIC POWER

Numerous authors have attempted to explain the phenomenon of bureaucratic power. This has been a common topic of discussion since the writing of Max Weber,[8] and it would require only a minor bit of mental exercise to argue that Machiavelli and many other political philosophers were vitally interested in either the power of the bureaucracy or, at least, how to control it. Most, if not all, of the factors contributing to the power of the bureaucracy can be grouped into five general categories:

1. The career bureaucrat, at every level of government, benefits from a *permanency* that is guaranteed to no other participant in the political system except federal judges. Chief executives come and go. Legislators also change regularly, although they often last longer than executives. Only the bureaucrats have tenure in their jobs, so they have a lasting impact on the decisions

---

[6] Peter Woll and Rochelle Jones, "Against One-Man Rule: Bureaucratic Defense in Depth," *The Nation, CCXVII*, 229 (September 17, 1973).

[7] Thomas E. Cronin, Speech at San Jose State University, San Jose, California, April 27, 1974.

[8] Max Weber, *The Theory of Social and Economic Organization*, trans. and eds., A. M. Henderson and Talcott Parsons, Oxford University, New York, 1947.

that are made and the actions that carry out those decisions. If the worst possible state of affairs occurs, and the political leaders seek to establish and carry out policies hostile to the bureaucracy, the bureaucrats can usually, over the long term, overcome the political leaders by carefully following the rules, keeping a low profile, and outlasting their opponents.

2. Just as important as the factor of permanency is the unrivaled *expertise* of the governmental bureaucracy. The staff of any executive agency will, over a period of years, become more knowledgeable and skilled in the subject area under consideration than any other group (with the exception, perhaps, of the clientele served when that clientele is a professional or skilled group itself, such as the radio and television industry). "In the modern state this expertise comes pre-eminently from the fact that a variety of highly trained elites practice their trade in public organizations."[9] These elites hold in their grasp the necessary skills and information needed to formulate and to implement public policy. Skill is important, but it is useless without the proper information. Thus, the control of information is power, just as the skill at using knowledge is power.

3. If the bureaucracy wishes to do so, it may use its expertise in a way that will guarantee it *outside support*. As Rourke says, "Through the assiduous cultivation of legislative and public support, it is possible for an administrative agency to establish a position of virtually complete autonomy. . . ."[10] The FBI accomplished this position during the days of J. Edgar Hoover; the Army Corps of Engineers also developed a position of autonomy from the presidency by emphasizing its ties to Congress. While not achieving total independence, other segments of the national bureaucracy, such as the Veteran's Administration, have also created a vociferous and loyal following that helps the agency to defeat its enemies and to win its battles in Congress. At the state and local levels, it is possible to identify departments that are equally successful in getting their way at budget time as well as at other times. Prime examples of these are local police departments and fire departments where their expertise, their internal organization, their reputations of public service, and their acts of heroism, which are often brought before the public through the news media, help to create a sympathetic public and legislature.

4. Another source of bureaucratic power is the *respect* in American society *for specialized professionalism*. As was noted in the second factor above, the governmental bureaucracy is filled with people from every profession that exists in our society. Douglas M. Fox argues that

the governmental specialist is well thought of not only for his reputed competence, but also because he contrasts favorably with those who hold office as a result of patronage. Professional bureaucrats have done their best to prop-

[9] Rourke, p. 42.

[10] *Ibid.*, p. 31.

best to propagate the myth that they are neutral in policy matters and simply act, to the best of their ability, as directed by political executives.[11]

Americans have always honored professionals as individuals who have a special position in society and who have, therefore, a special right to comment about a wide variety of political and social issues. Thus, while civil servants are not highly regarded by society, those civil servants who are also professionals have been able to combine the two factors to their advantage.

5. The bureaucracy gains much of its independence (which is not necessarily the same as power but is essential to power) from its *size*. The larger the organization, the more it can collect within it the expertise which is so important to gaining power. Size also allows most of the employees a greater degree of protection from publicity, which, in return, allows the bureaucrat to go about his or her job without fear of being singled out for blame or for praise. The national government's bureaucracy has long been considered "unmanageable" because of its size. The same criticism is now leveled toward most state bureaucracies and many of the larger cities throughout the country, for most of the growth in government employment has occurred at the state and local levels during the last twenty years. Although the chief executive is held responsible for the actions of these employees, there is no way for the executive to maintain surveillance and control of the employees' actions. For this reason, the presidents of the United States have become increasingly frustrated during the last two decades when attempting to create changes in national policy. Thomas Cronin claims that this is one of the factors that has caused the tremendous growth in the White House staff.

(O)ccupants of the White House frequently distrust members of the *permanent government.* Nixon aides, for example, have viewed most civil servants not only as Democratic but wholly unsympathetic to . . . objectives of the Nixon administration. . . . Departmental bureaucracies are viewed from the White House as independent, unresponsive, unfamiliar, and inaccessible.[12]

In like manner, many local governmental bureaucracies are considered to be uncontrollable, with New York City, for instance, being referred to as ungovernable. The inability of the mayor to "straighten out the mess in city hall" has led to the demise of several young, glamorous, and potentially powerful politicians.

---

[11] Douglas M. Fox, *The Politics of City and State Bureaucracy,* Goodyear, Pacific Palisades, Calif., 1974, p. 19.

[12] Thomas E. Cronin, "The Swelling of the Presidency," *Saturday Review of the Society, I,* 35 (February 1973). Emphasis added. The idea of the public bureaucracy serving as a "permanent government" is an interesting concept in and of itself.

# THE COOPERATING FORCES:
# FORMAL AND INFORMAL CONTROLS

In spite of the power that the public bureaucracy has in the United States, the bureaucracy has been held in check by our system of government. These checks have come from both outside and inside the bureaucracy and from outside and inside the bureaucrat as an individual. Each type of control is important; however, it is doubtful that any one type of control can function successfully without the others. Let us divide the control mechanisms into three categories: external system controls, internal system controls, and internal individual controls. We will discuss each category in turn, showing how the particular mechanisms function to limit the power and freedom of the bureaucracy, to guarantee that bureaucratic actions are not detrimental to the public, and to attempt to assure results that are beneficial to the people as a whole.

## Formal Control: Accountability

When the control over bureaucratic action comes from outside the individual or from outside of the particular part of the organization that is carrying out the operation, it is said that the bureaucrat is *accountable* to someone else. This accountability may be formalized through laws, rules, regulations, and court orders, or it may be based on an informal set of checks and balances developed through face-to-face confrontations, rumors of support, threats of opposition, or other similar types of clearly understood but unwritten formulas.

**Legislative Controls.**    The most widely recognized controls are those held by the legislature. The interaction of the executive agencies and the legislature has been discussed in preceding chapters of this book. While it is true that the bureaucracy influences many of the legislature's actions, congressmen and councilmen also influence and control the actions of the civil servants. Depending on the importance of the actions being taken (and other factors such as the technical knowledge required to understand the procedures), the legislature may demand a great amount of control over executive agency actions or may choose to give only minimal direction; however, Malcolm Jewell and Samuel Patterson note that all federal agencies receive some level of oversight.

When an individual legislator observes closely and becomes familar with the organization and policy implementation of an administrative agency, or when a legislative committee by contact, observation, or investigation places itself in the posture of a "watchdog" over agency activities, we speak of these legislative-executive relationships in terms of *oversight.* When the influence of individual legislators or legislative committees constitutes substantial involvement in the formulation or implementation of administration policy, producing changes in policy emphasis or priority, we speak of these relationships as legislative *supervision.* When the legislature directs administrative organization and policy, or requires legislative clearance for administrative decisions, it is meaningful to talk of the legislative-executive relation as one of *control.* [13]

At the state and local level, the same kind of phenomena occur regularly. It is common for a city council to allow purchases up to a specific limitation to be made by the manager or the manager's designee; above this limitation, the council must give approval before purchase. Such a policy allows the council to approve major decisions before they are carried out, yet relieves the council from having to make a constant stream of minor decisions. Debates often arise in council meetings as to which streets should be paved first, what busy corners should have priority for the installation of traffic lights, and what parks should be developed first or have special recreation programs. In each case, the council is attempting to control or to limit the choices open to the administrative agency involved.

Behind the "suggestions" made by the legislature are two formal weapons that may be used if informal controls do not work. First, the legislature approves the budget of each department on an annual basis. Second, the legislators may enact their suggestions as laws if such a step becomes necessary. The administrative officers receiving the advice recognize the possibility of negative legislative actions if they are not observant of and sympathetic to the suggestions of the lawmakers.

**Interest Group Controls.**    Closely allied to the legislative control of the public bureaucracy is the surveillance of the various interest groups. Of course, the interest groups are watching the actions of both public bodies, and these outside groups may well try to gain advantages by using either or both of the branches of government; however, we are primarily interested in the ways that the executive agencies are affected by this practice.

There are hundreds of organized groups that maintain lobbyists and professional staffs in the national and state capitals; there are also numerous similar arrangements in county courthouses and city halls. One of the major jobs of these lobbyists is to keep track of the actions of the bureaucracy. Whenever it is possible, these associations attempt to influence the decisions and performance of the agencies by testifying at legislative hearings and by feeding information into the decision-making system of the bureaucracy. Any time the interest groups appeal outside the executive structure, additional problems are created for the administrative organization; therefore, it is easier to cooperate and to assuage the interest groups when possible.

Because numerous interest groups exist and represent most of the segments of society, it is often taken for granted that, ultimately, everybody benefits from

[13] Malcolm E. Jewell and Samuel C. Patterson, *The Legislative Process in the United States,* Random House, New York, 1966, p. 484.

such an arrangement; however, some critics argue that certain groups, instead of benefiting, "get it in the end." There have been some groups, such as consumers and welfare recipients, who have not had organized representation in this system or who have only recently gained representation. It can be argued, therefore, that these groups have not had protection of this type against the bureaucracy. Although this charge may be true, the existence of such a system of control over public administrative action cannot be denied; where it does exist, it functions quite well.

**The Courts as a Control Agent.**   As was noted previously, it is possible to appeal administrative decisions and actions to the courts; thus, the courts are also involved in controlling the actions of the public bureaucracy. It is possible, through court order, to force the agencies to fulfill legal obligations. It is also possible to force the delay and perhaps the cancellation of proposed actions prior to or during their execution. Judges are limited in their control function because they must wait for someone to bring a particular issue to them. The courts cannot initiate action. However, this does not appear to be a serious drawback for the courts as they have become involved increasingly in the review of administrative actions. Judges are also limited in the actions that they can take against administrative officers because the courts generally rule only on the legality or illegality of the process used by the administrators. While courts may rule on the facts of a case, they usually shy away from such action. Thus, in most cases, the overview of bureaucracy carried out by the courts is rather narrow. On the other hand, if judges insist on becoming involved in the policymaking process, they may do so by broadly interpreting the intent of the law and by including in that interpretation the particular issue on which the judges wish to have input.

The involvement of the courts in the final outcome of administrative performance appears to increase as one moves from the national government to the local government level. More state agency actions are challenged than are national administrative actions, and the number of court challenges of local government actions again increases. The obvious reason for this is the larger number of state and local governments, with their proportionately larger bureaucracies which are involved in cases directly affecting the citizens. In addition, there are other reasons why the involvement of courts increases at the lower levels of government. Individuals generally feel that they have a better chance of challenging the rulings of local government and winning the challenge. The cases are likely to have less impact on government as a whole, although they may set precedents that can be used elsewhere; therefore, both the challengers and the courts may find it easier to involve themselves in the issues being considered, whereas cases with wide impact might increase the reluctance of everyone concerned to deal with the issue. Finally, local governments have less status than the states, and this may make it easier to attack the actions of the local governmental employees.[14] Whatever the reasons, local administrators appear to work under a greater threat of judicial interference with governmental bureaucratic actions.

**Open Hearings and Meetings as Control Mechanisms.**   Another popular method of controlling the bureaucracy is the utilization of open hearings or meetings where policies, rules, or regulations are being set by the agency. This procedure primarily applies to the regulatory agencies, but other administrative bodies are also affected. Regulatory agencies have always had to open their hearings to those groups that were directly affected by the decisions, but often rulings were made in executive session (a session closed to the public) after the open hearings were over, so that it was impossible to know how individual agency commissioners voted.

Now there is a concerted effort to force all sessions of legislatures and bureaucracies to remain open to the public. The laws requiring open meetings are generally called "sunshine laws." There are two interpretations as to why they gained this title; one states that they were so named because the first states to establish such laws were Florida and California; the second states that the passage of such a law lets in the "light of day" because decisions can no longer be made behind closed doors. The assumption behind such laws, of course, is that by opening the meetings to the public, the secret deals and compromises that have been made in the past will no longer be made because of the scrutiny of the press and of other interested groups. Therefore, the decisions will better represent the needs and desires of the general public. There are those who feel that such a maneuver only limits the amount of compromise possible on issues where it is essential to be able to compromise because interested parties will force those who are representing their views to take firm and unalterable stances. If the critics are right, of course, this means that the "open meeting" laws may lead to greater conflict in the political system, or they may force the compromises to be struck in a new way or in different settings. Who will finally be proved right cannot be known yet, but there will undoubtedly be more attempts to control the actions of bureaucrats through the utilization of open meetings.

---

[14] The lower status of cities and counties is based on "Dillon's rule," the classic statement on limitations on municipal autonomy, which states that

it is a general and undisputed proposition of law that a municipal corporation possesses and can exercise the following powers and no others: first, those granted in express words; second, those necessarily or fairly implied in or incident to the powers expressly granted; third, those essential to the accomplishment of the declared objects and purposes of the corporation—not convenient, but indispensable. Any fair, reasonable, substantial doubt concerning the existence of power is resolved by courts against a corporation, and the power is denied. (John F. Dillon, *Commentaries on the Laws of Municipal Corporations*, Fifth Edition, Little, Brown, Boston, 1911, p. 448.)

This very constrictive definition of municipal power is justified by Dillon by reasoning that since the city is merely a creature of the state, the city may also be limited *or done away with* by the state. Thus, the state, as a sovereign body, must have its laws broadly construed, while the city, as a creature of the state, must have its laws narrowly construed.

*The press as a watchdog.*   A major advocate of the idea of open meetings has been the news industry. Many of the major stories about politics and the bureaucracy are generated by news reporters. Every major agency maintains a public relations person who is expected to cooperate with the press insofar as possible, because public administrators know and respect the power of the news media in creating a positive image for an agency *or* in creating a negative image if the media gets hold of news of malfeasance or misfeasance in office by any public official.

*Citizen participation as a control agent.*   Citizen participation has long been used both for support by the agency and as a control device by the lawmakers. As was noted in the last chapter, the concept of citizen participation received a tremendous boost when President Johnson and the Congress included in the War on Poverty program a specific requirement that local governments should strive to achieve maximum feasible citizen participation in the development and administration of the various antipoverty programs.[15]   Further impetus was created for greater citizen input, especially in the previously ignored ghetto areas of the cities, when the report of the National Advisory Commission on Civil Disorders (the Kerner Commission) was released in 1968. The Kerner Commission suggested that

[a] lack of communication exists for all residents in our larger cities; it is, however, far more difficult to overcome for low income, less-educated citizens who are disproportionately supported by and dependent upon programs administered by agencies of local government.[16]

Numerous community councils began to emerge during this time, especially in the many Model Cities areas that were established in the larger cities. The success of these groups in allowing the local residents to gain some control over the bureaucracy has been mixed, but the idea has not lost any of its glamor; there will undoubtedly be a continuing desire for more programs of this kind. Since this is true, it might be interesting to examine one example of how these new bodies have functioned in one major city.

In 1970, after the publication of the Kerner Commission report, and after some serious discussion within city hall, the police department decided to establish an Internal Investigation Division which would be responsible for investigating any complaints brought against a police officer for actions taken while on duty. Police departments have a great amount of independent power because of specific authority given to the police by the laws of the state and the ordinances of the city. These powers are increased by the coalitions that the police are able to forge politically within the community and by the unique

---

[15] Public Law, 88-452, 88th Congress, 2nd Session, August 20, 1964.

[16] *Report of the National Advisory Commission on Civil Disorders*, New York Times, New York, 1968, p. 284.

type of function served by the police department. Because of the independent power of the police department and because of some tension between the police and the minority community of the city, the leaders of the Model Cities area proposed a civilian police review board. According to the proposal, the police review board would have had the right to hear and to investigate allegations from citizens, and when the review board felt it was appropriate, it would have had the power to provide money for civil suits in the courts. The police department, the council, and the manager were all opposed to such a review board, and after careful maneuvering everyone thought that the idea had been checkmated. However, as was noted above, the leaders of the drive for the police review board were also on the Board of Directors of the Model Cities corporation, which included much of the area of the city inhabited by the minority population. According to the rules that controlled the use of Model Cities' money, the Board of Directors was given "green light" authority over the use of these funds. This meant that although the directors could not originate expenditures, they had to approve the use of these funds. Since Model Cities' funds could be used as "seed money," through which the city and county could generate additional federal funds via the grant programs, the amount of money that the Board of Directors had some control over was approximately 11 million dollars. The proponents of the police review board were able to talk the directors into tying up all of these funds, which were to carry out several projects that both the city and county wanted to move forward on as quickly as possible. Obviously, some sort of agreement was going to have to be reached. After a series of bargaining sessions, a compromise was attained in which the city established an ombudsman's office. The minority community obtained the most important part of its goal in that the ombudsman had the right and duty to work with the Internal Investigation Division of the police department; thus, it guaranteed that the review of citizen complaints against the police would be thorough and objective. At the same time, the city administration was satisfied with the agreement because the ombudsman was empowered to serve the total population of the community, he was appointed to handle investigations because of his professional expertise, and he was able to act upon complaints against other departments of the city as well as the police department. The input of citizen desires, voiced through a council representing the minority populace of the city, forced both the politicians and the public administrators to change their policies and practices. Thus, the development of a neighborhood council which had the power to criticize and to make suggestions, as well as some strength to back their suggestions, led to a new method of controlling bureaucratic actions.

**The Ombudsman's Office.**   The establishment of an ombudsman's office in a city is a relatively new idea. However, the idea of such an office has been gaining support throughout the country. At least two states, Hawaii and Oregon, have state ombudsmen, and the idea was tried in a slightly different form by Pennsylvania's Governor Raymond Shafer, in 1967, when he established the Governor's

Branch Office in an attempt to allow citizens, who usually could not deal with the governmental bureaucracy, to have access to the services that they should be receiving.[17] There has been increasing pressure for ombudsmans' offices, or something similar to that concept, in several major cities.[18]

The name "ombudsman" and the concept of the office are borrowed from Sweden. An ombudsman is an official within the government, but he is separate in responsibility from the bureaucratic chain of command. His job is to accept complaints against the action or inaction of any government employee. Upon receiving a complaint from a citizen, the ombudsman has the duty of determining if the complaint is valid, and if so, he has the authority to carry out a thorough investigation and to help the citizen resolve the problem. In order to function effectively, the ombudsman must have the trust and support of both the citizen and the bureaucrat. Such a position requires an individual with special interpersonal skills, an individual of unquestioned honesty, and an individual with a high level of ingenuity. Usually, in America, the ombudsman has little power in the formal sense. The two powers that the ombudsman can use are his direct access to the top administrator in that particular jurisdiction and his power to publicize his findings. Since the ombudsman is appointed by the governor, city manager, or other top administrator at a similar level, the other bureaucrats in the organization recognize the value of cooperating whenever possible, for the ombudsman has direct communication links with the top official, and the ombudsman's word can carry a great deal of weight with that official. Second, public administrators wish to avoid adverse publicity, so they are usually willing to cooperate in finding equitable solutions to citizen complaints so that the issue will be resolved before getting out to the general public through the news media, council meetings, or other similar public forums. Finally, if the ombudsman is judicious in his actions, and if he attempts to develop a rapport with the administrators, then it is possible to convince the department heads that it is to their advantage to cooperate *because cooperation will help them to do their jobs better.* While the ombudsman is developing this kind of relationship with the bureaucrats, he must, at the same time, develop and maintain a rapport with the citizenry; he must convince them that he is an impartial, objective individual who will listen seriously to their problems and satisfy their needs.

These skills are apparently achievable, for the experiences with the ombudsman concept in the United States have generally led to positive reviews. So a

---

[17] William W. Vosburgh and Drew Hyman, "Advocacy and Bureaucracy: The Life and Times of a Decentralized Citizen's Advocacy Program," *Administrative Science Quarterly, XVIII,* 433-448 (December 1973).

[18] For an in-depth consideration of the ombudsman concept and how it is applied in practice, see: John M. Capozzola, "An American Ombudsman: Problems and Prospects," *Western Political Quarterly, XXI,* 289-301 (June 1968). See also: "The Ombudsman or Citizen's Defender: A Modern Institution," *The Annals of the American Academy of Political and Social Science, CCCLXXVII* (May 1968).

new method of attempting to control the power of the bureaucracy appears to be gaining ground in our political and administrative systems.

**Do the External Controls Work?** From our discussion, it becomes apparent that the public bureaucracy does not have absolute freedom of action. When bureaucratic actions get too far out of line with public desires and ideals, it is possible to bring pressure to bear through the legislature, the courts, the interest groups, and clientele associations. These external groups are also important to the bureaucracy because of the competition that occurs between governmental organizations. After all, the public bureaucracy is divided into competing businesses. Each particular department, agency, and bureau must compete for limited resources, just as is true for all the other organizations of society. The form of the competition may differ in that the organizations are competing for political support so that they can gain the resources that are needed through the budgetary and legislative processes, but it is competition nonetheless. Anyone competing with other groups for support will find that one of the most important factors in gaining that support *over the long run* is honesty; this fact is not lost on bureaucrats any more than it is on individuals in any other walk of life. Thus, competition helps to control the bureaucracy.

Whatever the number and intensity of external controls, which are the traditional and popularized protections against immorality in public administration, there is still a question as to whether or not they really work. Paul Appleby, in his lectures on *Morality and Administration in Democratic Government*, argues that these protections are not very effective and may be negative.[19] Instead of depending on legal controls, Appleby wants to make sure that administrative behavior will be judged in the ballot box. The ultimate external check must come from the electorate because

any effort to remove an area of governmental activity from general political responsibility—to "protect" it from politics is, per se, a threat to administrative morality since it encourages the administrator to approach his problems narrowly, to minimize or neglect or ignore the general interest.[20]

**Internal System Control: Hierarchy.** We have discussed methods of gaining and maintaining responsiveness and control over the public administrators, and it is obvious that those methods are important; however, Appleby argues that a second type of control is necessary, and this control is of vital importance although it is often forgotten when talking about this subject. This mechanism is the hierarchy within the administration. Hierarchy is often commented upon dis-

---

[19] Paul Appleby, *Morality and Administration in Democratic Government*, Louisiana State University, Baton Rouge, 1952.

[20] Frederick C. Mosher, *Democracy and the Public Service*, Oxford University, New York, 1968, p. 212.

paragingly by organization theorists and by those attempting to apply behavioral science methods to organizations through the techniques of "organizational development." In their rush to condemn the hierarchical structure of organizations, these critics may be overlooking one of the essential reasons as to why hierarchy is good in public administrative agencies. Appleby argues that if the hierarchy is effective, it "forces important decisions to higher levels of determination or at least higher levels of review where perspectives are necessarily broader, less technical and expert, (and) more political."[21] The hierarchy also adds another dimension of control to the actions of most bureaucrats, for they know that if clients or those receiving services are unhappy with the actions that are taken, those actions can be appealed to someone who is higher in authority in the organization. While the primary importance of hierarchy may lie in the area referred to by Appleby, both factors help to maintain the responsiveness and morality of the public bureaucracy.[22]

The additional controls mentioned by Appleby are important, but there is still a limit on what can be accomplished by checks external to the individual. In fact, in spite of all the talk about controls on the governmental bureaucracy, they have probably decreased in importance during the last several decades. Referring to this factor, Michael Harmon has commented that

since clearly defined external sanctions to govern behavior are becoming generally less evident, their existence cannot realistically be presumed in a theory of responsible behavior in any sphere of activity. Instead, we are required to turn increasingly to an existential concept of self-responsibility as the foundation of a new theory.[23]

### Informal Control: Responsibility

The new theory of public servant control is based on the concept that the most important and ultimate control is internal; Harmon referred to it as "self-responsibility." Such a factor is of extreme importance in maintaining the public bureaucracy's loyalty to the ideals and procedures of a democratic state. If a public administrator wants to subvert the law or take a particular matter into his own hands, it is often possible for him to do so. Thus, ultimately, "bureaucrats need to be imbued with the values of our constitutional democracy because, for the most part, the limits on them are those they impose upon themselves."[24]

---

[21] *Ibid.*

[22] See the chapter on "Control" for futher consideration of the usefulness and methods of internal control in a bureaucratic organization.

[23] Michael M. Harmon, "Normative Theory and Public Administration: Some Suggestions for a Redefinition of Administrative Responsibility," in Dwight Waldo, ed., *Toward a New Public Administration*, Chandler, Scranton, Penn., 1971, p. 179.

[24] Woll and Jones, p. 232.

Perhaps the problem that we face at this point is one of defining the difference between the responsiveness of the bureaucracy and the control of the bureaucracy. Control usually comes from outside the individual. It is important but is not enough in and of itself to guarantee that the bureaucracy will function in a way that is beneficial to the public. As Rourke notes,

Dissatisfaction with the adequacy of controls over bureaucracy in the contemporary world . . . springs from the fact that these controls are far more effective as checks than they are as spurs to action.[25]

Responsiveness, on the other hand, may be a spur to action *or* a check on action, depending on the particular circumstances. Responsiveness also connotes an acceptance of responsibility, whereas controls from outside are defined as connoting the idea of accountability to some person or to some thing outside the organization. An official is morally obligated (responsible) by his decision and by any actions emanating from it, even when he cannot be held legally accountable. For instance, a social worker, if he or she is carefully following the "rules and regulations," cannot be held legally accountable for causing welfare clients to suffer needlessly; however, if such officials could adopt a more flexible stance in handling the cases but do not do so, they are morally responsible for the impact of their inflexibility. The ultimate check, therefore, allows even greater control over the actions of the bureaucracy.

Public administrators feel a responsibility for their actions, and this feeling is often a more powerful deterrent to wrong actions and a greater stimulus to correct actions than any other type of control. If this is so, what composes this informal and internal, yet powerful control? It is composed of such things as the public administrator's attitudes toward the law, the value placed upon each individual as a human being, and the general personal moral hierarchy of the individual public administrator. The recognition of this internal control raises the following questions: (1) How are these elements developed within the public administrator, and (2) can these elements be changed in some way if such a course of action seems appropriate?

The attitudes and ideals that make up the public administrator's moral hierarchy are the culmination of his life experiences and training. The creation of the "final product" primarily involves three major factors: the socioeconomic background of the individual; the type and extent of education received by the individual; and the professional ties of the particular individual. These factors can be aggregated for all civil servants in order to get an overall picture of the composition of the total public bureaucracy and to begin to understand what kind of an effect these factors may have on the ability of the civil service to fulfill its role of carrying out the government's programs in a way that will benefit the public interest.

---

[25] Rourke, p. 148.

One of the most important factors in guaranteeing that the ideals of the public administrators match those of the public they serve is by making sure that the characteristics of the civil servants match the characteristics of the public. Civil servants' perceptions of the world are greatly influenced by factors in their backgrounds, such as the economic level and racial composition of their families; even their religious backgrounds will be an influencing factor. Each of these factors leads to different attitudes about the kinds of services that are needed and how those services should be delivered, as well as to basic differences in the way democratic ideals of the society are understood. The ideal that should be sought within the civil service is the development of a representative bureaucracy or one that contains the appropriate mix of the various social, ethnic, and economic backgrounds present in society. Paul P. Van Riper argues for such a representative bureaucracy, claiming that only through a representative bureaucracy can all the desires and needs of the total public be understood, considered, and met by the public bureaucracy; he states,

A representative bureaucracy is one in which there is a minimal distinction between the bureaucrats as a group and their administrative behavior and practices on the one hand, and the community or societal membership and its administrative behavior, practices and expectations of government on the other. Or, to put it another way, the term representative bureaucracy is meant to suggest a body of officials which is broadly representative of the society in which it functions, and which in social ideals is as close as possible to the grass roots.[26]

While this argument has not been accepted by everyone, it has been a central factor in the long and heated debate over affirmative action that has developed during the last decade. Unless this argument is accepted as valid, there is no reason to debate about the composition of the civil service or about the validity of the selecting mechanisms that are used to hire people into the system, because it would not be important to have a representative mixture in the public employ. Of course, it will never be possible to match the composition of the population perfectly; however, that is not the goal of those who support the idea of maintaining responsibility within the public bureaucracy. Among the supporters of the concept of representativeness in bureaucracy, mirroring the general populace is an ideal to work toward, and they believe that the closer the government bureaucracy comes to achieving this goal, the more responsive and responsible will be the bureaucracy.

Education is the second internal factor that influences the responsibility of public administrators. The importance of the educational process can be seen in sharp detail when the educational backgrounds of the civil servants of Great

---

[26] Paul P. Van Riper, *History of the United States Civil Service*, Row, Peterson, Evanston, Ill., 1958, p. 552.

Britain and the United States are compared. The top-level civil servants in Great Britain have come primarily from the best private schools (called public schools) of the country, and they have gone to one of the "Oxbridge" (Oxford and Cambridge Universities) colleges where their main course of study has been the humanities. In comparison with Britain, the top civil servants in the United States have come from a wide variety of professions after getting their elementary and secondary educations in the public schools. The difference in performance between the two sets of bureaucrats has been pointed out in several studies, with the researchers generally pointing to the greater generalist attitude and perception of the British civil servant and to the greater technical capabilities and more egalitarian attitudes of the United States' civil servant. Interestingly enough, critics in both countries have pointed to the other country's civil service as an example that should be followed at home. Apparently, there may be some balance between the two extremes that gives a public bureaucracy the proper mixture of generalist and specialist training and perception, but that balance has not yet been achieved.

There is a constant stream of criticism about the education of public administrators in the United States. At various times, the critics have argued for different types of education for the public bureaucracy's leaders, but the demands for change have taken on a particular emphasis during the 1960s and the 1970s. Dvorin and Simmons have sounded the cry for the entire movement when they comment that

to a considerable degree, colleges and universities have provided academic programs in public administration which are largely devoid of inspiration or intellectual content. The "span of control" has been seen as being of infinitely more importance than the "span of value commitment."[27]

This argument is further developed when they say that

concern with values and a central concern for the dignity of man should not be grafted as afterthoughts onto specialist bureaucrats. These concerns should be the core of the academic curriculum, and it is crucial that this approach be stressed in the earliest years of career preparation.[28]

Not everyone agrees with the goals of education spelled out by Dvorin and Simmons, but most agree that the education of the civil servant affects the ability and desire of the bureaucrat to deliver service in the manner most suited for a democratic state.

Closely allied to the problem of education is that of professionalism in the public service. Once again, there are two different attitudes toward this aspect of public administration. There are those who see the trend toward greater profes-

---

[27] Eugene P. Dvorin and Robert H. Simmons, *From Amoral to Humane Bureaucracy*, Canfield, San Francisco, 1972, p. 21.

[28] *Ibid.*, p. 51.

sionalism in the public service as a threat to democratic government, while a second group believes that professionalism will increase the quality of decision making and the quality of service to the public in addition to maintaining the democratic system.

Paul Appleby and his followers see the establishment of professional enclaves in the public service as a threat to the protective mechanism (open politics and a responsible hierarchy within the bureaucracy) that has been so painstakingly created. Most professionals are greatly influenced by the ideals, codes of ethics, and customs of the groups to which they belong and with which they identify; as Frederick Mosher has noted,

Most professions are at best ambivalent, at worst downright hostile toward government in general and politics in particular. Most seek to shield them-selves from politics, and this of course means that they oppose *open* politics.[29]

The result of professional attitudes toward politics has been that most profes-sionals in the public service seek protection from any and all political forces. This ties in with the problem of open politics as a control over the bureaucracy, because

by removing itself as far as possible from the normal channels of political com-plaint, debate, and appeal, a professionally dominated agency denies the general public the opportunity for democratic direction and decision.[30]

Although professionals abhor politics, those parts of the public service that have seen large influxes of professional employees have also seen those profes-sionals taking over many, if not all, of the positions of power within the hier-archy. Such a phenomenon occurs for at least two reasons. First, as the number of professionals becomes greater within a particular bureaucracy, the normal sta-tistical laws show that the odds increase for professional bosses. However, a second and perhaps more important factor usually is involved. As an agency be-comes populated with professionals, the argument is made that it is essential for the leaders of the agency to be drawn from the profession concerned in order that the leader can comprehend the problems of the agency and the perception of the members. A professional boss also increases the chances that the members of the agency will have the proper regard for their leader. This creates the second problem raised by Appleby:

By closing the elite of the hierarchy to all but professionals, it denies assurance of broadly based and disinterested judgement on problems.[31]

<hr />

[29] Mosher, p. 215. This and the following quotes are representations of Appleby's arguments by Mosher.

[30] *Ibid.*, p. 212.

[31] *Ibid.*

The proponents of professionalism, on the other hand, do not see the increasing number of professionals within the government service as a detrimental force either in policymaking or in responsiveness to the public. Professional codes of ethics, to which members prescribe, are important in creating the attitudes of the individual as he works within the public bureaucracy (whether the code has the power of coercion or persuasion). The professionals usually try to find ways of working with society and operating in the public sphere according to the democratic ethic, for as Rourke notes,

Codes of ethics adopted by administrative groups such as city managers characteristically accept a subordinate role for bureaucrats in the governmental process. To be sure this acceptance may be mere lip service, designed to disguise the extent to which bureaucrats actually control policy decisions. At the same time, however, it seems fair to assume that there will be some strain toward consistency on the part of administrative officials, and that a bureaucrat's conception of his role as a limited one will have a restraining effect upon his behavior in office.[32]

The use of professionals should improve the delivery of services, thus making the bureaucracy more responsive in that manner. The proponents of professionalism argue that the professional has an important place to fill in the policymaking process because of his expertise in the many subjects that require attention. These advocates of professionalism usually recognize the need for a change of perception from specialist to generalist as an individual moves up the hierarchical ladder. This change is not adequate in and of itself for those who feel that public administrators must move out of their professional shell and into a more advocative stance; these critics of professionalism believe that the various professionals must develop a closer identity with *public administration* as a profession, and then the public administrators must, as a group, become actively involved in the policymaking process. This sentiment is the basis for the following statement by Dvorin and Simmons:

The end of public administration is not to execute public policy with utmost dispatch, with maximum efficiency, or value neutrality—or any combination of the three. The refinement of technique is of low priority compared to the discipline's need to define the *public interest*. . . . Only by a fundamental and searching reevaluation of its role in the community of man can public administration become morally relevant. Unless the bureaucracy "throws its hat into the ring" of public controversy as an active participant which believes strongly in moral choices *of its own derivation*, it cannot justify its exercise of power.[33]

[32] Rourke, p. 146.

[33] Dvorin and Simmons, p. 50. Emphasis added.

The writers ignore the problem of how "the public interest" is to be defined when this approach to the role of the professional public administrator is proposed. Every reform that has led to greater participation of the public administrator in local government has been supported *and* attacked from this standpoint. Robert Lineberry and Edmund Fowler, in examining the effect of political reform on the political processes of cities found that

> . . . when a city adopts reformed structures, it comes to be governed less on the basis of conflict and more on the basis of the rationalistic theory of administration. The making of public policy takes less count of the enduring differences between White and Negro, business and labor, Pole and WASP. The logic of the bureaucratic ethic demands an impersonal, apolitical settlement of issues, rather than the settlement of conflict in the arena of political battle.[34]

This is exactly the result that is sought by many of the reformers who are seeking bureaucrats who will give less weight to the "private-regarding" and "artificial" cleavages in the population, and who will give more weight to the "public-regarding" and "totalistic" aspects of the community. Critics of this type of reform insist that no individual or group should be ignored, considered less important than any other segment of the population, or treated as less important than the "total population," which is a term that critics believe is euphemistic for the elite group that the reformers represent.

Thus, it is possible to see that professionalism is one of the important factors influencing the responsiveness of the bureaucracy; furthermore, there is a great deal of disagreement as to positive or negative influence. Apparently, a similar type of debate exists as to whether or not increased professionalism will improve the services delivered to the public. The central problem is to define what is meant by "improvement of services." Is improvement to be measured by statistical records as established within a profession or by the administrative organization involved in delivery of the service? The two types of evaluation may lead to totally different results. It is usually taken for granted that increased professionalism in any agency will improve the delivery of services; this is true if the standards of the profession are used as the main yardstick. It may also be true, however, that the general public is actually less satisfied with the service they are receiving, even though the department is becoming increasingly professionalized. Richard Chackerian reports that as police departments increase in professionalism, greater citizen dissatisfaction occurs, because the citizens evaluate the police department by a completely different set of criteria than is used by those who set the standards for "professional" police departments.[35] Whose standards are

---

[34] Robert Lineberry and Edmund Fowler, "Reformism and Public Policies in American Cities," in James Q. Wilson, ed., *City Politics and Public Policy*, Wiley, New York, 1968, p. 112.

[35] Richard Chackerian, "Police Professionalism and Citizen Evaluation: A Preliminary Look," *Public Administration Review, XXXIV*, 141-148 (March-April 1974).

right is another question, but the fact remains that a problem is created by the use of two standards for evaluation of responsiveness.

If the psychological inner check on the actions of the public servant is so strong, perhaps we can move further and further away from the legal, external controls. While it is true that "among the larger units of American government, the older and more overt violations of individual honesty and trust (among the bureaucracy) have been minimized,"[36] there is no guarantee that this will remain the case without the formal constraints that are currently in existence. As Herman Finer has pointed out,

Reliance on an official's conscience may be reliance on an official's accomplice, (since) the political and administrative history of all ages . . . has demonstrated without the shadow of a doubt that sooner or later there is an abuse of power when external punitive controls are lacking.[37]

Because of the tremendous power of the public bureaucracy and the reality of human nature, those who have argued for greater external control of the bureaucracy and those who want greater internal control agree that it is necessary to have both types of control:

Without the checks provided by either the law or the processes of professional socialization, the resultant behavior of administrators would be both selfish and capricious.[38]

## SUMMARY

The political impact of the bureaucracy is enormous. Top public administrators, especially, are involved in the policymaking process; all civil servants influence the implementation of public policy. The power of the bureaucracy is based on several factors, among the most important of which are permanency (based on tenure), expertise, outside support, respect for specialized professionalism, and the size of the bureaucracy. All this power creates a need for control over the bureaucracy.

Control of the public bureaucracy is based on both formal and informal elements (accountability and responsibility). Accountability is based on laws, rules, regulations, court orders, and other factors that make the public administrator answerable to someone else for his actions or the organization's actions. Among the external participants who help to control the public bureaucracy are the legis-

---

[36] Mosher, p. 211.

[37] Herman Finer, "Administrative Responsibility in Domocratic Government," *Public Administration Review, I*, 336-337 (Summer 1941).

[38] *Ibid.*, p. 337.

lature, interest groups, the courts, and ombudsmen; meanwhile, the hierarchy of the bureaucracy serves a similar function as an external control for the individuals of the administrative system.

Informal control (responsibility) is based on the concept that the most important and ultimate control on any public administrator is internal; it is the administrator's personal values and loyalty to democratic ideals that limits his actions. The administrator's "moral hierarchy" is created by the interaction of the socio-ethnic background of the individual, the type and extent of education received by the individual, and the professional ties of the particular individual. Each of these factors may lead to the civil servant's adherence to the public interest or a refusal to accept the public interest as defined by the policymakers.

The most volatile question that is considered by the public administration profession is that of how involved the civil servants should be in determining public policy, therefore, the definition of "the public interest." One segment of the profession wants public administration to take a more active part in the policy process, while the other segment believes that such an active role will destroy the public's respect for the profession. Whichever philosophy is accepted, it still remains true that society must depend on a combination of the two types of control instead of relying totally on one type of control.

# BIBLIOGRAPHY

Altshuler, Alan A., *The City Planning Process: A Political Analysis,* Cornell University, Ithaca, N.Y., 1965.

Benveniste, Guy, *The Politics of Expertise,* Glendessary, Berkeley, Calif., 1972.

Cater, Douglass, *The Fourth Branch of Government,* Houghton Mifflin, Boston, 1959.

Dunn, Delmer D., *Public Officials and the Press,* Addison-Wesley, Reading, Mass., 1969.

Frederickson, H. George, ed., *Neighborhood Control in the 1970's,* Chandler, New York, 1973.

Friedrich, Carl J., *The Public Interest: Nomos V,* Atherton, New York, 1962.

Gellhorn, Walter, *When Americans Complain: Governmental Grievance Procedures,* Harvard University, Cambridge, Mass., 1966.

Gilb, Corinne Lathrop, *Hidden Hierarchies: The Professions and Government,* Harper and Row, New York, 1966.

Goodnow, Frank, *Politics and Administration,* MacMillan, New York, 1900.

Harris, Joseph P., *Congressional Control of Administration,* Doubleday, Garden City, N.Y., 1964.

Herring, E. Pendleton, *Public Administration and the Public Interest,* Russell and Russell, New York, 1936.

House Committee on Governmental Operation, *Freedom of Information Act* (Compilation and Analysis of Departmental Regulations Implementing 5 U.S.C. 552), 90th Congress, 2nd Session, Government Printing Office, Washington, D.C., 1968.

Krislov, Samuel, *Representative Bureaucracy,* Prentice-Hall, Englewood Cliffs, N.J., 1974.

Marini, Frank, ed., *Toward a New Public Administration: The Minnowbrook Perspective,* Chandler, Scranton, Penn., 1971.

Martin, Roscoe C., ed., *Public Administration and Democracy,* Syracuse University, Syracuse, N.Y., 1965.

Meyerson, Martin, and Edward G. Banfield, *Politics, Planning, and the Public Interest: The Case of Public Housing in Chicago,* Free Press, Glencoe, Ill., 1955.

Redford, Emmette S., *Democracy in the Administrative State,* Oxford University, New York, 1969.

Rourke, Francis E., *Secrecy and Publicity,* Johns Hopkins, Baltimore, 1961.

Rourke, Francis E., *Bureaucracy, Politics, and Public Policy,* Little, Brown, Boston, 1969.

Rourke, Francis E., *Bureaucratic Power in National Politics,* Second Edition, Little, Brown, Boston, 1972.

Rourke, Francis E., ed., "A Symposium—Administrative Secrecy: A Comparative Perspective," *Public Administration Review, XXXV,* 1-42 (January-February, 1975).

Schubert, Glendon, *The Public Interest: A Critique of the Theory of a Political Concept,* Free Press, Glencoe, Ill., 1960.

Smith, Bruce L. R., and D. C. Hague, eds., *The Dilemma of Accountability in Modern Government: Independence Versus Control,* St. Martin's Press, New York, 1971.

Tullock, Gordon, *The Politics of Bureaucracy,* Public Affairs Press, Washington, D.C., 1965.

Waldo, Dwight, ed., *Public Administration in a Time of Turbulence,* Chandler, Scranton, Penn., 1971.

Wyner, Alan J., ed., *Executive Ombudsman in the United States,* Institute of Government Studies, University of California, Berkeley, 1973.

# DESCRIBING THE ADMINISTRATIVE MACHINE

*Good organizations are living bodies that grow muscles to meet challenges.*

*Peter Townsend*

The administrative machine was discovered concurrently in Europe and the United States. Although large organizations had functioned for several thousand years, they were first considered to be social phenomena worthy of in-depth study by scholar Max Weber and practitioner Frederick Taylor at the beginning of the twentieth century. Weber, a German sociologist, attempted to conceptualize the characteristics common to all large organizations; he developed a typology to define bureaucracy that is still the foundation for any discussion of complex organization theory. While Weber developed his typology of bureaucracy,

# CHAPTER 5

Frederick Taylor was beginning to examine organizations from exactly the opposite pole by looking at each individual and his particular job. Taylor's theory and practice came to be known as Scientific Management.[1] Actually, one gains the best understanding of the way an organization works by examining both extreme levels of the system as well as the factors in the intervening space.

In order to perceive properly the complexity of the public bureaucracy and to discuss the role of the public administrator in managing this system, it is necessary to review the development of organization theory, for management problems and solutions are all intimately related to the discoveries that have been made by these men and their followers. Therefore, this chapter presents and clarifies the historical development of thought concerning organizations.

## BUREAUCRACY: THE IDEAL TYPE

Max Weber was interested in the development and change of Western society, which is not an uncommon interest for a sociologist. After extensive study of the organizations that had existed throughout history, as well as those that influenced his immediate world, Weber came to the conclusion that a special kind of organization had come into being. Furthermore, the new organization was pervasive throughout society, and had become one of the most important factors influencing our culture. In order to understand exactly how this bureaucratic system worked, for that is what Weber called this organization, he developed a list of the characteristics that were common to the organizations that most typified this group. The most important aspect of this typology was his description of the internal structure of the organization. Weber explains that

the whole administrative staff under the supreme authority then consists, in the purest type, of individual officials who are appointed and function according to the following criteria:

1. They are personally free and subject to authority only with respect to their impersonal official obligations.
2. They are organized in a clearly defined hierarchy of offices.
3. Each office has a clearly defined sphere of competence in the legal sense.
4. The office is filled by a free contractual relationship. Thus, in principle, there is free selection.
5. Candidates are selected on the basis of technical qualifications. In the most rational case, this is tested by examination or guaranteed by diplomas certifying technical training, or both. They are appointed, not elected.
6. They are remunerated by fixed salaries in money, for the most part with a right to pensions. Only under certain circumstances does the employing authority, especially in private organizations, have a right to terminate the

---

[1] Perhaps something about the two cultures, European and American, can be understood by noting that Weber's theory was universal and abstract, while Taylor was interested in the specific and concrete problem of how to get the job done in the most efficient way.

appointment, but the official is always free to resign. The salary scale is primarily graded according to rank in the hierarchy; but in addition to this criterion, the responsibility of the position and the requirements of the incumbent's social status may be taken into account.

7. The office is treated as the sole, or at least the primary, occupation of the incumbent.
8. It constitutes a career. There is a system of "promotion" according to seniority or to achievement, or both. Promotion is dependent on the judgement of superiors.
9. The official works entirely separated from ownership of the means of administration and without appropriation of his position.
10. He is subject to strict and systematic discipline and control in the conduct of the office.

This type of organization is in principle applicable with equal facility to a wide variety of different fields. It may be applied in profit-making business or in charitable organizations, or in any number of other types of private enterprises serving ideal or material ends. It is equally applicable to political and religious organizations.[2]

When examining any public administrative organization, it is apparent that the characteristics described by Weber are applicable in describing its structure and the way it functions. The work of the agency is divided into specialized areas, with each employee becoming the expert in his job. The employees are chosen through a procedure that purports to be objective, one that is supposed to choose them on the basis of their ability. Neither the regular employees nor the administrators can claim ownership of their organization. Instead, they operate in an agency that has been established by an outside group (the legislature) to serve the general public, with the resources for operation also coming from that same public. Any public administrator is usually familiar with the hierarchical structure of his organization. He knows exactly where each office is placed on the organization chart and understands which particular duties and powers are spelled out for that office. The duties, powers, and objectives of each office are combined into the total organization structure; that structure and the organization's objectives are spelled out within the procedures manual and the laws pertaining to the organization; these rules may be used as the final arbiter in case of internal or external disagreement about actions that are to be taken. Finally, it is generally understood by all of the employees in any public agency that they are expected to remove their personal predispositions from any internal interactions as well as from their interactions with clients and other people external to the organization. Equal service to all, despite social, economic, sexual, or racial consideration, is the central tenet of any public bureaucracy.

---

[2] Max Weber, *The Theory of Social and Economic Organization,* trans. and eds., A. M. Henderson and Talcott Parsons, Oxford University, New York, 1947, pp. 333-334.

Even though the public bureaucracy closely follows Weber's typology, there has developed among the general public a negative connotation to the term. In fact, "bureaucracy" is often spit out as an epithet, and most employees mentally cringe when they are referred to as "bureaucrats" because of the overtones of inefficiency and inhumaneness that have settled around the term. Normative overtones are absent from Weber's discussions, however, as he is simply describing an existing phenomenon. Weber is careful to point out that bureaucracy is a necessary result of the technological revolution, for he states that technology has created an urgent need for stable, strict, intensive, and calculable administration. It is this need that gives bureaucracy a crucial role in our society as the central element in any large-scale organization. "It (bureaucracy) is superior to any other form in *precision,* in *stability*, in the stringency of its *discipline*, and in its *reliability*."[3]

Our current technological society demands a high level of rationality and predictability in order to function properly, and these are precisely the qualities most provided by bureaucracy. Peter Blau points out that even in most cases where people tend to complain bitterly about the inefficiency of the bureaucratic system, they are wrong. Those complaining about the way they are treated by the organization fail to consider whether the action complained about really was inefficient or irrational *from the viewpoint of the bureaucracy.*[4] If the action of the bureaucracy is examined in this way, it will usually be discovered that the action was efficient and rational *for the organization.* Complaints are really based on the feeling of impersonality and lack of individual consideration that is sensed when an individual is forced to respond to the bureaucratic system.

A second misconception has also developed around the concept of bureaucracy, and that misconception should be corrected immediately. Many critics of bureaucracy tend to connect it to the capitalist economic system and seem to think that bureaucracy does not exist under socialist or communist systems. Once again, the most direct way to respond to such claims is to quote Weber, for he says that

it makes no difference whether the economic system is organized on a capitalistic or a socialistic basis. Indeed, if in the latter case a comparable level of technical efficiency were to be achieved, it would mean a tremendous increase in the importance of specialized bureaucracy.[5]

---

[3] Weber, p. 339. (Emphasis added.)

[4] Peter M. Blau and Marshall W. Meyer, *Bureaucracy in Modern Society,* Second Edition, Random House, New York, 1971, pp. 148-151.

[5] Weber, pp. 337-338.

Such has been the case. Milovan Djilas has brought this point home in a profound work entitled *The New Class*, which is based on the thesis that the communist systems have created a new class (the bureaucracy) made up of technocrats who run the state and who actually have more power than any comparable class of prior times.[6]

## Bureaucracy: Its Dysfunctions

If bureaucracy could function in the ideal way contemplated by Weber, there would be little criticism of the system. However, it must be remembered that Weber presents his typology as an ideal; the ideal type is a picture that portrays the system being described, in this case the bureaucratic system, where every factor is developed to its logical extreme. Weber recognizes that it is not practical to expect any organization to match that ideal in the real world. He argues that the organization will function better as the ideals he states are approached, but *few* are approached in many organizations, and no organization achieves all of the ideal types. To the extent that the ideal bureaucratic system is not functioning, the organizations will have difficulty in efficiently and rationally carrying out their duties. At the same time, it has been discovered that for every strength attributed to the bureaucratic system, there is a concomitant weakness. Thus, every characteristic that Weber states as typical of bureaucracy may lead to a better functioning of the system or may, if not carefully watched, lead to a poorer functioning of the system.

Each bureaucracy has a clearly defined *hierarchy* of offices. Such a hierarchy is functional in that it creates a unity of command and designates to every individual in the bureaucracy the formal communication network. At the same time, the unity of command concept may create a situation where authority is misused, communication is ignored from lower offices in the organization, and the formal communication network may be blocked or become very inefficient. The informal authority system and communication system of the organization may be ignored because of the emphasis placed on the formal hierarchy. If this is true, there is a good chance that the formal and informal systems of the organization may work in different directions; in many cases, the two systems have been known to function in diametrically opposite directions, to the great misfortune of all concerned.

*Specialization* is essential to an organization in order to increase productivity and efficiency, but overemphasis on specialization may lead to competitiveness and a lack of coordination and common effort toward the organizational objectives. In a similar context, it is argued that the *separation of ownership from the official* helps to create a more rational decision-making process. Although

---

[6] Milovan Djilas, *The New Class: An Analysis of the Communist System,* Praeger, New York, 1957.

this may be true in part, it is also argued by many students of bureaucracy that such a separation, along with the merit system principles, leads to a conservative, inflexible type of leadership that in turn brings about an inability to cope with many of the major challenges facing bureaucracies today. Such a problem is serious for business, because it could mean the failure of a particular corporation with all of the difficulties involved for the participants, investors, and clients. But imagine the even greater impact of the failure of the government as a result of inflexibility, for in this case the organization upon which the social and economic system depends for continuity and the basic "rules of the game" would change in an unanticipated direction which might cause "system chaos." This is what has happened whenever a revolution occurs within any country.

The actions of the bureaucratic system are no longer based on the orders of an individual or on tradition; all *the offices, the actions, and the objectives of the organization are established by law.* Since the law is general by necessity, the bureaucracy then interprets the law to the particular case and, in time, develops a set of procedures that are themselves written down in a procedures manual or some similar document. The fact that such material is written down is useful in several ways. It is much easier to introduce new employees to the system of operation if they can read the procedures and then apply them to each new case. Written rules also help to guarantee equal treatment for clients, or equal delivery of services, because the knowledge of proper procedures is available to both the organization member and the public. While written rules may be a benefit for the reasons given, they may also lead to a serious dysfunction that has been pointed out by Robert Merton in his book, *Social Theory and Social Structure.*[7] Merton notes that the emphasis within bureaucracy is on discipline and reliability of response; he then points out that rigidity of rules often leads to rigidity of personality. In turn, rigidity of personality leads to timidity and conservatism within the bureaucrat. When this happens, members of the organization tend to transfer their interest and loyalty from the aims, or *ends*, of the organization to the particular details of behavior, or *means*, used within the organization. Timidity requires security, and the most secure way to act is "by the book" since it is difficult to criticize anyone for doing what the rules say should be done—even if the particular rule does not perfectly fit the desired end in the case being considered.

It would be possible to continue describing the dysfunctions of bureaucracy, but the point being discussed has been adequately presented so that the reader can carry the logic forward whenever necessary. The question that needs to be addressed is, What common elements exist in each of the dysfunctional cases that arises? When each of the cases mentioned is examined, there appears to be one common element that leads to dysfunctional developments within the bureaucracy. The intellectual construct is logical and complete. The difficulty does not exist within the model. The problems always occur because the rational

---

[7] Robert Merton, *Social Theory and Social Structure*, Free Press, Glencoe, Ill., 1949, pp. 153-157.

model is put into effect by *irrational human beings*. Many scholars have expended a great deal of effort attacking Weber's typology and criticizing its shortcomings. These criticisms have been summarized in the following way by Fred Luthans:

> ... During the past few years both theorists and practitioners have felt increasing dissatisfaction with classical bureaucratic concepts. The argument is not that the classical bureaucratic theorists were necessarily wrong but, rather, that the times have rendered their concepts and principles no longer relevant. Bureaucratic organization theory is said to be too inflexible to adapt readily to the dynamic nature and purpose of many of today's organizations.[8]

Such criticism would appear to be stated too generally. The problem is not with the concepts but rather with the individuals involved in the organization. The new theories of organization that have developed during the past few years have started with the positive aspects of the bureaucratic model and added new ideas that hopefully will overcome the dysfunctions that have been discovered in bureaucracy. In order to make the bureaucratic system function properly, it is necessary to consider the strengths and weaknesses of the individuals who fill the positions within that system.

## CLASSICAL ORGANIZATION THEORY

Weber studied organizations from an intellectual stance; he attempted as a sociologist to develop an understanding about the elements common to all bureaucracies. The men who studied organizations in the United States and who made up the major contributors to classical organization theory were scholars; however, many of them also had backgrounds as practitioners in the organizations they scrutinized. Their practical backgrounds in bureaucracies led them one step beyond the search for understanding. These gentlemen not only began to seek understanding but they also began to prescribe for the ailments of the organization. This prescription was further accentuated in the public sphere by the fact that their studies were taking place at a time when public indignation was building against the spoils system in government employment, as well as all the graft, corruption, and inefficiency in government that was thought to accompany the spoils system. Thus, while Weber's study was objective and scholarly, the studies of Frederick Taylor, Luther Gulick, Lyndall Urwick, James Mooney, Alan Reiley, Henry Fayol,[9] and other classical organization theorists were often subjective and always closely associated with the practical world. While different approaches to the problem were used by Taylor and by the other gentlemen,

---

[8] Fred Luthans, *Organizational Behavior: A Modern Behavioral Approach to Management*, McGraw-Hill, New York, 1973, p. 123.

[9] Henry Fayol was a prominent engineer in France, but he must be included as a leader of the administrative management school.

their work intermeshed around a common theme. These men were convinced that it was possible to develop a universal set of principles describing how best to organize any business or public agency. Taylor and his followers, seeking the "one best way" to do the job, carefully examined the work done by each individual. The other men analyzed the overall structure of the organization as they looked for the "one best way" to arrange the offices and tasks so that maximum organizational coordination and efficiency could be attained.

Taylor began his work at approximately the beginning of this century. After observing the individual performance of numerous employees, he became convinced that much greater efficiency could be achieved. Two major factors were essential to achieve his goal. First, the elements of each job had to be examined in detail, with the elements being rearranged in a manner that allowed the worker to produce the greatest amount with the least expenditure of effort. Second, the workers had to be convinced that they should use the new methods.[10]

In Taylor's writing, he insisted that improved productivity required scientific investigation. Taylor and his followers developed numerous job evaluation techniques that are still used today. It was taken for granted that machines could be made to function efficiently. Human beings were recognized as the weakest link in the production process, so the studies focused on the human aspect. Special studies were made in order to discover how to coordinate movements of people on assembly lines so that a minimum amount of effort would be required.[11] These studies led to specific suggestions as to how the arms and legs should work and how high from the floor working benches should be. The durability of human beings was also examined, with fatigue being defined according to the amount of time a given muscle group could work and the amount of rest that muscle group required. It was at this time that the use of stopwatches to check the speed of production became a common practice. From all these efforts, dramatic increases in productivity were possible and were recognized by many organizations.

The second part of the plan for success, getting workers to accept the new methods, did not seem difficult to accomplish. Taylor and his followers accepted an economic interpretation of human motivation. Therefore, the way to gain worker cooperation was to create the proper economic incentive, usually accomplished by establishing a piecework system whereby each employee was paid according to the amount of work completed. In many cases, this procedure was successful, but such an incentive system proved difficult to use in most government jobs. Not only was it difficult to measure productivity, but government employees rebelled against having production engineers snooping around with

[10] For greater detail of Taylor's argument, see: Frederick Taylor, *Scientific Management,* Harper and Brothers, New York, 1947.

[11] As a good example of the literature on time and motion studies, see: Frank B. Gilbreth and Lillian M. Gilbreth, *Applied Motion Study,* Sturgis and Walton, New York, 1917.

stopwatches and timing each particular activity. The introduction of the Taylor system into the arsenals in 1910-1911 led to such an outburst of indignation among the employees that, after congressional investigation, a law was passed that prohibited stopwatches in government arsenals, a proscription that was annually renewed until World War II. The congressional and government employee reactions may have caused Taylor's low opinion of the productivity of government employees (a low opinion shared mutually), for in an article published posthumously, he stated that ". . . the average government employee does not do more than one-third to one-half of a proper day's work."[12] Apparently, the Taylorites had miscalculated the total reaction of employees to the new methods. Not enough attention had been paid to the multifaceted behavior of the people that the theorists were attempting to change.

While Taylor and his followers were attacking the problem of maximizing production from each employee, another group of men was examining the structure of the organization, looking for the "one best way" to structure the offices and tasks. By following their universal rules of organization, these men believed that the functions of management would be made more efficient and successful. In 1931, James Mooney and Alan Reiley first presented the findings of this group in a book entitled *Onward Industry!*[13]; however, the classic statement of the administrative management school appeared in the *Papers on the Science of Administration*, edited by Luther Gulick and Lyndall Urwick.[14] It was in the *Papers* that Gulick coined the acronym POSDCORB, which has appeared regularly in literature on administration ever since.[15] POSDCORB stands for the first letters in the terms that Gulick used to describe the functions of management: *P*lanning, *O*rganizing, *S*taffing, *D*irecting, *C*o-*O*rdinating, *R*eporting and *B*udgeting. In order to accomplish these functions, the idea was accepted that the concepts of organization that had been developed must be applied. The number and order of these principles varied according to the author, but most of the rules were subsumed under the following five categories: unity of command; authority commensurate to responsibility; maximum delegation of authority; limited span of control; and power to organize.

Whereas Taylor argues for functional foremanship, where a worker can have as many as five supervisors, Fayol and Urwick argue vehemently for unity of com-

---

[12] Frederick Taylor, "Government Efficiency," *Bulletin of the Taylor Society*, pp. 7-13 (December 1916).

[13] James D. Mooney and Alan C. Reiley, *Onward Industry!*, Harper and Bros., New York, 1931.

[14] Luther Gulick and Lyndall Urwick, eds., *Papers on the Science of Administration*, Institute of Public Administration, New York, 1937.

[15] A variation of this acronym that is often used in management literature is PMOC: Planning, Motivating, Organizing, and Controlling.

mand.[16] It is their contention that each employee of the organization should be responsible to and receive orders from only one supervisor. Any variation from this principle can only undermine authority and discipline. Also any variation directly conflicts with the second principle that authority has to be commensurate with responsibility, for how can a supervisor be held responsible for those under his authority if his employees also are expected to obey another supervisor? Likewise, when conflicting orders are received by a subordinate from two supervisors to whom he or she is responsible, which order is the subordinate supposed to follow? However, the principle of equal authority and responsibility goes beyond employees. It means that if an individual is charged with the responsibility for any task, the authority needed to accomplish that task must also be given.

Since responsibility exists at each level of the organization, there must be authority at each level of the organization. The above principle appears to make such a statement true; however, the third principle carried that idea even further by stating that decisions should be made at the lowest possible level within the organization. Routine matters and matters that concern only a particular segment of the organization should be handled by the supervisors or employees who are immediately involved. The lack of ability to delegate power is decried as one of the major sins of administrators, and the inability is caused by the sense of responsibility each administrator feels for the programs under her control. Delegating that responsibility to subordinates requires both courage on the part of the administrator and a faith in the qualifications and quality of the subordinates to whom the authority is granted.

The fourth principle deals with span of control. After examining the number of subordinates that can be properly supervised by one administrator, the experts agree that the number should be limited. This idea is especially supported by V. A. Graicunas, who is responsible for a mathematical formula that shows the number of social relationships, or combinations of communications or interactions, that are possible in any span of control. For instance, if twelve subordinates are under a supervisor, there are over 20,000 relationships; twenty subordinates create over 10 million relationships. Such figures are nearly meaningless, but they still help to point out the complexity of social relations in an organization. The administrator is capable of keeping track of only a limited number of subordinates, and the usual number mentioned by the experts varies from three to six.

Along with the idea of limited span of control, it is essential that the manager has the power to organize the agency in any way necessary. Of course, the theorists have designed special rules for grouping the tasks in the organization, and Gulick discusses this theory in his "Notes on the Theory of Organization."

In building the organization from the bottom up we are confronted by the task of analyzing everything that has to be done and determining in what group-

---

[16]Gulick and Urwick, p. 15.

ing it can be placed without violating the principle of homogeneity. This is not a simple matter, either practically or theoretically. It will be found that each worker in each position must be characterized by:

1. The major *purpose* he is serving, such as furnishing water, controlling crime, or conducting education;
2. The *process* he is using, such as engineering, medicine, carpentry, stenography, statistics, accounting;
3. The *persons or things* dealt with or served, such as immigrants, veterans, Indians, forests, mines, parks, orphans, farmers, automobiles, or the poor;
4. The *place* where he renders his service, such as Hawaii, Boston, Washington, the Dust Bowl, Alabama, or Central High School.[17]

Additional "principles" of organization could be cited. The students of administrative management developed a principle for every problem that could be imagined. Just as with Taylor's principles, the principles that were developed by Fayol, Gulick, Urwick, and others who studied organizational structure were valuable and are still used by a majority of the managers who are active today.[18] However, there are two major problems with these principles. First, the authors of the principles of administrative organization passed off their ideas as universal truths, or truths that fit all occasions. Such is not the case. As Herbert Simon remarks:

It is a fatal defect of the current principles of administration that, like proverbs, they occur in pairs. For almost every principle one can find an equally plausible and acceptable contradictory principle. Although the two principles of the pair will lead to exactly opposite organizational recommendations, there is nothing in the theory to indicate which is the proper one.[19]

The principles are useful when their limitations are recognized, but the originators failed in their excitement of discovery to recognize the limitations of their ideas. Second, the principles of organization being considered are guilty of an error similar to that which exists in the principles espoused by Taylor; the principles of administrative management lack sensitivity toward the behavioral aspects of the organization. Ernest Dale summarizes the assumptions made by administrative management theorists as follows. He says that the top management must

1. Know what it wants done;
2. Arrange a structure in which the various tasks are exactly dovetailed;

---

[17] *Ibid.*

[18] Ernest Dale, *Organization,* American Management Association, New York, 1967.

[19] Herbert Simon, *Administrative Behavior,* MacMillan, New York, 1947, p. 20.

3. Provide for coordination through common superiors or some other formal arrangement;
4. Issue the necessary orders down through the chain of command; and
5. See that each person is held accountable for his part of the work.[20]

It is assumed that if these conditions are met, the organization will run smoothly. When applied to the real world, however, it is found that the theory is incomplete. A key element is missing!

## THE REDISCOVERY OF MAN

Each of the three theories that has been discussed in this chapter is logically derived, and when considered as theory, each proves to be useful to anyone trying to study or manage an organization. However, one problem is common to all three theories. When removed from the written page and applied to ongoing organizations, the theories do not work in the way they are expected to perform. According to one of the leading organization theorists of the day, James Thompson, the major reason that the three schools fail is because they are "closed system" models.[21] In each case, the authors attempt to rid their theories of all uncertainty by reducing the variables that are considered to only those factors *within* the organization. The environment of the organization is ignored; therefore, it is possible to develop a rational model, with all the alternatives and all the consequences of action known and understood, only to have it fail when the environment is reintroduced. Both the scientific management school (Taylor) and the administrative management school (Gulick and Urwick) assume that goals and tasks are known, resources are automatically available, and output disappears.[22] Bureaucratic theory also employs the closed system of logic by plugging the three holes through which Weber admits that outside forces might penetrate the system.

Policymakers, somewhere above the bureaucracy, could alter the goals, but the implications of this are set aside. Human components—the expert officeholders—might be more complicated than the model describes but bureaucratic theory handles this by divorcing the individual's private life from his life as an officeholder through the use of rules, salary, and career. Finally, bureaucratic theory takes note of outsiders—clientele—but nullifies their effects by depersonalizing and categorizing clients.[23]

Thompson's criticisms of the three theories have a central theme that explains their failure. *In each case, the theorists have ignored the implications of the fact*

---

[20] Dale, p. 199.

[21] James D. Thompson, *Organizations in Action,* McGraw-Hill, New York, 1967, pp. 4-6.

[22] *Ibid.,* p. 5.

[23] *Ibid.,* pp. 5-6.

*that they are dealing with human beings.* In order to improve the theories so that they are useful in managing the modern organization, it is essential to rediscover human beings.

It is impossible to recognize man as a sociological and psychological being who may be rational, but who may also be irrational, and to maintain the closed system concept for which the theorists are striving. Two aspects of the human factor must be considered: the biases, attitudes, and behavior of people outside of the organization who have grouped together in numerous ways to protect and promote their special interests; and the biases, attitudes, and behavior of the people inside the organization. In this section of the text, the emphasis is on the internal aspects of bureaucracy; therefore the accent is on the human factor *within* the organization. Before discussing the elements of modern management, in which an understanding of human behavior is central to most new theories, a brief history of the *reintroduction of man* into organization theory will be presented in order that the reader can comprehend the development of the modern perception of organizations.

## The Hawthorne Experiments

When people are dealing with scientific endeavor, an interesting phenomenon often occurs. Just as everyone becomes convinced that, finally, after great effort, man has solved all the problems surrounding a particular issue, thus creating a completed science (meaning that every detail about the subject is known and that all details fit neatly into a theory that allows total explanation and prediction), someone comes along with a discovery, or a new question, that totally destroys the logic of the system. For example, physicists were convinced that they had nearly completed explaining the laws of the universe and were preparing to pat one another on the back for a job well done, when Albert Einstein brought the whole system crashing down around everyone by presenting his theory of relativity, which forced a totally new set of circumstances and questions on the physicists of the world. Einstein did not present his theory because of an exciting new discovery; instead, he simply took all the theory previously developed, examined it carefully, and after deciding that there were questions that the present theory did not answer, developed a totally new theory by reconstructing the various parts in a new way. A similar kind of incident occurred in the scientific study of organizations. Shortly after Taylor published his works, and prior to the publication of *Papers on the Science of Administration* by Gulick and Urwick, a series of experiments began at the Hawthorne Works of the Western Electric Company which were to undermine the theories that had been developed.

It has often been said that the seeds of our own destruction lie within us, and this was certainly true of the *Papers on the Science of Administration.* Included in the book was one of the original reports on the Hawthorne studies.[24] Just as the proponents of the administrative management school produced the most

---

[24] L. T. Henderson, T. N. Whitehead, and E. Mayo, "The Effects of Social Environment," in Gulick and Urwick, pp. 141-158.

complete and profound exposition of their theory (in 1937), the experiments at Hawthorne pointed out the weakness and inadequacy of all the theories presented up to that time. Two years later, Fritz Roethlisberger and William Dickson presented a detailed account of the Hawthorne experiments in their work entitled *Management and the Worker.*[25] The findings of the experiments emphasized the lack of consideration for the human participants within the organization and made it clear that if a truly comprehensive theory about organizations was to be developed, the oversight had to be corrected. The first and perhaps most important experiment can serve as an example of the breakthrough that occurred at Hawthorne.

One of the major theses of the theory of scientific management was that individuals would perform optimally when their environment was controlled in a way that made work easiest to perform. The National Research Council sponsored a series of experiments to measure the effects of various levels of illumination on worker productivity. In order to test this hypothesis, two rooms were set up, with one group of female workers in a control room where all conditions were held constant and a second group of female workers in the test room where illumination was varied. It was expected that an optimum level of light would be discovered at which the women in the test room would maximize production. Changing the lighting to higher or lower levels was expected to decrease the level of production. Of course, by definition, no change was expected in the control room. As the investigators began to increase the light, the production increased just as expected. Looking for the optimum level of light, the investigators continued to increase the light in the test room. Production continued to increase. This continued even when the light became an obvious glare and created some discomfort. The investigators were puzzled by this result, so they changed their tactics and lowered the light to the original level. Once again production increased. The lights were dimmed by stages and at every stage production increased, even when the amount of light was so low that the workers appeared to be working in the moonlight. None of the results in the test room fit the hypothesized results, and what was even more disconcerting was the fact that all the time the experiment continued, *production in the control room was also rising!* As Fred Luthans summarizes this experiment:

Obviously, some variables in the experiment were not being held constant or under control. Something besides the level of illumination (independent variable) was causing the change in productivity (dependent variable). This something, of course, was the complex human variable.[26]

---

[25] Fritz Roethlisberger and William Dickson, *Management and the Worker,* Harvard University, Cambridge, Mass., 1939.

[26] Luthans, p. 24.

The results of the illumination experiments led to a series of further experiments that attempted to pinpoint the variables that were in action within each group, or production activity, studied. In some of the later studies, the investigators came upon blatant restriction of production. This proved that there was the possibility that the human factors being examined could operate in either direction—to increase or decrease productivity. The tests generally led to a new awareness of the individual and his sense of personal value, satisfaction with the type of job performed, the social interactions that developed for each individual, and the impact of supervisory style upon each individual. When production increased, the participants were highly motivated and had positive attitudes toward the group in which they worked, the type of supervision experienced, and the money they earned. The participants were especially influenced by the fact that they were treated and recognized as individuals who had something to contribute. In those experiments where production was restricted, the workers were dissatisfied and did not accept the company's goals. It was now evident that managers had to understand more than just the mechanical and structural aspects of their organizations. In order to manage any organization, it was apparent that the social and psychological factors of the employees must also be understood.[27]

There has been a steady outpouring of literature on organizations since the Hawthorne studies. Almost immediately, an attempt to examine leadership began, and other social scientists began to study the effects of small group structure on the completion of a variety of assigned tasks. Serious attempts were made to look at the way in which communications flowed through different organizations. The decision-making process also became a field of interest. In these and many more areas, it was discovered that the formulas and laws that had been developed were only generalizations about hypothetical cases; when these rules were juxtaposed against real-world situations, there were dramatic discrepancies between theory and reality. These discrepancies generally occurred because the human being was ignored. Therefore, people are the building blocks of which organizations are made.

This section of the text focuses primarily on the human side of public management. First, although we may refer to humans as building blocks, people do not have square sides similar to those possessed by most blocks. The human building block is quite asymmetrical, with each individual having particular strengths and weaknesses to offer to the organization. Thus, it is necessary to combine the individuals in any organization in the way best calculated to use everybody's strengths and neutralize each person's weaknesses. Second, to public

---

[27] There is debate over the Hawthorne studies and their validity. For a discussion of the experiment's advocates and opponents, see: Henry A. Landsberger, *Hawthorne Revisited,* Cornell University, Ithaca, N.Y., 1958. Whatever one's position on that debate, the importance of the studies and the issues they raised are generally accepted.

administration it is doubly important to understand the human side of any program, because it is essential to deal with the individuals within the organization while guiding the program through the shoals of the political environment.

## SUMMARY

Two major theories about complex organizations were developing at the beginning of the twentieth century. Max Weber, a German sociologist, developed a typology of bureaucracy that explained its commonalities when applied to the wide variety of modern organizations. The principle facets of bureaucratic organizations are that (1) career officers are (2) contractually chosen (3) on the basis of technical qualifications to fill a position (4) within a hierarchy of offices. Each official has (5) a clearly defined sphere of competence along with (6) official obligations that are based strictly on position because (7) the official does not own the organization he is administering. Finally, (8) the office is the full-time occupation of the incumbent because (9) there is a system of promotions built into the career, with (10) salaries based on the position with its commensurate duties and required skills. This typology describes the elements of organizations that have developed in an attempt to create precision, stability, discipline, reliability, and rationality in organizational decision making and activity.

Frederick Taylor and the "scientific" organization theorists of the United States developed a practical approach to bureaucracy—a view that focused on the individual and organizational structure with the intent to improve organizational efficiency and effectiveness. The original work of Taylor focused on the evaluation of jobs, individual performance, and the proper coordination of work processes that required the interaction of several people and machines. From these efforts, dramatic increases in productivity were possible. At the same time, the "administrative management" school was examining the structure of organization and the functions of management in an attempt to find the "one best way" to administer any establishment. The administrative management school developed a series of principles dealing with concepts such as: unity of command; authority commensurate to responsibility; maximum delegation of authority; limited span of control; and power to organize. Many of these principles are still used by managers today.

By combining the theories of Weber, Taylor, and the members of the administrative management school, many students of organization thought that all the problems of bureaucracy would be solved. However, at least one major internal factor had to be added to the formula before the expected results could be achieved. This factor was added to the formula when the Hawthorne experiments took place; these experiments introduced the human, psychological element of organizations that had been downplayed or forgotten in prior theories. Once the human element of organizations was reinstated into the formula, the study of organizations was ready to advance to the present "state of the art."

# BIBLIOGRAPHY

Blau, Peter M., and Marshall W. Meyer, *Bureaucracy in Modern Society*, Second Edition, Random House, New York, 1971.

Chandler, Alfred D., *Strategy and Structure*, Doubleday, Garden City, N. Y., 1963.

Crozier, Michel, *The Bureaucratic Phenomenon,* University of Chicago, Chicago, 1964.

Djilas, Milovan, *The New Class: An Analysis of the Communist System,* Praeger, New York, 1957.

Gilbreth, Frank B., and Lillian M. Gilbreth, *Applied Motion Study*, Sturgis and Walton, New York, 1917.

Gulick, Luther, and Lyndall Urwick, eds., *Papers on the Science of Administration*, Institute of Public Adminisration, New York, 1937.

Landsberger, Henry A., *Hawthorne Revisited*, Cornell University, Ithaca, N. Y., 1958.

Luthans, Fred, *Organizational Behavior: A Modern Behavioral Approach to Management*, McGraw-Hill, New York, 1973.

March, James G., ed., *Handbook of Organizations*, Rand McNally, Chicago, 1965.

Merton, Robert, *Social Theory and Social Structure,* Free Press, Glencoe, Ill., 1949.

Mooney, James D., and Alan C. Reiley, *Onward Industry!*, Harper and Brothers, New York, 1931.

Polenberg, Richard, *Reorganizing Roosevelt's Government*, Harvard University, Cambridge, Mass., 1966.

Roethlisberger, Fritz, and William Dickson, *Management and the Worker*, Harvard University, Cambridge, Mass., 1939.

Simon, Herbert A., *Administrative Behavior: A Study of Decision-Making Processes in Administrative Organization*, Second Edition, Free Press, New York, 1957.

Taylor, Frederick W., *Principles of Scientific Management*, W. W. Norton, New York, 1911.

Taylor, Frederick W., *Scientific Management*, Harper and Brothers, New York, 1947.

Thompson, James D., *Organizations in Action*, McGraw-Hill, New York, 1967.

Weber, Max, *The Theory of Social and Economic Organization*, trans. and eds., A. M. Henderson and Talcott Parsons, Oxford University, New York, 1947.

# DECISION MAKING

*No decision can be better than the information upon which it is made.*

An atomic bomb was dropped on the Japanese city of Hiroshima. The repercussions of that action are still felt throughout the world. People continue to debate the issue of whether or not the bomb should have been dropped, but few debate the question of whether or not President Harry Truman had the power to order the armed forces to carry out the act. President Truman was carrying out his duty to make a decision as commander-in-chief of the United States Armed Forces. Truman was fond of saying, "The buck stops here!" Regardless of the triteness of the statement, it was true, for his job as president required that he make the ultimate decision concerning the dropping of the bomb.

# CHAPTER 6

In Wilmington, Delaware, Mayor Thomas Maloney, after examining the findings and recommendations of a task force that he had established, decided that the scavenger service in his community could be cut by 40 percent without seriously impairing the health or quality of life in the community. When the order was received, the sanitation workers went on strike. After a period of time, the issue was resolved in a way that allowed the continued lower level of service. While there was controversy about the decision that was made, it was accepted by everyone that Mayor Maloney had the right to make that decision.[1]

The single most pervasive function of management is that of making decisions. In fact, it is so pervasive that some students of management equate all the tasks of the manager to the single process of decision making. According to these students, all the functions of planning, controlling, motivating, and leading the organization should be studied under the heading of decision making. While it is too simplistic to combine all the manager's tasks in such a way, decision making is so central to all these processes that it seems appropriate to begin our discussion of the functions of management with an in-depth look at the way decisions are made by public administrators. First, decision making is defined, followed by a discussion of several decision-making models that attempt to describe the process used by individuals when decisions are made. Finally, the major portion of the chapter is devoted to an analysis of the problem of rationality in decision making and deals with the following two questions: What factors within human nature and the political system limit rationality in decision making? and How can the rationality of decision making be increased?

## DEFINITION AND PROCESS

Regardless of the simplicity or sophistication of any decision-making model, its definition boils down to the basic concept of *choosing between alternatives.* The public administrator is seldom faced with situations where only a single alternative is available, even though the rationale presented to the elected officials after a choice has been made often attempts to justify that choice by arguing that the alternative picked is the *only real* choice available given the circumstances. In actuality, Chester Barnard is correct in stating that the processes of decision making are largely techniques for narrowing choices among the several available alternatives.[2]

The process of choosing between alternatives is broken down into sequential steps. Theories vary from the three-step models of John Dewey and Herbert Simon to more elaborate five-step models, such as the one developed by the systems theorist, Alvar Elbing. Disequilibrium may come to the attention of the public administrator because of pressure from either inside or outside the organization. The problem may become apparent within the bureaucracy before it is

[1] "200 Faces for the Future," *Time,* p. 54 (July 15, 1974).

[2] Chester Barnard, *The Functions of the Executive,* Harvard University, Cambridge, Mass., 1938, p. 14.

ever noticeable to those outside. However, problems often occur because of political pressure created by city council members, state and national legislators, interest groups, or clients of the public agency. Wherever the controversy originates, the administrator should immediately begin to sift through the available information, attempt to clarify the situation, and separate the claims into fact and fancy. Once an understanding of the existing situation has been developed, the decision maker can determine what alternative courses of action are available and what the results of each alternative may be. Such a choice also implies that

## DECISION-MAKING PROCESS

| Dewey[3] | Simon[4] | Elbing[5] |
|---|---|---|
| 1. Controversy— consisting of opposite claims regarding the same objective situation | 1. Intelligence activity— searching the environment for conditions calling for decision | 1. Disequilibrium— recognition of problem situation |
| 2. Clarification— defining and elaborating claims | 2. Design activity— inventing, developing, and analyzing various possible alternative courses of action | 2. Diagnosis— developing assumptions about the underlying causes of the problem |
| 3. Choice— which is the decision between claims, closing the current dispute, *and* serving as a precedent or rule for the future | 3. Choice activity— selecting the particular course of action to be followed from all available analyzed alternatives | 3. Definition— specific statement of the problem as diagnosed |
| | | 4. Discovery— selection of a method of solution |
| | | 5. Doing— the implementation of the selection in 4 (and which, through feedback, may lead back to disequilibrium) |

[3] John Dewey, *How We Think*, D. C. Heath, Boston, 1933, p. 120.

[4] Herbert A. Simon, *The New Science of Management Decision*, Harper and Row, New York, 1960, p. 2.

[5] Alvar O. Elbing, *Behavioral Decisions in Organizations*, Scott, Foresman, Glenview, Ill., 1970, p. 13.

a desired level of improvement or solution has been established; it may be established before beginning to examine alternatives, or, more likely, it will emerge in some way while the alternatives are being scrutinized. At some point, the decision maker will discover the most appropriate alternative. Once this alternative is authenticated, the decision maker will act or give the appropriate orders for action, so that the selection will be implemented, hopefully reestablishing equilibrium. That decision will stand as precedent for future action until, at some time in the future, it does not achieve the desired results when it is used. At that point, equilibrium is once again created and the decision-making process is reactivated.

The same procedure is followed whether the decision is one made by a single administrator or is a policy decision that involves major segments of the community. If the decision to be made is that of finding a way to integrate the school system of a metropolitan area, the same general steps are involved, but the number of participants and the complexity of the process are greatly increased. In this case, the decision may have to be made by a group of people (the school board) and the situation that must be understood includes the attitudes and activities of a wide variety of citizen groups as well as the quantifiable facts such as demographic characteristics and the availability of physical facilities, special educational programs, and finances. While it is usually stated that "the school board has to make the final decision," a great many individuals and groups will be involved in making the decision; vital among these participants are the school administrators and the consultants who are expected, as full-time employees and specialists, to understand why and how the problem arose and what alternatives for solution are available and appropriate. If an alternative is not authenticated, the issue may be brought to the attention of officials in a different segment or at a different level of government (the city council, state or national legislature, or the federal court system). Ultimately, a solution will either be accepted by or imposed on the community, and the school board will operate under that decision until new demands develop in relation to the racial balance in the schools. (In this case, many decisions are made with the understanding that they are temporary solutions and that they are not satisfactory to any segment of the population as an ultimate decision.) The important point is that even though the process involves large numbers of people and many organizations, it remains approximately the same as that described for the single decision maker.

### Programmed Versus Nonprogrammed Decisions

The frequency with which disequilibrium is created may be important to the decision-making process and to the concerned organization. If the decision does not have to be "remade," it tends to become routine, and it is usually turned over to individuals at lower levels of the organization (see Figure 4). If the process can be routinized to the point that virtually no new decisions have to be made, the tasks involved may be set up on an assembly-line basis where every

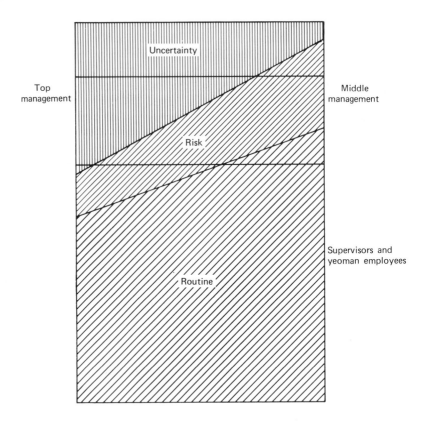

**Figure 4**

Types of decisions made by different levels of employees. The lower area of the illustration represents the type of decisions made by line employees and their supervisors. The middle area represents the type of decisions made by middle-management employees. The area at the top includes top management's area of decision. *Risk* refers to those decisions where there is an element of prior experience that may be turned to, or where there is some knowledge of the probabilities of success when a particular alternative is taken. *Uncertainty* refers to those decisions where there is no prior knowledge or experience that may be turned to in making the decision, and where there is no prior knowledge of the probabilities of success when a particular alternative is chosen.

step of the process is programmed in detail and carried out repetitively. The epitome of this system is the modern factory, such as an automobile plant, but the same type of process is used in many governmental offices. For example, when you take your driver's examination, the work may be divided between several employees, with the first administering the written questions, a second examining your eyesight, a third giving the actual driving test, a fourth completing the license application and photographing the applicant, and a fifth accepting the license fee. The employees who are involved in these processes seldom have the need or opportunity to make important decisions concerning the welfare of the organization or the direction of its policies (although those citizens turned down in their quest for a driver's license are convinced that these employees do make important decisions).

In contrast, nonprogrammed decisions, those that have a key impact on the organization, are usually handled by administrators at the higher levels of the organization. These decisions require analysis that cannot be based on prior circumstances; therefore, they include a level of risk or uncertainty. There is usually some experience from the past that is valid, or there is some capacity for predicting the outcomes of the alternatives that are being considered. Nonetheless, there seems to be a correlation between the degree to which a decision is basic to the organization and the amount of uncertainty that is involved. Dalton McFarland proposes that basic decisions require a long-range commitment or a major investment of the resources of the organization in such a way that a mistake might jeopardize the welfare of the organization.[6] Almost any governmental official will agree that such a commitment usually entails a high level of uncertainty. If a city operates under a merit system, the normal decision as to whether or not to hire a particular individual does not entail great risk for the personnel office of a city; therefore, such a decision can be made by a personnel analyst without the involvement of the head of the personnel department. But when a decision has to be made as to how the rules should be changed in order to assure that the city is in compliance with the Equal Employment Opportunity guidelines of the national government, there are numerous variables involved that may affect the city's future policies regarding testing, recruitment, appointment, promotion, training, and all other functions of the personnel office. These factors, in turn, may lead to new definitions of the terms "civil service" and "merit"; the repercussions from these problems may lead to confrontations with the city manager or mayor, the council, the civil service commission (if one exists), state and national agencies and officials, the courts, and citizen groups from the community. It is necessary for the consequences of any changes to be mapped out to the greatest degree possible so that the proper decision (the one that will allow the type of result desired) can be formulated and put into effect. Although the personnel analyst may be able to have some input into the decision process, the decision will ultimately be made by the top administrator in the department; if the decision is considered a volatile enough subject, it may even be taken out of the personnel director's hands and decided at the very top of the organization by the manager, or mayor, and the council. It is easy to see why such basic decisions are made by the top administrators and why they are made only after careful analysis of the required commitment.

[6] Dalton McFarland, *Management,* Third Edition, MacMillan, New York, 1970, p. 83.

## DESCRIPTIVE MODELS OF DECISION MAKING

Three models help to describe the development of decision-making theory during the twentieth century. It is necessary, therefore, to look briefly at (1) the economic model of decision making; (2) the incremental model; and (3) the mixed-scanning model, which attempts to combine the best aspects of the first two models.

### The Economic Model Versus the Incremental Model

Bringing the theory of decision making, as developed by scholars, into harmony with the practice of decision making as carried out by public administrators has taken time and effort on the part of both groups. The perception of the way decisions are made has been constantly changing, and it will continue to change for a long time. The original perception of the procedure through which public officials and administrators made decisions was based on the idea of "economic man," much in the same way Frederick Taylor based his theory of motivation solely on economic principles; therefore, for obvious reasons, it was called the economic model. First, it was taken for granted that the decision maker clearly understood the problem being considered. Second, all available alternatives were spelled out with the costs and consequences of each alternative calculated. Third, it was assumed that the decision maker had established a utility ordering, or a priority listing, of the desired outcomes. Fourth, with these three factors as a foundation, it was relatively simple to develop a theory of decision making that accepted the principle of maximization of benefits, or the *best possible solution*, and presumed a "scientific" process of decision making.[7]

The "economic" model of decision making works only when the solutions being sought are relatively simple; the problem must be quantifiable, or expressable in numbers, and there must be very few human factors or values (which are nonquantifiable) involved; at least, human values must not be very significant to the people affected by the decision. The situations in the political world usually are not that simple. This may be especially true as one considers the larger jurisdictions of government because of the greater scope of the issues and the larger populations served. Even at the local level, it is difficult to think of situations in which the head of a program or a department, much less a mayor or manager of a city, can know all the available alternatives, comprehend the costs and benefits (tangible and intangible) of the consequences of each alternative, and be sure about which combination of costs and benefits is the best possible solution. The "economic" model does not work in the real world. Instead, Anthony Downs notes that the realistic world of the public official places many limitations upon the decision maker because

---

[7] For a description of this decision-making process, see: John M. Pfiffner, "Administrative Rationality," *Public Administration Review, XX,* 125-132 (Summer 1960). See also: Charles Lindblom, "The Science of Muddling Through," *Public Administration Review, XIX,* 79-88 (Spring 1959).

1. Each decision maker can devote only a limited amount of time to decision making.
2. Each decision maker can mentally weigh and consider only a limited amount of information at one time.
3. The functions of most officials require them to become involved in more activities than they can consider simultaneously; hence, they must normally focus their attention on only part of their major concerns, while the rest remain latent.
4. The amount of information initially available to every decision maker about each problem is only a small fraction of all the information available on the subject.
5. Additional information bearing on any particular problem can usually be procured, but the costs of procurement and utilization may rise rapidly as the amount of data increases.
6. Important aspects of many problems involve information that cannot be procured at all, especially concerning future events; hence many decisions must be made in the face of some ineradicable uncertainty.[8]

Added to the criticisms made by Downs must be those of Charles Lindblom, who disapproves of the "means-ends" analysis, which he calls the "rational-comprehensive" model, that is inherent to the economic model of decision making. If there is a "best possible solution," that means there is also an agreement as to what end is being sought among the decision makers. There must be agreement on the proper end for the decision so that the means to achieve that end can be chosen. But in making decisions dealing with public policy, there is seldom any agreement on the goals, nor is it possible to get such agreement; therefore, the incremental model of decision making is used. Since there is no agreement on the end sought by a policy, the rational, ends-means analysis cannot be used by the person or group having to arrive at the decision. Instead, adjustments are made in both ends and means while the decision is being made. These adjustments appear as compromises and redefinitions of the problems, and ultimately, "the test of a good policy is typically that various analysts find themselves directly agreeing on a policy (without their agreeing that it is the most appropriate means to an agreed objective)."[9] In such a decision process, no decision is the ultimate solution. There is usually a series of attacks on a problem, and each attack makes only incremental changes in the status quo, with everyone involved in the process evaluating how that small change affected their position or the end they desired. Once that evaluation is completed, the problem will often be attacked anew by those who feel that further remedial action should be attempted.

[8] Anthony Downs, *Inside Bureaucracy*, Little, Brown, Boston, 1967, p. 75.

[9] Lindblom, p. 81.

Since analysis is limited and since only incremental decisions are made, the decision process as described by Downs and Lindblom is primarily geared toward the alleviation of present, concrete social problems and may not apply as adequately when the purpose is the promotion of future goals. However, these "current affairs" are those on which administrators spend most of their time, so it may be a valid description of the way decisions are made, especially in a political setting. As Lindblom notes, the process of making decisions through "successive limited comparisons is . . . a method or system; it is not a failure of method for which administrators ought to apologize."[10] Other supporters of the incrementalist decision-making process have gone beyond the point of using it as a descriptive tool; instead, they argue (as, indeed, does Charles Lindblom) that it is a normatively "good" model which should be used by public administrators as they consider public policy. Aaron Wildavsky is the leading proponent of this school of thought, as is shown in his article entitled "Toward a Radical Incrementalism," for he says that public officials

. . . soon discover that ends are rarely agreed upon, that they keep changing, that possible consequences of a single policy are too numerous to describe, and that knowledge of the chain of consequences for other policies is but dimly perceived for most conceivable alternatives. . . . All that is accomplished by injunctions to follow a comprehensive approach is the inculcation of guilt among good men who find that they can never come close to fulfilling this unreasonable expectation. . . . What . . . officials need are not injunctions to be rational but operational guides that will enable them to manage the requisite calculations.[11]

### A Third Approach: "Mixed Scanning"

Although the incremental model of decision making has found much favor in the eyes of many scholars, there are critics who propose that the model is inadequate both in *explaining* the process and in *prescribing* how decisions should be made. Amitai Etzioni, who is one of the critics of the incremental model, points out that the model is not applicable to fundamental decisions—those decisions that are so unique or so basic to the direction of subsequent events that the entire issue at stake must be evaluated. While the supporters of the incremental model argue that there are few such decisions, Etzioni argues that

. . . the number and role of fundamental decisions are significantly greater than the incrementalists state. . . . While incremental decisions greatly outnumber

---

[10] *Ibid.*, p. 87.

[11] Aaron Wildavsky, "Toward a Radical Incrementalism," in Alfred deGrazia, ed., *Congress: The First Branch of Government*, American Enterprise Institute, Washington, D. C., 1966, pp. 121-122.

fundamental ones, the latter's significance for societal decision-making is not commensurate with their number; it is thus a mistake to relegate nonincremental decisions to the category of exceptions. Moreover, it is often the fundamental decisions which set the context for the numerous incremental ones. Although fundamental decisions are frequently "prepared" by incremental ones in order that the final decision will initiate a less abrupt change, these decisions may still be considered relatively fundamental.[12]

As proof of Etzioni's proposal, it is only necessary to look at two of the many examples that might be presented. As Franklin Roosevelt faced the specter of having to bring the United States into an active role in World War II, he, at some point, had to come to the conclusion that involvement was inevitable. To the uninitiated, the point of entry into the war appeared to have occurred immediately after Japan's attack on Pearl Harbor. To the isolationists, who struggled to keep the United States from becoming involved in the war, the decision for active involvement came with the sale of fifty old destroyers to the British in September of 1940, more than a year before the Japanese attack on Pearl Harbor. However, Roosevelt had made a fundamental decision, long before any actions were carried out committing the United States, as to which side the United States must ultimately support during the early stages of the war.[13]

In a similar way, the environmental and energy crises that are currently facing the United States are forcing policymakers to develop fundamental changes in our patterns of transportation and in our life-style. The changes will take place, however, in smaller, incremental steps. Within each metropolitan area, the transportation system will move only gradually from dependence on the automobile to greater dependence on some type of mass transit; the fundamental decision will have occurred, and it will be the motivating influence behind the series of incremental decisions that take place. Similar policy processes will be occurring in a number of areas that affect all of our lives (housing, career opportunities, leisure activities, etc.); the changes will have been instigated by fundamental decisions regarding the future availability of resources, the effect of human activities on the environment, and the current ideas of society as to what comprises "the good life."

If the incremental decisions are not influenced by the fundamental choices, *the basic societal innovations*, then Etzioni believes that an even more serious problem may appear; when fundamental decisions are missing, "incremental decision-making amounts to drifting," and this leads to a focus on the short term. Etzioni says,

---

[12] Amitai Etzioni, "Mixed Scanning: A Third Approach to Decision-Making," *Public Administration Review, XXVII,* 387-388 (December 1967).

[13] For a good description of Roosevelt's thinking toward the Second World War, see: James MacGregor Burns, *Roosevelt: The Lion and the Fox,* Harcourt, Brace and World, New York, 1956.

While an accumulation of small steps could lead to a significant change, there is nothing in this approach to guide the accumulation; the steps may be circular—leading back to where they started—or dispersed—leading in many directions at once but leading nowhere.[14]

Therefore, Etzioni argues that two sets of mechanisms are needed to make public policy. First, fundamental decisions will require a high order of attention to detail; they will require consideration of the effect of different alternatives, for long periods of time into the future, upon the goals of the organization or society. Second, the incremental process can be used most of the time "to prepare for fundamental decisions and work them out after they have been reached."[15] The combination of these two processes Etzioni calls "mixed scanning."

Under the "mixed scanning" process, the decision maker scans the total organization regularly but does not attempt to digest the overwhelming amount of detail that is generated. As long as no in-depth examination appears to be necessary, the decisions of the organization can be made on an incremental basis; on the other hand, if any new, unexpected, or significant details appear while the perfunctory scanning is occurring, the decision maker can zero in at a level of intimate detail in order to observe the occurrence and to make any basic decisions that are required. Etzioni describes how the process works by using as an example a proposed plan for a weather observation satellite system which would photograph the weather patterns of the earth by producing a composite, but nondetailed picture of the total system. Whenever the first camera revealed the need for a more in-depth examination, a second camera, creating greater detail but having a narrower range of view, could be brought into focus, giving the observers the information that they sought. The goal of mixed scanning is to produce flexibility. Etzioni believes that mixed scanning combines the best parts of both the economic, or rational, model and the incremental model of decision making, because

in the exploration of mixed-scanning, it is essential to differentiate fundamental decisions from incremental ones. Fundamental decisions are made by exploring the main alternatives the actor sees in view of his conception of his goals, but—unlike what rationalism would indicate—details and specifications are omitted so that an overview is feasible. Incremental decisions are made but within the context set by fundamental decisions (and fundamental reviews). Thus, each of the two elements in mixed scanning helps to reduce the effects of the particular shortcomings of the other; incrementalism reduces the unrealistic aspects of rationalism by limiting the details required in fundamental decisions, and con-

[14] Etzioni, p. 387.

[15] *Ibid.*, p. 388.

textuating rationalism helps to overcome the conservative slant of incrementalism by exploring longer-run alternatives.[16]

A similar type of approach to all of management (which some people define as decision making) has been suggested by other practitioners when they discuss the concept of "management by exception." The system of control that they propose works on the same principle as that mentioned by Etzioni, except that in this case the manager scans the information fed back to him, looking for any part of the organization, or any activity, that does not appear to be functioning as expected. The manager then focuses on those cases where the abnormal is occurring, giving more direction and correction to those programs.

# THE LIMITS ON RATIONALITY IN PUBLIC DECISIONS

Students of public administration, as well as political reformers, have constantly argued that the goal of their research, training, and reform is to improve the rationality of decision making. Before one can accept their statement at face value, it is necessary to agree on a definition of rationality—a task that is exceedingly difficult—and then to agree that rationality is indeed an appropriate goal in the political world—a task as thankless as the first. Before dealing with the issue of improving rationality in the decision-making process, two steps appear to be necessary. First, it is essential to attempt to clarify what is meant by the term "rationality." Second, it is necessary to consider several factors, some within the individual decision maker and some that can be best referred to as "system problems," that limit our ability to achieve rationality.

### Definition of "Rationality" in Decisions

When dealing with the actions of people and organizations existing in a political environment (and remember that there is politics *within* an organization just as there is politics around and between organizations), it is extremely difficult to gain agreement on what is meant by the term "rational." Different practitioners and scholars define the term in widely divergent ways. For this reason, any attempt to define rationality is usually attached to the process by which the decision is made. (This is true in the literature that has been reviewed earlier in this chapter.)

Because of the difficulty in arriving at a commonly acceptable definition of rationality and because of the differing situations to which the definition must be applied, an adequate definition of rationality must include both a consideration of the decision-making process *and* the result of the decision (where it is possible to examine the effect of the decision on the ongoing situation). When examining the process for rationality, it is necessary to find out if the decision makers objectively considered all possible aspects of the problem including the

[16]*Ibid.*, pp. 389-390.

quantifiable factors, those that can be defined monetarily or in designated units of measurement, and the factors that are only qualifiable, those for which measurement is impossible, such as philosophical and attitudinal factors. To the extent that decision makers quantify all the factors possible, *but only those factors*, and then consider all the subjective factors that can be developed, the decision-making process can be considered rational. However, it must be pointed out that there is always an area of unforeseeable variables and consequences that must be accounted for; therefore, the process is rational only to the extent that the problems of uncertainty and ignorance are also taken into consideration by the decision makers.

If the question of rationality is being considered after the decision has been made, it is possible to include in the definition an evaluation of the success of the decision. If the results of the decision are those things that are desired by the decision makers, and there are no negative side effects or unanticipated consequences, such a result appears to further verify the rationality of the decision. Since most decisions do not fall into such a clearly favorable position, it is usually necessary to compare the positive results of the decision with the negative effects (similar to "after the fact" cost-benefit comparison) and to judge the rationality of the decision according to the positive or negative balance when costs and benefits are totaled.

Such an evaluation can be challenged on at least two grounds: (1) even if agreement can be reached as to what level of achievement is considered "a success," the balance sheet may vary depending on who is in charge of the evaluation; (2) it may be possible for decisions that have followed the process spelled out above to have negative results, just as split-second, totally uninformed decisions may be quite successful. However, since the evaluation of the results of the decision can occur only after the fact, it should be possible to use the decision maker's statement of expected results as a yardstick against which the actual results are measured. (It is taken for granted that the decision being considered is of sufficient importance to have elicited a public pronouncement from the decision maker; it would appear to be a waste of time to attempt such an analysis on most minor decisions.) In relation to the second criticism, such an occurrence may happen occasionally, but the issues involved are so complex that the probability of making the right choice purely by chance is almost nonexistent, and the repetition of such a feat on a regular basis would be impossible.

Thus, rational decisions are those that are based, to the greatest extent possible, on means-ends processes but that also recognize the severe limitations on such processes in a political world; therefore, rationality depends on the idea of reasonableness *given the particular situation*. Actually, the political world is one of the most severe "system" limitations on "pure" rationality. One final word of clarification should be added. The barriers to rationality that are considered below are discussed in the singular—as if they are affecting a single public administrator. While this approach is taken in order to simplify the discussion, it should be understood that the barriers apply equally to groups and organizations when decisions are being made by more than one individual. The material may be "pluralized" very easily; in fact, the reader should attempt to apply each of the following factors to groups as an exercise to further his or her understanding of the barriers.

## Psychological Barriers to Rational Decisions

One of the important factors that must be considered when discussing the limitations on rationality in decision making is that of the personal, or psychological, factors that influence the decision maker. These factors vary from individual character traits and personality dynamics brought to the organization by the executive to the habits and behavior that are instilled in the individual by the other members of the organization to which he or she belongs. These personal characteristics may, on occasion, be the single most important variable in understanding why a particular decision is made; at other times, personality may play only a minor role in the final outcome, but it cannot be dismissed as unimportant. Thomas Mongar has written a thought-provoking article entitled "Personality and Decision-Making: John F. Kennedy in Four Crisis Decisions," in which Mongar argues that quite often "the decisional process of executive systems can be reduced to the personality dynamics of chief executives." Mongar says,

The primary reason for this assumption is that one man (the executive) must ultimately determine the course of action of the system he heads. Buried in this assumption is the further implication that the decisional processes of the personality and the executive system are basically the same.[17]

The similarity between the executive system and the personality of the executive can be better understood if it is remembered that chief executives are usually given some margin of freedom to choose their subordinates. In most cases, the executive will choose people who have the same philosophy toward life and who agree with the executive as to how various policies and activities should be carried out. When this is true, the staff, or the executive system, becomes an extension of the personality of the executive, and decisions will tend to reflect the personality of the executive, even if they are made by other members of the executive staff. In most basic decisions, there is a thin margin between success and failure; yet it is extremely easy for irrational forces to creep into the choice process.

The most common types of psychological barriers can be grouped into five general categories: (1) the determination of thought by position in social space; (2) the projection of attitudes and values; (3) over-simplification; (4) cognitive

---

[17] Thomas Mongar, "Personality and Decision-Making: John F. Kennedy in Four Crisis Decisions," *Canadian Journal of Political Science, II,* 212 (June 1969).

nearsightedness; and (5) identification with outside groups. Let us look briefly at each type of barrier in order to see what kinds of problems they cause for public administrators and to decide if there are ways to overcome the difficulties.

**The Determination of Thought by Position in Social Space.** The way that one thinks and the type of decisions one makes are often influenced by one's position in social space. This position is decided by one's level within the hierarchy of the organization, the prestige level of the organization in society, and the peer group that surrounds the individual. Many of our attitudes and perceptions of the world are influenced by those with whom we associate daily. These are the people whom we usually wish to impress, and they are the group that is most likely to give us the information on which we base our decisions. If the information that is received is valid, there is no problem with such an arrangement; however, all too often the information that is passed on becomes, over a period of time, distorted by any particular group so that it fits their special needs and desires. Once such a procedure has begun, it becomes increasingly harder for those involved in the group to perceive the truth and even more difficult to get the group to retrace its steps so that the misconceptions and distortions can be corrected. William H. Whyte pictured the epitome of this type of problem in his book, *The Organization Man,* in which Whyte argued that the manager of the 1950s and 1960s was a direct reflection of the cultural values that Whyte called the "social ethic."[18] This ethic taught that the two most important things that any individual could do were to be loyal to the organization and to sacrifice individuality for the sake of the group and the organization. A natural corollary of this idea, of course, was that the group was the source of creativity; therefore, a manager was expected to go along with the group consensus.[19]

A good example of the social ethic in action has been the U.S. Department of State. The advice that was most commonly given to young State Department employees who wished to get ahead was "Don't make waves." It was assumed that those who were promoted had been socialized into the system, had made decisions in the "proper way," had presented the "proper image" to the public, and had agreed with the decisions and policies of their superiors—or at least had carried out those decisions without becoming vocal in their opposition. In 1967, Chris Argyris found that the State Department, in general, and the Foreign Service, in particular, had developed norms that stopped the confrontation of

---

[18]William H. Whyte, Jr., *The Organization Man,* Doubleday Anchor, Garden City, N. Y., 1956.

[19]*Ibid.,* pp. 7-8.

difficult problems and penalized those willing to take a risk.[20] Argyris charged that this culture

... rewards certain types of interpersonal styles, helps to create a perception of the Foreign Service as being a rather closed club, induces a degree of blindness on the part of the members concerning their impact on each other and "outsiders," and generates an intricate network of organizational defenses that makes the members believe that changing it may be very difficult if not impossible.[21]

In order to overcome this serious problem, the State Department established a task force on "Stimulation of Creativity"[22] which concluded, after additional research into the problem, that the charges leveled against the service were correct; the task force suggested a series of changes to the structure and personnel policies of the department in an effort to overcome these difficulties.

Before the reader takes pleasure in the troubles of the State Department, it should be pointed out that exactly the same type of problem exists (although perhaps on a different scale) in many of the departments of state and local government. Similar charges have been leveled against police departments in particular. It is argued that since policemen work at odd hours and since, for various reasons, they tend to socialize with each other when not at work, the police department develops a social system that protects its own members at all costs. It is also argued that the decisions of policemen, both as patrolmen on the beat and as administrators in headquarters, are strongly affected by their membership in such a close-knit group.

**Projection of Attitudes and Values.** Many decisions are doomed to failure at the instant they are made because the decision maker has based the final choice on the attitudes and values he holds and takes it for granted that the other individuals involved agree with these ideas. Attitudes and values are often projected (as this procedure is named) from one individual to another; however, attitudes are deeply personal and differ to some extent for each individual. A presumption that the attitudes of administrator and client or of different sets of bureaucrats working in separate offices are the same is almost certain to cause faulty judgment in the making of decisions. To believe that the values of social

[20] Chris Argyris, *Some Causes of Organizational Ineffectiveness Within the Department of State*, Center for International Systems Research, Occasional Papers Number 2, U. S. Department of State, Washington, D. C., 1967.

[21] *Ibid.*, p. 2.

[22] *Diplomacy for the 70's, A Program of Management Reform for the Department of State*, Government Printing Office, Washington D. C., December 1970, pp. 290-339.

workers, urban planners, or policemen in any way closely resemble those of the citizens of the urban ghetto is ridiculous. There will generally be enough of a difference that the actions of such professionals are likely to have unanticipated consequences unless an extra effort is made to understand the attitudes, values, and motivations of the people with whom they are working. Of course, the same kind of value disparity has been one of the causes of controversy throughout the history of federal grant-in-aid programs to the state and local governments, because the values of the national politicians and administrators vary from those of their counterparts at the state and local level. This has led to charges at the national level that funds have been misused by local officials, while the local officials respond by charging that the federal government places local officials in a straitjacket, which limits the capability of local government to meet its most pressing needs.

Surprisingly enough, especially after the comments on group socialization in the prior section, one of the best ways to counteract the problem of the projection of attitudes is to use the combined knowledge of groups when making decisions. Such a tool must be carefully utilized, however, for the desired end of such a practice is that the group will be able to introduce into the decision process, and to the decision maker, the various ideas, attitudes, and values that exist within the affected segments of society, so that the tendency to project may be overcome with large doses of reality.

**Oversimplification.** A common charge leveled against politicians is that they attempt to present all problems and the solutions to those problems, in overly simplistic terms. Public administrators also may fall prey to that temptation because simple problems are more likely to be solved by simple answers. Since most decisions must be made within a specified time limit, one of the easiest ways to narrow down the variables being considered and the number of alternatives being evaluated is to reduce the problem to a simple model of its complex reality. Such simplification may occur in several ways.

First, there is often a tendency to picture political issues in a dichotomized way. When a political issue arises, one of the opposing sides ends up wearing the white hat and riding the white horse, while the other side gets the villain's garb; there is often an attempt by each side involved in an issue to paint a picture of their particular group as being the champion of society while picturing the other side as self-interested and uncaring about the needs of society. It is very easy for administrators to fall prey to this rhetoric, but issues are seldom so clearly drawn; decisions based on such information almost always lead to even further problems in the future.

Second, if a public administrator gets too far away from the problem that must be faced, there is a tendency to see the various segments of the problem in an undifferentiated way. If the head of a welfare program does not keep in contact with the many citizens that are served by the agency, the administrator may begin to forget the unique characteristics that must be taken into account while handling cases involving dependent children. Instead, a stereotype of mothers and fathers who require aid in order to feed and clothe their children develops in the mind of the administrator, and the decisions that are handed down in reference to these cases will fail to meet the requirements of the clients. In a similar way, a mayor may begin to think that "all unions are the same," an attitude that creates additional difficulties for the negotiators on both sides of the table when contract time rolls around.

A third example of oversimplification often occurs because administrators work under the assumption that the future will repeat the past. Perhaps the most dramatic case of this error was presented by the French General Command between the two world wars when they assumed that the next war would be fought like the prior war—in trenches on the ground—and expended millions of francs to build the Maginot Line along the border with Germany. When the Germans attacked with their *Blitzkrieg* through neutral countries, the Maginot Line proved to be absolutely worthless as a defense mechanism for the country. The tactics of war had changed, but the assumptions of the generals had not.

It is easy to apply the same idea to urban problems. For instance, Thomas P. F. Hoving, the director of the Metropolitan Museum of Art in New York, points out that the prevailing ideas about parks and recreation in New York City must change in order to meet the needs of the citizens. Hoving states that "despite the dizzying pace of change nowadays—in art, politics, culture—the nature of our parks has remained the same, lifelessly suspended in time like the pyramid of Cheops."[23]

With the vanishing of large open spaces in the heart of the city the time is long overdue for a redefinition of our concept of a park and the role of the Parks Department. . . . A great deal of New York's available open land now consists of small parcels, many of them junk piles, garbage heaps and slum backyards. . . . Reclaimed as joint ventures by local community groups . . . and the Parks Department, the vacant lots can be filled with purpose: to put . . . parks where the people are. . . . As far as the city's available park land is concerned, it means that to think big we must also think small.[24]

There are other causes of oversimplification in addition to those already mentioned. It is common for decision makers to mistake the more obvious symptoms of problems for the less obvious causes. This was one of the initial problems that existed when the federal government began to attack the problem of urban renewal. Initially the program set out to rebuild housing in the central cities. Such a program was needed, but in order to attack the causes of urban blight, it was necessary to recognize and deal with several other problems that were equally as important as the physical condition of housing. The problems of education, underemployment, ill health, and other social and economic

[23] Thomas P. F. Hoving, "Think Big About Small Parks," in Ray Ginger, ed., *Modern American Cities*, Quadrangle, Chicago, 1969, p. 189.

[24] *Ibid.*, pp. 189–200.

ills had to be attacked in concert with the problem of housing or little could be gained regardless of the amount of money spent on the housing program.

This difficulty might have been recognized more quickly had not another problem in decision making been present. There is a tendency for technical experts to have "tunnel vision" when looking at a problem. Quite often, these technicians try to alleviate the problem only through the use of their skills and their agencies. This is where the role of a higher administrator in the decision-making process is obvious. Since the higher level administrators are able to seek the advice of a cross section of the bureaucracy, they should be able to avoid the oversimplified solution by combining all the various relevant factors in a broad-based program dealing with the total problem.

**Cognitive Nearsightedness.** In political systems, it is often necessary for the elected officials to show those who elected them that they are interested in the problems that the citizens consider to be most important. A common adage among politicians says that the citizens, when election time nears, always ask, "What have you done for us lately?" The natural result of such pressures on politicians is that they, in turn, push the public administrators who work for them to produce solutions that give "instant" results. It is easy for either political or administrative decision makers to suffer from "cognitive nearsightedness" under so much pressure from the public. It is often argued that the United States presidents have generally sought solutions that would achieve the desired effect by the next election rather than long-term solutions to economic problems. On numerous occasions, economists have argued that these short-term solutions have led to additional economic turbulence at later times. When decisions are made, it is important to consider both short-term and long-term results of the alternative under consideration. If this is not done, the result may be short-term solutions that lead to even greater problems in the future. As we increasingly face new problems because of the shrinking base of resources in relation to the amount of resources that we are using, it will become more and more important not to fall into the trap of trying to achieve instant solutions.

**Identification with Outside Reference Groups.** In 1965, a Legal Services Program was inaugurated as a new division of the U.S. Office of Economic Opportunity. This program made available to the poor free legal services in *civil* cases. The concept of free legal aid in *criminal* cases had been accepted for some time and had been confirmed by the Supreme Court,[25] but the idea of free legal services for civil cases was relatively new. The lawyers implementing the program were faced with a constant dilemma as they attempted to carry out their duties. How closely would they cooperate with the local and state bar associa-

---

[25] The U. S. Supreme Court was cementing the concept of free legal aid for indigent defendants in criminal cases at just this time. The landmark cases were: *Gideon v. Wainwright* (1963)—the Fourteenth Amendment requires free legal counsel for all indigent defendants in criminal cases; *Escobedo v. Illinois* (1964)—a suspect is entitled to confer with counsel as soon as police investigation focuses on him; *Miranda v. Arizona* (1966)—a suspect must be informed, before he is questioned, of all his constitutional rights, including the right to counsel and to remain silent.

tions? Should the lawyers in the Legal Services Program identify with the Office of Economic Opportunity and those that it served, or should their decisions and actions be primarily influenced by their fellow lawyers?

This is a problem that is faced by every professional in public service at some time during that service. The influence of outside groups may be subtle and hardly recognizable even to the individual public administrator, or it may be an openly recognized factor that constantly impinges on the choices that are made by public servants. In most cases, the dual identification probably causes little difficulty, because the goals of the outside groups may coincide with the goals of the public organization. The goals of most public professional associations, for instance, are centered on the delivery of needed public services. However, some groups will not agree with the goals of the public agency, and even when they do, there may well be disagreement on the means for achieving the best possible results for the public. In such a case, how much should public health doctors allow their decisions to be influenced by the American Medical Association, or how much should a social worker's decision on a case be influenced by the American Social Work Association?

There is no single answer as to how much outside groups should be allowed to impinge on the decision-making process of either an individual or a total public agency. The influence of an outside group may prove to be rational if that group is knowledgeable and powerful enough to help the decision maker. However, when such a group is used by the decision maker, the group often has little, if anything, to contribute. This is especially true when dealing with the question of "what is best for the public?" In this case, the only thing such outside groups can contribute is personal vindication for the decision maker through rationalization of the official's choice in case that choice is attacked. Such support is important; this is not an attempt to downgrade the value of such support whenever it is available, nor is this discussion meant to infer that there is always such a dichotomy between public policy and the program advocated by professional organizations. However, it is meant to point out that such differences do occur on occasion, *and when they do occur,* the public administrator must be cognizant of the disparity so that a more rational decision can be made.

In the case of the Legal Services Program, the local programs had occasional conflicts with their bar associations; where such opposition arose, it was usually obviated when it became clear that the local program would not mean an economic loss for the practicing attorneys in the area, and the program was able to go ahead to win some landmark cases while representing the clients of the Office of Economic Opportunity. In fact, when the program was attacked politically in California and in Congress, the American Bar Association supported the OEO and helped to defeat crippling legislation. The American Bar Association also supported the California Rural Legal Assistance Program when it was charged with improper conduct.[26]

---

[26] For a brief description of the battle over the California Rural Legal Assistance Program, see: Larry L. Wade, *The Elements of Public Policy*, Charles E. Merrill, Columbus, Ohio, 1972, pp. 78-86.

## System Barriers to Rationality

In addition to the many psychological barriers to rational decision making is a variety of factors that are outside the control of the individual decision maker. Some of the prior discussion could be rewritten with a different emphasis, and it would fall into this segment of the chapter as easily as the section on psychological problems; it is often difficult to tell where many of the forces cease being problems internal to the decision maker and become part of the environment in which the decision maker must operate. It is difficult to know when, for example, the pressure of outside loyalties changes from a personal problem, created by the individual's identity with a particular group, to a pressure subtly or forcefully placed upon the decision maker in an attempt by that organization to sway the final decision. Therefore, it would behoove the reader to reconsider the prior discussion dealing with barriers to rationality, bearing in mind where such differences of emphasis could be applied.

**Form of the Question.** It should be noted that the political system places many limitations on the rationality that can be achieved by the public administrator. Many of the most important decisions that are faced by public administrators are placed before them by other people such as legislators or citizens who are making demands; therefore, the public administrators have only limited control over the way that questions are asked. There is a big difference between asking, What would be the best mass transit system for the cities of California? and asking, What would be the best fixed guideway mass transit system for the cities of California? The first question leaves all alternative modes of transportation open to the decision maker, whereas, the second has limited the choices. By stating the question in the latter form, the political system may have forced the decision maker to arrive at a choice that, while feasible to operate, does not meet criteria of maximum efficiency, comfort, or social equity. This may be exactly the problem faced by transportation experts if the political system freezes funds into particular categories or if the law is frozen into the constitution, as occurs in many states. Therefore, two important factors may influence the ability of the public administrator to respond in the most rational way: the first factor is whether or not the form of the question is formulated inside or outside the bureaucracy; the second factor is whether or not a specific kind of response is mandated. These are not hypothetical cases, for it is important to remember that there is a great deal of disagreement as to what the ends of programs should be; when such disagreement exists within the political system, it is a common practice for the interested parties to write such limitations into the law, so that the majority group may guarantee that their interests and ideas will be protected.

**Time as a Limiting Factor.** Perhaps the single most important limitation on rationality in decision making is the matter of time; it is impossible to carry out a rational decision-making process if there is only a short time to arrive at the conclusion of a conflict or problem. Academicians often forget that this problem exists because they live in an environment that rewards preciseness and completeness in solving problems. On the other hand, the public administrator operates in an environment that rewards the individual who has the ability to make decisions quickly. Thus, the successful manager in the public sphere must either have or develop the ability to pick out the most important variables affecting a problem, to zero in quickly on these issues, and to arrive at a decision within the amount of time available. Such decisions cannot be made according to preset formulas, and for this reason, the decision is not always going to achieve the best possible result. In cases where immediate response is essential, the decision maker is not rewarded for his ability to arrive at the *best possible* solution; instead, rewards are allocated according to his ability to find an *acceptable* solution within the allotted time.

Other limits on rationality, such as the pressure for finding the conspicuous answer rather than the basic answer, could be discussed; however, the fact that there are limitations has been made adequately with the several examples previously given. Now it is time to consider some of the techniques that are being used by those in authority to improve the rationality of their decisions.

## THE SEARCH FOR MORE RATIONAL DECISIONS

The type of decision making that takes place is usually determined by the situation that exists when that particular decision must be made. For this reason, Etzioni's "mixed-scanning" model, which was described earlier in this chapter, is perhaps the most useful picture of decision making that we have discussed, primarily because it allows all the other models to fall within its boundaries. Even though the public administrator must operate in a volatile environment, and rationality is *not* one of the characteristics for which the political world is known, there has not been a movement away from the rationalistic attempts at decision making. On the contrary, there is an increasing interest in processes that will allow more rational choices to be made within public agencies; such an interest will undoubtedly continue and increase in the future. It is true that decision makers must consider innumerable variables with unknown consequences for countless alternative courses of action, but such conditions do not let the administrator off the hook. Those decisions still must be made, with the public and the politicians all watching and waiting to judge the results. Is it any wonder, then, that the public administrator is looking for help from whatever source it may be available?

Two major approaches have been developed that are designed to bring greater attention to a wider variety of details as a decision is made and to introduce hitherto undiscovered alternatives and solutions into the decision arena. These new methods, in some cases, allow the use of a group of people; in other cases, the use of computers and mathematical formulas allow calculations on the effects of decisions to an extent deemed impossible before these techniques were invented.

## Group Decision Making

The most difficult aspect of decision making is the generation of creativity. Our ability to develop creativeness lags behind all other techniques now used by managers, but "it is creativity which is desperately needed to solve the important basic, nonprogrammed, risk-uncertainty types of decisional problems" that face us in our modern society.[27] The few theories that apply to creativity have been around for some time, and little significant information is being added to the area. Only two approaches, "brainstorming" and "synectics," have been formally treated by authors.

*Brainstorming* was developed to help trigger creative ideas in advertising. The idea behind the system is to bring a group together and to establish an environment where individuals within the group can present *any* idea that seems even remotely to apply to the subject being considered, with the understanding that criticism will be withheld unless it can somehow improve on the original idea.[28] The practitioners of brainstorming have been able to determine some specific procedures that improve the effectiveness of the brainstorming sessions. For instance, Charles Whiting suggests the following guidelines.

1. The sessions should last forty minutes to an hour, although brief ten- to fifteen-minute sessions can be effective if time is limited.
2. Generally, the problem to be discussed should not be revealed before the session.
3. The problem should be clearly stated and not be too broad.
4. A small conference table which allows people to communicate easily should be used.[29]

This approach can be useful in dealing with many public policy or administrative problems. When the major problem is one of discovering new ways to deal with a situation, brainstorming may prove useful. One of the most difficult aspects of brainstorming, however, is creating a situation where it can occur, for the "rules of the game" are based on an implicit level of trust between individuals that often does not exist in the politically volatile public organization. This kind of trust must be developed in order for the procedure to be successful; thus, people tend to become freer and better able to use the process as they participate in repeated experiences and accept the validity of the process.

*Synectics* is a form of creative decision making that is based on the concept of using analogies to help in the two processes of (1) making the strange familiar,

---

[27] Fred Luthans, *Organizational Behavior: A Modern Behavioral Approach to Management*, McGraw-Hill, New York, 1973, p. 223.

[28] Alex F. Osborn, *Applied Imagination*, Charles Scribner's Sons, New York, 1953.

[29] Charles S. Whiting, "Operational Techniques of Creative Thinking," *Advanced Management, XX,* 28 (October 1955).

and (2) making the familiar strange.[30] Each phase is important to the process of creativity in decision making. It is necessary to make the strange familiar in order that a common understanding can be developed of the subject under discussion. Then, the creative solutions are usually developed as the familiar is made strange, for during this period those involved in the decision-making process make a conscious effort to look at the problem from a completely different viewpoint. Synectics is a more difficult tool to use than regular brainstorming, even though there are many similarities in the two processes, because it requires specialists who have been trained in the procedure and who understand its philosophy; still, it has proved useful in many cases where technical difficulties in scientific programs have needed to be overcome.

Both brainstorming and synectics may be useful to public administrators at various times as they attempt to derive new and unique solutions to pressing problems. However, there are drawbacks that limit their usefulness. Both systems may prove to be quite expensive, for they require the involvement of several people, who are often well paid, over an extended period of time. The solutions may prove to be only superficial after closer examination. Also, the more successful of the two systems at developing substantive answers to technical problems is synectics, which requires a great deal of special training. Still, both processes have proved useful to government officials when they have been faced with decisions that were filled with uncertainty. Under the proper rules, many minds do appear to be better than one.

The *Delphi* technique, which was named after the oracle at Delphi in ancient Greece, has been used on an increasingly larger scale during the last decade to assist in making decisions where there is a need for forecasting over the long range. Variations of Delphi have now moved into a variety of processes where it is desirable to have the input of a number of individuals.[31] The basic rules of the technique are as follows.

1. A panel of experts on the particular problem at hand is drawn from both inside and outside the organization.
2. Each expert is asked to make anonymous predictions.
3. Each panelist then gets a composite feedback of the way the other experts answered the questions.
4. Based upon the feedback, new estimates are made and the process is repeated several times.[32]

The key to the process is the anonymity of all participants, for when names are not attached to ideas, there is no need to "defend one's expertise" against

---

[30] William J. J. Gordon, *Synectics*, Collier-MacMillan, London, 1961.

[31] During 1974, one university even used a modified Delphi technique to help define the curriculum for a new undergraduate program in Public Administration.

[32] "Forecasters Turn to Group Guesswork," *Business Week*, p. 130 (March 14, 1970).

the ideas of others. To state this another way, there is no problem with "losing face" before others. Thus, the information received can be treated more flexibly, and it is easier to move toward a consensus based on the expertise of all the participants.

Good decisions require good forecasts. No system has been developed that can forecast the future perfectly, but the Delphi technique has proved to be as successful as any forecasting techniques currently known. As would be expected, however, the system can be criticized, for it is expensive and time-consuming; however, the major criticism directed toward it is one called the "Ouija-board effect." According to this criticism,

. . . Delphi can claim no scientific approach or support. To counter this criticism, Rand has attempted to validate Delphi through controlled experimentation. The corporation set up panels of nonexperts who use (sic) the Delphi technique to answer questions such as "How many popular votes were cast for Lincoln when he first ran for President?" and "What was the average price a farmer received for a bushel of apples in 1940?" These particular questions were used because the average person does not know the exact answers but knows something about the subjects. The result of these studies showed that the original estimates by the panel of nonexperts were reasonably close to being correct, but with the Delphi technique of anonymous feedback, the estimates were greatly improved.[33]

Upon completion of the study, the Rand Corporation felt that the Delphi technique had been proved successful, but the difficult task of convincing the scientific community that it was useful was not so easily accomplished. Now, however, the use of Delphi is common in the Defense Department, and it is spreading among other federal departments. Undoubtedly, Delphi will become a common term at the state and local government level during the next decade.

Public administrators have also turned increasingly to *citizen participation* as a means of arriving at better decisions, at least as far as aligning decisions more closely with the desires of those the public administrators serve. The use of citizens to help *initiate* policy and to advise on decisions has come into special popularity since 1960, with "citizen participation" being the rallying cry of interest groups, minority groups, and many politicians and public administrators. The idea has spread from the office of the president to the office of the mayor in most cities.

At the national level, the idea of citizen participation had its initial impetus with the inauguration of President John F. Kennedy. Until that time, the legislative program was formulated almost exclusively by the departments and agencies, who prepared and submitted the proposals to the president through the Bureau of the Budget.[34] Critics were contending that new ideas were adulter-

---

[33] *Ibid.*, p. 134.

[34] Richard E. Neustadt, "The Presidency and Legislation: Planning the President's Program," *American Political Science Review, XLIX,* 980-1018 (December 1955).

ated, and often emasculated, by the internal bureaucratic politics, while other proposals were repeated until they won acceptance by attrition. In many cases, the rationale for a proposal had disappeared by the time it was accepted, and in the majority of cases, "agency-oriented proposals . . . tended to be unimaginative, remedial, and incremental rather than broadly innovative."[35] Kennedy commissioned 29 task forces composed of leading Democrats to study the areas of foreign and domestic policy. The task force reports helped the new administration to think through several of the problems that it was facing, eventually resulting in a series of legislative proposals.

President Lyndon Johnson carried on the tradition established by President Kennedy. Perhaps the most famous of the commissions established by Johnson was the Commission on Civil Disorders (the Kerner Commission) whose report in March of 1968 led to great amounts of criticism and support for its conclusions and recommendations. The use of task forces continued into the Nixon administration with the most well-known task force once again leading to animated debate, this time over the issue of decriminalizing marijuana.[36]

At the local level, the idea of participation by the citizens in setting goals and priorities for the community was becoming accepted at the same time it was developing at the national level. The concept of citizen participation was given tremendous impetus by President Johnson's "War on Poverty" program, which had as one of its goals "maximum feasible participation" among the groups that were served through the federal funds. At the same time, city councils and city managers began to make use of groups of citizens drawn from throughout the cities (usually a combination of volunteers and representatives of various community groups) to establish the goals of the cities. Many of these bodies have gained some semblance of permanence because the revenue-sharing programs of the national government require a citizen review board before the local governments can receive their share of the available money.

The major thrust of citizen participation has been to gain a better understanding of the wants and needs of citizens. Any time such a procedure is used, however, the administrator may find that the decisions made by those groups do not match the decisions that the administrator would have desired. This is a fact that may occur any time decisions are delegated to other individuals or groups. Of course, the same result may occur when the administrator proposes actions or policies to the legislative body. The problem is with the definition of rationality as it applies to decisions in public agencies. We will return to this subject after discussing the most "rational" decision-making tools—models, mathematical techniques, and other computer-assisted devices.

The most dramatic advances in public administration have occurred in con-

[35] Norman C. Thomas and Harold L. Wolman, "The Presidency and Policy Formulation: The Task Force Device," *Public Administration Review, XXIX*, 459 (September-October, 1969).

[36] *Report of the National Advisory Commission on Civil Disorders*, New York Times, New York, 1968. *Marihuana: A Signal of Misunderstanding*. U. S. Superintendent of Documents, U. S. National Commission on Marihuana and Drug Abuse, Washington, D. C., March 1972.

junction with the use of the computer. The ability of the computer to carry out complicated calculations, which could not be done prior to its invention, has allowed a tremendous increase in the complexity of problems that can be tackled through mathematical representation. These tools are especially useful when a problem is being faced that is primarily made up of factors that are divisible and quantifiable. Let us suppose that the decision being faced by a city government is that of making a choice among possible sites for a new airport. There are numerous problems that must be worked out, including where to place the airport and how the facilities should be arranged once the site is chosen. The choice of the site will be influenced by many factors: the local air traffic patterns that will be affected by the new airport; the overall pattern created by other already existing airports; the availability of the airport to its potential users; the effect of the airport on the physical environment; and the effect of the airport on the quality of life of those people living in close proximity to the site. The model must answer many specific questions about each area of concern, such as How many people will be living under the corridors at each end of the runways? What effect will the airport have on noise levels in the occupied areas around its perimeter? How will the airport affect air and water quality? and What types of traffic will the airport generate? All these questions must be answered, because it is essential to design the internal operation of the airport in a way that allows maximum efficiency in utilizing the facilities while guaranteeing everyone at least a minimum of safety and convenience.

Such questions can best be solved by applying such management science techniques as linear programming, queuing theory, the Monte Carlo technique, and other similar mathematical models to the problem. If necessary, it is possible to simulate the total system of such an airport in order to discover how the particular choices being considered may operate in reality.[37] The implementation of the final decision may also be improved through the use of such planning and control models as the Program Evaluation Review Technique, Critical Path Method, and other similar models. It would be impossible for a single individual, or any group of people, to make all the calculations connected with any of these programs manually; however, with the aid of computers, it is possible to arrive at a conclusion that is rational *from a quantitative point of view.*

Of course, there are other models beside those that are of a mathematical nature. Models may be in the form of a drawing or may take the more realistic form of a scaled replication of the expected end product. Most people are familiar with the scale model of urban renewal projects or with the "campus of the future." These models help to fill the void left by limited imagination, and they allow a full appreciation of the physical and aesthetic potential of the proposed construction.

Also included under the general rubric of "models" are games and simulations of reality that may be used either to train individuals in a particular process or, in many cases, to allow the decision makers the opportunity of seeing their pro-

[37] Richard A. Johnson, Fremont E. Kast, and James E. Rosenzweig, *The Theory and Management of Systems*, McGraw-Hill, New York, 1963.

cess and choices in a manner as nearly replicating the real world as possible. The most well known of the simulations, or games, are the frequent war games that are carried out by the military both as a training device and as a means of keeping their active forces at peak efficiency during peacetime. Games are now being used in the classroom and in the training of professionals and executives, so that they can develop a sense of the way the processes work in which the individuals function. Through such games the various major forces that impinge on any decision can be brought to light, and the decision maker can examine the interaction of these forces in a neutral, learning environment where mistakes and new approaches to old problems are not rewarded and punished in a way that limits innovation. Again, computers have allowed this type of gaming, or modeling, to develop to the level of complexity and sophistication that they have now achieved, for the computer can carry out the mathematical calculations needed to give a feeling of reality to the game.

## THE COMPUTER: BOON OR BANE?

It is impossible to discuss decision making without commenting on the impact of computers. In general, the development of the computer has been the most important occurrence in the history of organizations, particularly of public bureaucracies. The impact of the computer has been so great in this area that Herbert Simon can say with a great deal of justification that

the major problems of governmental . . . organizations today are not problems of departmentalization and coordination of operating units. Instead, they are problems of organizing information storage and information processing.[38]

The computer is capable of handling repetitive tasks in a fraction of the time that such transactions once took; also, the computer has become increasingly available to all levels of government as time sharing has become a reality. This means that city administrators may benefit from the same rapid response to queries about the status of programs and accounts that has been the boon of state and federal administrators. These factors, plus many others have improved the sophistication of the decision-making process; therefore,

with the rapid development of information-processing technology, the . . . public decision-making processes are becoming immensely more sophisticated than they were in past eras. . . . We have a growing capacity to consider interactions and tradeoffs among alternatives and consequences; to cumulate our understanding of fragments of the whole problem by embedding these fragments in comprehensive models.[39]

---

[38] Herbert Simon, "Applying Information Technology to Organization Design," *Public Administration Review, XXXIII,* 276 (May-June, 1973).

[39] *Ibid.*, pp. 276-277.

However, every new advance in technology creates a greater opportunity for the misuse of that process. The strength of the computer is also its weakness. The capacity for combining diverse bits of information into comprehensive models is useful, but such a capacity can be easily misused. This consideration takes on critical importance when the information that is being collected and disseminated is of a social nature. In her lectures on *Systematic Thinking for Social Action*, Alice Rivlin directly faces this problem. She notes that

there is pressing need for longitudinal information to help us understand, for example, what happens to children as they move through a school system. Are children who have serious deficiencies in first grade necessarily the ones who are deficient in high school? What happens to people with health problems? To what extent do people move in and out of poverty?

The technical capacity to answer these questions now exists. Individuals and families can be assigned identifying numbers, such as the social security number that most people already hace, which can be used to match data from different sources or on the same persons at different times. The crucial questions now are not so much technical as organizational. Can the collection of information, especially information on individuals at different points in their lives, be organized to be useful to policy makers without undue inconvenience or danger to privacy?[40]

In the past, there have been major abuses of such privacy ideals by credit bureaus and other types of corporations. Today, there is a great fear among civil libertarians about the ability of the federal government to combine the numerous files that are currently available into a composite record on citizens.[41] In the future, it is likely that we will continue to curse the tool that blesses us. An answer to the problem of how to control our capabilities so that they do not affect our liberties will not be easily found. It is a certainty that we will not be able to arrive at a commonly accepted ground on the issue of how much individuality we are willing to give up for the sake of increased rationality in decision making. The fact that we cannot agree may be a healthy sign.

## IS RATIONALITY POSSIBLE?

Throughout this chapter, the central theme has been the quest for more rationality in the decision-making process. The problem lies in the definition of rationality as it applies to decisions bearing on the public sphere. A rational decision in

[40] Alice M. Rivlin, *Systematic Thinking for Social Action*, Brookings, Washington, D. C., 1971, p. 15.

[41] *The Computer and Invasion of Privacy*, Hearings Before a Subcommittee of the House Committee on Government Operation, 89th Congress, 2nd Session, 1966; *The Coordination and Integration of Government Statistical Programs*, Hearings Before the Subcommittee on Economic Statistics of the Joint Economic Committee, 90th Congress, 1st Session, 1967; see also: Alan F. Westin, *Privacy and Freedom*, Atheneum, New York, 1967.

the public sphere is one that meets both the logic of the public administrator and the logic of the politician. The administrator places more emphasis on the quantifiable aspects of the problem, while the politician places more emphasis on the nonquantifiable aspects. Thus, when one is talking about a public decision, rationality contains within it a proper understanding of the political conditions that are involved in its acceptance and implementation. A decision is *not* rational, regardless of how well it fits group consensus among administrators or the equations of mathematics, if the proposal does not take into account the political ramifications of the alternative selected for action. Logic and analysis are important, but their significance is limited within the "real" world. This fact is made clear by James Schlesinger, who has held a variety of high-level posts in several federal agencies. He points out that while analysis is able to sharpen and educate the judgments and intuitions of decision makers, and while analysis may smoke out ideologies and hidden interests, these additional benefits of the process may not be persuasive when the time comes for the final choice. According to Schlesinger,

Systems analysis cannot achieve wonders: it cannot transmute the dross of politics into the fine gold of Platonic decision-making, which exists in the world of ideas rather than the world of reality. Political decisions in a democratic society can hardly be more "rational" than the public, the ultimate sovereign is willing to tolerate.[42]

Some public administrators (fortunately they are in a minority and their future rise to greater positions of authority is undoubtedly limited) have not realized the validity of Schlesinger's pronouncement; these administrative decision makers have fallen into the trap of being overly impressed by the beauty and logic of numbers. These administrators, ignoring the nonquantifiable, thus troublesome, political factors and giving too much weight in their calculations to the quantifiable and "provable" part of the decision process, present to the public policymakers a beautifully prepared and documented program only to have it rejected. In the ensuing period of consternation, the public administrator may, publicly or privately, complain about the irrationality of the legislative body; on the contrary, the decision may be perfectly rational from the viewpoint of the legislators. The definition of a rational policy or a rational act may be different for the elected official. For this reason, the public administrator must include in his calculations the *political feasibility* of the selected alternative whenever that choice must be sanctioned by politicians. The same is true, although perhaps to a lesser extent, when any decision does not go before the elected officials. If the citizens become unhappy about the decision, they can make that fact known by going directly to the administrator, their elected officials, or the courts. Thus, in the end, the public administrator as decision maker

---

[42] James R. Schlesinger, "Systems Analysis and the Political Process," in Louis C. Gawthorp, ed., *The Administrative Process and Democratic Theory*, Houghton Mifflin, Boston, 1970, p. 352.

must have the ability to consider and use her knowledge of human nature and the political system, and these skills will be every bit as important to the administrator's success as will be her ability to understand the latest and most sophisticated analytic techniques.

Many students of decision making take the argument about the limit on rationality a step further and point out that, since the administrator or agency is but one participant embedded in a political system, rationality is an improper goal. In the political world of the public agency, decision making is the product of interaction between numerous participants (both individuals and organizations) in that system. Viewed from this perspective, the problem of decision making is not so much a problem of "rationality" versus "incrementalism" as it is a problem of interaction among all parts of the system in such a way that the decision-making process is responsive to a wide array of desires and demands and yet "gets things done." Balancing the desires and demands while fulfilling the aims of the agency is the primary goal of the public administrator; therefore, these two ideas would appear to be central to any definition of rationality when discussing decision making. This argument, instead of denying the possibility of rationality, helps to clarify what that term must mean when one is discussing decision making in a political world. All the tools and processes that have been discussed in this chapter are, when properly used, primarily aimed at helping the decision maker (whether a single individual or agency or a group of participants interacting in a political system) reach decisions that achieve these two goals.

Undoubtedly, rationality in the decision-making process of the public administrator has been, and will continue to be, increased, but pure rationality will never be achieved, and that is as it should be. The achievement of such a goal would be a catastrophe.

## SUMMARY

Decision making, the process of choosing between alternatives, is the single most pervasive function of management. The process of choosing between alternatives is broken down into sequential steps (three or five steps, depending on the particular model) that move from the initial recognition of a problem, through the clarification and analyzation of the alternative courses of action, and on to an ultimate choice of action. Although this basic process is repeated in every decision situation, some decisions are repetitive and programmed, while other decisions are either so unique or so basic for the organization that the entire process must be completed before the action alternative can be chosen. Normally, the higher one's position within the public bureaucracy, the more nonprogrammed and the more encumbered with uncertainty are the decisions that must be made.

Decision theorists have presented at least three major models of the decision-making process. The first descriptive model was based on the familiar tenets of the "economic man." The assumptions of perfect knowledge about both the problem and the available alternatives were soon discounted as too simplistic.

The second model, based on the concepts of limited knowledge and narrow spans of attention, proved more realistic, but it still proved to be unsatisfactory to those attempting to improve the process. The third model, which attempts to combine the best of both systems, is known as the "mixed-scanning" approach; it may prove to be the most useful model for public managers.

Rationality is the key to good decision making for public managers; however, in the political world of public administration, there are numerous factors that limit rationality. There are several psychological barriers to rational decisions that can be grouped into five general categories: the determination of thought by position in social space, projection of attitudes and values, oversimplification, cognitive nearsightedness, and identification with outside reference groups. There are also system barriers to rationality that include such factors as the form of the question given to the public manager and the limitation placed on the time for selection of a response. In order to improve rationality, a variety of techniques has been developed. Some techniques, such as brainstorming, synectics, and the Delphi system, have tried to use the combined creativity of a group when making decisions. Of course, when material is quantifiable, the computer has also opened a variety of new techniques to decision makers; however, some students of decision making consider the computer a bane as well as a boon.

Every available tool that will improve rationality should be used as long as the decision maker remembers that the definition of rationality varies when one moves from administration to politics. Decisions, if they are to prove useful and acceptable to everyone concerned, must include an ample understanding of political rationality.

# BIBLIOGRAPHY

Art, Robert J., *The TFX Decision: McNamara and the Military*, Little, Brown, Boston, 1968.

Barnard, Chester I., *The Functions of the Executive*, Harvard University, Cambridge, Mass., 1938.

Bross, Irwin, D. J., ed., *Design for Decision*, MacMillan, New York, 1953.

Cronin, Thomas E., and Sanford Greenberg, *The Presidential Advisory System*, Harper and Row, New York, 1969.

Dewey, John, *How We Think*, D. C. Heath, Boston, 1933.

Downs, Anthony, *Inside Bureaucracy*, Little, Brown, Boston, 1967.

Elbing, Alvar O., *Behavioral Decisions in Organizations,* Scott, Foresman, Glenview, Ill., 1970.

Gore, William J., *Administrative Decision-Making: A Heuristic Model,* Wiley, New York, 1964.

Hein, Leonard W., *Quantitative Approach to Managerial Decisions*, Prentice-Hall, Englewood Cliffs, N. J., 1967.

Johnson, Richard A., Fremont E. Kast, and James E. Rosenzweig, *The Theory and Management of Systems*, Second Edition, McGraw-Hill, New York, 1967.

Katz, Daniel, and Robert L. Kahn, *The Social Psychology of Organizations*, Wiley, New York, 1966.

Kepner, Charles H., and Benjamin B. Tregoe, *The Rational Manager*, McGraw-Hill, New York, 1965.

Levin, Richard I., and Rudolph P. Lamone, *Quantitative Disciplines in Management Decisions*, Dickenson, Belmont, Calif., 1969.

Luce, Robert D., and Howard Raiffa, *Games and Decisions*, Wiley, New York, 1957.

Luthans, Fred, *Organizational Behavior: A Modern Behavioral Approach to Management*, McGraw-Hill, New York, 1973.

March, James G., and Herbert A. Simon, *Organizations*, Wiley, New York, 1958.

McFarland, Dalton, *Management*, Third Edition, MacMillan, New York, 1970.

Miller, David W., and Martin Starr, *The Structure of Human Decisions*, Prentice-Hall, Englewood Cliffs, N. J., 1967.

Neuschel, R. F., *Management by System*, McGraw-Hill, New York, 1960.

Pfiffner, John M., "Administrative Rationality," *Public Administration Review, XX*, 125-132 (Summer 1960).

Raiffa, Howard, *Decision Analysis*, Addison-Wesley, Reading, Mass., 1968.

Rivlin, Alice M., *Systematic Thinking for Social Action*, Brookings Institution, Washington, D. C., 1971.

Simon, Herbert A., *Administrative Behavior: A Study of Decision-Making in Administrative Organization*, Second Edition, Free Press, New York, 1957.

Simon, Herbert A., Donald W. Smithburg, and Victor A. Thompson, *Public Administration*, Alfred A. Knopf, New York, 1950.

Stein, Harold, ed., *Public Administration and Policy Development, A Casebook*, Harcourt Brace Jovanovich, New York, 1952.

Thompson, James D., *Organizations in Action*, McGraw-Hill, New York, 1967.

Wilensky, Harold L., *Organizational Intelligence: Knowledge and Policy in Government and Industry*, Basic Books, New York, 1967.

# PLANNING: DECISION MAKING FOR THE FUTURE

*Planning is doing something by which you bring the future into existence. It is not forecasting the future and adjusting to it.*

Approach any public administrator and ask if he has a plan for the organization that he is managing, and most likely the answer will be an immediate and resounding "Of course." If you are persistent in your questioning and ask for detailed information about the extent and content of the plan, the manager is likely to refer you to the planning document, which may have to be hurriedly and surreptitiously dusted off by the secretary once its place on the shelves has been rediscovered. If you are allowed to continue your interrogation of the manager, you will probably receive an apologetic explanation of why that par-

# CHAPTER 7

ticular position leaves the manager little time for planning due to the crush of everyday problems. Quite often, the fact will also be pointed out to you that the organization under discussion has a special group or department that handles the planning end of the business.

Planning is one of the major roles of any public administrator, and the higher the administrator's position is in the organization, the more important becomes the role that must be played by the administrator in the planning process. In this chapter, we attempt to understand what is involved in the planning process and to see why planning is so important to the successful formulation and implementation of public policy. First, it is necessary to define what we mean when we speak of planning and then to examine the steps that occur in the planning process. After these two factors have been clarified, we will examine several special problems that must be considered when one is discussing planning. Most of these problems occur in any kind of an organization, but some are unique to public administration, while others are exacerbated by the fact that the planning is occurring in a political environment. After having discussed planning in this detail, you will be better equipped to see why the public administrator, who you were interviewing, responded as he did and why those responses point to problems in his management style.

## PLANNING DEFINED

The word "planning" is on everyone's tongue in our modern world. Most people recognize that planning is necessary as a result of the highly interdependent and technological world in which we live. There is seldom any complaint about corporate planning; indeed, it is the mark of good business. However, there is less agreement on the value of planning by the government. Public administrators unanimously accept the necessity of such a process in government. Legislators are increasingly considering a plan as a necessary aspect of policymaking and generally wish to know how their legislation, or that suggested by outside interest groups or internal administrative organizations, will affect the long-term goals of the community or nation. Even the general public has now come to accept the necessity of planning *at the theoretical or conceptual level*, but a great debate springs up the minute the theory starts to become reality.[1] At its most elementary level, planning is merely thinking ahead to the future with the intent of influencing the outcome of events in a particular way. In this sense, "Planning is such a common type of activity that it may take longer to describe

---

[1] There are those who see planning as a tool for limiting freedom. For a classic statement of this position, see: Friedrich A. von Hayek, *The Road to Serfdom*, University of Chicago, Chicago, 1944. For a discussion about a current program, see: Jeun J. Couterier, "Manpower Revenue Sharing—Federalizing State and Local Government," *Good Government*, *XC*, 13-15 (Fall 1973). Couterier argues against the national government's plans for state and local government manpower programs; these programs are seen as further limitations on the freedom of the lower level governments.

the process than it does to carry it out."[2] However, such a general definition is too broad to be useful in most cases. A more helpful definition of planning describes it as

. . . that activity that concerns itself with proposals for the future, with the evaluation of alternative proposals, and with the methods by which these proposals may be achieved. Planning is rational, adaptive thought applied to the future and to matters over which the planners, or the administrative organizations with which they are associated, have some degree of control.[3]

The debate about planning occurs because plans ultimately affect human behavior. As long as planning is being discussed on a theoretical level, no one feels directly threatened; but whenever a plan begins to take on form and substance, some individuals begin to realize that the plan is going to force them to act differently than they have in the past, and in many cases the new behavior that is required of them is considered less desirable by those individuals. Whatever the cause of their feeling, the individuals who see themselves in a losing position will automatically fight back and blame the *process being applied* as well as the *people who have won* within the process. When a person's behavior is affected, one of the most intimate and jealously guarded aspects of that individual is being attacked. In this case, an extreme reaction in regard to the idea of planning should not be surprising.

Planning can and does take on many forms, and it is applied to almost all parts of our lives as citizens. Much *social planning* is carried out by all levels of government in the United States, but the citizenry as a whole is most aware of the social planning that is carried out at the state and national levels, primarily because it is specified as such by the legislators and administrators actively involved in making it.[4] In 1946, the Congress declared that the national government had a general responsibility for maintaining a stable and prosperous economy.[5] The government was already involved in social security, unemployment, and welfare programs of various types, and each of these programs required a comprehensive plan. (There are often claims that each plan is prepared without consideration of the other programs in the general area of concern, and some-

---

[2] John K. Parker, "Administrative Planning," in James M. Banovetz, ed., *Managing the Modern City*, International City Management Association, Washington, D. C., p. 238.

[3] Herbert A. Simon, Donald W. Smithburg, and Victor A. Thompson, *Public Administration*, Alfred A. Knopf, New York, 1950, pp. 423-424.

[4] Over the last three decades, we have become increasingly aware of the fact that all types of planning have tremendous social impacts, but city planners and other planners who did not have to deal directly with human beings tended to ignore the social implications of their plans until such a position became impossible.

[5] *U. S. Code*, 1970, Title 15, Section 1021.

times with counterproductive results.) The Old Age, Survivors and Dependents Insurance program, better known to many as "Social Security," is a complex plan for taking care of many individuals who might otherwise become wards of the state. One of the major reasons for acceptance of the Social Security system was that Congress decided that this plan was a more humane, more psychologically acceptable, and perhaps a more efficient way of providing for the social welfare of the participants than any of the other alternative plans proposed for taking care of those being served.

Another form of plan with which most individuals are familiar is the *budgetary plan*. In the budget, a plan is prepared that shows how the expected revenues for the year will be spent. A step above the budget in the hierarchy of economic planning is the fiscal policy or plan of the country, which is primarily prepared by the national government. The national government spends much time and effort planning whether more or less money should be flowing through the economic system, whether taxes should be equal to the amount spent in the budget, and whether the other factors that affect the maintenance of a healthy national economy should be juggled.

When the word "planning" is used at the local level, most people immediately think of city planning or the *physical land use plan* for the community. Not only is this the most commonly understood type of planning but it is also the type of planning that raises the most controversy because this plan tells people how they may use the land that they own. Such a plan places limits on the economic gain that owners can expect to receive from selling or using their property; thus, such a plan becomes a very hot political issue, and both the local politicians and administrators must be very careful about the way such plans are developed and implemented.

Finally, two additional kinds of plans should be mentioned because they are the primary responsibility of the administrator. The two are *crisis planning* and *management planning*. One type of crisis planning that is familiar to most people is disaster planning. Depending on the area in which one lives, it is common to have annual trial runs of plans established to cope with earthquakes, tornadoes, hurricanes, floods, and other natural disasters. All too often, however, organizations suffer a constant barrage of crises that is not caused by wind, fire, rain, or earthquake. These crises occur simply because the managers of the organizations have not thought ahead or made adequate managerial plans for the various changes and crises that may occur as a result of the growth of the community, changes in the composition of the population, technological change, or other similar occurrences. On the other hand, many of the better administrators measure their success by how often they are able to avert a crisis or have a plan ready to be implemented in case crisis cannot be averted. One of the most successful ways to avert crises and to guide the government smoothly and securely is to have a plan that attempts to forecast the future of the organization and also attempts to prepare for the situations that are predicted. As new situations arise, the plan must suggest how the organization will need to be rearranged and how the people and their skills can be developed to meet the needs of the organization.

The public administrator is involved in all the types of planning that have been discussed in this chapter. As will become apparent in the following discussion of the planning process, there is a tremendous amount of effort involved in planning regardless of the level of government with which the administrator is concerned. Since it is difficult to plan and since there is so much to be done in order to keep the organization operating every day, why should a department head, governor, or city manager go to such effort? This question was well answered by a New England city manager who said,

The average city council seems to thrive on details. Frequently these details have no relationship to long-range policy, but represent a common vocabulary that can be easily grasped by officials and the public. Absorption in trivia is the best assurance of continuing the status quo, and thwarting desires to improve the community, the council, and the employees. The short term security gained is seldom worth the intolerable knowledge that growth and renewal are being suffocated.

The most successful method to break away from the routine cycle is through city planning, be it with professionals, lay boards, or the manager himself. Four important results can be attained.

First, routine decisions can assume relevance in terms of articulated goals, thus making these decisions important to the community.

Second, a skillful program can translate judgements based on experiences of line personnel into accepted guidelines, preventing the accusation of arbitrary and erratic actions. Planning can convert accumulated wisdom into defensible policies.

Third, a planning program can create a background of long-term perspectives against which to judge the performance of both employees and elected officials. Properly constructed, this tool will enable the public to recognize the quality of its government.

Fourth, planning, and its processes of discussion and debate, can serve as a forum for community involvement and future leadership.

Every city, large and small, must establish planning and its many variations as one of its primary programs of communicating internally and externally. To paraphrase Charlie Brown, "Planning isn't everything, but no planning is nothing."[6]

## Steps in the Planning Process

Although there are many types of plans, there is generally one process for the making of those plans. Numerous descriptions of the process have been pre-

---

[6] James Hobart, in "What is the Importance of the Planner to City Management," *Public Management, LI,* 3-4 (December 1969).

sented. By combining these ideas, it is possible to develop a comprehensive picture of the planning process which includes eight steps.[7]

**Recognizing the Need for Planning.** Before planning can occur, there must be a recognition of the need to have planning, and then a systematic attempt to carry it out can be established. The best time to plan is when things are calm. Administrators always bemoan the lack of adequate planning during times of crisis; however, the crisis is often caused by the lack of planning in the first place. Once the crisis is over, the administrators tend to congratulate themselves for having survived the storm, and they soon become reimmersed in their day-to-day activities. If administrators can be shaken out of their bad habits and made to recognize the need for planning, the organization is ready to begin the planning process.

**Determining the Objectives.** It is impossible to start the planning process without having some idea of what particular objectives are being sought and when those objectives are to be obtained. The goal may be to maintain a nuclear striking power equal to that of the Russian military, to reduce welfare rolls in the county by 15 percent during the next year through permanent job placements, or to remove or rehabilitate all substandard housing within the city during the next five years. Whatever the particular objectives may be, it is essential that they are stated in a clear and concise manner. This is a principle that is much more easily suggested than carried out, for the objectives are "those underlying ends which society expects of its . . . institutions if they are to survive."[8] If you visit a New England town meeting or a rural county board of supervisors meeting, you *may* find some unanimity about objectives, but as governments become larger and more complex, the things citizens want from government become more numerous and often contradictory. For instance, the citizens of many cities want mass transit systems but demand more highways and low-density housing; they cry for more police protection but complain about police harrassment; they want lower taxes but do not want industrial or commercial establishments near their homes. From this mass of relatively inarticulate demands, the city councils and the city administrators must create some kind of acceptable statement of objectives.

**Forecasting the Future.** Once the objectives have been established and before any plans can be prepared, it is necessary to look at the future in order to predict and describe the factors that are going to affect the possibility of achieving

---

[7] There are several statements of the planning process that may be examined by the reader; for example, see: John Argenti, *Corporate Planning: A Practical Guide*, Richard D. Irwin, Homewood, Ill., 1969; Argenti, *Systematic Corporate Planning*, Wiley, New York, 1974. See also: Ignacio G. Moreno, *Top Management Long-Range Planning*, Vantage, New York, 1963; and George A. Steiner, *Top Management Planning*, MacMillan, New York, 1969.

[8] Steiner, p. 32.

those objectives. Of course, the first task is to define where the organization and its environment are at the present time. Then predictions about the future will extend from the present situation. The forecast must predict the future of the organization, the future state of the particular community that the organization serves, and the future of the other environmental factors that are influential.

A cardinal purpose of planning is to discover future opportunities and make plans to exploit them. Correspondingly, basic to long-range planning is the detection of obstructions that must be removed from the road ahead. The most effective plans are those which exploit opportunities and remove obstacles on the basis of an objective understanding of the strengths and weaknesses of the (organization).[9]

Future technological breakthroughs may have a dramatic influence on the accomplishment of an objective, but we cannot know when and if a particular breakthrough will occur. This is pointed out as an extreme example of how the environment around any particular organization may affect the plans that are being developed. It might be a useful exercise for the reader to choose a particular public agency at random and to enumerate the environmental factors that might impinge on any plans that are made by that agency. Perhaps you can begin to see the task facing the forecaster.

**Setting Priorities.** When setting objectives, it is necessary to remember that the resources that are needed to carry out programs are limited. It is the limitation on resources that originally creates the need for planning and forces the creation of priorities among goals. First, there must be an ordering of the various objectives that are established, since some are more important than others. The most important objectives must be taken care of before the next group is considered; the remaining objectives can be considered if there are still available resources. Second, the length of time required to complete a particular program, or a phase of that program, may influence the priority of the objective. Politicians often must think as much about the timing of delivery as about the long-range value of the program. All politicians hope that their constituents see current fulfillment of promises, for if they do not see immediate results, the politicians may not remain in office long enough to work on the long-range plans. Public administrators must be aware of the importance of both types of priorities if they are making plans that must be approved by their political bosses.

**Developing Action Plans.** Now that objectives and priorities have been set, it is possible to develop the action plans. All of the prior steps are preparatory to this stage. The action plan lays out the steps that will be followed in implement-

[9] *Ibid.*

ing the program in such a way as to achieve the desired goals. There have been numerous techniques developed to help carry out this process. Examples of these techniques include processes such as Program Evaluation Review Technique (PERT), Critical Path Method (CPM), and other formalized planning and decision-making models that can be "customized" for almost any complex planning process. On the other hand, many times such sophisticated methods are not necessary. Local governments, for example, may need only a simple time-line plan which specifies the steps or phases of the particular program being considered and projects the time when each step must be reached if the objective is to be completed on the desired date.

Perhaps the single most important plan that is prepared by all levels of government is the budget. The budget is a plan in the sense that it establishes objectives and priorities through the allocation of available resources. The budget also includes a forecast of revenues (resources) available to that government during the year of the budget. One of the weaknesses of the budgetary process has consistently been the inadequate comprehension of the budget as a plan by those who prepared and ratified it. New budgeting techniques are attempting to expand the planning role of the budget, requiring projections of available financial resources and expenditures for several years into the future.

**Implementing the Plan.** All too often, the planning process stops with the development of the plan. There is a staggering number of plans sitting on organization shelves waiting to be implemented. Hopefully, some plans, such as those to be used in the event of a world war, major accident, or natural disaster will never be needed; many others should never be used because they were ill-devised in the first place. However, many plans remain unimplemented simply because managers never get around to carrying out the plans that they have developed. Unless someone sees that the plans that have been developed are carried out, they are totally useless; it would often be better if they had not been established, because the hopes and desires of interested citizens are raised when the announcement is made that the plan has been prepared only to be deflated by the following inaction.

**Evaluating the Plan.** Immediately upon commencing the program, it is necessary to start evaluating the success of the plan. Only lately has the importance of program evaluation been recognized. The national government is becoming especially interested in the evaluation of programs at the local level as more of the money going to state and local governments is being released in the form of federal block grants or general revenue sharing. Under these new forms of federal aid, the national government does not tell the local governments exactly how they must use the funds that are given to them; however, since all the ancient distrust of local officials and politicians by Congress has not been overcome, the local governments must present plans for the expenditure of the funds and must carry out periodic evaluations which are reported to the financing departments in Washington, D. C. Of course, there are special difficulties involved in evaluating many of the new social programs that are being established by local governments, but attempts at evaluation must be carried out in order to allow the completion of the final step in the planning cycle.[10]

**Revising the Plan.** Every plan requires revision, regardless of how well it is prepared. Nobody likes to do this "hard work," and often change is seen as an admission of prior mistakes. Rather than being an admission of failure, revision of plans is the step that assures continued success in the future. Once a plan is devised, it cannot remain unchanged for an indefinite period of time; the lack of constant updating, in order to react to continuous environmental changes, exposes the organization to difficulties that may lead ultimately to ruin.[11] At this point, the planning cycle has made one full revolution and has already started to retrace the steps that have been described.

## Special Problems in Planning

When we speak of planning, most citizens perceive a process that is objective, rational, and scientific. Such a perception may be even stronger in a discussion on planning than in a discussion on decision making, because planning refers to a process that includes a series of decisions and is usually understood to include a number of specialists (which is also true of decision making but is often not recognized by the general public). However, the perception of rationality is only partially correct. Scientifically developed plans, which are both rational and objective, may be the goal of administrators, but numerous elements thwart the realization of the dream. It is necessary to examine some of the problems that must be faced as the planning process spins its web for the future; planners— whether they are administrators, politicians, or citizens—must recognize the constant presence of the problems in planning. First, it is important to note that, due to the similarity between the decision-making process and the planning process, most of the factors noted in the prior chapter as limitations on the rationality of the decision maker also apply to the planner. The obstacles that must be considered in this section are too abundant to consider individually; however, as a sample of the problems facing planners in the public sphere, let us consider three issues: (1) the importance of "means" as well as "ends"; (2) the implications of local government structure; and (3) the influence of personal values held by the planners.

[10] For a recent discussion of the problems of evaluation, see: Harry P. Hatry, Richard E. Winnie, and Donald M. Fisk, *Practical Program Evaluation for State and Local Government Officials*, The Urban Institute, Washington, D. C., 1973. See also: John Van Maanen, *The Process of Program Evaluation*, National Training and Development Service, Washington, D. C., 1973.

[11] Moreno, p. 17.

**"Means" and Their Effect on Citizens.** Human beings can be only partially controlled. Although a plan may be ingenious and thorough, someone (or some group) will be working hard to find a way of subverting the plan or turning it to his advantage. One of the most intricate and painstakingly exact plans has been established with the intention of getting each citizen to do his or her share in supporting the government; it is known as the Internal Revenue Code. In response to this carefully prepared plan, which has a tremendous control and enforcement unit working to see that its goals are accomplished, there has sprung into existence a special group (made up of individuals from the same general profession, accounting, as the control and enforcement unit) which has as its primary interest helping individuals to avoid doing their share in supporting the government. Otto Eckstein notes that those in the profession of tax accountant spend much, if not most, of their time helping those who can afford to pay taxes avoid doing so.[12] Similar types of problems face any planner as he or she attempts to control human behavior on a grand or minor scale.

To those individuals who accept and defend the democratic ethic, such a problem is not really a "problem" at all; it is an absolute blessing. Of course, such a feeling does not hold without the democratic ethic. In those countries where the "state" is recognized as being of greater worth than any of the individuals within it, or where the individual is less significant than a particular political ideology, the problem of lack of control over the "human variable" is considered to be a great difficulty that must be surmounted through behavioral modification or manipulation. In this case, the leadership must seek ways to overcome the eccentricity of individuals so that it will be possible to achieve what is best for the state. However, in the United States, the ideology proclaims that all persons are created equal, and that they have certain rights which even the state may not take away. The individual is the basis of policy and the reason for the existence of the state. This belief leads to a twofold emphasis for the planner. First, the ends that are chosen must improve the condition of the citizens as individuals; it is not acceptable to improve the position or condition of the state if, at the same time, it impairs or erodes the condition of the individual citizen. Second, and equally as important, the means by which the plan is put into action must also be considered with the idea always in mind that *the way individuals are treated by the system may be as important as the end that is being sought.*

These two issues have been central to the welfare debate that has raged for at least the last decade.[13] While Congress has talked about setting a goal of holding down or decreasing welfare rolls, the critics of the welfare system have argued that perhaps the nicest thing that can be said about the welfare program in the United States is that it really has had no goal. The more bitter and vocal critics have suggested that the current welfare program is a calculated plan to maintain

---

[1,2] Otto Eckstein, *Public Finance*, Prentice-Hall, Englewood Cliffs, N. J., 1973, p. 79.

[13] A. Dale Tussing, "The Dual Welfare System," *Transaction: Social Science and Modern Society, II,* 50-57 (January-February, 1974).

those on welfare at a subsistence level while keeping them from having a chance to rise higher in society. At a different level of debate, many critics of the welfare system argue that the means used by the program are dehumanizing, requiring clients to suffer indignities and invasions of privacy that are improper in a democracy. Because of the dual failure of the welfare program, there has been a general feeling of uneasiness by both the administrators and the politicians, while on the other side, the clients of the program have banded together in welfare rights associations and other similar groups. There would be no debate of this type if the ideology of individual dignity and worth was not a basic part of our political heritage. In the Soviet Union, where individual rights are not honored to the extent that they are in the United States, there are no such debates; in many cases, those who are found not to be holding jobs that the state considers "useful to society" are sentenced to work camps for the crime of "social parasitism."

**Types of Government Structure.** The problem of government structure and its effect on planning is common to all levels of government; for instance the federal system has a dramatic effect on how plans are prepared at each level of government. The effect of this system on the tasks of public administrators, and the development of public policy, has already been discussed in Chapter 3. However, a special problem exists for planners at the local level, because the planning process may be affected by the form of government used in a particular location. The function and result of planning may differ if there is a council-manager form of government from that which would exist if there was a council-mayor form of government. This has been proven true in research dealing with the outputs of public policy by city legislative bodies where a correlation was shown between the level of reform in city government structure and the laws passed by the city councils, and it seems logical to believe that a similar type of result occurs in the planning process which is closely allied to the policymaking process.[14] It can be argued that city managers, because of their professional background and because they do not have to face a public election, can afford to take a longer view toward plans and the planning process than can mayors who must think more in terms of what can be done by the next election. On the other hand, this is not a claim that either type of local leader can go to extremes. The manager serves at the pleasure of the council, while the mayor may have the expectation of being reelected, and both mayors and managers want to be remembered kindly by citizens in the future. The political system of reformed cities, those with city managers and council members elected at large, appear to offer a better environment for planning than those cities where the political atmosphere is closer to the surface in all of the actions that are taken. However,

[14] Robert L. Lineberry and Edmund P. Fowler, "Reformism and Public Policies in American Cities," in James Q. Wilson, ed., *City Politics and Public Policy*, Wiley, New York, 1968, pp. 97-123.

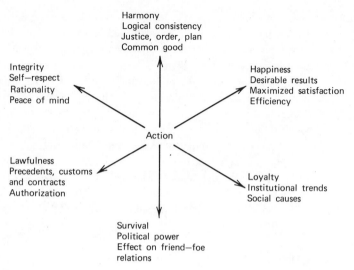

**Figure 5**

Values and the decision maker. (Source: Wayne A. R. Leys, in Mailick and Van Ness, eds., *Concepts and Issues in Administrative Behavior*. Prentice-Hall, Englewood Cliffs, N.J., 1962, p. 88.)

none of these issues may have as much ultimate influence on the planning process as another and more intangible variable, one over which the political system may have very little control; that variable is the personality of the individual who heads the government.

**Values of the Top Public Administrator.** Perhaps the most important factor influencing the planning process is the set of values held by the public administrator who is ultimately in charge of the organization (see Figure 5). He or she is the individual who gives full attention to the organization, who has the respect and support of the elected officials, and who often has a tenure in office that extends beyond the normal politician's term in office. Not only does the manager influence the planning process but the result in each case is also unique because his values, ideas, and moral standards are themselves unique; such values, ideas, and moral standards are the basic premises of planning, because

values are injected into all of the important elements of . . . planning. They may concern which objectives are to be sought. (Also) the means chosen to achieve these ends are influenced by his values. . . . Sometimes . . . the major values of top managers are expressed in written statements. Most values, however, are not. But whether written or not, they are of fundamental significance in the planning process.[15]

[15] Steiner, pp. 32-33.

The validity of this statement is supported by the experience of one of the major cities of northern California. It has been suggested that the reason for the uncontrolled growth of the city during the 1950's and 1960's was the lack of adequate planning. However, the city doubled in size each decade, not because of a lack of planning, but because of the deliberate plan of the city manager. During the 1960's, a controversy developed over the effects of uncontrolled growth upon the previously agricultural valley. The major complaint of the proponents of controlled growth was that if the community continued to grow at its current speed and in the present manner, the city would soon become "the Los Angeles of northern California." Of course, this comment was meant to be interpreted as a negative value statement with continued growth expected to bring about bad results for the environment and for the citizens of the community. Such statements did not have the expected effect on the city manager. He went on record publicly with several statements to the effect that he considered such charges to be praise instead of criticism, because he could see nothing wrong with Los Angeles. In.fact, he said that it was his goal to turn the city into "the Los Angeles of northern California."

Obviously, the value structure of the city manager, the top public administrator of that governmental unit, had a major impact upon the planning process and the results of that process. The policy of the city began to change only after the city manager resigned. It is true that the city manager remained in power because many people in the community agreed with his philosophy of unlimited growth, but is is also true that he established the basic premise around which everyone argued and acted; the premise was that "growth is a sign of a healthy community."

It is impossible to remain aloof from politics and at the same time to be active in the planning process. City managers have recognized, at least to a limited extent, their role in policymaking; however, the debate about the political role of the public administrator has not been permanently settled. Especially among urban planners, the debate continues at a heated level. John Dyckman, writing in the *Journal of the American Institute of Planners* in 1961, noted the reluctance of urban planners to admit their political role, for he somewhat skeptically commented that

. . . the prestige of the city planner may hinge on the remoteness of promised results, as with the clergy. But the prestige must be defended on occasion by walling off the operational role of the planner from the world of practical affairs. This segregation of operations is glorified as a rejection of politics.[16]

Such a stance is impossible according to Dyckman. Francine Rabinovitz supports Dyckman's thesis, for she argues that "although the myth of apolitical action remains, the success of planning is tied to the operation of the political sys-

---

[16] John W. Dyckman, "Planning and Decision Theory," *Journal of the American Institute of Planners, XXVII,* 166 (November 1961).

tem."[17] Since the political system is often weak or disorganized with varying groups counteracting each others' policy proposals and does not stimulate support for any particular action, Rabinovitz argues that the urban planner must stir an otherwise static system.

The important issues in such a situation are how far a planner can carry the political role and who the planner represents in the role of advocate. During the last decade, there has been an increasing cry for "advocacy planning" among those in the planning profession. The idea of the planner, whether an urban planner or a manager filling a planning function, as an advocate for the rights and needs of the less privileged in our society has a distinct appeal for many in the public administrative professions. The proponents argue that such a stance will allow those groups who have until now been unrepresented to have their interests considered in the planning process. It is suggested that an advocacy position will lead to more equitable social plans. As social plans become more equitable, this will lead to greater participation in the political system by disadvantaged citizens who will become more interested in that system as they recognize the fact that they can influence the outcome of the policy process; therefore, advocacy planning will lead to a "truly democratic" system that will produce social and political peace over the long run.

Those opposing advocacy planning argue that if professional administrators take a political stance in the planning process, especially a stance consistently favoring the disadvantaged groups in society, the administrators will quickly lose their legitimacy in the eyes of the majority of the populace. Once that legitimacy has been lost, the administrator becomes merely one of the numerous interests attempting to influence the policy process. Such a fate destroys the role of the planner at any level of government.

The resolution of this debate will not occur within the foreseeable future for both sides have a partially valid argument; Francine Rabinovitz effectively elucidates this problem by noting that a

. . . series of profound questions arises with respect to the desirable limits on political action by professionals, the advisability of giving planners very broad discretion and power to shape cities, and their capabilities to determine community goals democratically. However, while a decision to move toward (a politicization of the planning profession) will certainly raise new and difficult problems, the alternative to these changes is not pleasant to contemplate. For, if planners avoid the hard choices required, they may begin to find that as respect for their profession grows, its utility as a mechanism for effecting urban development is withering.[18]

This stern warning may be applied to all public managers who are involved in the planning process, both within and outside their organizations.

[17] Francine Rabinovitz, "Politics, Personality, and Planning," *Public Administration Review,* XXVII, 21 (March 1967).

[18] *Ibid.*, p. 24.

## SUMMARY

After having digested this information on planning, let us look back at the introduction to this chapter and see if we can spell out in some detail the problems facing a public administrator who operates in the manner described. These problems are going to relate to every aspect of his or her task! Proper planning is essential to any organization, and any administrator who does not recognize the centrality of this function will probably fail to achieve the maximum performance possible from the agency or department; then the public, the citizens, will have every right to demand an accounting. At some time, they will demand exactly that.

The planning process is central to all the functions of a public manager. The process is concerned with generating proposals for the future, looking at and evaluating different alternatives, and finding methods by which these proposals may be achieved. Of course, there are various types of plans that are of interest to the public administrator; these vary from social plans such as Social Security and Medicare to plans for city land use. However, the type of plan that must be considered by all top public managers is the plan for the administrative organization over which he or she operates.

In order to plan properly, a regular cyclical process must be followed. The first, and sometimes the hardest, step in the process is that of simply recognizing the need for planning. Once that has been accomplished, it is possible to determine the objectives of the organization, to forecast the future, and to set priorities among the objectives. With all of this information, the planner is ready to examine the alternative action plans and choose one for implementation. After implementation has begun, there is a need for a constant control system that allows evaluation and revision of plans on a regular basis.

Any planning procedure is going to be faced with difficulties, but special problems arise when an attempt is made to plan in a democracy. In a democratic state, the means that are used in implementing a plan are just as important as the end of the plan; therefore, public administrators are limited in both the means and ends that they may consider when attacking the many social, economic, physical, and political problems of our country. The structure of government also creates a variety of problems for planners. Ultimately, however, the most important ingredient that influences the planning process may be the most abstract and ephemeral of all the elements considered; this is the set of values held by the top public administrator, who establishes the tenor, or tone, for the planning process. Central to this set of values is the attitude of the administrator toward taking a neutral or advocate role in the planning process.

# BIBLIOGRAPHY

Altshuler, Alan A., *The City Planning Process: A Political Analysis,* Cornell University, Ithaca, N. Y., 1965.

Anthony, Robert N., *Planning and Control Systems: A Framework for Analysis,*

Division of Research, Graduate School of Business Administration, Harvard University, Boston, 1965.

Benveniste, Guy, *The Politics of Expertise*, Glendessary Press, Berkeley, Calif., 1972.

Cleland, David, and William R. King, *Systems Analysis and Project Management*, McGraw-Hill, New York, 1968.

Dale, Ernest, *Planning and Developing the Company Organization Structure*, American Management Association, New York, 1952.

Emery, James C., *Organizational Planning and Control Systems*, Collier-MacMillan, London, 1969.

Ewing, D.W., ed., *Long-Range Planning for Management*, Harper and Brothers, New York, 1960.

Gass, Saul I., and Roger L. Sisson, eds., *A Guide to Models in Governmental Planning and Operations*, Sauger Books, Potomac, Md., 1974.

Gulick, Luther, and Lyndall Urwick, *Papers on the Science of Administration*, Institute of Public Administration, New York, 1937.

Johnson, Richard A., Fremont E. Kast, and James E. Rosenzweig, *The Theory and Management of Systems*, McGraw-Hill, New York, 1967.

Meyerson, Martin, and Edward G. Banfield, *Politics, Planning and the Public Interest: The Case of Public Housing in Chicago*, Free Press, Glencoe, Ill., 1955.

Miller, George A., Eugene Galanter, and Karl H. Pribaum, *Plans and The Structure of Behavior*, Holt, Rinehart and Winston, New York, 1960.

Quade, E.S., and W.I. Boucher, eds., *Systems Analysis and Policy Planning*, American Elsevier, New York, 1968.

Rivlin, Alice M., *Systematic Thinking for Social Action*, Brookings Institution, Washington, D.C., 1971.

Simon, Herbert A., Donald W. Smithburg, and Victor A. Thompson, *Public Administration*, Alfred A. Knopf, New York, 1950.

Steiner, George A., ed., *Managerial Long-Range Planning*, McGraw-Hill, New York, 1963.

Warren, E. Kirby, *Long-Range Planning*, Prentice-Hall, Englewood Cliffs, N.J., 1966.

# CONTROL: PLANNING'S "OTHER FACE"

*A little neglect may breed great mischief.*

*Ben Franklin*

The most beautiful and perfectly prepared plan will be wasted unless a system is developed "which provides direction in conformance to the plan, or in other words, the maintenance of variations from system objectives within allowable limits."[1] That special system fulfills the control function, and this function

[1] Richard A. Johnson, Fremont E. Kast, and James E. Rosenzweig, *The Theory and Management of Systems*, McGraw-Hill, New York, 1963, p. 38.

# CHAPTER 8

makes up one of the important tasks of any public manager. The control function, according to Herbert Hicks, makes up "the part of the manager's job in which he checks up on assignments, sees what is being done, compares it with what ought to be done, and does something about it if the two are not the same."[2] Although there are few defenders of control systems, we should be thankful for the fact that they exist, because they are a symbol of man's very humanness, which includes a propensity to error. Control systems allow flexibility; without the feedback and correction available through such systems, it would not be possible to react to the changing conditions surrounding any organization.

It is true, however, that the necessity for a control system points out a weakness that exists in organizations, for the procedure implies that the decision-making and communication processes are not perfect; therefore, the plans that have been made may be either poorly prepared or inadequately understood by the public employees who are putting the plans into action. Thus, the control process is a major step in the total cycle that makes up the planning process.

The success of the control function depends on how well the objectives and standards of performance have been spelled out within the plan. It is impossible to check on the assignments of employees or to compare what is being done with what ought to be done, unless the objectives, or final goals, of the agency have been stated in relatively explicit terms. Likewise, after the objectives of the agency have been specified, the level and type of performance required from each employee can be established. Only when these steps have been taken will it be possible to have adequate control over the programs and employees of the agency.

Because of a heightened recognition of these preliminary requirements, many governmental units have gone to the use of a management system generally known as Management by Objectives.[3] With this system, which has been applied by a variety of public organizations ranging from the U.S. Department of Health, Education and Welfare[4] to local municipal governments and school districts, there is an explicit attempt to state publicly the basic goals and quantifiable objectives of the organization. Priorities are then established for these goals and objectives, which are used as guides for allocating the organization's resources during the time for which the organizational goals apply. These goals and objectives also give the organization a "yardstick" against which the success of the year's activities may be measured.

[2] Herbert G. Hicks, *The Management of Organizations,* McGraw-Hill, New York, 1967, p. 205.

[3] Peter F. Drucker, *The Practice of Management,* Harper and Row, New York, 1954; John W. Humble, *Improving Business Results,* McGraw-Hill, London, 1968; Humble, *Management by Objectives in Action,* McGraw-Hill, London, 1968; George S. Odiorne, *Management by Objectives,* Pitman, New York, 1965.

[4] Rodney H. Brady, "MBO Goes to Work in the Public Sector," *Harvard Business Review, LI,* 65-74 (March-April, 1973).

In many cases, perhaps in most cases, the problem of control is still confused and complicated by the fact that, in spite of the use of new management systems, it is not possible to establish clear, concrete, and permanent goals for a public agency. For the sake of convenience and clear discussion, the policy process is viewed as a series of stages with a definite beginning and a definite end. There is a danger of oversimplification in such a view. As Charles Jones says, "If one does not resist, it is possible to envisage public officials perceiving a problem, determining what course of action to pursue in solving the problem, seeking to implement their course of action, then moving on to the next problem."[5] But such a clearly defined process is seldom the case, for as Charles Lindblom notes, "Policymakers are not faced with a given problem."[6] Every set of circumstances can create a number of problems with many different policymakers getting involved in deciding on a course of action. Quite often, different parts of an agency or different agencies may be working toward contradictory or conflicting goals; furthermore, the next problem comes along before the current one is resolved. All these problems complicate the control problems of the public manager.

In order to understand the process of control, from the perception of the public manager, the following discussion will refer to the simpler situation; however, the above paragraph should help to remind the reader that a more complex situation usually exists. The first part of the chapter deals with the problem of measuring performance, with the types of control broken down into three categories: system controls, impersonal controls, and personal controls. The latter part of the chapter considers the issue of how to take corrective action when the controls show improper deviation from the norm or plan. Central to this discussion is the concept of "authority" and how differing types of authority create the need for differing control and correction systems.

## MEASUREMENT OF PERFORMANCE

Once the goals and objectives have been clarified, the control function begins to operate in earnest. There are three basic types of control; one primarily involves system control and the other two deal with the control of the individuals within the particular system.

### System Control

In any public agency, numerous plans are being made and implemented at any one time. A particular department, such as a local public works department, may have scores of separate plans in various formative or operative stages, while a

---

[5] Charles O. Jones, *An Introduction to the Study of Public Policy,* Duxbury, Belmont, Calif., 1970, p. 48.

[6] Charles E. Lindblom, *The Policy Making Process,* Prentice-Hall, Englewood Cliffs, N.J., 1968, p. 13.

city government will have hundreds of plans, and a state or the national government will have plans numbering in the thousands. Every program that is in operation will have been planned in some detail; therefore, it is possible, and more comfortable, to shift to the term "program" in the discussion of control, while keeping in mind that the discussion accepts as implicit the fact that *each program is the implementation of a plan.* No plan, or program, is comprehensive; some programs are short range, others are long range. Of course, there is no magic yardstick or calendar that places each plan in its proper category, but most managers can classify the plans with which they are working on the continuum of short-range to long-range plans.

The important thing to remember is that the short-range programs become stepping stones on the way to accomplishing the long-range programs that lead to the goals of the organization. This creates at least two major problems for the public manager. First, the manager must coordinate all these programs so that the various subgoals will be focused toward the same ultimate ends, or else it would be easy for the programs, at best, to go in unrelated directions and, at worst, to go in absolutely contrary directions. A common complaint by citizens is that, due to lack of coordination, the municipally owned utilities manage to cut up newly paved streets within weeks of the resurfacing. Similar complaints about the lack of systemwide coordination include situations where the new construction within a community outstrips the water supplies and the sanitary systems, which lead to unhealthy and inconvenient conditions for the citizens. All of these inconveniences and hazards are caused either by plans that are not adequately prepared or by plans that lack proper controls to see that they are carried out. Good streets and improved utilities are both worthy goals, just as proper housing and industry are vital to economic health; however, all of these various programs must intermesh with the other ongoing activities of the government (and private organizations to the extent possible) or else they may very easily cancel out each other.

Plans and programs are usually more contradictory than would initially seem to be the case. This is especially true because of the use of specialized units for planning, with several departments having their own planners. In medium sized cities (over 100,000 citizens), it is not uncommon to find several major departments with their own planning shops. As units of government grow larger, planning groups proliferate. Without coordination, these specialized units tend to create plans that mirror the professional perspective of the involved department and the desires of its clientele. To counteract this tendency, someone must operate out of the manager's, or mayor's, office in order to oversee the consistency and coordination of the planning goals being developed and the programs being delivered throughout the organization.

Even if all of the plans are aimed toward the same goal, there is a second "system" control that must be applied. Since the plans intermesh, with some serving as stepping stones to other longer range plans, it is essential that the *timing of* the plans be coordinated so that the various steps of the process are completed at the most appropriate time for the over all plan. In many cases it is not possible to start or continue one part of a program until the prior steps have been completed, and such a difficulty can completely foul up the most beautiful plan. In order to attack this problem, a variety of methods have been developed in recent years that allow the planning, scheduling, and control of projects to be combined through processes that are called "network techniques." The most important of these techniques is referred to as PERT/CPM (Program Evaluation Review Technique/Critical Path Method).[7] John K. Parker describes the process in the following way:

PERT/CPM identifies the individual activities which must be accomplished to complete a project, which may be anything from writing a report through construction of a complex of buildings. The activities are then shown on a diagram, illustrating the sequence in which activities are scheduled. The length of time required to complete each activity, the manpower and other resources needed for each activity, and the cost of each activity are estimated. Then the network diagram is modified until a desirable combination of time, resources, and cost is found. Responsibilities for accomplishing each activity are assigned to appropriate managers and supervisors, and the network is used to control the progress of the work. Delays in accomplishment of activities, excessive expenditure rates, or changes in the availability of resources are reported and the network is used to analyze the implications for the project as a whole. As often as is necessary . . . the network is "up-dated" to reflect current accomplishment, the remainder of the project is replanned as necessary, and the network is revised.[8]

## Impersonal Controls

System controls are vital, but at some point control must move from the system level to the level of the individual within the system. These control systems may involve personal contact; in fact, some personal contact is essential. We shall discuss that matter in the next section and focus for the moment on the impersonal means of control that are regularly used by bureaucratic organization.

It is important to understand exactly what is meant by "impersonal control." Peter Blau and W. Richard Scott explain this concept by pointing out that

the concept of "impersonal authority" in formal organization is usually interpreted to mean hierarchical relations free of personal involvement, in contrast,

[7] For a general introduction to PERT/CPM, see: John Dearden and Warren McFarlan, *Management Information Systems,* Richard D. Irwin, Homewood, Ill., 1966.

[8] John K. Parker, "Administrative Planning," in James M. Banovetz, ed., *Managing the Modern City,* International City Management Association, Washington, D.C., p. 252. For some examples and discussion of administrative uses for PERT/CPM, see: Mary F. Arnold, ed., *Health Program Implementation Through PERT,* Western Regional Office, American Public Health Association, San Francisco, October 1966.

for example, to charismatic authority where personal ties bind the followers . . . But impersonal authority may also mean management through nonhuman mechanisms of control. It is possible for management to design and install an impersonal control system in such a manner that it, rather than the hierarchy, exerts continuous constraints on the performance of subordinates.[9]

An example of a simple but efficient impersonal control system of the second type mentioned by Blau and Scott (which is the type of impersonal control in which we are interested) is the time card and the punch clock that record when employees arrive at and leave work. A record, or control, of employee action is kept without the controller and the controllee ever having to experience any personal contact. Assembly lines also function in a similar way, with the production process forcing employees to work at a set speed. Both of these impersonal control systems generate negative reactions among employees unless great pains are taken to overcome the normal attitudes that develop because employees believe that "people do not count around here any more."

There is one type of impersonal control that has special importance to public administrators because it is applicable to the service-oriented programs that are so common in governmental agencies. The evaluation and control of performance are often accomplished on the basis of statistical performance records. How useful these performance records can be is best illustrated by quoting at length from the research of Blau, as reported in his book written in collaboration with Scott. In the research, Blau considered as a prime item of study the use of performance records in a state employment agency. He found that

the agency developed performance records as an indirect means of control—to provide the supervisor with information which would serve as a basis for the evaluation and guidance of workers. But once introduced, the records themselves became a direct mechanism of control.[10]

The records were public; therefore, employees knew exactly how their performance compared with that of their fellow workers. Many of the employees with below average records were motivated to improve their performance; hence, public records controlled employee behavior without any direct intervention on the part of supervisors. By using a little ingenuity in determining which statistics were collected and reported, it was possible to measure the quality as well as the quantity of work.

For example, to measure how carefully interviewers selected qualified applicants for jobs in the employment agency, the proportion of referrals who actually

---

[9] Peter M. Blau and W. Richard Scott, *Formal Organizations,* Chandler, San Francisco, 1962, p. 176.

[10] *Ibid.,* p. 178.

obtained the job to which they had referred was computed. By including some statistical measures in the performance record and not others, and by placing more or less emphasis on any one measure, management could regulate the amount of effort interviewers would devote to various aspects of the work.[11]

The performance records also had an effect on the way that the supervisor had to control subordinates. The supervisor no longer had to keep a constant check on the employees, yet the job performance evaluation was easier. The records could be used as proof that employees had problems when a supervisor consulted with a subordinate about inadequate performance, and, often, the subordinates came to the supervisor for help when they saw their performance was lagging. Thus, the use of proper performance records changed the style of supervisor—subordinate relations throughout the organization, for

even when the supervisor talked to an interviewer with a poor record about improving his performance, the existence of statistical records completely changed the nature of the conference. In the absence of performance records, the supervisor would have to start the conference by first telling the interviewer that his performance was inadequate. The existence of public records made this opening superfluous and, consequently, transformed the supervisor's discussion from a criticism that was likely to be resented to an offer to help the subordinate improve his record. Still another function of statistical records was that they served as an instrument for evaluating the work of interviewers on the basis of accomplished results and thus enabled management to permit officials more discretion in their work. The freedom from close supervision and from rigid operating rules that performance records make possible tends to enhance work satisfaction.[12]

On the other hand, performance measurements are not without their difficulties because focusing on single measures of performance may lead to consequences that are quite dysfunctional for the organization. A single criterion was used for a while in the employment agency that was studied by Blau.[13] When the number of interviews conducted by the employment counselors was used as the criterion, the interviewer was motivated to complete as many interviews as possible without spending adequate time in locating jobs for the candidates. In an attempt to correct that problem, the criterion was changed to the number of job referrals and placements. Counting referrals and placements led to two unanticipated consequences. First, the interviewers tended to generate wholesale and indiscriminate referrals, which were damaging to the agency's screening function. Second, interviewers tended to focus on the easier cases

[11]*Ibid.*

[12]*Ibid.*, p. 179.

[13]Peter M. Blau, *The Dynamics of Bureaucracy*, University of Chicago, Chicago, 1955.

in order to make a "good record"; thus, at times, they slighted those individuals who most needed in-depth counseling and aid.

In an article on the "Dysfunctional Consequences of Performance Measurement," V. F. Ridgeway noted several additional cases where organizations found that single measures of performance led to serious difficulties. Apparently this problem is universal, for Ridgeway reported on two studies of Soviet management that showed how an emphasis on production records and quotas led to neglect of repairs, allowed fluctuations in the flow of products, and, in the case of individual workers, permitted the output of the entire plant to fall off in order that the proper conditions could be established for one worker to set a production record.[14]

Recognition of the inadequacies of a single measure of success has occurred everywhere. In the Soviet Union, the manager works under several measures of success, "and the relative influence attached to any one measurement varies from firm to firm and month to month."[15] In the employment agency studied by Blau, the performance records were evaluated according to multiple standards (ratios of referrals to interviews, placements to interviews, and placements to referrals) in an attempt to stress the qualitative aspects of the interviewer's job.

Regardless of the way in which people react to these impersonal controls, increasing use of such techniques is to be expected in the future as governments grow in size and as the complexity of the services they offer also increases. Impersonal control is so important to any public agency that it led to a comment by Blau and Scott that:

it appears that management's primary significance is no longer as the apex of the authority pyramid; rather its central function is to design, in collaboration with a staff of experts, appropriate impersonal mechanisms of control.[16]

## Personal Control

While impersonal methods of control are vital to the modern public administrator, and while systems must have overall control, the place of personal control through direct interaction with employees and the public will never disappear. Leon Hay argues very cogently for this position by noting that "both logic and observed practice of managers support the view" that much needed information for an organization cannot be processed electronically or mechanically.[17] In addition,

---

[14] V. F. Ridgeway, "Dysfunctional Consequences of Performance Measurement," *Administrative Science Quarterly, I,* 240-247 (September 1956).

[15] *Ibid.,* p. 244.

[16] Blau and Scott, p. 185.

[17] Leon E. Hay, "What is an Information System: The Legal, Conventional, and Logical Constraints," *Business Horizons, XIV,* 65 (February 1971).

The information a manager needs to measure his success in motivating employees can come much more swiftly (and, perhaps, more accurately) from his own observation of the reactions of employees, his sense of their esprit de corps (or lack of it), his conversations with individual employees, or the conversations he overhears in the cafeteria, than from formal written reports or cathode ray tube displays.[18]

The problem that must be faced when we are dealing with personal control is one of deciding how much personal contact is best for the individuals and for the organization. This problem is commonly referred to as finding the proper span of control. The term "span of control" can have two definitions. First, it can refer to the number of subordinates over which a supervisor has some authority, responsibility, or control. This was the original concern of the management scientists during the early part of the century. V. A. Graicunas first discussed this problem in his article on "Relationship in Organization," which appeared in 1937 in the *Papers on the Science of Administration.*[19] Graicunas was especially interested in the complexity of social interactions that, theoretically, could occur as a group was expanded. Because of the potential for interactions, Graicunas came to the conclusion that the optimum number of employees that could be supervised by one boss was between five and ten. Most of the early studies agreed with the idea of a limited span of control; later it became apparent that such studies had to consider not only the number of employees supervised but also the closeness of contact between the superior and the subordinates.

The amount of contact that is required can dramatically affect the number of employees that a supervisor can properly control. The complexity of tasks within the organization, the professionalism of the employees, the physical distance between employees, and the importance of the employees' decisions to the continued existence of the organization are among the types of factors that will influence how closely employees need to be controlled.[20] When jobs have been routinized, a superior can control the operation of large numbers of employees. The same is true if the employees work in relatively close proximity and if their decision-making power is relatively limited. However, in most public organizations, none of these rules can be generalized for there is as much diversity in public employment as can be imagined.

Public administrators are, to a great extent, involved in the delivery of

[18] *Ibid.*

[19] V. A. Graicunas, "Relationship in Organization," in Luther Gulick and Lyndall Urwick, eds., *Papers on the Science of Administration,* Institute of Public Administration, New York, 1937, pp. 183-187.

[20] For a discussion of how these factors affect the span of control, see: William G. Ouchi and John B. Dowling, "Defining the Span of Control," *Administrative Science Quarterly, XIX,* 357-365 (September 1974).

*services* to the public. It is much harder to establish an "assembly-line" approach to such programs, and it is necessary to use many employees who have professional training and who must use that professional background in the completion of their assigned tasks. Also, it is often necessary for employees to function in situations that are outside of an office or a specific location. All these factors confuse the issue of exactly how the employees should be controlled; there is no pat answer to the question. Instead, all the decisions must be based on the particular situation that is being faced. Rigid discipline stifles professional judgments. Conversely, hierarchical control is weakened by increasing technological complexity in an organization, with its resulting emphasis on technical expertness for all personnel, including those on the lowest operating levels. Within these two statements lie the dilemma for the public administrator. How far can technological or professional judgment be turned loose in a democratic government? Maximum feasible freedom must be given to public employees; at the same time, some minimum level of control must be maintained in order to be sure that the desires of the citizens are being met. Blau and Scott have a general "rule of thumb," which they offer to all managers, and which might serve as a "first guide" to public administrators. According to their rule,

A flat structure—an obtuse hierarchical pyramid—by increasing the number of their subordinates, prevents superiors from supervising too closely and thereby alienating their subordinates. At the same time, this flat structure prevents them from leaning too heavily on their own superiors and thus losing their independence and the respect of their subordinates. Further, it makes it less likely that superiors become over-involved with their subordinates, simply because there are so many of them, and it consequently promotes detachment.[21]

## OBTAINING THE PROPER MIX

The problem of the proper control within a political system still exists, and the only honest answer to this question is that no precise rule exists. Herbert Kaufman reported on the ways the United States Forest Service attempted to cope with the problem of control in a public agency that was dispersed over the entire country; this report gave some insight into how the problem was attacked.[22] During the early years of their ranger training, the Forest Service attempted to build into the rangers a set of internal constraints. Badges and uniforms set the rangers apart as a special corps; in addition, the corps held a position of high status. These factors helped to create an *esprit de corps* and a strong identification with the organization. Promotions were made only from within and were relatively slow, so the ranger had acquired considerable experience and had become properly socialized before he was given much responsibility. All of these facts were made known to the potential recruit before he

---

[21] Blau and Scott, p. 238.

[22] Herbert Kaufman, *The Forest Ranger,* Johns Hopkins, Baltimore, 1960.

joined, so it was doubtful that an individual would select a career in the agency without some commitment to the goals of the Forest Service. Thus, self-selectivity also helped in controlling the actions of the rangers.

Once in the field, another set of control mechanisms was set into motion. Rangers were located in remote areas, so it was difficult to maintain any centralized control over their actions. Elaborate manuals and guides were promulgated so that there would be a known, standard way in which to handle different situations as they arose. Rangers were asked to submit regularly written reports and to keep an official diary within which they were to record, to the nearest half-hour, their activities for each day. The central office processed many of the statistics collected and used by the rangers in the field. This was a service for the ranger, but it was also a device whereby the regional headquarters could keep track of the activities of the ranger. Field inspections were regular, and the public had the right to appeal decisions by rangers to the regional office. Finally, the Forest Service had a policy of frequent transfers, a practice that reduced loyalty to any specific community while increasing the rangers' dependence on the Forest Service.

In the above example, it is possible to see how the proper level of control, and the proper methods, have to be tailored to the situation. This is where the skill of the administrator must exert itself. Two organizations that appear to be carrying out identical roles, but that exist in different cities or states, may require quite different levels and types of control because of differing environmental characteristics. William Turcotte, in his research dealing with state-operated liquor monopolies, has pointed out the diverse characteristics that can clothe control systems.[23] While the two operations appeared to serve the same general function, the control systems were operated under dramatically different philosophies. In one state, the liquor monopoly was depended on to raise a substantial portion of the state's revenue. Demanding objectives for output were established and understood by the executive branch, the legislature, and the agency. As Turcotte notes, the "explicitness of objectives was especially important when ambiguity existed between social or economic purpose[24]; in this case, the mission of the stores was economic, since the various decision makers had apparently concluded that the amount of alcohol consumed would vary little in spite of social pressures. The managers of the state-operated stores had to compete, in many cases, with cut-rate liquor stores just across the state boundary, so

(in this state) an automated inventory control system paced both the store managers and the director. . . . The system was designed to minimize manual reports and bookkeeping by the store manager. Concentration was on overall output and error was tolerated (though not encouraged).[25]

[23] William E. Turcotte, "Control Systems, Performance, and Satisfaction in Two State Agencies," *Administrative Science Quarterly, XIX,* 60-73 (March 1974).

[24] *Ibid.,* p. 72.

[25] *Ibid.,* pp. 66-67.

In contrast, the liquor stores in the other state produced only a minor portion of the total state revenue. In this state, the control system concentrated on after-the-fact accountability. Increased output, which created more state revenue, was not as important as being able to account for every penny. "The directors regarded the low error rate as one of their fundamental achievements,"[26] for it was impossible for anyone to create political headlines because of missing money. The store directors received detailed instructions on how to deal with every eventuality. "The directions on how to take care of the store safe alone exceeded in page count the directions on how to calculate and obtain inventory requirements."[27] The number of written reports was fifteen times as great in this state as it was in the one discussed above.

Size and not the fundamentally simple task of the state . . . agency yielded a perceived top management need for many staff specialists. These specialists required expression of their professionalism and a demonstration of their value to the agency. Systems and programs that they designed were of individual high quality and were therefore imputed to be contributive to store operations effectiveness. Close review indicated that . . . (the staff) introduced programs that tended to add to the complexity of the store manager's task and detracted from his real output effectiveness.[28]

Thus, because of a different type of political emphasis, the control system of the state, while costing twenty times as much, served as a policing agent instead of actually aiding the store managers to accomplish greater sales. This means that the emphasis in operation was on accountability rather than profitability; therefore, the successful manager adjusted his or her style of management to fit the surrounding political pressures.

## TAKING CORRECTIVE ACTION: WHY EMPLOYEES DO NOT LIKE CONTROLS

When controls show a noticeable variation from what was prescribed in the original plan, it is necessary to take some sort of corrective action. One of several conclusions may be reached, in which case appropriate action will be taken. First, it may be decided that the plan is wrong and corrections may be adopted. If this is done, there will probably be no great difficulty with employees, *as long as* they recognize the necessity of the change and understand its implications for them. There may be some difficulty in getting the changes accepted outside the organization, however, for every change usually means that some groups in the political environment gain, while some other groups lose. Such changes in

[26] *Ibid.*, p. 67.

[27] *Ibid.*, pp. 66-67.

[28] *Ibid.*, p. 68.

benefits and costs may lead to political battles, and, in extreme cases, they could lead to a realignment of the political forces surrounding programs and agencies.

A second conclusion might be that the standards are right and should be maintained. Then there are two possible courses of action open to the decision maker: (1) there may be a need to "tighten up" and obtain greater conformance between the standards and performance or (2) new motivational techniques may be needed to gain compliance with standards. The term "tightening up" means that closer controls may be needed and employees may be reprimanded or even fired. This step is undoubtedly necessary on occasion, but all too often it is the type of reaction that occurs and leads to what Fritz Roethlisberger has referred to as "the vicious-cycle syndrome," where

... the breakdown of rules begot more rules to take care of their breakdown or the breakdown of close supervision and as a result, the continuous search and invention of new control systems to correct for the limitations of previous ones.[29]

Such a procedure becomes a vicious cycle because the process is based on a negative style of management in which there are only further and further attempts at limitations with no positive incentives involved. Such procedures generally create more opposition to control, and they often lead to a greater effort being applied to the process of subverting or beating the control system than is being applied to getting the work done. Even when the controls are accepted as essential, there will probably be some opposition to the standards that have been set, the reporting procedures (including the amount, nature, and frequency of reports), and the interpretation of the information generated by the system. If, in addition, the control system creates fears of retribution and punishment, the opposition of employees can be expected to be unanimously negative.

The ultimate success of the control system and compliance with the plan can be traced directly to the type of authority that is used by the manager when corrective action is taken. The authority of a manager can be defined as his or her "capacity to evoke compliance in others."[30] According to Robert Presthus, whose definition of authority has been used here, authority is a relative, fluid, "subtle interrelationship whose consequences are defined by everyone concerned."[31] According to this view, authority is a transactional *process* that is just as dependent on the individual who is controlled as it is on the controller. In such a case, authority has to be accepted by the subordinates rather than

[29] Fritz J. Roethlisberger, "Contributions of the Behavioral Sciences to a General Theory of Management," in *Toward A Unified Theory of Management*, McGraw-Hill, New York, 1964, p. 54.

[30] Robert V. Presthus, "Authority in Organizations," *Public Administration Review, XX*, 86 (Spring 1960).

[31] *Ibid.*, p. 87.

being forced on them by the superior[32]; the process by which the "authority is accepted may be called legitimation, which is roughly synonymous with 'sanctioned' or 'validated'."[33]

Four bases for legitimation are suggested by Presthus: the formal role, a generalized deference to authority, technical expertise, and rapport. Regardless of the way these factors are intermixed in most situations, the relative weight of each will vary in each organization and in each situation. The formal role is very significant as a basis for legitimizing authority; this was forcefully pointed out by Max Weber in his description of bureaucracy. The structure of the organization gives those who are at the top of the organization more information, greater flexibility of action, and ready access to decision-making centers. In addition, Presthus notes that "the formal allocation of authority is also reinforced by various psychological inducements; including status symbols, rewards, and sanctions."[34] In such a situation, the authority does appear to be flowing down from the position even though it is recognized as legitimate by subordinates.

The recognition of authority attached to a specific role is further legitimated by a generalized deference to authority that is instilled in individuals from infancy. From the moment one is old enough to recognize authority, he or she is taught that deference should be shown to these "superior" people, whether they are parents, teachers, religious leaders, or politicans. (Remember that only a tiny child was willing to tell the emperor that he was not wearing any clothes.) In many instances, positive and negative sanctions are attached to the behavior patterns that occur when dealing with these people of authority; therefore, people become conditioned to giving deference to those in authority.

These two factors form the foundation through which a minimal level of authority is created. In cases where authority is based only on these factors, however, the style of control and the corrective processes applied will tend to be negative—the "tightening up" and "rule creating" types of actions mentioned earlier—because authority based on such principles does not motivate that part of the subordinate's personality which leads to initiative and inventiveness. The natural instinct of an individual under such circumstances is to make sure that he or she has done nothing that can lead to trouble or negative sanction.

Authority is based on factors other than the superior's role and the subordinate's deference to such positions. It can be expanded and the style of control systems modified if the authority is based on factors such as expertise and rapport. Expertise, technical skill, and ability to do the job are probably the most pervasive legitimating criteria for authority that exist in our society.

[32] This is also the idea developed by Chester Barnard in *The Functions of the Executive*, Harvard University, Cambridge, Mass., 1938.

[33] Presthus, p. 87.

[34] *Ibid.*, p. 88.

Presthus notes that

respect for the superior's expertise as a source of validating his authority is particularly effective where his expertise is the same as that of his subordinate's only greater. This source of legitimation has been strengthened by specialization, which in turn, has been reinforced by the professionalization process.[35]

Subordinates will turn for advice and help to an individual who is known for his knowledge in an area when, in similar circumstances, they will resist or ignore the orders and ideas of an official who lacks experience and proven knowledge.

Legitimation of authority by expertise can be further enhanced through the application of interpersonal skills and maintenance of sympathetic human relations. Such behavior on the part of those in positions of authority can lead to the development of rapport or a feeling of harmony, intimacy, and affinity between themselves and the employees they control. In such a case, the type of control system, and the corrective action that must be taken, may vary greatly from that required under conditions of minimal legitimation of authority. For example, if a superior is recognized as knowledgeable in her field and has a close rapport with subordinates, she may be able to take corrective action by suggesting a new procedure or a new way of viewing a problem. Employees are motivated to act because they have a feeling of affinity for their superior instead of, or in addition to, simply wanting to protect themselves from the negative sanctions that may be applied when work is inadequate.

The importance of expertise and rapport as factors in successful control systems cannot be overstressed, because the type of control and correction system developed directly spills over into the management functions of motivation and leadership (which are discussed later in this section of the text.) Regardless of the field under consideration, the added impact of these two factors can be noted. In sports, Vince Lombardi was more than a figurehead coach; he was revered because of his knowledge and ability to develop an intense rapport with his team. Similar examples may be drawn from the military, business, and the public bureaucracy. When authority is augmented in this way, it is possible to deal with the new incentive systems and management styles that are able to bring programs not only into compliance with plans but also into a state where flexibility and innovation can actually improve the ability of the public organization to meet the myriad and often conflicting demands of the public that it serves. Perhaps the reason that many managers use negative control systems instead of positive motivational systems is that the change of incentive or management requires that the manager's style and philosophy must change. This type of change is a difficult one for many managers to make, because they consider the recognition of a need for change as an admission of guilt, weakness, or failure, and they find it easier to try to make others change than to change their own behavior.

[35] *Ibid.*

## SUMMARY

Plans are useless unless there is a control system to guarantee that the plans are followed. Once the objectives have been established and the program is underway, it is essential that adequate measurements of performance be established and that these measures be used to maintain the direction of the organization. Such a control system must apply to the total organization, whether it is a department or a total governmental jurisdiction (the type of system varies for each level of organization.) At the same time, many aspects of the system help to maintain overall control within the organization. The controls must also apply to the individuals within the organization. Individuals may be directed by using either impersonal or personal controls, and in most cases some balance must be maintained between the two techniques of control.

Whatever the balance, there will usually be some behavioral reaction among the employees to the control system; such a reaction is often decided by the type of control system used and the kind of corrective action that is taken by those in authority. When superiors depend on their formal positions, and the general deference given to high positions, to legitimate their authority, it is likely that control and correction systems will be of a negative nature. If those in authority have been able to reinforce the legitimacy of their position through expertise and a close rapport with their subordinates, they will use more positive control and correction systems. If positive rather than negative motivation can be used to keep employees and the organization on course, there is a greater chance that the organization will be able to carry out its plans and achieve its goals.

# BIBLIOGRAPHY

Anthony, Robert N., *Planning and Control Systems: A Framework for Analysis,* Division of Research, Graduate School of Business Administration, Harvard University, Boston, 1965.

Bittel, Lester R., *Management By Exception,* McGraw-Hill, New York, 1964.

Blau, Peter M., and W. Richard Scott, *Formal Organizations: A Comparative Approach,* Chandler, San Francisco, 1962.

Brady, Rodney H., "MBO Goes to Work in the Public Sector," *Harvard Business Review, LI,* 65-74 (March-April, 1973).

Cleland, David I., and William R. King, *Systems Analysis and Project Management,* McGraw-Hill, New York, 1968.

Dearden, John, and Warren McFarlan, *Management Information Systems,* Richard D. Irwin, Homewood, Ill., 1966.

Dunbar, Roger L. M., "Budgeting for Control," *Administrative Science Quarterly, XXVI,* 88-96 (March 1971).

Emery, James C., *Organizational Planning and Control Systems,* Collier-MacMillan, London, 1969.

Evarts, Harry F., *Introduction to PERT,* Allyn and Bacon, Boston, 1964.

Gulick, Luther, and Lyndall Urwick, eds., *Papers on the Science of Administration,* Institute of Public Administration, New York, 1937.

Holden, Paul E., L. S. Fish, and H. L. Smith, *Top Management Organization and Control,* McGraw-Hill, New York, 1951.

Humble, John W., *Improving Business Results,* McGraw-Hill, London, 1968.

Humble, John W., *Management by Objectives in Action,* McGraw-Hill, London, 1968.

Johnson, Richard A., Fremont E. Kast, and James E. Rosenzweig, *The Theory and Management of Systems,* McGraw-Hill, New York, 1967.

Jun, Jong S., ed., "Symposium of Management by Objectives in the Public Sector," *Public Administration Review, XXXVI,* I- 45 (January-February, 1976).

Kaufman, Herbert, *The Forest Ranger,* Johns Hopkins, Baltimore, 1960.

Leonard, William P., *The Management Audit,* Prentice-Hall, Englewood Cliffs, N. J., 1962.

Odiorne, George S., *Management by Objectives,* Pitman, New York, 1965.

Ridgeway, V. F., "Dysfunctional Consequences of Performance Measurement," *Administrative Science Quarterly, I,* 240-247 (September 1956).

Rowland, Virgil K., *Managerial Performance Standards,* American Management Association, New York, 1960.

Schell, Erwin H., *Technique of Executive Control,* Eighth Edition, McGraw-Hill, New York, 1957.

Seashore, Stanley E., *Assessing Organizational Performance with Behavioral Measurements,* Foundation for Research on Human Behavior, Ann Arbor, 1964.

Simon, Herbert A., Donald W. Smithburg, and Victor A. Thompson, *Public Administration,* Alfred A. Knopf, New York, 1950.

Tannenbaum, Arnold S., *Control in Organization,* McGraw-Hill, New York, 1968.

Thompson, James D., *Organizations in Action,* McGraw-Hill, New York, 1967.

# COMMUNICATION

*Communication in organization is not a means of organization.*
*It is the mode of organization.*

*Peter Drucker*

If an organization can be said to have a nervous system similar to that of a biological organism, the communication system fills that description. The role of the communication system is similar to that of our nerves in that it keeps the decision-making apparatus within the organization informed about the status of both internal and external occurrences and variations that are of interest to the organization. The importance of communication cannot be overstated! This

# CHAPTER
# 9

point is made by Norbert Wiener when he says that "communication is the cement that makes organizations."[1] No group of people can function in a coordinated way when they are attempting to achieve a common goal unless they are able to communicate. Communication enables a group to think together, to reach agreement, and to act together. Even two people must be able to communicate if they are to cooperate. In his book, *Rules for Radicals,* Saul Alinsky notes the importance of good communication for community organizers by pointing out that

one can lack any of the qualities of an organizer—with one exception—and still be effective and successful. That exception is the art of communication. It does not matter what you know about anything if you cannot communicate to your people. In that event you are not even a failure. You are just not there.[2]

This is a very nonradical statement. It is just good common sense, which is the point that Alinsky is attempting to combine with radical political ideas. One can go a step further and note the importance of communication from "the people" to the leader, which is as vital as the message from the top down. Pearl Harbor is an example of a failure to communicate up. A minor officer at a radar sight discovered the approaching Japanese airplanes, but he could not get his message up "through channels" in order to inform the appropriate authorities; therefore, the Japanese attack, although discovered, was a complete surprise to the American armed forces. This chapter is devoted to the study of communication within the public bureaucracy. After defining communication, the chapter focuses primarily on the way communication takes place inside the organization. First, we examine the various types of communication networks that exist in the public bureaucracy, and then look at the most common problems associated with the different communication networks.

## THE DEFINITION OF COMMUNICATION

The term *communication* is freely used by everyone in modern society, but very few people have a firm definition of the concept. Falling into the general area of communication are several disciplines and activities that are all considered to be a part of the "communication sciences." Among these are the studies of interpersonal communication, including such esoteric fields as body language, gestalt, and transactional analysis, which are examples of useful and interesting but quite specialized parts of communication theory. At the organizational level, the study of communication encompasses such diverse topics as public relations, systems

---

[1] Norbert Wiener,    *Communication,* Massachusetts Institute of Technology, Cambridge, 1955, p. 1.

[2] Saul Alinsky, *Rules For Radicals: A Practical Primer for Realistic Radicals,* Vintage, New York, 1971, p. 81.

theory, and management information systems. All these topics make important contributions to the public administrator; however, in order to give direction to the discussion in this chapter, it is important to define communication as it applies to the administrative functions of a public bureaucrat.

Since organizations are composed of people, it will be useful first to define communication as it occurs between individuals and to define communication within the administrative context. *Communication occurs between individuals as ideas, feelings, and attitudes are transmitted—either verbally or nonverbally— from one person to another in such a way that the transmitted message produces a response.*[3] Often, communication is defined as the *act of transmission,* but it seems inadequate to argue that communication occurs unless the transmission produces a response in the receiving individual, even if that response is only a recognition of the message and a storage or dismissal of the information without any visible reaction. If a fire captain asks for a ladder to aid in the rescue of people from a burning building, but the request is not granted because no one reacts in *any way* to the request, it is difficult to describe it as a completed act of communication. It is a completed communication if someone replies in any fashion, including "Get the ladder yourself," for at least some reaction has been instigated, even if the response is inappropriate. A more specialized definition of communication, which takes into account the functions of management, states that, "Administrative communication is a process which involves the transmission and accurate replication of ideas ensured by feedback for the purpose of eliciting actions which will accomplish organizational goals."[4] This definition by William Scott allows consideration of personal communication where two people within an organization deal directly with one another; it also allows us to look at all of the formal and impersonal methods of communication that are used by the various governmental bureaucracies.

## TYPES OF COMMUNICATION NETWORKS

Communication allows the public manager to collect the information that is necessary in order for adequate and relevant decisions and plans to be made. Communication allows those plans to be made known to the rest of the organization, and it is also required if the manager is to maintain control and to see that the parts of the organization are working together for the common achievement of the public policies that have been established as the department or agency goals. At the same time, the employees at all levels of the agency depend on the communication network in order to know exactly what they should be doing and to communicate their information and attitudes back up through the system.

[3] This definition is similar to that of Norman B. Sigband, *Communication for Management,* Scott, Foresman, Glenview, Ill., 1969, p. 10.

[4] William G. Scott, *Organization Theory,* Richard D. Irwin, Homewood, Ill., 1967, p. 153.

The complexity of the communication network can be best described by looking at a single program within a city government and noting both the types of required information and the sources of that information. Good examples of such a program are any of the public employment programs that have operated during the 1970s. Once a city learns of the program, which in itself requires a communication link with Washington, D.C., it must collect the appropriate data about the number of unemployed persons in the city, the size and types of industries and businesses within the area, the size of the city budget, and the number of city employees; all of this information is needed to see if the city is eligible to participate in the program. Once this relatively easy task is completed, the city must decide if it is qualified to join in the program and if it wishes to participate. If the decision is made to participate, the city must examine its resources and needs so that a decision can be made about the size of the program desired. (The biggest program is not always the best, so sometimes it pays not to take all the federal funds available for special programs.) All these bits of information come from an internal information network.

Adequate administration of such a manpower program requires the development of an intricate network of communication that will furnish the following kinds of information.

1.  The information should note where the special employees can be placed within the city bureaucraey so that the program will optimize the advantages to the city *and* the individual. This calls for information about the priorities of city programs, shortages in manpower in various departments of the city, and the current skills and expertise of the new employees.
2.  The information should show how the city can meet its obligation to aid in the training or retraining of those special employees who need help. To carry out this obligation, information must be communicated about the types of final placements desired by these employees, as well as their current jobs for the city, the kind of skill development or new knowledge the employees need to do their current job adequately and to achieve their final placement goal, and the availability of training from within the city or the necessity to obtain training from an outside source.
3.  The information should clarify the ways in which the city can meet its obligation to place a certain percentage of these special employees in permanent jobs. Such placements will require information from outside the organization about possible jobs for the special employees, while on the inside of the organization, the city may have to bargain with a variety of groups (unions, the council, department heads, and the civil service commission) in order to achieve the necessary changes in the system so the special employees can be placed in permanent jobs with the city.

The network for a communication system that will allow the achievement of the goals of such a program, even in a moderate-sized city, is amazingly intricate and encompasses most of the city's bureaucracy as well as the rest of the city, including business and industry. The amazing thing about such a network is that a good public administrator creates it without thinking of the action as being unique in any way, for the establishment of such a network is a natural part of administration.

How many types of networks exist for such a program? If the head of the public employment program stops and categorizes the various networks that have been established, he may break all the types of communication into two categories, the formal and informal communication systems. To the two categories that are usually recognized by practitioners must be added a third type of communication network, which is called the interpersonal communication system.[5] It is closely allied to both of the others and may overlap with them both; however, it must be considered separately because of its unique characteristics.

## Formal Communication

The formal communication network is recognized by everyone who works in an organization and by many who regularly deal with that office or department. The formal network is explicitly spelled out by the administrative manual, and messages that come to anyone through the formal communication network are recognized as "official" by the receiver. The formal channels of communication substantially coincide with the official structure of the organization as spelled out by the organization charts. This network carefully specifies who may communicate with whom, when and how such communication must or should take place, what procedures and forms should be used, who can see the communications, and who can give out information on particular subjects. The attempt to control communication in this way is found in its most elaborate form in the military, "where extremely intricate patterns of communication are incorporated into formal rules and where channels are rigidly enforced."[6]

The closest approximation to the military in local government is the police department, which operates under many of the same constraints that affect the armed services. For example, each police officer operating a patrol car is provided with a manual that formally communicates to the officer what the approved procedures are while on duty. Upon arriving at work, the officer may receive a special briefing that includes instructions on activities and people to watch for during the day. The police officer patrolling in a car may be given a list of license numbers to watch for while cruising. Of course, the officer is also able to communicate via radio, so that new information will be handed on as it becomes available. Even the use of the radio is carefully controlled, with priorities being established as to which types of messages will receive attention first. In return, the officer is expected to file the appropriate forms at the end of each

---

[5] This discussion is based, in part, on: Anthony Downs, *Inside Bureaucracy*, Little, Brown, Boston, 1967, pp. 112-131.

[6] Herbert A. Simon, Donald W. Smithburg, and Victor A. Thompson, *Public Administration*, Alfred A. Knopf, New York, 1950, p. 222.

shift as well as to keep in constant contact via radio. Any time a car is stopped for a traffic violation, the officer may be expected to check the license number to see if, by chance, there is any official reason for impounding the auto and arresting the driver and occupants of the car. While investigating any crimes or dealing with the public in any other way, the officer has been trained to collect certain types of information that are required by other parts of the police department and, at the same time, to release only certain restricted types of information to the public. Any other requests for information from the police officer are diverted by a statement that such questions must be answered by a superior officer within the department. In other words, a police officer operates in a system where much of the communication occurs in a highly formalized network.

A formal communication network is an essential part of any public bureaucracy.[7] Since the formal network closely follows the hierarchical structure of the organization, the authority of superiors within the organization is enhanced by the use of formal communications. When a superior needs a record of an order so that there can be no doubt as to whether or not such an order has been given, it is best to communicate formally, usually in writing. Such a step is necessary when the particular order is of great importance (e.g., an order is given by the mayor or city manager to increase the number of fire inspections in buildings that have more than four floors because of an increase in fires in the downtown area of the city) or when an order is likely to meet with explicit or implicit resistance (e.g., an order by the mayor or manager to limit all coffee breaks to 15 minutes). Also, those individuals who work in areas of functional specialization can be given, by a formal grant, enhanced authority to communicate on issues within their spheres of competency.

Not only does a formal communication system allow better and more authoritative communication but it also allows the top officials to maintain a good control system. Periodic reports in a required form allow the interested parties to prepare the control information and, at the same time, make the process of "keeping tabs on what is going on down below" easier for higher level managers. Control over many of the actions of civil servants is maintained by the formal communication network, because the rules for formal communication specify the form and content as well as the channels that are to be used. Not only do these rules allow a quick check on what is going on within the organization but they also keep everyone in the organization from being overwhelmed by the masses of information that are generated by any ongoing governmental operation.

Although the formal communication network is important, it is necessary to recognize the limitations that are inherent to such a system. Because of the limitations of the formal communication system, Simon, Smithburg, and Thompson say that

[7] *Ibid.*, pp. 222-226.

it is not the complete answer to an organization's communication needs. Every happening in the organization cannot be foreseen so that it can be formalized. The "channels" cannot be expressive of the wide variety of human need for communication. Nor can communication through channels always give "the sense" of what is intended to be conveyed. Formal communication tends to be stiff, slow, inflexible. Often it cannot express the real needs and demands of the organization.[8]

It is for this reason that a new executive feels inadequate in his knowledge about the new system. The formal network fails to communicate much important information to the executive; therefore, a major task of any new executive is that of developing the contacts that are essential to find out what is really going on inside the particular organization and how the organization fits into the overall scheme of the government.

## Interpersonal Communication

Most governmental agencies have developed adequate formal communication tools to pass on the information that is required for the minimal operation of the organization. There is the employee handbook that spells out employee rights and obligations, the newsletter that keeps everyone up to date on the latest policy changes and the activities of both the organization and other employees, the procedures manual that explains how each particular case should be handled, and the forms and reports that control the actions of the government employees and protect them if their actions are challenged. These are the important mediums for communication downward and to a certain extent across the organization, but they do not supply an adequate level of communication at either of these levels. In order to develop *adequate communication in all directions* throughout the organization, the interpersonal and informal communication systems must be functioning effectively.

The substance that holds together the formal framework of the organizational communication network is close personal relations. Interpersonal communication is vital to both the formal and informal networks, for it is the major element in two-way communications. All other methods of communication are supplemental aids to this basic process. In the end, the principle method of two-way communication is personal discussion between first-line supervisors and employees, between supervisors at the same level whose departments or sections interact in the production of a product or the delivery of a service, and among various levels of the hierarchy of the organization up to and including the top executives and the elected officials. No form of printed communication can match the personal meeting in importance or value.[9]

---

[8] *Ibid.*, p. 225.

[9] Harold P. Zelko and Harold J. O'Brien, *Management-Employee Communication in Action*, Howard Allen, Cleveland, 1957, pp. 21-24.

Although personal communication may follow the formal channels, it does not have to do so; most of the informal communication network is built around the personal communication system. While the information received through such contacts is not official, it does reveal much about the attitudes of a variety of people toward the activities of the executive's organization, and therefore may serve as a check on activities and a guide toward new or different activities in the future. If personal communication is used, it is important to realize its strengths and limitations.

First, personal channels of communication are primarily used for reports and suggestions. Orders and directives are given through the formal channels. Personal messages are transmitted by people who are acting as individuals rather than as officeholders, even if they are communicating along formal channels. Anthony Downs states that in this case, such officials are acting in a *subformal* way with the message being "transmitted by individuals acting in their official capacity—but not for the record."[10]

Second, the personal network can transmit messages with amazing speed because there is no delay for verification. Herbert Kaufman and Michael Couzens comment that

there is evidence that this channel is impressively active, both downward and upward. In one (federal) bureau, for example, an official reported to us that he contrived a false memorandum describing some technical changes and "incidentally" announcing his own "transfer" to Alaska; (they were talking to an official in Washington, D.C.) by the end of the same day that he put it in his out-box, he began to get calls from friends in Albuquerque, a major field center of the organization. . . . Similarly, in another bureau, officials said that personnel decisions made in the central office commonly evoked reactions from the field before they were officially announced. The point is not that items were "leaked" but that knowledge of them spread via these informal pathways, and very swiftly.[11]

When speed in communicating is necessary, the interpersonal and informal networks are often the most efficient and effective systems that can be used.

Third, the interpersonal network allows maximum upward communication as well as downward communication; although there is no verification mechanism, there may be, and often is, a high degree of accuracy in the network. For example, in his investigation of "Rumors in War," Theodore Caplow found that the rumor network maintained great accuracy in detail even after messages had passed through hundreds of persons.[12] Of course, anyone who has ever

---

[10] Downs, p. 115.

[11] Herbert Kaufman and Michael Couzens, *Administrative Feedback: Monitoring Subordinates' Behavior*, The Brookings Institution, Washington, D.C., 1973, p. 34.

[12] Theodore Caplow, "Rumors in War," *Social Forces*, XXV, 298-302 (March 1947).

participated in the parlor game of "Gossip" (a message is whispered by each participant to the next until it has made the complete circuit of everyone in the room) knows that messages can be badly garbled. Therefore, the sign of a good administrator is the ability of that individual to maximize the information coming "up" from the organization through the personal communication network and the ability to "separate the chaff from the wheat," or to recognize the valid information while discarding the obviously wrong or suspicious information.

Fourth, because of limitations, administrators must usually verify any information received from personal communications before acting on it in an official way. On occasion, however, officials have to act so quickly that there is no time for verification; it is in these cases that the skill and judgment of a public administrator are put to the extreme test. A wrong estimate of the level of crisis or the acceptance of faulty information can lead to irreparable public damage and loss of trust in the ability of the public official.

## Informal Communication

Formal networks do not fully describe the important channels of communication within any government organization. In order to understand fully the communication network within any agency, it is necessary to include an examination of the informal communication system. The informal communication system is made up of all those channels of communication that fall outside the officially designated channels that are spelled out in the rules, regulations, and manuals of the organization. For example, in addition to the formal communication system, police officers will probably receive a tremendous amount of information each day from the informal network in which they function. While preparing for the day's work, they are probably going to hear quite a bit of "office scuttlebutt," which may vary from rumors about disciplinary and promotional actions to the latest information about some cases that are of mutual interest with several other officers. Once the morning's briefing is completed, the officers may communicate informally with numerous people both in and out of the police department. While carrying out their normal duties, the officers may come into contact with employees from other parts of the governmental bureaucracy. Such contacts may allow discussion on a variety of topics, including such items as the expected settlement of a complaint against the police department by a civil rights group and the amount of pay increase that will be demanded by the bargaining committee for the police when the new budget is prepared. The officers may get in touch with special informants who regularly help them on certain types of criminal cases. Finally, they may use the informal communication channels to let the police chief know about a problem that is developing in their neighborhood because of rivalry between the juvenile authorities and the narcotics squad.

Each of these uses of the informal communication system occurs because there is a functional need for communication, but no formal channel exists by which the particular information can be passed. The need may be one of making sure that important information is not blocked by recalcitrant superiors or subordinates. There may be a need for greater speed in transmission of information than can be achieved through the formal channels. The informal channels may allow individuals to develop power and authority that they could not otherwise gain, thus leading to their assiduous development of the informal communication system. Above all, the formal system may not answer questions to which employees feel they should receive responses. In reference to this particular problem, Eugene Walton notes that the "organization's informal communications network begins to hum whenever the formal channels are silent or ambiguous on subjects of importance to its members."[13] Thus, whatever the reason for their existence, the informal networks play an important role in the public bureaucracy.

An informal communication network has a structure, just as does the formal network, although there are differences in the structure's development and stability. Whereas the structure of the formal communication system is established by the orders of the legislative body and the top administrators, the informal network derives its principle channels from social groups that develop within the organization. If relationships remain stable in a bureau for any length of time, a grapevine is sure to result as the personal contacts develop. Such factors as the degree of interdependence among activities and the level of organizational uncertainty, or ambiguity, will influence the amount of interaction among employees and the structure of the functioning network.[14] Close proximity leads to greater development of informal contacts, while physical or hierarchical distance or any type of conflict may lead to less interaction. With such a variety of relationships influencing the growth and continuation of any informal communication network, it is understandable that any network is in a constant state of fluctuation, with that fluctuation having an impact on everyone that the system touches.

How pervasive are these informal networks? How many people are affected by them and how many actively participate in the network? The answer to the first question is relatively easy because of its generality. Informal communication networks are all-pervasive; therefore, it follows that all public employees are affected by the grapevine, as it is commonly called. However, it is more difficult to ascertain how many employees are active participants in the passing of information through the grapevine. In the studies that have been done, it has been difficult to arrive at any common conclusions, but one finding that is gener-

---

[13] Eugene Walton, "How Efficient is the Grapevine," *Personnel, XXXVIII,* 45 (March-April, 1961).

[14] Downs, pp. 113-115.

ally accepted is that the predominant flow of information takes place within a group rather than between groups in a bureaucracy.[15] That is, employees who receive a piece of information through the grapevine are more likely to tell other people who work in the same office and have similar jobs.

While studying how information was passed through a government agency, Harold Sutton and Lyman Porter found an amazing variation in the amount of informal information received and passed on to other employees. One-third of the rank and file employees heard less than half of the rumors that made their way through the organization. Of the 67 percent who received a majority of the information, 57 percent of them passed on *less* than one-third of the information. Thus, only 10 percent of all the employees were active "liaisons" who regularly served as the linkages in the "grapevine." Caplow found a similar pattern when he studied the transmission of rumors in twelve company-size units that were operating as a regiment during World War II. This study led him to the conclusion that ". . . only a few of the members of each group habitually communicated the rumors originating in their own group to members of the other, and these few habitual contacts . . . were the only bridges by which most rumors passed from one group to the other."[16] Other studies have shown that the liaison persons varied according to the type of information that was involved,[17] but in each case only a minority of the employees were actively involved in passing on news, even though everyone received at least some of the information.

When the focus of the research moved from the rank and file employees to those in supervisory and managerial positions, an interesting phenomenon occurred; a growing involvement in the grapevine was seen. Sutton and Porter commented that while there was a wide divergence in involvement among the rank and file employees, the findings showed a significant trend for individuals higher in the organization hierarchy to be more informed concerning grapevine information.[18] Even more interestingly, the researchers found that 100 percent of the individuals in supervisory positions functioned as liaisons in the grapevine.

Such findings are not surprising given the realization that most administrators place some importance on the informal communication network as an aid to the success of any operation. There is no guarantee that the formal and informal communication systems will necessarily compliment one another (they may operate in direct opposition to one another); yet organizations that are successful in developing such a supplementary arrangement are able to function better and faster, to improve the morale of the employees in the organization, and to

[15] Harold Sutton and Lyman Porter, "A Study of the Grapevine in a Governmental Organization," *Personnel Psychology, XXI*, 223-230 (Summer 1968).

[16] Caplow, p. 299.

[17] Keith Davis, "Management Communication and the Grapevine," *Harvard Business Review, XXXI*, 43-49 (September-October, 1953).

[18] Sutton and Porter, p. 226.

meet their obligations efficiently and effectively. Since the leaders are aware of the benefits of such coordination, they take an interest in the grapevine; they listen carefully to the information that is flowing through it, while, at the same time, they use the grapevine to send out messages that can be best handled in an informal way. Above all, the leaders attempt to influence the form of the network and the stance that it takes toward the formal structure of the bureaucracy; if they can influence the informal communication network in a way that leads to its being a complementary tool for management, a major administrative victory has been won. Open, free, and satisfactory communication requires the maximum utilization of all three of the communication networks that exist in the bureaucracy.

## PROBLEMS IN COMMUNICATION

There are two major factors that influence the types of problems that occur in bureaucractic communication. The first factor is the direction of communication; does the particular information move upward, downward, or laterally within the bureaucracy? Of equal importance is the second factor; does the information, which is considered important to someone else in the organization, move through the organization as a command, advice, or data about the "state of the world"? These two variables, either separately or combined, tend to generate or exacerbate the difficulties that are generally pointed out as "problems in communication."

### Downward Communication

The downward information system is dominated by formal communications, such as orders, directives, and policy statements, although informal links also exist in this direction. The downward communication system has five major goals according to Katz and Kahn; these goals are:

1. To give specific task directives about job instructions.
2. To give information about organizational procedures and practices.
3. To provide information about the rationale of the job.
4. To tell subordinates about their performance.
5. To provide ideological-type information to facilitate the indoctrination of goals.[19]

Most governmental bureaucracies concentrate on the first two goals, as do the students of administration. Traditionally, management theory has been interested in finding the most efficient method for passing communiques from superior to subordinate until the information reaches the bottom of the bureaucracy. In addition, after the Hawthorne study found that effectiveness of com-

---

[19] Daniel Katz and Robert L. Kahn, *The Social Psychology of Organizations*, Wiley, New York, 1966, p. 239.

munication was as important as the efficiency of communication, a great deal of time was spent on determining the way to create the most impact with messages. Chester Barnard has suggested four criteria that determine when a command message will be accepted as authoritative:

A person can and will accept a communication as authoritative only when four conditions simultaneously obtain: (a) he can and does understand the communication; (b) *at the time of his decision* he believes that it is not inconsistent with the purpose of the organization; (c) *at the time of his decision,* he believes it to be compatible with his personal interest as a whole; and (d) he is able mentally and physically to comply with it.[20]

In spite of Barnard's stress on the individual within the organization, and the individual's attitudes and understanding of the organization, the usual recommendations to public managers have stressed clarity, unambiguity, unequivocalness and detail in orders. For this reason, many of the most common complaints about communication in public agencies deal directly with the last three goals spelled out by Katz and Kahn. The comments of public employees are (1) I am constantly given orders to do a task without being told why that job needs to be done; (2) I am not told whether or not my performance is satisfactory; and (3) no one has explained the philosophy of this agency to me. Surprisingly, in a political world, the third complaint is especially prevalent. The philosophy of a public bureaucracy is extremely important. Such information may be made available initially, but continued reaffirmation of the philosophy often tends toward lip service or else is completely forgotton in the rush of everyday affairs. Therefore, it must constantly be repeated that

communicating to personnel the rational for the job, the ideological relation of the job to the goals of the organization, and information about job performance, if properly handled, can greatly benefit the organization.[21]

Lack of communication may not be an accident, of course. There are cases where the head of an agency and his or her associates may have a clear understanding about the particular goals of a program, but they may not want to present those goals to the total organization or to the outside world. "The matter may be delicate; it may imply an admission of partial failure; it may require the equivalent of talking 'among ourselves' in the family circle."[22] The serious ques-

[20] Chester I. Barnard, *The Functions of the Executive,* Harvard University, Cambridge, Mass., 1938, p. 165.

[21] Fritz M. Marx and Henry Reining, Jr., "The Tasks of Middle Management," in F. M. Marx, ed., *Elements of Public Administration,* Prentice-Hall, Englewood Cliffs, N.J., 1959, pp. 378-379.

[22] *Ibid.*

tion in this type of case is, how many times can top management get away with this type of behavior? For instance, almost all public employees will occasionally forgive their manager for operating in such a manner; however, the word "occasionally" must be stressed, and it must be apparent *after the fact* why such silence is necessary in the first place. If such is not the case, the trust in the communication from the top of the organization will rapidly deteriorate.

Of course, the other problem that is likely to occur, especially as an attempt is made to correct an inadequate flow of information, is that people at the lower levels of the organization may be inundated under torrents of information. As Marx and Reining state,

Downward communication may be a meager trickle from sheer timidity, but it may also suffer from torrential abundance. The policy announcement is followed by an interminable series of clarifications, or the administrative order carries in its wake a whole string of implementing instructions, one more detailed than the other. The essential economy of communication lies between these two extremes. . . . Most middle managers consider themselves victims of either too little or too much. They may not always be the best judges of the "golden mean," but all too often they can make a good case to demonstrate that they are "left high and dry" or altogether "snowed under."[23]

Downward communication often fails for another reason. Quite often, distortion occurs in the transmission of information because of the excessive levels of hierarchy through which the message travels. Messages are "reinterpreted" by each intervening level of management until, in many cases, any resemblance between the original message of the top official and the information received by the employees is coincidental. Perhaps the only way to solve this problem is to flatten the hierarchy by removing some of the levels of midmanagement. This has been accomplished with some difficulty in several public agencies; however, the result has been an improvement in communication that has generally convinced the top administrators that the effort was worth it.[24]

There is no final solution to the problem of improving downward communication. The best advice is to observe what is going on below in the bureaucracy and to see if the actions of the employees match the instructions that have been communicated to them; at the same time, managers should follow the rules for giving effective instructions developed by Lee Thayer, who says that both procedures and instructions should be

---

[23] *Ibid.*

[24] There are several case studies of government reorganization in which the hierarchy has been flattened. For example, see: Frederick Mosher, ed., *Governmental Reorganization: Cases and Commentary*, Bobbs-Merrill, Indianapolis, 1967. For an interesting example drawn from business, see the discussion of Sears, Roebuck and Co. in: Alfred D. Chandler, Jr., *Strategy and Structure*, Massachusetts Institute of Technology, Cambridge, 1962.

1. Unambiguous.
2. Unequivocal.
3. Detailed only to the extent of precluding any unnecessary ambiguity—of content, situation, or intention.
4. Specific as to time and place, both beginning and ending.
5. Consistent with the functions, the capabilities, and the judgment-abilities of the receiver.
6. Consistent with other procedures and instructions.
7. Consistent with the goals and objectives of the organization.[25]

## Upward Communication

There are two types of upward communication within the bureaucracy. Management solicits one set of information; at the same time, employees voluntarily send a second set of information toward the top of the organization. The information that is solicited through surveys, formal and informal meetings (the "rap sessions" between management and employees that are in vogue now), and suggestion and gripe boxes is quite useful to top management. This information can be used to aid in attacking problems that are developing inside the organization or to prepare for environmental issues that may influence the success of the bureaucracy in meeting its goals.

The truly important information that may move upward through a governmental bureaucracy is not always solicited; these are the messages that top management most needs if it is to be successful. Complaints, suggestions,[26] "intelligence" reports, and innovative ideas start upward regularly, but top management receives only a minute portion of these messages. Of course, only a small number of the items should be considered by top officers, such as governors or city managers, for they have many important tasks that require their time. The vital issue deals with information as it is being transmitted and the use of that information once it is received.

Adequate and important information fails to reach top administrators for two major reasons: (1) top managers fail to listen to those below them in the hierarchy; and (2) the information that does make it through "the channels" is distorted. Few managers are psychologically prepared to listen well; therefore, it is much easier for an official to give orders than to listen carefully to advice. Marx and Reining not only describe this problem but they also manage to categorize this type of "boss" when they say

A feeble or small-minded top management, offended by any "criticism" from within, is obviously unable to foster . . . habits of consultation, however much

[25] Lee Thayer, *Communication and Communication Systems in Organization, Management, and Interpersonal Relations,* Richard D. Irwin, Homewood, Ill., 1968, p. 216.

[26] It is interesting to note that "orders" move downward in an organization, while "suggestions" move upward or laterally.

lip service it may pay the abstract principle. Helpful suggestions and new ideas will not come forth when they fail to find eager takers.[27]

Anyone with experience in the public service can recall situations with managers who, after declaring an open-door policy, take any suggestion for innovation or change as a personal affront or as a tacit criticism of past practices. A proposal for a new outreach program in the city's personnel department in not perceived by the personnel director as an attempt to meet new demands, to serve better the needs of the population, or to fulfill obligations of the Affirmative Action and Equal Employment Opportunity Programs; rather, the personnel director sees the proposed program as an attempt to force him or her to admit that prior programs were inadequate and did not meet the demands of the citizens. Granted, either interpretation can be made in such a situation; however, it is fair to say that the interpretation accepted by the director is, subconsciously, a self-definition of prior motivation and policy.

Upward communication can work only when the leader of the organization sincerely wants it to work. Even then the manager must make sure that the information received is adequate and accurate, because the propensity toward distortion is greatest when communication is moving upward; now the trans-mitter is influenced not only by his or her perception of the world but also by a tendency to phrase the communication in a way that is most pleasing to the superior. This retranslation occurs even when a superior is *not* surrounded by "yes-men"; a department head must actively seek ways of counteracting the overly optimistic and positively distorted information that superiors are likely to receive. Thus, the wise manager establishes a strategy of "counterbiasing" received information.[28]

The first method, the use of distortion-proof messages, should be used whenever possible. The military and paramilitary organizations find such messages especially important; however, there are very limited uses for such a system, because such messages can be used only when the information being conveyed is unambiguous and does not require qualitative exposition.

The second method that is used is based on the experience of the manager. As Downs notes, "Every general was once a lieutenant and remembers the type of distortion he used when he forwarded information to his own superiors."[29] Therefore, every general, president, mayor, city manager, or department head can counterweigh the information received and remove those biases that creep into information. A police chief forwards information to the mayor or manager in a form that makes his department appear to be operating at peak efficiency

---

[27] Marx and Reining, p. 381.

[28] Downs, pp. 118-127.

[29] Downs, p. 121.

and effectiveness; at the same time the information will portray the need for additional officers, support staff, and equipment. The police chief has received the same type of biased information from his captains, who have received biased reports from their lieutenants, who have sergeants and patrolmen reporting biased information to them; in every case, "Full and objective reporting is difficult, regardless of the organizational situation; no individual is an objective observer of his own performance and problems."[30]

Third, it is often possible to receive the same type of information from more than one source. Overlapping or redundant channels allow a comparison of facts that often leads to additional or conflicting interpretations of the same facts or to totally new information that would not be available under any other system. The easiest way to create such redundancy is to create overlapping areas of responsibility. President Franklin D. Roosevelt was especially adept at maintaining control over programs and assuring himself of the validity of all the information by creating areas of overlapping responsibilities. By arbitrating the conflicts that regularly occurred between his subordinates and Cabinet members, Roosevelt was assured that he would receive all the pertinent information as interpreted by more than one individual; in addition, he knew that he would make the final decision on those programs that created conflict within his administration.[31]

When such a system is used, it is extremely important to reduce the penalties for conflicting reports. If the subordinates find that disharmony is reprimanded, conflict is eschewed, and someone will be a "winner" while another will be a "loser," they will quickly learn to cover over any debate by either refusing to participate or by working in collusion in order to present a united front to their superiors.

If a manager suspects that there is any incompleteness or bias in the communications, an immediate check should be made through the internal informal communication system (the "grapevine") and through the external contacts that are available. The grapevine should be cultivated rather than castigated, especially since its continuation is assured regardless of what the boss says or does. The grapevine cannot be ordered out of existence. However, the grapevine offers the wise manager a tremendous chance to check and countercheck "the facts." Outside contacts can also furnish the official with a fresh perception of activities that are going on in the organization from the view of someone who is unattached to the normal bureaucratic loyalties (although any such outside view must be weighed carefully for biasing influences that may exist in that individ-

---

[30] Katz and Kahn, p. 246.

[31] President Roosevelt is reported to have said, "There is something to be said for having a little conflict between agencies. A little rivalry is stimulating, you know. It keeps everybody going to prove that he is a better fellow than the next man. It keeps them honest too. An awful lot of money is being handled. The fact that there is somebody else in the field who knows what you are doing is a strong incentive to strict honesty." Arthur M. Schlesinger, Jr., *The Coming of the New Deal,* Houghton Mifflin, Boston, 1958, p. 535.

ual's background). Drastic action may be needed at times in order for public officials to determine exactly what the situation is in a particular segment of a program under their jurisdiction. Sometimes the only way to understand the conditions is to move totally outside the upward communication system and go to the problem in order to experience it directly. When, for example, a 10 million dollar public housing project in Atlanta was apparently falling apart four years after it was built, Mayor Maynard Jackson spent a weekend as the guest of a widow and her seven children. Jackson wandered around for two days observing the unhealthy living conditions, the general disrepair, and the poor workmanship. He talked to residents about their problems and came away saying, "Last weekend I spent a month as a resident of Bankhead Courts. . . . We wonder why people get mad living there. . . . I only spent one weekend there and I'm mad already."[32] After his visit, Mayor Jackson promised more federal funds and city services to improve the conditions at Bankhead. Mayor Jackson could understand, in a poignant and experiential manner that would have been unachievable in any other way, the information that he was receiving. Biases or incompleteness in reports about the housing project could be much more easily spotted by the Mayor after he learned in a firsthand manner about the existing state of affairs.

Finally, the elimination of middlemen, of the extra layers in the hierarchy of the organization, will accomplish a great deal toward opening the lines of upward communication. Thus, reorganization, properly conceived and consummated, improves both upward and downward communication, and therefore maintains open channels and welcomes both the good news and the bad, *but only if management sincerely desires improvement.*

## Lateral Communication

In many cases, the most important type of communication that occurs in the bureaucracy takes place laterally. Lateral communication is the passing and receiving of communication between employees at approximately the same level within the organization, or directly between employees who do not report to one another through the normal hierarchical channels of the organization. These communications may also be with individuals inside or outside of the same particular bureaucracy.

The rules of classical organization theory have taken little note of the need for horizontal, or lateral, communication. Henri Fayol was the lone early student to consider this problem of organizations.[33] Fayol argued that if a "gangplank" could be established between employees F and P, instead of forcing them to work up and down through the formal hierarchy, great benefits in time and productivity might accrue (see Figure 6). The gangplank would

---

[32] "A Long Weekend," *Time*, p. 12 (November 4, 1974).

[33] Chester Barnard was the first major contributor to the theory of organizational communication.

allow the two employees F and P to deal at one sitting, and in a few hours, with some question or other which via the scalor chain would pass through twenty transmissions, inconvenience many people, involve masses of paper, lose weeks or months to get to a conclusion less satisfactory generally than the one which could have been obtained via direct contact as between F and P.[34]

Horizontal communication is necessary for the overall coordination of the organization; the more interconnected and interdependent the parts of a bureaucracy, the greater will be the need for such communication, for in such cases there is a need for rapid, direct, and unambiguous information.[35]

As an example of the usage of horizontal communication systems, Chorness, Rittenhouse, and Heald note in their study of educational program planning and curriculum development that, although federally funded programs and structured information are used, the most frequently used sources of information include colleagues in one's own school system, principals and vice-principals, contacts at professional meetings, superintendents, and curriculum

[34] Henri Fayol, *General and Industrial Management,* trans., Constance Storrs, Sir Isaac Pitman and Sons, London, 1949, p. 35.

[35] James D. Thompson, *Organizations in Action,* McGraw-Hill, New York, 1967, p. 62.

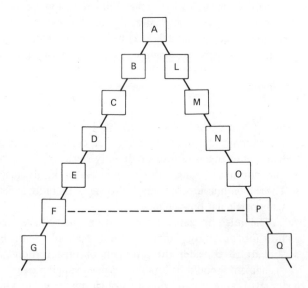

**Figure 6**

Fayol's gangplank concept. (Source: Henri Fayol, *General and Industrial Management,* trans., Constance Storrs. Sir Isaac Pitman and Sons, London, 1949, p. 34.)

specialists. Decision makers emphasize sources of information that are easily accessible.[36]

There are several reasons for horizontal communication in addition to the need for coordination between separate units of the bureaucracy. Communication with peers from other parts of the organization provides social support for the individual. It is also easier to turn to a peer for advice and consultation on a problem than it is to approach a superior. In such cases, lateral communication can be healthy and productive for the organization; however, if the communication is not guided in some way toward attaining the goals of the organization, the communication can just as easily take forms that are "irrelevant to or destructive of organizational functioning."[37] Thus, public managers should observe how lateral communications develop and how such systems are used with the ideal, not of stopping these informal communication systems, but of using the lateral systems in a way calculated to improve the total bureaucracy.

Two major problems may arise when managers attempt to deal with lateral communication. There may be a problem of understanding the language that is used by the different segments of the bureaucracy, or employees may misunderstand a message because of the particular frame of reference that they have when considering an issue. Of course, the problems may exist in upward or downward communication, but they tend to be especially prevalent when considering communication that occurs across the organization.

Bureaucracies tend to develop their own languages. Public agencies develop a stilted use of the language that is referred to either as "officialese" or "gobbledygook." To anyone not immersed in the bureaucracy, such language can be both confusing and repugnant. Simon, Smithburg, and Thompson deal with this particular communication phobia by pointing out that

consciously or unconsciously most organizations develop their own peculiar modes of speech. Further than that, specialized units within organizations also develop new words and new meanings from old words. Very often this movement goes so far that official interpreters have to be employed in order to communicate effectively with outsiders.[38]

Lawyers, accountants, scientists, personnel officials, and other public professionals have been guilty of this type of behavior. Perhaps police officers have taken the most ribbing for this habit; their critics often picture the English

---

[36] M. H. Chorness, C. H. Rittenhouse, and R. C. Heald, *Decision, Process, and Information needs in Education: A Field Survey,* Far West Laboratory for Educational Research and Development, Berkeley, Cal., 1969, p. 10.

[37] Katz and Kahn, p. 244.

[38] Simon, Smithburg, and Thompson, p. 232. See also: Stuart Chase, *The Power of Words,* Harcourt, Brace and World, New York, 1953.

language as losing ground among a group of people who talk in numbers. They answer calls to crises that are described by numerical code. They arrest citizens and hand out citations, all based on violations of civil and criminal codes described in a special system based on numbers. If such a practice is carried to an extreme by the police, citizens may feel that they have been cited for having committed an unmentionable act upon a set of numbers. An individual from another part of the city bureaucracy may have a difficult time understanding a conversation that is carried on with police officers about their business. Of course, the same thing may be true of the language used by engineers who are discussing the construction of roads and bridges or by public health employees who are explaining their attempts to control rats or mosquitoes.

The obvious answer to such a problem in communication, whether lateral or vertical, inside or outside of the organization, is to make the specialist see the necessity of making others understand what the specialist is doing. Refresher courses in "how to write in plain English" may not be required, but constant vigilance against the use of needless gobbledygook must be maintained if communication between parts of the organization is to be successful.

Once the language of communication between departments and specialists has been clarified, approximately half of the problem has been corrected. Specialization has a tendency to create a second problem. Individuals with training, experience, and therefore conditioning in an area of expertise of a profession tend to develop a "mental set" that influences what messages are received and how they are received. The problem of what messages are received is caused, first, by the selective perception of each information receiver, wherein the individual tends to pick from among the myriad communications that are available those that fit what the receiver wants to read or hear. This does not mean that a receiver deliberately screens out information; however, people tend to accept those parts of information that fit comfortably into their general mental set.

In addition, individuals develop preconceptions about situations; in other words, they make up their minds in advance about an issue. Even though, as in the case of selective perception discussed just above, there is no conscious effort to accept or interpret information in any particular way, individuals with preconceived ideas at first tend to ignore contradictory facts until they become so prominent that they cannot be escaped; even then the information is interpreted, whenever possible, to fit the mental set of the individual.

Let us suppose that it has come to the attention of the city manager of a city of 200,000 that there is a sudden upsurge in the level of juvenile delinquency within the community. In an attempt to control the increase in delinquency, the manager calls a meeting of four department heads who, it is assumed, have an interest in the problem and may have some ideas about how to control it. Thus, the manager meets with the heads of the police department, the recreation department, the local school district, and local welfare department. Since they have been informed of the purpose of the meeting, each administrator arrives at the meeting with an explanation for the origin of the problem and a potential solution.

The police chief suggests that the major reason for the problem is the increasing number of young people who are hanging out in a variety of night spots. Increased free time leads to additional opportunities for getting into trouble. He suggests that the police department be given greater financial resources so that it may assign several young officers, in plain clothes, to patrol the areas suffering from the higher incidences of vandalism and juvenile crime.

The recreation director suggests that the problem is created by a lack of recreation facilities and programs that should be available during evening peak hours of juvenile usage. Since there are no organized activities available, the young people create their own diversions, some of which are frowned on by adults. She suggests that the recreation department be given more funds so that it can rent facilities and develop some supervised activities for youths.

The superintendent of the school district believes that the major contributing factor to the increase in juvenile delinquency is the inability of the school to offer an adequate number of extracurricular activities, as well as the lack of adequate counseling for the students who have family and emotional problems. He is convinced that more funds for these two programs would dramatically cut into the incidence of juvenile delinquency.

The director of the local welfare department is convinced that the major causes of the accelerating incidence of juvenile delinquency are the inability of the welfare department to offer proper family counseling services and the necessity of many welfare mothers to work, therefore leaving their families unattended except for informal arrangements the mother may make with friends or relatives for major periods of the day (especially in the evening when many service jobs are available for the untrained worker). She believes that a major improvement can be made in the problem of juvenile delinquency if her department has additional financial support for family counseling and is able to establish child-care centers for working mothers.

You will notice that each definition of the problem being discussed, and each potential solution offered, is colored by the particular background of the individual involved in the discussion. Such a reaction is perfectly normal for each individual is most familiar with, and can therefore best prescribe action for, her own organization. However, the most appropriate response to the situation will *not* be any of the proposals but will be a plan based on the combination of all these suggestions in addition to other ideas that may be available from interested parties. The final solution might include a short-term plan for increased patrol by the police while the recreation department develops a crash program of youth activities using available facilities in a few of the school buildings. At the same time, a plan for coordinated counseling programs might be established with the schools and the welfare department both specializing in segments of the total counseling program, with each department referring individuals to the other when a case is diagnosed as being in the other department's area of expertise. Finally, long-range plans for child-care centers and permanent recreation and craft programs can be planned so that the problem can be addressed throughout the future.

Lateral communication is essential to the solution of any such problem; in order for the communication to be successful, the viewpoints and biases of the different specialists must be overcome so that they have a common understanding of the total issue. The manager is responsible for gaining cooperation and maintaining coordination. Maintaining a good lateral communication system that is functioning in a timely way and producing useful and understandable information is as essential as the maintenance of the upward or downward systems.

The public manager's success or failure may very well be determined by the functioning capabilities of the communication system. This is frightening to many administrators, for they realize that they control only part of the development of that system. March and Simon point out that "in part, the communication network is planned; in part, it grows up in response to the need for specific kinds of communication; in part, it develops in response to the social functions of communication."[39] The manager must maintain as much influence over the communication system as possible, for it "will have an important influence on decisionmaking processes, and particularly upon nonprogramed activity."[40] These two areas of organizational activity are elemental to the success or failure of any public agency.

## SUMMARY

The communication system of an organization is comparable to the nervous system of a biological organism. Communication allows the members of the organization to know what is happening internally and externally, to think together, and to act as a unit working toward a common goal. Communication occurs between individuals in the organization as ideas, feelings, and attitudes are transmitted—either verbally or nonverbally—from one person to another in such a way that the transmitted message produces a response.

There are several types of communication networks, and each is necessary if the organization is to function efficiently and effectively. The most important of these networks are the formal system (explicitly spelled out by the administrative manual and by law), the interpersonal system, and the informal system (the last two are created by the social structure of the organization and by situations where extra-formal communication is essential to the operation of the bureaucracy). The wise leader accepts the presence of all three networks and attempts to utilize all three in guiding organization thoughts, decisions, and activities.

The problems that develop in communication systems are usually attached to two major factors—the direction of the communication and the type of communication being transmitted. Downward communication is composed primarily of formal directives, orders, and policy statements. Downward communication may be too scarce or too abundant; even when the volume of information is properly adjusted, there is still a danger of distortion during the transmission of

[39] James March and Herbert A. Simon, *Organizations,* Wiley, New York, 1958, p. 168.

[40] *Ibid.*

the information. Upward communication has the hardest time surviving, or remaining intact, during transmission. The information fails to reach top administrators because top administrators often fail to listen; when they do listen, the information is often distorted. If the manager sincerely wants the information, it can be received and corrected for biases by using distortion-proof messages, prior experience to make corrections, and overlapping sources of information. Lateral communication aids the organization in maintaining coordination and in sharing knowledge; however, such communication can be incomplete or misunderstood because of the use of private languages by transmitters or because of the application of special frames of reference by the receivers.

# BIBLIOGRAPHY

Barnard, Chester, *The Functions of the Executive,* Harvard University, Cambridge, Mass., 1938.

Bassett, Glenn A., *The New Face of Communication,* American Management Association, New York, 1968.

Berlo, David K., *The Process of Communication,* Holt, Rinehart and Winston, New York, 1960.

Chandler, Alfred D., *Strategy and Structure,* Doubleday, Garden City, N.Y., 1963.

Dearden, John, and Warren McFarlan, *Management Information Systems,* Richard D. Irwin, Homewood, Ill., 1966.

Deutsch, Karl W., *The Nerves of Government,* Free Press, New York, 1963.

Dippel, Gene, and William C. House, *Information Systems,* Scott, Foresman, Glenview, Ill., 1969.

Downs, Anthony, *Inside Bureaucracy,* Little, Brown, Boston, 1967.

Huseman, Richard C., Cal M. Logue, and Dwight L. Freshley, eds., *Readings in Interpersonal and Organizational Communication,* Holbrook Press, Boston, 1969.

Katz, Daniel, and Robert L. Kahn, *The Social Psychology of Organizations,* Wiley, New York, 1966.

Kaufman, Herbert, and Michael Couzens, *Administrative Feedback: Monitoring Subordinates' Behavior,* Brookings Institution, Washington, D. C., 1973.

Luthans, Fred, *Organizational Behavior: A Modern Behavioral Approach to Management,* McGraw-Hill, New York, 1973.

March, James G., ed., *Handbook of Organizations,* Rand McNally, Chicago, 1965.

March, James G., and Herbert A. Simon, *Organizations,* Wiley, New York, 1958.

Myers, Charles A., ed., *The Impact of Computers on Management,* Massachusetts Institute of Technology, Cambridge, 1967.

Pierce, J. R., *Symbols, Signals and Noise: The Nature and Process of Communication,* Harper and Brothers, New York, 1961.

Redfield, Charles E., *Communication in Management,* University of Chicago, Chicago, 1958.

Sigband, Norman B., *Communication for Management,* Scott, Foresman, Glenview, Ill., 1969.

Simon, Herbert A., Donald W. Smithburg, and Victor A. Thompson, *Public Administration,* Alfred A. Knopf, New York, 1950.

Sutton, Harold, and Lyman Porter, "A Study of the Grapevine in a Governmental Organization," *Personnel Psychology, XXI,* 223-230 (Summer 1968).

Thayer, Lee, *Communication and Communication Systems in Organizations, Management, and Interpersonal Relations,* Richard D. Irwin, Homewood, Ill., 1968.

Weiner, Norbert, *Communication,* Massachusetts Institute of Technology, Cambridge, 1955.

Wilensky, Harold L., *Organizational Intelligence: Knowledge and Policy in Government and Industry,* Basic Books, New York, 1967.

Zelko, Harold P., and Harold J. O'Brien, *Management-Employee Communication in Action,* Howard Allen, Cleveland, 1957.

# CONFLICT IN BUREAUCRACY

*(I)t is . . . to be hoped that we shall always have conflict; the kind which leads to invention, to the emergence of new values.*

*Mary Parker Follett*

Peacemakers are important to our society, as is the circumstance that they bring; however, the desire for peace, socially and organizationally, has been stressed to such an extent that we have failed to recognize the necessity and value of the opposite condition—that of *conflict*. Conflict is a valuable part of our environment. In and of itself, conflict is neither good nor bad, just as is true of many other aspects of society. Ethical judgment can be made only during or

# CHAPTER 10

after the particular conflict, unless the conflict is one of those larger and more obvious battles such as war; even in these cases there is disagreement among the judges as to the positive or negative evaluation of the conflict, although particular *participants* in the conflict may be judged harshly or leniently. Conflict is an integral part of our daily life; it is also an integral part of the public agencies that govern everyone's daily life. Mary Parker Follett, who was forty years ahead of her time in recognizing the utility of conflict, as well as its danger, pointed out the way in which conflict should be regarded by saying that

as conflict—difference—is here in the world, as we cannot avoid it, we should, I think, use it. Instead of condemning it, we should set it to work for us. Why not? What does the mechanical engineer do with friction? Of course his chief job is to eliminate friction, but it is true that he also capitalizes friction. The transmission of power by belts depends on friction between the belt and the pulley. The friction between the driving wheel of the locomotive and the track is necessary to haul the train. All polishing is done by friction. The music of the violin we get by friction. We left the savage state when we discovered fire by friction. We talk of the friction of mind on mind as a good thing. . . . We have to know when to try to eliminate friction and when to try to capitalize it, when to see what work we can make it do.[1]

In this chapter, we attempt to follow the advice of Mary Parker Follett by examining in some detail the role of conflict in the public bureaucracy. First, it is necessary to define what we mean by the term "conflict." Second, we discuss the effect of conflict on the individual and the way the effect differs when shifting to an "organizational conflict" context. Third, we examine the negative and positive aspects of conflict on public bureaucracy; and, fourth, we review methods of managing conflict.

## DEFINITION OF CONFLICT

Conflict is one of those phenomenon that is experienced by everyone but that can be defined completely and accurately by no one. An individual knows when conflict occurs, and he knows, within the limits of psychology, why the conflict was caused, how the scenario of the situation progressed, and what the final conclusion of the conflict was. Most people can, in most cases, say that a situation either is or is not conflictive. It is another matter, however, to define conflict. What are the elements that always exist in a conflict? This is the question that must be answered before an adequate definition of conflict can be presented. What elements are necessary in order for a situation to be considered a conflict, and which elements may be present but not necessary? We are interested in the essential features that make conflict the unique experience that it is, regardless of the type of conflict being considered.

[1] Henry C. Metcalf and Lyndall Urwick, eds., *Dynamic Administration: The Collected Papers of Mary Parker Follett,* Harper and Row, New York, 1940, pp. 30-31.

Conflict is the struggle over resources or ideas, between two or more parties, caused by the perception on the part of the contending parties that both or all cannot have what they desire. Conflict usually occurs when one or more parties believe the normal channels of grievance resolution are closed to them, and conflict, therefore, requires extra-normal procedures for its resolution. H. Randolph Bobbitt, Jr., and his co-authors have found that the term "conflict" is used to define a variety of *conditions, perceptions, feelings, actions,* and *processes.* In order to understand adequately the concept of conflict, all of these elements must be considered.[2]

*Latent conflict* refers to the *antecedent conditions* that always exist when conflictful behavior occurs. Examples of these latent factors or conditions are scarcity of resources, different goals, or different opinions. Actually these conditions always exist in any public agency. Resources are always scarce when considered in relation to demands, whether one is considering the national government, a major city such as Chicago, or a smaller area such as Pocahontas County, West Virginia. Governments suffer from the problem of limited resources because they must depend on taxes rather than on the revenue-generating services that give businesses some greater flexibility in resource generation and utilization. The goals accepted by the politicians, the public, and the bureaucrats within the government may differ widely; within the bureaucracy, where unanimity might be expected, differences in goals may lead to violent struggles in which the participants attempt to direct the governmental service toward widely divergent ends. For instance, there has long been a battle within the bureaucracy of the national government as to how the lands held by the government should be used: Should grazing be allowed on grasslands, and, if so, how much? Should the trees on government land be logged, or should the land be maintained as virgin, natural forest? Even when there is agreement of these goals, there is still a difference of opinion as to how these goals can best be achieved.

*Perceived conflict* refers to the way people apprehend or understand conflictful situations. Some people perceive a conflictful situation at a time when others do not see the situation as unusual, tense, or discordant. Such a situation is not too uncommon, nor is it uncommon for such a situation to develop into a conflagration of immense size and intensity once the unknowing party finally realizes that the other side has been treating the ongoing interaction as a conflict; by that time, the unknowing party is likely to feel that she has been taken advantage of in an underhanded way, and that she must now overcome a decisive disadvantage.

Open conflict may still be perceived in a variety of ways by observers and participants. The process of a conflict may be seen in a dramatically different light, depending on the preconceptions of the passive perceiver or the actions, gains, losses, and values of the participant. Political battles are regularly perceived differently by the two or more sides that are involved. The tactics used by

[2] H. Randolf Bobbit, Jr., Robert H. Breinholt, Robert H. Doktor, and James P. McNaul, *Organizational Behavior: Understanding and Prediction,* Prentice-Hall, Englewood Cliffs, N.J., 1974, pp. 137-138.

Mayor Daley of Chicago are praised by his supporters as "truly representative of the desires of the citizens who elected him," while the liberal Democrats of the city (and elsewhere) consider Daley to be a throwback to the days of evil big city bosses who were prevalent at the turn of the nineteenth century. At the same time, the Republicans of the area respect Daley's political clout, strongly dislike his somewhat ruthless handling of elections, and probably secretly envy his political power and ability. It would be easy to include federal and state officials in any listing of groups involved in the conflicts swirling around the mayor's office. It is also easy to imagine the different perceptions of the conflicts that are held by the individuals who are either involved or who are observing, whether the conflict is over the placement of public housing, the repair of streets and highways, garbage collection, or the efficiency and honesty of the public employees.

Generally, two major views of conflict have prevailed. On the one hand, conflict has usually been perceived as dangerous and deleterious to the individuals or organizations that are involved, and it is believed almost any step is justified that represses or puts a stop to conflict. This view has the added weight of majority opinion behind it. On the other hand, a minority of advocates has always held that conflict is normal, healthy, and useful if it is controlled and properly channeled. Both views are still in evidence, with the latter interpretation gaining in respectability but still not being as popular as the idea of repressing conflict.

*Felt conflict* is the third part of the total definition of the topic being discussed. This part of the issue specifically deals with the way individuals react to conflictful situations. Depending on the individual's particular personality and the circumstances under which the conflict occurs, the feelings that are generated may be tenseness, hostility, anxiety, exhilaration, camaraderie, or anticipation. Regardless of the type of conflict, it does affect the individual participants; hence, their reactions must be carefully considered.

All of the conditions, perceptions, and feelings lead directly to the fourth part, which is *manifest conflict*. This part of the definition deals with the way people behave in a conflictful situation, that is, with their *actions*. Manifest conflict may vary from the minimal action of inaction (withholding information from another person or group who needs it and therefore influencing the outcome of a conflict by doing nothing when "doing something" is the expected behavior) to the action of verbally attacking another's position, or in extreme cases, physically fighting it out (a behavior that is usually frowned upon by even the most ardent advocates of conflict).

The term "conflict" refers to specific situations where it is believed that conditions are such that some individuals cannot have what they desire; the participants perceive this problem and feel that the issue is important enough that they must get involved in an active way. The manner in which the conflict develops depends on the particular issue, the individuals or organizations involved, and the "rules of the game" under which the conflict takes place.

Therefore, the fifth part of the definition deals with conflict as a *process*. The way in which a conflict is carried out is important because it defines who will be involved, what the outcome of the conflict will be, and whether or not the issue will be terminated in a way that will either settle the matter or allow it to arise again in the near future.

## EFFECTS OF CONFLICT ON THE INDIVIDUAL

In order to limit the discussion, we will consider the causes of conflict in an individual within the organizational context and individual reactions to that situation. Within the organizational context, the most influential factor in creating conflict is the "role" of the individual. Every individual is expected to fulfill certain functions within the organization. Attached to the position (see Max Weber's ideal typology of bureaucracy) are a series of duties and powers that lead everyone who comes into contact with that particular individual to expect him to behave in a certain manner. This *expected behavior* is one's role, for a role is assigned to a person by others, even though each individual has a perception of his or her own role. We all expect city managers to behave in a certain way when they are operating within the city's bureaucracy, for managers are expected by everyone concerned to fill a place of leadership, decision making, and dignity that helps to set the tone for the entire city employee force. The expected role of a recreation specialist is quite different; and the role of a janitor, a personnel analyst, or a building inspector will vary accordingly.

Conflict occurs when an individual senses an inconsistency in the designated role or when that role is not clear. Geoffrey Cornog divides this situation into two types of problems: role ambiguity and role conflict.[3] *Role ambiguity* occurs when an individual lacks information that is necessary in order for him or her to perform that role properly. For example, if a man takes a job as community relations specialist in the mayor's office, he wants to know what the mayor expects him to do; also, if possible, he wants to know what is expected of him by the community. If adequate information concerning his expected behavior and required duties is not available he is faced with a personal conflict that is caused by uncertainty,[4] because he does not know what will be the outcome of any actions that he takes. A new employee desires a condition of certainty and knowledge about his position; yet, in this case, the community relations

---

[3] Geoffrey Y. Cornog, "All the World a Stage, But Who Writes the Roles?" *Personnel Administration, XXXIII*, 26-31 (November-December, 1970).

[4] According to James March and Herbert Simon, there are three ways in which conflict arises:

1. *Unacceptability*, in which the individual knows the probable outcome associated with each alternative of action. In addition, he may be able to identify a preferred alternative, but the preferred alternative is *not good enough*.
2. *Incomparability*, where the individual knows the probable outcomes but cannot identify a most preferred alternative (the old problem of comparing apples and oranges).
3. *Uncertainty*, because the individual does not know the probable outcome of the possible alternatives.

March and Simon, *Organizations*, Wiley, New York, 1958, p. 113.

specialist perceives that such information is not being made available (either purposely or by accident); this leads to a feeling that the situation must be remedied in some way. If the mayor wishes to maintain this ambiguity, and there may be some justification for doing so in the eyes of the mayor, a conflict has begun.

If, on the other hand, the community relations specialist learns exactly what his role is expected to be, the problem may not have been solved. Instead, he may have solved the problem of role ambiguity and discovered that he now has a problem of role conflict. *Role conflict* exists when "two or more role demands are made and when compliance with one makes it impossible to fill the others."[5] After some parrying between the specialist and the mayor, the specialist may finally get a statement of what the mayor expects of him. In this case, the community relations specialist has already read the job specifications that were published with the job announcement and the position description that is on file in the personnel office; he finds that the mayor expects him to spend most of his time in personal contact with citizens and organizations explaining city policies and programs and serving as a feedback mechanism to bring back to city hall citizen ideas and complaints. It becomes clear that the citizens expect a high level of objectivity in the specialist's comments and a sympathetic ear for their ideas and complaints, while the mayor expects him to present the city's activities in the best light possible, always defending the mayor. There is conflict in such a situation, because it is difficult, if not impossible, to satisfy one group while fulfilling the expectations of the others. And, of course, "the difficulties people have with their organizational roles increase as conflict and ambiguity increase."[6]

How common is such conflict in the roles performed by public servants? Quite common! At one time or another, and in many cases regularly, employees are uncertain about the way their supervisor is going to evaluate their work, their scope of responsibility and authority, and their chances for advancement. At the same time, supervisors are constantly "caught in the middle" between the employees they supervise and the managers above them in the bureaucracy. Many, if not most, public servants work in positions that force them to "cross organizational boundaries," where they have contacts with the public. In this case, "the greatest tension is experienced by those who have discontinuous contacts outside the organization,"[7] so that absolute frequency is not an accurate measure of the conflict and tension faced by a public employee because of outside contacts. The amount of innovative decision making required of an em-

---

[5] Cornog, p. 29.

[6] Robert L. Kahn, "The Management of Organizational Stress," in John M. Thomas and Warren B. Bennis, eds., *Management of Change and Conflict*, Penguin, Baltimore, 1972, p. 422.

[7] *Ibid.*, p. 428.

ployee also affects the amount of conflict that an employee experiences, because any individual placed in a position that requires innovation will "become engaged in conflict primarily with the organizational old guard—men of greater age and power, who want to maintain the status quo."[8] Finally, rank also brings conflict with it. Kahn and his co-authors claim that:

The often heard assertion that the lowest levels of supervision are subjected to the greatest conflict is not borne out by (the) data. Rather, there is a curvilinear relationship in which the maximum conflict occurs at what might be called the upper middle levels of management.[9]

Therefore, if all the causes of conflict that are listed here are combined (along with the many others that can be thought of), one can see that conflict is a common experience in the life of a public servant. This is especially true when the new guidelines for citizen involvement in public policymaking are considered, for there has been a dramatic increase in the expectations and demands of citizen groups.

Since conflict is a regular part of the individual public servant's career, how does an individual react to it? While many people try to suppress and ignore conflict, others seem to thrive on it by actively seeking the "hot spots" and jobs that throw them into the thick of the fray. An individual can initially attempt to suppress or ignore the situation as long as possible by smoothing over the differences that are the basis of the conflict. In fact, this is the most usual approach as long as it is a viable alternative. Think once again of the new community relations specialist; he may try to downplay the existence of the problem he is facing by reinterpreting his working relationship with the mayor. He may be especially reluctant to admit to members of the public, such as the press, that any problem exists; it may be hard for him to convince even himself that the situation is serious. At some point, however, the conflict becomes threatening to his personal values; at that point the attempt to suppress the conflict fails.

## Resolutions to Conflict

Robert Blake and Jane Mouton suggest that there are five ways to resolve conflict once suppression has failed,[10] and the way that the individual chooses to resolve the issue is a major factor in deciding whether or not conflict hurts or helps an individual to grow and develop. First, people often withdraw from the

[8] *Ibid.*

[9] *Ibid.*, p. 429.

[10] Robert R. Blake and Jane S. Mouton, *Building a Dynamic Corporation Through Grid Organization Development,* Addison-Wesley, Reading, Mass., 1969, pp. 65-68.

conflict. If it is no longer possible to suppress the conflict between the community relations specialist and the mayor over the role the specialist is to play, he may try to withdraw from the conflict. One method of withdrawal is most decisive; he may quit or resign, thus ending the conflict and terminating his job. If this is the procedure he chooses, however, he should be sure that the economy is expanding and other means of employment are readily available; otherwise, he must be prepared for the trials of unemployment. In other words, withdrawal in this manner is not often a viable choice. At a less dramatic level, he may withdraw by attempting to avoid the mayor and by retreating into a position of performing his job "according to the book." Even though this action may lower the level of open conflict, neither the specialist nor the mayor (not to mention the other groups who may be interested in the issue) will be satisfied with the situation and with the way the job is being performed. This kind of defensive withdrawal position is the one that is portrayed by most critics of the public bureaucracy as "the normal procedure" of civil servants. This criticism goes back to Max Weber, the developer of the typology of bureaucracy. Although withdrawal may occasionally be successful, in most cases it is not a satisfactory resolution to conflict.

A second approach to resolving conflict is that of trying to smooth over the differences that are at the basis of the issue. Such an approach is almost tantamount to ignoring the issue, for to smooth over the differences means that people must be convinced that the factors over which they have been fighting are not important enough to continue the battle. Undoubtedly, this may be true in some cases, and when it is true, such a tactic, if handled properly, will resolve the conflict, with both sides vowing to "forgive and forget." In reality, this solution is neither practical nor ideal in most situations.

Third, one or more parties in a conflict may force a win or lose resolution. This is an especially enticing solution to the situation, if one side is strong enough to be sure they will win. If, for example, the community relations specialist is able to gain the support of the city council, the civil service commission, and the citizens' groups that he is working with, and if the mayor is not able to counterbalance those forces with any comparable coalition of power, the specialist may be tempted to force the issue of what his duties are as community relations specialist, because he knows that he can probably force the mayor to back down and accept his interpretation of the job requirements. As Mary Follett says, "This is the easiest way of dealing with conflict, the easiest for the moment but not usually successful in the long run. . . ."[11] While the issue may appear to be resolved, this type of resolution guarantees that at least one party involved in the conflict is going to be very dissatisfied. In such a case, the "defeated" party will usually attempt to develop a realignment of the coalitions, so that the conflict may be reopened with a resolution more favorable to the defeated party or one that will completely reverse the situation. After all, what self-respecting mayor would accept such public humiliation? The mayor can always point to the com-

[11] Metcalf and Urwick, p. 31.

munity relations specialist as the one who forced the conflict into the win-lose mode. A temporary victory is very likely to bring about a period of extended discomfort and a fear of future retribution if the tables are ever turned. A forced win-lose mode of resolution for conflicts may be unavoidable at times, but such a procedure is not always the best possible alternative when looking for methods to resolve conflict.

The fourth method of resolving conflict is the most commonly used approach, and it may be the best possible alternative in a majority of conflictful situations. This resolution is known as compromise. To again quote Mary Parker Follett:

(Compromise) is the way we settle most of our controversies; each side gives up a little in order to have peace, or, to speak more accurately, in order that the activity which has been interrupted by the conflict may go on.[12]

If neither the community relations specialist nor the mayor has the power to force a decision that would be totally satisfactory, the two of them may attempt to reach a compromise. According to the compromise, the community relations specialist may agree to spend half his time working directly for the mayor, while the mayor accepts the argument that the specialist needs to spend half of his time in direct communication with the citizens. It is also agreed that the specialist will attempt to present the mayor's programs to the public in these meetings, and that he will report directly to the mayor the feedback that is received while dealing with the public. In order to achieve this compromise, the community relations specialist gives up some of his freedom to speak openly to the public. Also, he is committed to release all information through the mayor's office, although the original job description stated that he was to represent all of the city organization and was to have full authority to release information for all departments. The mayor has given up his claim to the specialist's full-time efforts, instead agreeing to the concept of the specialist spending half his time in the field.

Most conflicts are resolved in this way. Compromise is often described, for instance, as being at the heart of politics, so much so that one of the most common definitions states that "politics is the art of compromise." It cannot be expected that those involved in administration, or implementation, within the political system will be involved any less in compromise. Even so, compromise may not be the ultimate and best resolution of the issue at hand. Compromise means that *everyone* involved in the battle has given up something that he or she desires; perhaps no one is totally satisfied with the agreed upon solution. Therefore, the agreement may not be a solution. The issue will probably be raised again at a future date, and this may lead to further conflict and the establishment of new compromises.

Herein lies the major problem with the four types of resolution that have

[12]*Ibid.*

been discussed. In every case, except perhaps in the case of total withdrawal, the conflict is allowed to be a recurring phenomenon. It will arise again, and the same issues will have to be confronted and resolved. In order to make progress and move on to new issues that need to be considered, a permanent resolution must be found for the current conflict in a way that will satisfy the combatants and allow them to spend their time on other issues. The way to accomplish this is to resolve the conflict in a fifth way in which the conflict is openly confronted by everyone involved and there is an attempt to employ a problem-solving attitude in attacking the situation. This is an attempt to achieve what Mary Parker Follett calls an "integrative" solution to conflict. When an integrative solution is achieved, it means that a solution has been found in which both or all of the combatants have found a place so that neither side has had to sacrifice anything.[13] Such a solution may sound like a dream, but there are occasions when integrative solutions can be found (although, admittedly, they cannot be found in a majority of cases); whatever the result, such a solution would appear to be a worthwhile goal to establish.

How can the community relations specialist and the mayor arrive at an integrative solution to their problem concerning the way the specialist is to fulfill his duties? After some discussion, they may arrive at a solution to their dilemma that is mutually satisfactory to both of them; one that allows both of them to achieve the basic goals that appeared to be placing them in conflict. First, the mayor may accept the idea that the community relations specialist needs to spend a majority of his time working directly with the citizens of the community, but the mayor may ask the specialist to be familiar with the mayor's policy stance and his reasoning so that the specialist can present them to the public. At the same time, the mayor may agree to the idea that the community relations specialist should represent the views of other elected officials and employees as long as he agrees to clearly identify the author of the view. Thus, the specialist can openly present the views of all city officials without negatively affecting the image of the mayor. Second, the community relations specialist may retain the right to feed back information from the community to any bureaucrat or official in the city, but he promises to make that information available to the mayor at the same time it is given to the others (usually through duplicate memoranda). In this manner, the mayor can be assured that he is receiving the maximum amount of information from the specialist while not being embarrassed by a lack of knowledge that is available to others. Finally, the problem of publicity might be solved by allowing the specialist to prepare press releases and other public information for anyone in the city, with a proviso that the mayor or his designee be given a copy of the information prior to its release (far enough in advance so that the mayor's office will have time to study the information involved). With such a proviso, the mayor's office will have the opportunity to join the other officials in sponsoring the release if he and the other officials so desire (although the mayor cannot remove the other officials'

---

[13] *Ibid.*, p. 32.

names). The mayor will also have a chance to attempt to stop releases or change them under these circumstances; but he will have to do so by contacting the originating officials, not by ordering the community relations specialist to stop the release. Once again, the mayor will have a chance to influence publicity or to prepare a proper rebuttal, thus being saved from unexpected embarrassment, while the specialist's ability to work with and for other officials in the city will be protected.

If such a solution to the conflict can be achieved, all sides will be benefited, for with a solution that meets the basic needs of everyone, the conflict should be resolved in a manner that will permanently resolve the issue and allow everyone involved to move on to other pressing problems. Conflict resolution of this sort is also the type of activity that enables an individual or organization to make the adjustments that are necessary in order to keep up with the changing environment of the world and its constantly shifting demands upon everyone and everything.

## CONFLICT AND THE ORGANIZATION

Individuals are regularly placed in conflictive situations. Organizations, as well as individuals, appear to be placed in conflictive situations; however, can the theory that is applied to conflict between individuals also be applied to conflict between and in organizations? A search of the literature shows an amazing similarity between discussions on these two types of conflict. This point has been stressed by Boulding in his book, *Conflict and Defense,* when he says,

Much of the theory of conflicting organizations . . . applies equally well either to organizations or to persons. The main difference lies in the greater capacity of organizations for growth and, therefore, for incompatability in their self-images. Persons are sharply limited in extent by their biological structure; organizations are much less limited in this way, though, even here, the biological limits on the capacity for the receipt of information and for the elaboration of images may be important. For this reason, organizational conflict is likely to be more extensive, more diffuse, and perhaps more dangerous than the conflict of persons. It is not, however, an essentially different system.[14]

It must be remembered, of course that two types of organizational conflict can occur: conflict *between* organizations and conflict *in* organizations. Both types are of great importance in deciding the success or failure of an organization and its manager. However, most of the current discussion will deal with conflict *in* organizations, because the focus of this part of our discussion deals with the internal aspects of the public bureaucracy at the departmental, or single organization, level.

[14] Kenneth Boulding, *Conflict and Defense.* Harper and Row, New York, 1963, p. 165.

Conflict is common between organizations; it is accepted as a natural occurrence. As was discussed in Chapters 2 and 3, our most accepted theory of politics (the pluralist approach) is based on the idea of competing interest groups, while the basic philosophy of our economic system (free enterprise) is based on the philosophy of business competition. In both cases, the basic premise or assumption that underscores all the rest of the logic states that competition guarantees that, in the case of politics, the largest possible number of citizens will have their interests represented, and that, in the case of business, those products desired by the public will be made available at the lowest price possible. Conflict is one of the vital factors leading to the proper functioning of the systems and the satisfaction of those people who are served.

These conflicts appear to occur for approximately the same reasons as those that lead to conflicts between individuals. The underlying sources of conflict can be condensed into three general categories: (1) competition for scarce resources (rivalry for a share of limited resources that are doled out by elected officials); (2) drives for autonomy (the attempt to gain control over programs and organizations so that outsiders cannot force "undesirable" ends or means on the public administrators or their bureaucracies); and (3) divergence of goals (differences of opinions among the various groups as to the goals of the government, as well as to the subunit goals of the divisions and departments). Not only are the reasons for the conflicts the same but also the reactions of the organizations are the same, although, as was noted above, organizations have to deal with a greater number of conflicts, many of which are of great intensity. For this reason,

Organizations are characteristically faced with more conflicts than can be dealt with, given available time capacities. The normal reaction is to focus attention on only a few of these, and these tend to be the conflicts for which short-run, routine solutions are available. For organizations successfully to confront the less programmed conflicts, it is frequently necessary to set up separate sub-units specifically to deal with such conflicts.[15]

When discussing conflict in a public agency, we are primarily interested in the way conflict affects three facets of that organization.[16] The first facet of importance is productivity—both quantitative and qualitative. The public organization is "better" if it produces more of a product or service that the public wants, if it is more innovative in finding out what the public wants and discovering ways to fulfill those desires, and if its output meets higher standards of quality than those of other similar organizations. The second important facet of the public agency that is affected is stability. Generally, an organization improves if it can increase its cohesiveness internally, and at the same time, increase

---

[15] Louis R. Pondy, "Organizational Conflict: Concepts and Models," *Administrative Science Quarterly, XII,* 301-302 (September 1967).

[16] *Ibid.,* p. 308.

its. "solvency" by developing additional support from interest groups and politicians who are outside the organization, thus assuring adequate political and financial support in the future. Third, adaptability is an essential facet of a successful public agency. The successful public agency will learn from its past experiences and improve its performance by changing to meet, understand, and use to its advantage various internal and environmental pressures. The important question is, What are the effects of internal conflict on the people in the organization and on the effectiveness of the bureaucracy? There are both negative and positive effects, and which outweighs the other will depend on the way the conflict is handled by the managers and employees of the agency. An examination of some of the negative and positive aspects of conflict in the organization will help to highlight the importance of properly managing conflict in a public organization.

## The Negative Effects of Conflict on Bureaucracy

Each of the three facets of organizational effectiveness can be, and often is, negatively influenced by conflict. Productivity is a measure of benefits produced for the cost incurred. Conflict regularly affects this equation in ways that either raise costs or lower benefits. Conflict is often negatively valued by organization members, because most people do not like to be placed in the uncomfortable position of having to confront a situation that they realize may change the balance of power and responsibilities for everyone concerned. Of course, there are always those individuals who thrive on conflict, but they are in the minority unless the organization is managed in a manner that encourages open conflict. Even though individuals do not care to deal with conflict, they can be induced to do so for a price. Increased rewards help to counterbalance the costs to the individual, but increased rewards affect the productivity of the organization, for in order to increase rewards, the organization's costs go up without a guaranteed increase in benefits that are produced.

By the same token, once a conflict is in existence, the people who are involved may become so absorbed in the issue that they neglect their normal duties and throw themselves into the conflict with furious abandon. College professors have been known to become so inflamed over an issue that they have spent weeks writing nasty, detailed, and lengthy memos back and forth; at the same time, they attempt to gain academic allies through other types of persuasion, and fail totally to carry on their other duties of teaching, counseling, and research. Any employee of governmental organizations can recite similar experiences, where a conflict has become so central to those participating that work has been put aside until the battle is won or a truce is declared. In such cases, it is obvious that productivity, in the form of services produced, has been affected negatively.

Conflict also affects the interaction of the participants. Withdrawal is a common reaction in organizational conflict just as it is in personal conflict. Individuals, different departments, or battling segments of the organization often stop communicating when conflict occurs. Such a reaction has several negative impacts on the organization. Coordination ceases or is significantly decreased; therefore, the problem remains unresolved and may, in addition, set off a chain reaction of derivative conflicts that complicate an already murky situation. The communication that does occur takes place in the form of written communication; in addition, Berelson and Steiner note that

. . .conflict between leaders and subordinates tends to increase the number and concreteness of the organization's regulations, and vice versa—i.e., regulations go along with conflict.

Conflict can refer here not only to overt disagreements but even to differing perceptions of what various people are supposed to do.[17]

All these problems, in turn, have a negative impact on the stability of the organization. Personalities become involved, and the opposing parties in the dispute develop a dislike for each other. If personality is introduced into the conflict, the internal cohesiveness of the organization is often permanently damaged. This is a factor that has had dramatic illustration in the world of sports, but it has not been publicly noted in many other areas of life.

Internal conflict often leads to the wrong use of external contacts while affecting internal stability. Instead of using the good will and "I.O.U.'s" that have been developed with outside interest groups to help the organization achieve its goals within the political system, the various individuals or factions of the conflict will often attempt to use their resources to force their particular solution upon the other participants in the conflict. While this tactic may lead to "victory" for one group in the organization, the resources that were available for fighting the political battle with other competing organizations may have been depleted, often making the victory rather hollow, for it is then necessary to redevelop all the contacts, favors, and other elements that add up to "solvency" in the political world.

As productivity suffers, stability decreases, and organizations get locked into noncommunicative stances, with everyone working under a system of specific rules and regulations, it is inevitable that the organization's adaptability will be diminished. A "win-or-lose, all-or-nothing" attitude in a conflict means that very little learning can take place. In order to learn, one must not "know everything" or already have all the answers; it must be possible to admit incomplete knowledge and errors. This is not possible if the conflict has taken a negative twist. Without learning, the public agency cannot change, and change

---

[17] Bernard Berelson and Gary A. Steiner, *Human Behavior: An Inventory of Scientific Findings,* Harcourt Brace and World, New York, 1964, p. 377.

is one of the constant necessities of political reality. Thus, according to this doctrine, conflict is once again detrimental to the organization.[18]

Because of an overemphasis of the negative effects of conflict, a set of assumptions has developed that has influenced the way managers have run their agencies. These assumptions have held that (1) conflict can and should be avoided; (2) conflict primarily comes from personality problems in the organization; (3) conflict causes the people involved to react inappropriately; (4) conflict results in polarization of perceptions, sentiments, and behavior; therefore (5) conflict is "bad" for the organization, and conflict is a sign of poor management.[19]

## The Positive Effects of Conflict on Bureaucracy

Partially in reaction to this philosophy and partially because of further development of behavioral understanding of conflict, a newer set of assumptions has begun to gain acceptance. According to the new assumptions: (1) conflict is inevitable; (2) the causes of conflict can be found only by examining the total situation; (3) conflict is one of the primary elements in bringing about needed change; therefore (4) conflict may be "good" for the organization and may be a sign of proper management.[20] One way to understand the views toward this positive approach to conflict is to quote directly from the writings of two authorities in the study of conflict management. Joe Kelly states that

research evidence suggests that tension needs to be reappraised and that the exploitation of *healthy* tension can (a) stimulate learning, (b) serve to "internalize" the problems of other managers, (c) increase critical vigilance and self appraisal, and (d) induce decision makers to examine conflicting values more discerningly (including their own) when they are making decisions. . . . In a positive sense, conflict may be deliberately created to compel the organization to define goals, change processes, and reallocate resources.[21]

In the same general vein, Morton Deutsch maintains that

---

[18] Many organizations attempt to deal with this problem of conflict by having special officials, whose sole or primary duty is to take over the conflictive situations, thus relieving the other managers of this task. Many governments have, for example, special labor negotiators who spend a major portion of their time hammering out and interpreting contracts.

[19] Joe Kelly, *Organizational Behavior,* Richard D. Irwin, Homewood, Ill., 1969, p. 501.

[20] *Ibid.,* pp. 503-505.

[21] Joe Kelly, "Make Conflict Work for You," *Harvard Business Review, XLVIII,* 103-113 (July-August, 1970).

it (conflict) prevents stagnation, it stimulates interest and curiosity, it is the medium through which problems can be aired and solutions arrived at; it is the root of personal and social change. Conflict is often part of the process of testing and assessing oneself and, as such, may be highly enjoyable as one experiences the pleasure of full and active use of one's capacities. Conflict, in addition, demarcates groups and personal identities; external conflict often fosters internal cohesiveness.[22]

From these two quotes, it becomes obvious that those who accept this philosophy toward conflict feel that it is not only inevitable but that it is also an essential part of management in any organization in the modern world. When once again examining the three facets of the organization that were discussed from the negative viewpoint (productivity, stability, and adaptability), it is possible to see that a positive interpretation can be made for the effects of conflict; this positive interpretation can be defended just as strongly as was the negative view.

Productivity need not be diminished either in quantity or quality by conflict. Indeed, competition, one type of conflict, has regularly proved to increase both the quantity and quality of a product or service. One of the constant complaints raised by detractors of the public bureaucracy is that the security and lack of competition, which are common conditions of governmental organizations, lead to complacency, inefficient service, and a general lowering of performance among civil servants. In such cases, when the criticisms are appropriate, conflict, at least in the form of competition, is probably necessary in order to improve governmental service; other types of external or internal conflict may help to bring about the level of service that is expected. Both Deutsch and Kelly point out several ways that conflict may help to bring about greater stability and adaptability within organizations. Chief executives often utilize conflict situations by making dramatic organizational changes, which they may have been mulling over for some time. Adaptability is served because a time of conflict or crisis creates a need for reexamination of "the way things are done," and it allows all sides of an issue to be considered under the stark light of necessity. In such a case, the various sides are necessary to a proper resolution of the problem. In his book, *Thirteen Days,* Robert Kennedy leaves the careful reader with the impression that the situation required a polarization of ideas and individuals into "Hawks and Doves." Had the Hawks not existed, it would have been necessary to invent them, so that the Kennedy–McNamara team could test their ideas against an opposing perspective, thereby having the rationality of their proposals probed to the fullest extent possible. In such a situation, President Kennedy needed alternatives that he could follow if the original plans failed. Conflict within the National Security Council was an essential part of Kennedy's ability

[22] Morton Deutsch, "Conflicts: Productive and Destructive," *Journal of Social Issues, XXV,* 19 (January 1969).

to deal with an even bigger and unimaginably more dangerous world power confrontation.[23]

The secret to meaningful and positive conflict in the organization is the management of the conflict. If the conflict is properly handled by those who run the organization, the result should be beneficial to the organization, its members, and the public it serves. Productivity should be maintained or improved and stability increased; the organization should make the appropriate adaptations to inside and outside pressures. Internally, especially, the result should be constructive, leading to a more cooperative relationship and allowing the participants to focus on latent issues not previously perceived and dealt with. All of this requires special skills on the part of the manager, however, and these skills apply to all of the management operation, not just those periods filled with conflicts.

## METHODS FOR MANAGING CONFLICT

Two of the accepted aspects of public administration in the current era are confrontation and conflict. A city manager spends a portion of every day dealing with conflicts that arise between city departments; city, state, or national officials and programs; city administrators and elected officials or citizens; city employees and management; and competing interest groups in the community. The city manager must accomplish this, and, at the same time, maintain a reputation for being nonpolitical (at least in a partisan sense). As the level of government involved in the conflict rises to the state or national level, there is no lessening of the conflict that must be managed. Perhaps the type of confrontation and conflict varies as officials at different levels of government do their work, but the amount of conflict and the intensity of the issues in no way diminish.

The way the conflict is resolved and the effect of the conflict on the well-being of the bureaucracy are directly traceable to the way the organization is equipped to cope with the problem. In turn, the organization's ability to cope with conflict is controlled by the personality and skills of the top manager. Deutsch has pointed out that

. . . a conflict is more likely to be resolved cooperatively if powerful and prestigeful third parties encourage such a resolution and help to provide problem-solving resources (institutions, facilities, personnel, social norms, and procedures) to expedite discovery of a mutually satisfactory solution.[24]

[23] Robert F. Kennedy, *Thirteen Days; A Memoir of the Cuban Missile Crisis,* W. W. Norton, New York, 1969.

[24] Deutsch, p. 29.

The "third party" in a public agency is most often the manager. Although the city manager, for example, may be a party to the conflict on occasion, her role is most often that of conciliator or mediator. The manager may have to act as arbitrator also on occasion, but this role must be played as sparingly as possible if she is to maintain the trust and support of everyone concerned. It must always be understood, however, that the public manager's task is not to eliminate conflict and ambiguity from the city organization. Instead, the manager's job is the containment of these conditions at levels and in forms that are at least humane, tolerable, and low in cost; more hopefully, the conflict will be channeled into forms that might be positive in contribution to the government, its employees, and ultimately to the citizens and taxpayers.

## Organizational Controls over Conflict

Conflict has a great potential for destruction or for strengthening the organization. In order to minimize the destructive potential, institutional structures are established, roles are developed, norms of behavior are evolved, and rules and specific procedures are promulgated and spelled out in a written manual. The *structure* of the city, state, or national bureaucracy is established in a manner that shields most employees, allowing them to go about their jobs while reporting to a single superior. For this reason, some of the employees at the lower levels of the bureaucracy fail to recognize and appreciate the problems facing their supervisors. These first-line employees do not face the diverse pressures that build as one moves up through the system. Again, supervisors report to managers, allowing the managers to handle the negotiation and competition for resources and support among the various groups influencing the organization. The hierarchical concept, which is at the foundation of Weber's typology of bureaucracy, divides the task of dealing with conflict among the employees of the government; this limits the amount of conflict handled by each individual while giving that person the power needed to handle the conflict with which he is faced.

Every public jurisdiction has numerous people in the *role* of conflict handler. Among these individuals are mediators, conciliators, referees, judges, or police officers; their primary job is to see that conflicts are resolved. Likewise, these public employees have other public employees who carry out similar tasks for them inside the bureaucracy. While one police officer is attempting to resolve domestic squabbles and trying to break up fights between gangs of youths, another officer is at the city council meeting representing the police officers association in the negotiations over pay raises for next year. In fact, the officer on the street will have both the internal organizational authorities (the police chief and his staff) and the employee representatives (association officials) present at any such meeting. This guarantees police officers that they can go about their jobs and be assured that any conflict arising about the conditions under which they work or the way in which they do their jobs will be handled by competent representatives in a fair and equitable manner.

The manner in which the conflict is handled will depend to a great extent on the *norms* that have been accepted by those involved in the confrontation. These norms include such ideas as "fairness," "justice," and "nonviolence." When the Afro-American Police Officers Association decided to fight the racial bias of the hiring policies of the Chicago Police Department, the issue was not settled by a shoot-out on the streets of the city. Instead, the officers acted in a way that was prescribed by the norms of the organization in which they worked, with the officers appealing through the normal channels while continuing their routine on the job. The norms of the city government, and of the police profession, required that the conflict should not interfere with their work. This also kept the conflict from becoming "personalized"; the individuals involved on both sides did not attach the issues to specific officials or allow attitudes toward individuals to affect the ability to function as a department. The norms limited the kind of actions and statements that were acceptable; thus, these norms led to a series of court battles that culminated in the freezing of funds from the federal government until appropriate corrections were made in the city's hiring practices. Today, the greatest example of the use of norms in this way is in the United States Senate, where debate is unlimited but where norms for the conflict maintain the conflict at a level that allows the senators to continue and solidify their relationships over long periods of time.

Finally, specific *rules and procedures* for the handling of conflicts must be accepted by all the participants. The Afro-American Police Officer's Association knew when and how to present their demands. They first appealed through the police department, and then they appealed to the city government, and especially Mayor Daley, who they realized wielded an inordinate amount of power over such issues. The association also knew the rules for handling the expansion of the conflict. They very quickly moved from "hinting" that they would take action outside the city structure to "explicitly communicating" that they were taking the case to the federal courts. Once in the courts, both sides hired experts in handling this type of legal conflict, so that each side could be assured that their position would be properly presented and that the actions of the other side would be properly checked.

These structures, roles, norms, and rules are built into every organization; in some cases, they regulate how force may be used (in sporting events, such as football and hockey, or in the rules of business competition) to measure the power relations of the disputants without resorting to force (as in collective bargaining) or removing power as the basis for determining the outcome of the conflict (as is often the case in judicial decisions or in arbitration). Without such systems for channeling and limiting conflict, any public agency could be torn apart by the many forces that constantly battle for control. Numerous functions and processes in the normal operation of the organization help in achieving the proper balance between the competing forces. The entry and exit systems of public agencies help to insulate the organizations. Employees in any government agency usually self-select the organization to which they owe allegiance, so this selection controls their actions; if it does not, the threat of expulsion or separation may accomplish what loyalty cannot achieve. Other kinds of sanctions, both formal and informal, can help to limit conflict. Quite often the informal sanctions applied by surrounding employees may be more successful in limiting aggressive action than any formal steps available to the manager. Other procedures and documents, such as the budget and its annual cycle, help to maintain the organizational equanimity. In the end, though, all of these procedures and systems for maintaining a healthy type of conflict are dependent upon the top management of the agency.

### Managerial Rules for Conflict Situations

The most critical influence serving to guide and control conflict in any public organization is the manager. The manager sets the tone of interpersonal relations for employees, as well as for contacts between the agency and the public that it serves. This is true whether the official being considered is a university president, a department head in a large governmental jurisdiction, or the head of a seven-person operation in a small town. The attitude taken by the manager when he or she is faced by a conflict gives clues to all of those observing as to how they should handle similar situations. Also, the manager is the individual who ratifies the rules and structures that are used to carry out any battles that develop.

The ideal toward which the manager should strive is that of creating a situation within the organization in which there is a basic understanding of the goals of the organization and a confidence in the ability of the organization to attain those goals; there must also be an acceptance of debate as to what means are best for achieving the goals, because there has not been the development of a dogma surrounding the processes of the agency. This ideal situation, which applies to both individuals and organizations, has been described by Deutsch in the following way:

Neither undue smugness for satisfaction with things as they are, nor a sense of helplessness, terror or rage are likely to lead to an optimal motivation to recognize and face a problem or conflict. Nor will a passive readiness to acquiesce to the demands of the environment; nor will the willingness to fit oneself into the environment no matter how poorly it fits oneself. Optimal motivation, rather, presupposes an alert readiness to be dissatisfied with things as they are and a freedom to confront one's environment without excessive fear, combined with a confidence in one's capacities to persist in the face of obstacles.[25]

In this kind of atmosphere, it is possible for people to expend their aggressions and at the same time to withstand a fair amount of anxiety. Public managers,

[25] *Ibid.*, p. 21.

especially, can then welcome uncertainty as an opportunity to restructure their environment.[26]

In order to create an atmosphere that functions positively in situations of conflict, the public manager must have a personality that contains at least four important traits.[27] First, the leader must be high in tolerance of conflict. In other words, she will not shun or avoid conflict but will instead face and deal with conflict openly and readily. Second, an integrative leader must be low in authoritarianism; the manager should have a participative management style that welcomes suggestions and constructive criticism, and she should be directive and supportive in giving orders rather than following a rigid, militaristic order style. Third, a successful manager of conflict should have distinctive proclivities for bargaining. This is harder than it seems because bargaining, which involves a great deal of persuasion and reconsideration of issues, can take much longer than simply giving an order that must be followed. Finally, the first three characteristics all bespeak a fourth, which is that an integrative manager must be able to recognize the legitimacy of her opponent (not necessarily the opponent's position on the issue but always the legitimacy of the individual and his *right to hold an opposing position*). Managers who successfully cultivate these characteristics in their own personalities (and these characteristics can be at least expanded through training if the individual sincerely wishes to do so) will also cultivate the same kind of characteristics in the organizations that they manage. This is true even though public agencies have the additional problem of having to deal with political overseers, for managers who have this type of personality will apply these rules to dealings with political "superiors" just as they do to internal subordinates. This has been shown on numerous occasions at all levels of government.

However, it takes more than the proper personality on the part of the manager if conflict is going to be positively used by a public agency. In addition to a desire and the ability to cope with conflict, a set of ground rules is useful, as well as a chance to practice the use of those rules. Two sets of ground rules have

---

[26] Kelly, "Make Conflict Work for You." This idea is further developed by George Labovitz when he makes the following criticism of industry that is equally applicable to government.:

Psychologists tell us when a confident, secure person meets a frustrating obstacle, he will be likely to aggressively strike (sic) out when he encounters it. On the other hand, an individual who is pessimistic about his own ability tends to get aggressive inwardly. The paradox . . . is that although industry prefers the solid, confident individual especially for executives, it does not provide, or tolerate, outlets for emotional manifestations of frustrations. . . . All of which may explain why the public image of corporation presidents is one of robust health and confidence, born of happy meeting of aspirations and abilities. The junior executive, however, is seen in gray flannel, overworked, and nursing an ulcer; the result of frustration from unsatisfied needs.

Labovitz, "The Individual Versus the Organization," *Advanced Management Journal, XXXV*, 63 (January 1970).

[27] Managerial style is discussed in greater depth in the next chapter of this text.

been developed, one for individual managers and one for use in organizational conflict; while these sets of rules are incomplete (primarily because of incomplete knowledge), they are at least a foundation on which the practice of positive conflict resolution can begin; the rules may be expanded as new ones are proven to be effective.

Joe Kelly has established a series of ground rules which he says should help the "hard-pressed executive" to apply the theories about conflict in a way that will help the individuals who are involved to achieve "a creative, acceptable, and realistic resolution of conflict."[28] Every executive will play one of three roles in a conflict and, at one time or another, will undoubtedly be placed in all of the roles. The executive can be the initiator, the defendant, or the conciliator. The rules for each are as follows:

*. . . for the initiator*

Start at a low level and advance on a narrow front on one or two related issues, following a well-documented route.

Maintain second-strike capability.

Pick the terrain with care; where and when the case is heard is vital.

Be prepared to escalate, either to a higher level in the organization or to a meeting of peers.

Make it objective, private, and routine; above all, keep it formal.

Search for reaction; remember that you may have to settle for token conformity in the first instance.

Reinforce success and abandon failure.

*. . . for the defendant*

Do not overreact; keep your cool; let the initiator state his case; listen carefully and neutrally.

Ascertain scale of the strike; try to build a decision tree with "go/no go" decision rules.

Ask for the name of the game (e.g., Is it a courtroom? If yes, ask for the counsel of the defense.)

Ask not only for an exact definition of the charge, but also for the evidence with, if possible, identification of the sources.

If it is a "minor crime," be prepared to plead guilty.

Ascertain the various lines of appeal.

Consider the option "Waiting Brief" and be prepared to reserve your defense; take notes, above all, let the initiator score somewhere—and then try for informality.

*. . . for the conciliator*

Get the parties of the dispute to realize that conflict is not only universal but a necessary requisite of change.

Break down the attitudinal consistency of each disputant (belief that his attitudes do not contain contradictory elements).

---

[28] Kelly, "Make Conflict Work for You," p. 111.

After breaking down frozen but antithetical attitudes of the disputants, minimize their individual "loss of face."

Break the conflict into fractional workable components.

Consider common enemy, high interaction, shared subordinate goal strategies. Remember, nobody loves a go-between.[29]

When these rules are followed, the public administrator may find that the debates, confrontations, competitions for scarce resources, and other types of conflict which he or she regularly faces are not only kept within bounds but are also helpful in maintaining a vital and responsive public bureaucracy.

Conflict follows a predictable pattern in an organization just as it does between individuals, with the group working through three phases: (a) clarification of the issue; (b) evaluation of the issue; and (c) the decision of what to do with the issue. Mary Parker Follett worked out a set of meaningful regulations for making organizational conflict constructive. That set of rules is summarized in the following generalizations.[30]

1. Be open. All sides must put their cards on the table, thus uncovering the conflict or bringing the real issue(s) into the open. When this is done, "evaluation often leads to reevaluation," and when a reevaluation of interests has occurred, it often leads to realignment of groups involved in the conflict.
2. Search diligently for the significant rather than the dramatic features of controversy. "There is too great a tendency (perhaps encouraged by popular journalism) to deal with the dramatic moments, forgetting that these are not always the most significant moments."[31]
3. Take the demands of all sides and break them up in their constituent parts. Included in this step is the examination of symbols, that is, the careful scrutiny of the language used to see what it really means.
4. Clarify all the issues and try to find ways to resolve the conflict that will allow all sides to achieve their significant desires. This is often impossible at the rhetorical and theoretical levels (and may be impossible at any level); but such a solution may be found by focusing the attention of the disputants on concrete proposals for action to resolve the conflict. Quite often, "disagreement disappears when theorizing ends and the question is of some definite activity to be undertaken."[32]
5. Make sure that an individual who specializes in handling conflicts is available to all combatants; this person can anticipate the responses that each side will

---

[29] *Ibid.*

[30] This discussion is based on: Metcalf and Urwick, pp. 38-45.

[31] *Ibid.,* p. 40.

[32] *Ibid.,* p. 46.

carry out to various alternatives so that many of the steps in settling the conflict may be passed over or at least accelerated. All sides should recognize the need for such an individual, and should agree to the use of a conciliator/ mediator when the conflict reaches the appropriate stage of deadlock.

These rules are the classic set of regulations that have been applied to labor negotiations in both the private and public sphere. They are also applicable to most other conflict situations. A final element, the willingness of the parties in conflict to adhere to the rules, will influence the success or failure of regulating and guaranteeing constructive conflict. In the political world of public administration, there are numerous temptations to break the rules. When negotiating with labor organizations, management negotiators have been known to agree to higher wage settlements than was expected the council could or would agree to; in these cases, management hoped that they could escape the onus of employee disfavor while claiming to the council that they would go along with whatever the council finally decided. Public officials have been known to make promises to community groups that could not be fulfilled. Instead of squarely facing the issue, many public conflicts get embroiled in irrelevant issues, much to the pleasure of those who stand to gain by diverting attention from the more basic issues. In each of these cases, however, the conflicts ultimately tend to get out of hand, to take destructive routes, and often to lead to the downfall of political and administrative leaders. Thus, it behooves those who are committed to a policy of constructive conflict to establish the "rules of the game" in a way that will lead to acceptance of, and adherence to, the rules. This is most likely to occur when:

1. The rules are known to all, unambiguous in interpretation, consistent throughout, and unbiased;
2. It is expected by everyone that all sides will adhere to the rules;
3. Violators are quickly publicized, therefore known by all significant parties interested in the particular issue *or in maintaining a system of fair play*;
4. There is significant social approval for adherence to the rules and significant social disapproval for violators;
5. Adherence to the rules has been rewarding to those involved, while uncontrolled conflict has proven to be expensive in the past;
6. The parties involved believe it would be profitable to be able to apply the rules in future conflicts.[33]

Not only are these conditions essential to the acceptance of the rules of conflict but also within the conditions are the reasons for believing that the rules will be approved. Most parties to a conflict see the value of a consistent and enduring set of regulations governing conflict. As long as such a sentiment continues among participants in an organization, conflict can be used as a positive tool for improving the delivery of services to the public.

[33] Deutsch, p. 25.

## SUMMARY

Conflict is an integral part of our daily life, as it is of any public agency. Its value or cost to everyone concerned is decided by the way the conflict is defined and handled and the result that follows the conclusion of the conflict. Conflict is the struggle over resources or ideas, between two or more parties, caused by the perception on the part of the contending parties that both or all cannot have what they desire. Conflict usually occurs when one or more parties believe the normal channels of grievance resolution are closed to them, and conflict, therefore, requires extra-normal procedures for its resolution. The definition of conflict must include references to the *conditions* that cause it to occur, the *perceptions* that individuals have of the situation and its participants, the *feelings* that the situation generates in the observers and participants, the *actions* that take place, and the *processes* that are established to channel the activities.

Individual conflict is usually based on role ambiguity or role conflict; this is true because conflict is a social phenomenon, and role theory deals with the individual in a social context. Individuals usually react to conflict by attempting to suppress or ignore the situation as long as possible. If it cannot be ignored, the conflict will eventually be resolved by: (1) withdrawing from the situation; (2) smoothing over the issue; (3) forcing a "win or lose" resolution; (4) compromising; or (5) employing a problem-solving attitude in seeking an "integrative" solution.

Within an organization, we are interested in the way that conflict affects productivity, stability, and adaptability. Whether the conflict has a positive or negative impact on the organization depends on the way that management handles the situation. If the conflict becomes personalized, if it causes people to neglect their normal tasks, or if it leads to a proliferation of rules, regulations, and written communication, the conflict is deleterious to the organization. If, on the other hand, the manager is able to use skillfully the structures, roles, norms, and rules that exist within the organization to control conflict, the conflict will lead to healthy, meaningful, exploratory behavior that is a tonic for both the organization and the individuals involved.

# BIBLIOGRAPHY

Anderson, Harold H., ed., *Creativity and Its Cultivation*, McGraw-Hill, New York, 1958.

Bennis, Warren G., *Changing Organizations*, McGraw-Hill, New York, 1966.

Bennis, Warren G., Kenneth D. Berne, and Robert Chin, eds., *The Planning of Change*, Holt, Rinehart and Winston, New York, 1964.

Berelson, Bernard, and Gary A. Steiner, *Human Behavior: An Inventory of Scientific Findings*, Harcourt Brace and World, New York, 1964.

Blake, Robert R., and Jane S. Mouton, *Building a Dynamic Corporation Through Grid Organization Development*, Addison-Wesley, Reading, Mass., 1969.

Boulding, Kenneth, *Conflict and Defense*, Harper and Row, New York, 1963.

Deutsch, Morton, "Conflicts: Productive and Destructive," *Journal of Social Issues, XXV*, 5-41 (January 1969).

Downs, Anthony, *Inside Bureaucracy*, Little, Brown, Boston, 1967.

Follett, Mary Parker, *Creative Experience*, Peter Smith, New York, 1924.

Follett, Mary Parker, *Dynamic Administration: The Collected Papers of Mary Parker Follett*, Henry C. Metcalf and Lyndall Urwick, eds., Harper and Brothers, New York, 1940.

Kahn, Robert L., et al., *Organizational Stress: Studies in Role Conflict and Ambiguity*, Wiley, New York, 1964.

Katz, Daniel, and Robert L. Kahn, *The Social Psychology of Organizations*, Wiley, New York, 1966.

Kelly, Joe, *Organizational Behavior*, Richard D. Irwin, Homewood, Ill., 1969.

Kennedy, Robert F., *Thirteen Days; A Memoir of the Cuban Missile Crisis*, W.W. Norton, New York, 1969.

March, James G., *Handbook of Organizations*, Rand McNally, Chicago, 1965.

March, James G., and Herbert A. Simon, *Organizations*, Wiley, New York, 1958.

Moynihan, Daniel P., *Maximum Feasible Misunderstanding*, Free Press, New York, 1969.

Rapaport, Anatol, *Fights, Games, and Debates*, University of Michigan, Ann Arbor, 1960.

Schelling, Thomas C., *The Strategy of Conflict*, Harvard University, Cambridge, Mass., 1960.

Scott, William G., *The Management of Conflict: Appeals Systems in Organizations*, Richard D. Irwin, Homewood, Ill., 1966.

Simon, Herbert A., Donald W. Smithburg, and Victor A. Thompson, *Public Administration*, Alfred A. Knopf, New York, 1950.

Thomas, John M., and Warren G. Bennis, eds., *Management of Change and Conflict*, Penguin Books, Baltimore, 1972.

# MOTIVATION: MODELS OF INCENTIVES FOR PUBLIC EMPLOYEES

*The noblest motive is the public good.*

*Sir Richard Steele*

Earlier chapters of this section on management have dealt with several of the processes that must be understood by a public administrator who wishes to be successful in his chosen profession. This chapter changes from a focus on process to the problem of understanding and working with other people. In the end, no manager can accomplish the complex tasks placed before a public agency unless the manager is able to motivate the other civil servants to work at their fullest potential; only then is it possible to lead them in a meaningful, coordinated attack on the goals that have been established for the agency by the policy-makers.

# CHAPTER 11

Success or failure is only partially dependent on the technical expertise of the manager. Much of the success or failure depends on the manager's understanding of the people surrounding his or her position. This statement is not meant to denigrate the necessity of understanding of the various skills essential to the operation of a modern city or state, but it is important to comprehend the idea that is being expressed. For example, city managers are seldom released from their positions because they lack technical skills. It is possible to buy good accounting, engineering, or public health skills. City managers usually lose their jobs because they do not know how to get along with city employees, the council members, or the local constituent groups, such as the neighborhood associations or the businessmens' clubs. Similarly, complaints registered against employees working within the bureaucracy are usually not complaints about the lack of expertise; instead, the complaints deal with the way other employees, or the public, are treated by the individual against whom the complaint is lodged. This is especially true when employees complain about their superiors. Some of the bitterest strikes by public employees have centered on complaints about the way the managers have handled their employees rather than on wages. In other words, human relations skills are among the most important tools required for a public administrator to be successful.

An important step in becoming a successful manager is to develop an understanding of motivation, which is that force within an individual that incites or impels him or her to action. This chapter deals with two types of theories about motivation—human-relations theories and rational theories—and then considers the role of money, or material rewards, in the total concept of motivation.

## DEFINITION

No one has ever observed a motivation. Motivation is a construct that is used by those who study human behavior to explain why people act as they do; therefore, it is a meaningful and useful way to talk about behavior. Three elements—needs, drives, and goals—interact in motivation, and together they make up the complete cycle regardless of how complicated the theories become that relate the cycle to human beings.

Needs are created whenever an individual has either a psychological or physiological imbalance. Psychologically, an individual experiences an imbalance, for instance, when he misses the social interaction of other people because of some type of isolation. An example of a physical imbalance may be recognized the next time you are hungry.

A drive is created because of the imbalance that exists within the individual. This drive may be consciously recognized; however, in many cases, a drive may develop subconsciously. An individual may recognize the sense of loneliness and may purposefully set out to find companionship. On the other hand, companionship may be a subconscious goal, with an individual looking for interaction with another person without the realization that another's company is being sought. The need for nourishment will create a drive to find food. (It is important in this case to appreciate the difference between eating out of habit and eating because one is really hungry.)

The drive moves one toward a goal, which is at the end of the cycle. (Actually, the word "end" is improper, because there is usually no "end" to a cycle; rather, the cycle repeats after an interval of time because most needs are only temporarily satisfied.) The goal can be almost anything that will alleviate the need. A period of social interaction with friends will usually remove the feeling of loneliness. Eating will mitigate the sense of hunger. Thus, social interaction, and food and drink can be said to be the goals in these examples.

At no point in the cycle, or in the examples given, is it possible to see the motives; only the behavior of the individual can be perceived. The explanation behind the behavior is what we refer to as the motive; still, this model seems to be valid since it allows us to both explain behavior and to predict how individuals will behave under certain given circumstances. With this very elementary definition of motivation, let us move on to a discussion of motivation and its influence on workers in the public bureaucracy.

## THEORIES OF MOTIVATION

Early theories about motivation—assumptions used by the Taylorites—were simple and easy to apply. In fact, Fred Luthans, in describing this period, says that the assumptions are "as simple as one, two, three."

1. Personnel primarily are economically motivated and secondarily desire security and good working conditions. (A nonauthoritarian type of supervision is considered as part of conditions.)
2. Provision of the above rewards to personnel will have a positive effect on their morale.
3. There is a positive correlation between morale and productivity.[1]

The early theorists felt that the answer to solving all problems of motivation, to raising productivity, and to delivering a better product or service to the public was to make sure that employees were happy, and the best way to make employees happy was to reward them economically.

Unfortunately, these early theories, while being dramatically successful for a short while, soon reached the limit of their ability either to explain motivation or to serve as useful theories for practicing managers. As these factors were developed and applied to management, and as the limits of their impact were reached, it was discovered that the fulfillment of these goals led to the appearance of a whole new set of needs with their reciprocal drives. New problems were created for management as the old ones became less important. These mounting problems led to a renewed interest in motivation among behavioral

[1] Fred Luthans, *Organizational Behavior: A Modern Behavioral Approach to Management*, McGraw-Hill, New York, 1973, pp. 482-483.

scientists and management researchers; from this continuing research has come a series of new theories.

Although all theories of motivation attempt to explain why people work and what will increase their inclinations to function efficiently and effectively within the organization, not all the theories view the motivational process in the same way. Two major approaches to an explanation of motivation have developed during the last thirty years; much of the basic material overlaps, but the differences that do exist are significant. For want of better names, the two schools of thought are called the "human relations school" and the "rational school." Each helps to explain the idea of motivation, but it is likely that any final theory of motivation (the idea that a "final theory" is possible is itself theoretical) will include major aspects of both schools, because neither is complete in and of itself. Therefore, a discussion of additional models of motivation that have appeared during the last decade, and that draw upon both schools, will follow the discussion of the two major schools.

## Motivation as the Result of Human Relations

The human relations school advocates believe that motivation to work for the organization is directly attached to the morale, satisfaction, or happiness of the employee. Since this is true, when attempting to motivate people, the important fact to understand is what creates a sense of high morale within people; the answer to this question is found in two theories of motivation—those of Abraham Maslow and Frederick Herzberg (see Figure 7).

**Maslow's "Hierarchy of Needs."** The first reinterpretation of human motivation came from Abraham Maslow.[2] After observing reactions of the many people that he had worked with in a clinical setting, Maslow came to the conclusion that the human being is a perpetually wanting animal. It is impossible to satisfy all the needs of an individual because an individual has a hierarchy of needs. This hierarchy can be broken into five major categories: (1) physiological needs; (2) security (Maslow uses the term "safety"); (3) affiliation (Maslow uses the term "love")[3]; (4) esteem; and (5) self-actualization.

*Physiological* needs are the most basic needs of the individual; these are the basic requirements of food, clothing, and shelter. Such basic needs are necessary to the proper functioning of the body, and the majority of an individual's time will be spent in fulfilling these needs until they have been satisfied. Once this level of needs is temporarily and adequately satiated, the next level of needs

---

[2] Abraham Maslow, "A Theory of Human Motivation," *Psychological Review, L,* 370-396 (July 1943).

[3] These two terms have been changed because Maslow's terms can lead to a misunderstanding of the hierarchy as it applies to organization theory.

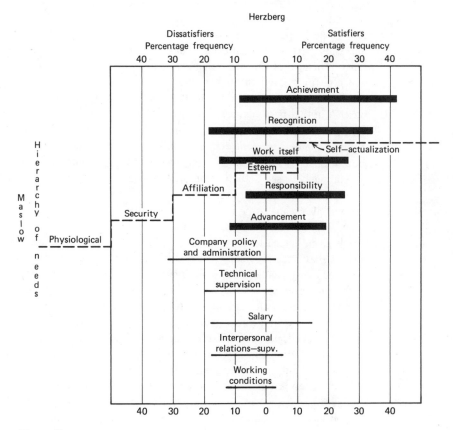

**Figure 7**

will become important. This leads to an attempt to satisfy the newly dominating needs. (This is true at each level; as the current level of needs is satisfied, the next level becomes dominant.)

*Security* needs are essentially the needs for physical safety and the desire to be free from the fear of deprivation of the physiological needs. In other words, the second level of needs is concerned with the future availability of present physiological necessities. Such problems as maintaining property, obtaining permanent shelter, and guaranteeing the availability of food are the prominent factors at this level of the hierarchy.

Once physiological and security needs are adequately satisfied, *affiliation* becomes the most important factor influencing behavior. Since humans are social creatures, they want to develop meaningful relations with other people or groups of people. It is important for a human to feel he or she belongs to, and is accepted by, other humans.

*Esteem* becomes the dominant need soon after one is accepted as a member of a group. Once an individual is accepted within the group, a desire for recognition and respect from other group members is generated. Not only is it important to be "a part of the team" but it is also important to feel like a useful and necessary part of the team and to have the other members recognize that importance. The goal of this need, then, is a feeling of self-confidence, prestige, power, and control created through meaningful contributions to the group; contributions recognized as meaningful by both the individual and by the "significant others" in that person's surroundings.

Once esteem needs are adequately satisfied, the ultimate need, *self-actualization*, becomes prepotent. Self-actualization refers to the need to maximize one's potential. It is not enough to be recognized as a competent musician, for the person seeking self-actualization strives to be the best musician that his or her talent allows. A professor will want to be known as an "authority in the field"; he will also want to be recognized as an excellent instructor. A self-actualizing manager will want to achieve the maximum level of managerial skill that she can reach given her particular capabilities. The interesting thing about self-actualization is that once a person reaches this level, apparently there is no fulfillment of this need that is adequate to assuage the drive. A person at this level will recognize, and react to, a variety of goals, for there are innumerable areas in which one may attempt to maximize potential. It is equally important to realize that the possibility of achieving one's maximum is unlikely, for once a particular goal is reached, new capabilities and new weaknesses are recognized.

In considering Maslow's theory of motivation, it is important to note at least two qualifying factors. First, Maslow does not argue that one need has to be completely satiated before the next need is activated. In fact, he says that for the average member of our society (and it is important to note that he is talking about Western societies, especially the society of the United States), the individual is usually partially satisfied and partially dissatisfied in all of his wants. Second, although the order of needs is usually in the progression stated above, there are occasions, or special conditions, that lead to the reversal of the order or the deletion of some steps in the progressions. Acts of heroism by police officers or fire fighters, for example, are considered to be heroic precisely because the individual acts in a way that ignores personal safety in order to help another person. A civil servant who refuses to follow orders, gives up a job rather than break an ideal, or makes public illegal activities when her supervisor is attempting to hush up any public information is performing in a way that does not fit the hierarchy. Other examples are readily available, but the point has been made that Maslow does not mean for the theory to be absolutely inflexible. Even so, his work helps to improve our understanding of motivation, and his ideas have had a tremendous impact on modern management.

**Herzberg's Two-Factor Theory.** While Maslow was developing his general theory about motivation, Frederick Herzberg was doing an intensive study of about 200 accountants and engineers who worked in the Pittsburgh, Pennsylvania area; he was trying to find out what made these employees feel exceptionally good or bad about their jobs.[4] The responses that Herzberg obtained from the participants in his research were both interesting and consistent. The answers were also categorizable into two groups. The first group of responses dealt with, or described, *how the workers related to the environment in which they worked.* These "hygiene" factors, as Herzberg referred to them, can be grouped under five general headings: company policy and administration; supervision; salary; interpersonal relations; and working conditions. Surprisingly, these factors all tend to be mentioned in negative ways; they are the factors that lead to bad feelings on the part of the respondents. Therefore, Herzberg refers to these issues as "dissatisfiers," meaning that these factors seldom seem to motivate people positively. On the other hand, poor handling of hygiene factors leads to low morale because of the unpleasant situation created by mismanagement.

The second group of five factors stands out as strong determiners of job satisfaction. These are achievement; recognition; the work itself; responsibility; and advancement. The last three are of greater importance in creating a lasting sense of positive motivation. These "motivating" factors, or "satisfiers," are descriptive of what a person does on the job. Thus, the motivating events seem to be satisfying because they allow the opportunity for growth and self-actualization. In fact, the two categories described by Herzberg are closely allied to the hierarchy developed by Maslow; much of the new literature on management uses the research of these two men as the foundation from which further discussion commences.

Herzberg's two-factor theory has been challenged by numerous academicians; however, it has also been accepted by many management practitioners. It is important to note the contributions that Herzberg made to the theory of motivation within the human relations school. This contribution was great because

he extended the Maslow need-hierarchy concept and made it more applicable to work motivation. Herzberg drew attention to the importance of job-content factors in work motivation which previously had been badly neglected and often totally overlooked. The practical motivation technique of job enrichment is also one of Herzberg's contributions. Overall, he added much to the better understanding of job satisfaction but, like his predecessors, fell short of a complex human motivational process. Probably his contribution should be thought of in terms of a theory of job satisfaction, not a comprehensive theory of work motivation.[5]

Within both theories that make up the core of the human relations school doctrine, the focus is on the individual alone; the major question becomes,

[4] Frederick Herzberg, Bernard Mausner, and Barbara Block Snyderman, *The Motivation to Work,* Second Edition, Wiley, New York, 1959.

[5] Luthans, pp. 489-490.

What is the key to motivating the individual *as an individual*? It is a simplification, but not a distortion, of these theories to say that they appear to pit the individual against the organization; the key to guaranteeing high morale, therefore high productivity, among employees is to remove, inasmuch as possible, any organizational structure or shackles from the individual. High morale is correlated with participation in decisions by employees, resolution of conflict, organizational harmony, and other factors that will create "happy employees."

The human relations school of motivation was not seriously attacked for over a decade after it first appeared following the Hawthorne experiments. Now, after three more decades, there is an intense battle occurring between those who base their motivational theories primarily on interpersonal relations and those who base their theories on organizational structure and rationality. The theories of Maslow and Herzberg, as well as the other theories of the human relations school, have not been tested scientifically on a large scale for several reasons, the most significant of which, according to Charles Perrow, is the fact that

the social sciences, at least in the area of complex organizations, have been desperate for *ideas*, not data. The practitioners seize upon concepts which will make sense of the world; if the concepts make sense, the social scientists do not inquire too carefully into the empirical support for these ideas or concepts. For those who find the ideas repugnant, the most pressing thing to do is to respond on ideological grounds; only later do some have the "luxury" of patiently reexamining the empirical documentation of the new idea.[6]

### Motivation as the Result of Rational Organization Structure

Now that considerable research has been done, attacks on the individual-oriented theories have gained in strength, and the attacks are based on the theories of the rational school. The attacks occur at two levels: on the first level (the objective level), the rationalists argue that there is no scientific proof that "happy workers are productive workers"; on the second level (the normative level), the rationalists argue that the representation of "man against the organization" is false. Let us look at both criticisms of the theories of the human relations school and the opposing ideas of the rationalists.

Numerous studies have tried to measure the correlation between job satisfaction and productivity; little correlation has been found. Victor Vroom was the most successful in finding studies that showed such a correlation, but the results were not impressive.[7] Vroom examined twenty studies where he found a positive correlation, however, the correlation only explained 2 percent of the relation-

---

[6] Charles Perrow, *Complex Organizations: A Critical Essay*, Scott, Foresman, Glenview, Ill., 1972, p. 103.

[7] Victor Vroom, *Work and Motivation*, Wiley, New York, 1964. See also: Arthur H. Brayfield and Walter H. Crockett, "Employee Attitudes and Employee Performance," *Psychological Bulletin, LII*, 396-424; and Abraham Korman, "Toward an Hypothesis of Work Behavior," *Journal of Applied Psychology, LIV*, 31-41.

ship between satisfaction and productivity. Similar results have regularly appeared in the literature. In fact, Lyman Porter and Edward Lawler decided that the causal relationship should be reversed.[8] They came to the conclusion that satisfaction might result from high performance *if the employee was rewarded for that performance.* They concluded that organizations should spend more time worrying about how to reward high performance and less time worrying about maximizing satisfaction among employees. After examining the literature on human relations and productivity, Charles Perrow came to the conclusion that

> one cannot explain organizations by explaining the attitudes and behavior of individuals or even small groups within them. We learn a great deal about psychology and social psychology but little about organizations per se in this fashion.[9]

All of these findings help to justify the motivational theory of the rational school, which is based on the idea of an inducements-contributions equilibrium within the organization.[10] According to this theory of motivation, individuals are motivated to participate in an organization because they receive more inducements from that participation than they have to give as contributions. The greater the surplus of inducements over contributions (in whatever form the inducements and contributions may take), the more willing the individuals are to continue their affiliation and the greater the contributions they can be expected to make. According to this theory, the ability of the organization to furnish rewards equal to, or in surplus of, the cost of membership is the central factor determining the members' motivation; therefore, the organization's structural and functional rationality are central to the success of motivation, because it is the rationality of structure and function that guarantees the surplus of inducements over contributions.

The idea that a rational structure is essential to the organization if an individual is to be motivated, first, to stay in the organization and, second, to be a productive member, flies in the face of the "man against the organization" stance that the rationalists claim the human relationists maintain. The strongest and most eloquent attack on the position of the human relationists and, at the same time, an exposition of the rationalists' ideas, is made by Herbert Simon in a published debate with Chris Argyris.[11] Simon says that the productivity of the

---

[8] Edward E. Lawler, III, and Lyman W. Porter, "The Effect of Performance on Job Safisfaction," *Industrial Relations, VII,* 20-28 (October 1967).

[9] Perrow, p. 143.

[10] James G. March and Herbert A. Simon, *Organizations,* Wiley, New York, 1958, pp. 84-110.

[11] Herbert A. Simon, "Organization Man: Rational or Self-Actualizing?" *Public Administration Review, XXXIII,* 346-353 (July-August, 1973).

United States is directly traceable to the rational structure of our industry, and he wonders what will happen to that productivity if we deemphasize the use of formal authority in search of self-actualization. He continues by saying,

But of course the issue is not crucial if we are mistaken in taking self-actualization—in the form in which it is described by Maslow and Argyris—as the main goal of . . . reform. If many or most can live the good life, not in a state of complete "freedom," but in a social environment that establishes various rules for their game of life at the same time that it is meeting their physical . . . needs; if Man is much more like the social animal . . . who finds pattern and meaning from his participation in social systems that possess a certain amount of structure, and that can offer him ideas and values; if much of self-actualization consists in acting with skill and purpose in a well-written play—if this is the kind of world we have and the kind of Man, then there is no basic conflict between Man and Organization. In this kind of world, Man is no more alien to organization or to society than he is to organic and physical nature. Man has weight, and so is acted upon by gravity; he metabolizes, and so he must eat; he responds to his fellows, and so he must live in social systems; he exercises reason, and so must be provided with an environment sufficiently simple and stable for the limits of his reason.[12]

Simon argues that Argyris and Maslow paint an overly romantic picture of Man, who is portrayed as a heroic and inexhaustibly creative being in need of absolute freedom and "a blank wall of infinite size in order to paint on it an unimaginably beautiful picture."[13] However, Simon believes that this portrayal of man is wrong, for he says,

All the evidence from the fine arts suggests that unlimited freedom is not the best condition for human creativity. The Gothic cathedrals were created not out of unlimited freedom, but out of the stern physical constraints imposed by gravity acting upon masonry walls, and the equally severe social constraints of the Catholic liturgy. Man creates best when he operates in an environment whose constraints are commensurate with the capacities of his bounded rationality. More constraint restricts his creativity, less throws him into confusion and frustration.[14]

For an individual to develop his or her capacity for legitimate self-assertion, there must be an institutional order or a public process that allows such action. Participation as such is not the single most important factor in self-actualization; of equal importance is the clarity of the organizational goal and the clarity of

[12] *Ibid*, p. 350.

[13] *Ibid*.

[14] *Ibid*.

one's role in the organization. The last two factors are positively correlated with job satisfaction and high motivation.[15] Therefore, structural and functional rationality once again become the key elements in the motivational process, because such a "process does not mean conflict and struggle as such, but a setting for ordered controversy and accomodation."[16]

## New Theories of Motivation

In order to combine the useful concepts of both the human relations school and the rationalist school, it is necessary to examine the theories of motivation that have been developed by several other researchers, specifically, the theories of Victor Vroom, David McClelland, and Lyman Porter and Edward Lawler.

Vroom has developed a general theory that does not specify which particular things motivate humans in organizations.[17] Instead, his theory attempts to show how the characteristics of the individual (whatever they are) combine to create a *reason for the person to make the necessary effort to complete a sequence of actions*. The model is built around the concepts of valence, expectancy, and force. By "force," Vroom means approximately the same thing as motivation, and force is shown by the algebraic sum of the products of valences and expectancies. Valence is the strength of an individual's preference for a particular outcome. That strength may be negative (the fear of being fired) or positive (the hope of being promoted). If the individual has no preference, the valence is zero. The hope for promotion, however, is at least a second-level goal, for it cannot be achieved except through a more primary goal (under the direct influence of the individual), such as superior performance on the job. Thus, the individual will be motivated to high performance because of his desire to be promoted.

However, the strength of the motivation will depend on a second factor. Not only must the goal be present in some strength but the individual must also have some expectancy of achieving the goal. Hence, the strength of the desire and the expectancy of seeing the desire satisfied combine to create the force, or motivation, to do the necessary work.

By combining Vroom's ideas with those of the two schools discussed above, it is possible to piece together a rather complete picture of motivation. The method of calculation discussed by Vroom is used by individuals to decide when and where they want to place their efforts; the rewards of goals toward which they are working are usually valued according to the hierarchy developed by Herzberg and Maslow; the feasibility of achieving the goals is based on the structural and functional rationality of the organization and the employees' expectancy that the organization can and will reward appropriate behavior. This proposition seems to be supported by the research of David McClelland and his

[15] Thomas Lyons, "Role Clarity, Need for Clarity, Satisfaction, Tension and Withdrawal," *Organizational Behavior and Human Performance, VI,* 99-110 (1971).

[16] Perrow, p. 142.

[17] Vroom, *Work and Motivation.*

compatriots,[18] as well as the findings of Lyman Porter and Edward Lawler. [19]

For over twenty years, David McClelland and his associates have been studying the "urge to achieve." They have concluded that a person with a high desire to achieve has certain characteristics that enable him to work best in certain types of situations. McClelland, in discussing the high achiever, notes that

1. To begin with, he likes situations in which he takes personal responsibility for finding solutions to problems. The reason is obvious. Otherwise, he could get little personal achievement satisfaction from the successful outcome. No gambler, he does not relish situations where the outcome depends not on his abilities and efforts but on chance or other factors beyond his control.
2. Another characteristic of a man with a strong achievement concern is his tendency to set moderate achievement goals and to take "calculated risks." Again his strategy is well suited to his needs, for only by taking on moderately difficult tasks is he likely to get the achievement satisfaction he wants. If he takes on any easy or routine problem, he will succeed but get very little satisfaction out of his success. If he takes on an extremely difficult problem, he is unlikely to get any satisfaction because he will not succeed.
3. The man who has a strong concern for achievement also wants concrete feedback as to how well he is doing. Otherwise how could he get any satisfaction out of what he had done?[20]

These rules are very nearly duplicated by the findings of Porter and Lawler; they found that there are three characteristics that are essential to the work situation if the job is to arouse higher order needs and to elicit good performance from the workers. First, the individual must receive meaningful feedback about her performance on the job. Second, the individual must believe that the job being performed requires the use of abilities which she considers to be valuable. This particular issue leads to low morale on many occasions, for people often feel "that they can be replaced by a machine," which means that their jobs are repetitive or do not call for great skill. Third, the individual must feel that she has a high degree of self-control in the setting of goals and in the way those goals are to be achieved if higher order needs are to be fulfilled.[21]

[18] David C. McClelland, J. W. Atkinson, R. A. Clark, and E. L. Lowell, *The Achievement Motive,* Appleton-Century-Crofts, New York, 1953. See also: David C. McClelland, *The Achieving Society,* D. Van Nostrand, Princeton, N.J., 1961.

[19] Lyman W. Porter and Edward E. Lawler, III, *Managerial Attitudes and Performance,* Richard D. Irwin, Homewood, Ill., 1968.

[20] David C. McClelland, "Business Drives and National Achievement," *Harvard Business Review, XL,* 103-105 (July-August, 1962).

[21] Edward E. Lawler, III, "Job Design and Employee Motivation," *Personnel Psychology, XXII,* 426-435 (Winter 1969).

## Money and Motivation

One final topic must be examined before discussing motivation in public agencies, and that is the topic of money as a motivator. At one time, it was taken for granted that the solution to any problem of morale or productivity could be found in the magic elixir, liquid cash. If morale was bad, the answer was to raise pay. If production was lagging, the solution was to change to some form of piecework pay incentive plan and employees would immediately improve performance. Now it is recognized that money is not "the almighty motivator"; however, no one is quite certain what its role is in employee satisfaction and morale.

The results of research on the importance of pay have been widely divergent. Nancy Morse and Robert Weiss found that 80 percent of the employed men they questioned said they would keep working even if they were independently wealthy; of this 80 percent, two out of three men gave positive reasons for continuing in some kind of work, such as claiming that work keeps one occupied, work gives one an interest, work keeps one healthy, or work is good for a person.[22] A twelve-year study of Sears employees found pay, and "rates of pay," to be ranked relatively low on their scale of factors important to job satisfaction.[23] Other studies, in different cultures and among skilled and semiskilled workers in the United States, have found pay to be the single most important factor to the workers.[24] All of these differing results lead one to the conclusion that, while few people suffer from the "Midas syndrome," the desire to have money for its own sake, they are probably interested in what money can furnish them, whether it is the security of money in the bank and a home that is paid for or the ability to participate in, and be accepted by, the right social groups. Once an individual perceives his present pay as adequate to achieve material, psychological, and social goals, the matter of rate of pay becomes relatively less important than it would be if the pay was too low to achieve these goals (this explanation fits neatly into Maslow's hierarchical theory). The most subtle and

---

[22] Nancy C. Morse and Robert S. Weiss, "The Function and Meaning of Work and Job," *American Sociological Review, XX,* 191-198 (April 1955).

[23] J. C. Worthy, "Factors Influencing Employee Morale," *Harvard Business Review, XXVIII,* 61-73 (January 1950).

[24] H. C. Ganuli, "An Inquiry Into Incentives for Working in an Engineering Factory," *Indian Journal of Social Work, XV,* 30-40 (1943). Ganuli found pay to be the most important of eight factors about which he asked employees in a Calcutta, India, engineering firm. D. Graham and W. Sluckin, "Different Kinds of Rewards as Industrial Incentives," *Research Review, Durham, V,* 54-56 (1954). They surveyed skilled and semiskilled workers in England, finding "pay" to be the most important factor to these workers. L. T. Wilkins, "Incentives and the Young Male Worker in England," *International Journal of Opinion and Attitude Research, IV,* 541-562 (1950). He found "pay" to be second only to "friendly workmates" as a morale factor amoung 18-19 year olds going into the British Army. All of these cases are noted in: Robert L. Opsahl and Marvin L. Dunnette, "The Role of Financial Compensation in Industrial Motivation," *Psychological Bulletin, LXVI,* 94-118 (August 1966).

important characteristic of money is its power as a symbol.[25] As Paul Hersey and Kenneth Blanchard note,

It is what money can buy, not money itself, that gives it value. But, money's symbolic power is not limited to its market value. Since money has no intrinsic meaning of its own, it can symbolize almost any need an individual wants it to represent. In other words, money can mean whatever people want it to mean.[26]

Thus, the effect of money on morale is important when considering employee satisfaction, but it is also vital to keep from oversimplifying the issue into an economic interpretation of motivation.

## Motivation Theory and Public Employees

For public managers, the focal question is, How does all of this theory about motivation apply to employees in the public sphere? The best way to deal with this question is to compare the results of various studies among governmental employees against similar findings in private industry. In this way, it is possible to see if the factors that appear to increase morale among public employees are the same as those in private industry; at the same time, one can compare how the various factors rank in importance. From this data, it is possible to make a judgment about the validity of general motivation theories when they are applied to public employees.

Several attempts have been made over the past fifty years to measure the attitude of the general public toward government employment and employees.[27] Most of this research has found that employment in the public bureaucracy generally is not considered a very prestigious job. Those in the lower socio-educational-economic levels of society give government employment relatively good ratings because of good pay and security; individuals in the higher socio-educational-economic levels of society prefer private employment because of better salaries, greater freedom in work, better chances for advancement, and greater recognition of prestige in the private sphere of society.

The most extensive study of attitudes among civil servants toward their work was reported by Franklin P. Kilpatrick, Milton C. Cummings, Jr., and M. Kent

---

[25] Saul W. Gellerman, *Motivation and Productivity,* American Management Association, New York, 1963. See also: Gellerman, *Management by Motivation,* American Management Association, New York, 1968.

[26] Paul Hersey and Kenneth H. Blanchard, *Management of Organizational Behavior: Utilizing Human Resources,* Prentice-Hall, Englewood Cliffs, N.J., 1969, pp. 33-34.

[27] The early efforts in the area of measuring attitudes toward government employment were carried out by Leonard D. White, in his books: *The Prestige Value of Public Employment in Chicago,* University of Chicago, Chicago, 1929; and *Further Contributions to the Prestige Value of Public Employment,* University of Chicago, Chicago, 1932.

Jennings in 1964.[28] As part of their analysis of the image of federal employment, these men inquired of the 948 civil servants who were interviewed what factors were positive and what factors were negative about their work. In a separate but closely related study by David T. Stanley, in which he studied the attitudes of the higher civil servants in the federal government, similar responses about positive and negative factors were solicited.[29] From these responses among both groups, it becomes apparent that "significant numbers find factors such as autonomy, variety, opportunities for self-expression and creativity, challenging work, a sense of doing something that is worthwhile and constructive, interesting work—all these, and more, in their job as a federal employee."[30] These are the needs and drives that fall at the higher end of Maslow's hierarchy, or that Herzberg refers to as motivators. Therefore, it would appear that these types of motivators are just as important to public employees as they are for private sector workers.

The issues of pay and security are important to people even though other factors are ranked higher. Among the general population and the general sample of federal employees, good pay and job security are among the top seven factors mentioned. The interesting fact to note is that the issue of pay is not even mentioned in the list of satisfiers among the higher civil servants, while job security is the last on the list. The four grade levels (GS 15-18) interviewed by David Stanley are the top levels within the federal civil service, with only the politically appointed department secretaries and their immediate assistants above the civil servants. While few civil servants, even at this level, are going to become independently wealthy, they make a salary that allows them to live well; thus, the factors that tend to motivate them in their work are factors at the upper end of Maslow's hierarchy. They have satisfied their physiological and security needs to a great extent, and they are now concentrating on the "top three" factors. Kilpatrick, Cummings, and Jennings found that the higher civil servants felt that adequate prestige (esteem) was not attached to public service, especially among other people at comparable levels in the private sector of society. It would seem from this research that the theories about motivation apply equally to public or private workers. The following two excerpts from Stanley's interviews bring out this point.

Defense official: Most of ____'s satisfactions with a federal career can be rounded up under the heading of professional opportunities. For someone of his background and interests there have been tremendous challenges and lots

---

[28] Franklin P. Kilpatrick, Milton C. Cummings, Jr., and M. Kent Jennings, *The Image of the Federal Service,* The Brookings Institution, Washington, D.C., 1964.

[29] David T. Stanley, *The Higher Civil Service: An Evaluation of Federal Personnel Practices,* The Brookings Institution, Washington, D.C., 1964.

[30] Kilpatrick, et al., p. 137.

of room both to make a contribution and to get involved in solving a variety of problems and having new experiences all around. He also derives satisfaction from knowing that he is really on the frontiers of the most advanced management practice. He compares this favorably with the rather more remote academic life which he had originally intended to pursue.

Program officer in a Cabinet department: My satisfactions have been primarily the opportunity to deal with matters of great importance and the fact that responsibility has been delegated in such manner that I've been free to go ahead and do a job. The fact too that I feel that the business of government is important to our society and the orderly disposition of problems is worth the effort and highly satisfying.[31]

The structure of the organizations allowed the employees to have a maximum amount of freedom within rational and supportive environments. The two interviews stress the importance of challenge and freedom within an orderly system; once again the findings appear to support a "combined theory" (made up of both human relations and rationalist ideas) of worker motivation and satisfaction.

In a similar manner, an examination of the factors that create dissatisfaction among civil servants points out the similarity between the private and public employees. When federal employees were asked to note the factors that dissatisfied them about their jobs, the responses primarily centered around poor pay, poor supervision, and other environmental factors. This was especially true of the higher civil servants.

From the results of this research, two facts become apparent. First, in spite of the stereotypes about civil servants, there is really little difference between the attitudes and values of public and private employees. Second, since there is little difference between public and private employees, there should be little or no difference in the applicability of motivation theories to the various work groups.

## SUMMARY

Motivations cannot be seen, but they are extrapolated from observation of the ways in which individuals behave. Motivation theory is based on three factors: (1) need—a sense of psychological or physical imbalance; (2) drive—a conscious or unconscious search for ways to satiate the need; and (3) goal—a situation that will alleviate the need. A variety of theories have been developed to explain how these elements interact within an individual. The earliest theories were based upon the "economic man" model; however, these theories proved to be inadequate to explain or predict behavior. Currently, two major schools of thought

[31] Stanley, p. 60.

exist that attempt to explain motivation; these schools can be entitled (1) the human relations school and (2) the rational school.

The human relations school is based primarily on Maslow's "hierarchy of needs" (physiological, security, affiliation, esteem, and self-actualization) and Herzberg's "two-factor theory" (hygiene factors and motivators). On the other hand, there are a variety of proponents of the rational school including March and Simon and Charles Perrow. The basis for their theory is the "equilibrium of inducements—contributions theory" and the "rational structure and function theory." When both of these schools are combined with the theories of Vroom (motivation is a combination of valence, expectancy, and force) and McCelland (the "urge to achieve"), the ability to explain worker motivation and satisfaction is greatly enhanced, although no complete theory has yet been developed.

When rewards are examined as motivators, it is found that money has less impact as one moves up through an organization or society; however, money maintains some subtle and important characteristics. Money can symbolize almost anything that an individual wishes it to represent, and it can allow an individual to achieve a variety of materialistic or nonmaterialistic goals.

The theories about motivation appear to apply equally to private or public employees. Ultimately, whether one works for private organizations or for the government, the work situation, with its combination of skill requirements, self-control, organizational structure, and feedback about performance, is a vital part of the total motivational process.

# BIBLIOGRAPHY

Arensberg, Conrad, ed., *Research in Industrial Human Relations; A Critical Appraisal*, Harper and Row, New York, 1957.

Berelson, Bernard, and Gary A. Steiner, *Human Behavior: An Inventory of Scientific Findings*, Harcourt, Brace and World, New York, 1964.

Gellerman, Saul W., *Motivation and Productivity*, American Management Association, New York, 1963.

Hersey, Paul, and Kenneth H. Blanchard, *Management of Organizational Behavior: Utilizing Human Resources*, Prentice-Hall, Englewood Cliffs, N. J., 1969.

Herzberg, Frederick, *Work and the Nature of Man*, World Publishing, Cleveland, 1966.

Herzberg, Frederick, Bernard Mausner, and Barbara B. Snyderman, *The Motivation to Work*, Second Edition, Wiley, New York, 1959.

Homans, George, *The Human Group*, Harcourt Brace Jovanovich, New York, 1950.

Katz, Daniel, and Robert L. Kahn, *The Social Psychology of Organizations*, Wiley, New York, 1966.

Kilpatrick, Franklin P., Milton C. Cummings, Jr., and M. Kent Jennings, *The Image of the Federal Service*, Brookings Institution, Washington, D. C., 1964.

Lansberger, Henry, *Hawthorne Revisited*, Cornell University, Ithaca, N. Y., 1958.

Likert, Rensis, *New Patterns of Management*, McGraw-Hill, New York, 1961.

Likert, Rensis, *The Human Organization*, McGraw-Hill, New York, 1967.

Luthans, Fred, *Organizational Behavior: A Modern Behavioral Approach to Management*, McGraw-Hill, New York, 1973.

Mann, Floyd C., and L. Richard Hoffman, *Automation and the Worker*, Holt, Rinehart and Winston, New York, 1960.

March, James G., ed., *Handbook of Organizations*, Rand McNally, Chicago, 1965.

March, James G., and Herbert A. Simon, *Organizations*, Wiley, New York, 1958.

Maslow, Abraham H., *Motivation and Personality*, Harper and Brothers, New York, 1954.

Maslow, Abraham H., *Toward a Psychology of Being*, D. Van Nostrand, Princeton, N. J., 1962.

Maslow, Abraham H., *Eupsychian Management*, Richard D. Irwin, Homewood, Ill., 1965.

McClelland, David C., *The Achieving Society*, D. Van Nostrand, Princeton, N. J., 1961.

McClelland, David C., et al., *The Achievement Motive*, Appleton-Century-Crofts, New York, 1953.

McGregor, Douglas, *The Human Side of Enterprise*, McGraw-Hill, New York, 1960.

Miles, Raymond E., "Human Relations or Human Resources," *Harvard Business Review, XLIII*, 148-155 (July-August, 1965).

Palumbo, Dennis J., "Power and Role Specificity in Organization Theory," *Public Administration Review, XXIX*, 237-248 (May-June, 1969).

Perrow, Charles, *Complex Organizations: A Critical Essay*, Scott, Foresman, Glenview, Ill., 1972.

Porter, Lyman W., and Edward E. Lawler, III, *Managerial Attitudes and Performance*, Richard D. Irwin, Homewood, Ill., 1968.

Roethlisberger, Fritz, and William Dickson, *Management and the Worker*, Harvard University, Cambridge, Mass., 1939.

Simon, Herbert, *Models of Man*, Wiley, New York, 1956.

Simon, Herbert, "Organization Man: Rational or Self-Actualizing?" *Public Administration Review, XXXIII*, 346-353 (July-August, 1973).

Stanley, David T., *The Higher Civil Service: An Evaluation of Federal Personnel Practices*, Brookings Institution, Washington, D. C., 1964.

Strauss, George, "Human Relations, 1968 Style," *Industrial Relations, VII*, 262-276 (May 1969).

Task Force to the Secretary of Health, Education, and Welfare, *Work in America*, Massachusetts Institute of Technology, Cambridge, 1973.

Vollmer, Howard M., and Donald L. Mills, eds., *Professionalization*, Prentice-Hall, Englewood Cliffs, N. J., 1966.

Vroom, Victor H., *Work and Motivation*, Wiley, New York, 1964.

Vroom, Victor H., and Edward L. Deci, eds., *Management and Motivation*, Penguin Books, Baltimore, 1970.

White, Leonard D., *The Prestige Value of Public Employment in Chicago*, University of Chicago, Chicago, 1929.

White, Leonard D., *Further Contributions to the Prestige Value of Public Employment*, University of Chicago, Chicago, 1932.

# LEADERSHIP

*The best executive is the one who has sense enough to pick good men to do what he wants done, and self-restraint enough to keep from meddling with them while they do it.*

*Theodore Roosevelt*

The ultimate success of any public agency rests upon the leadership of that organization; this statement applies to all agencies—large, small, state, local, or national. The reason for this very broad statement is the central aspect of leadership to all the functions of the agency. Before discussing leadership, however, it is essential to define what we are talking about. Sven Lundstedt states that

leadership is the ability to influence the behavior of others in a group or organization, set goals for a group, formulate paths to the goals, and create some social norms in the group.[1]

[1] Sven Lundstedt, "Administrative Leadership and the Use of Social Power," *Public Administration Review, XXV*, 156 (June 1965).

# CHAPTER 12

This definition points out the centrality of leadership to every activity of a public agency. The best qualified and most highly motivated employees can be stifled in their work if the leadership of their agency is primarily interested in the wrong goals and the wrong paths to those goals; this is especially true if the leaders also insist on behavior and norms that are incongruent with the expectations of the other employees in the agency. When the employees of an agency, which has been established to guarantee equal opportunity for all citizens, attempt to perform their jobs in a professional manner, but the leaders of the agency insist that no cases involving the local government should be encouraged or investigated, there cannot be a successful fulfillment of the initial goals of the organization. If, when the employees ignore these "unwritten rules," the supervisors reprimand them through implicit or explicit actions, the organization will quickly revert to the level desired by the leaders because the employees will conform to the desires of the leaders, be removed from the organization (known in vulgar terms as "being fired"), or will remove themselves by quitting.

Vigorous and competent leadership can be a guiding light in the improvement of skills, understanding, and motivation of employees; therefore, there is hope for an organization that has the proper leadership. The only hopes for an organization with incompetent or timid leaders are that either a miracle changes the skills and attitudes of the leaders or that there is a change in leadership. Thus, good leadership is the most essential element in the human side of any public enterprise. This chapter discusses the various theories that have developed around the idea of leadership. First, it is necessary to consider the role of "power" in leadership. Second, a discussion of leadership traits is included before, third, noting the importance of situational factors in deciding the success of leadership. Fourth, the interrelationship between motivation theory and leadership style is considered, and, fifth, the importance of leadership of the public bureaucracy within a democratic political system is considered.

## THE INTERRELATIONSHIP
## OF LEADERSHIP AND POWER

It is natural that leadership has been the focus of a multitude of studies in which an attempt has been made to categorize and to explain what makes one individual successful while another fails. Several of the attempts to explain the intricacies of leadership are quite useful to the public administrator. All of these theories are built around the concept of power, whether it is the theory of Max Weber or Peter Drucker; hence, an explanation of power is appropriate. Actually, French and Raven describe five categories of power, and each of the five categories is basic to leadership.[2]

---

[2] These five categories are developed by: John R. P. French and Bertram Raven, "The Bases of Social Power," in Dorwin Cartwright, ed., *Studies in Social Power,* Institute for Social Research, Ann Arbor, Mich., 1959, pp. 150-167.

1. *Reward power* is based on the belief that another person has the ability to give one pleasureable compensation for obedience and loyalty.
2. *Coercive power* is based on the perception that another person has the ability to inflict psychological or physical pain if obedience and loyalty are non-existent.
3. *Legitimate power* is founded on the acceptance of the idea that another person has a legal right to prescribe behavior for a particular situation when that prescription of behavior is done in the proper manner.
4. *Referent power* is founded on one's psychological identification with a particular individual, group of individuals, or a particular goal or ideal that is embodied in the individual or group.
5. *Expert power* is embodied in a recognized skill or knowledge.

Within these five categories of power lie the bases for the various types of leadership that have been established by different writers. Max Weber, who was among the first to popularize the study of leadership through his writing on bureaucracy, does not speak of leadership by that term; instead, he uses the term "authority" in describing how organizations are led.[3] Weber categorizes all organizations into three groups, which are based on the type of authority used by the leader at the "top" of the organization. The first type of leader that he discusses is the *charismatic leader* who gains power through personal "gifts of grace," such as physical prowess, persuasive abilities in speaking, or the ability to perform miracles. History is replete with examples of charismatic leaders. Some have been a positive force, others have had a negative effect on history, but they have all shared these gifts in some form, and they have used these gifts to develop a large and devoted following. Recent examples of charismatic leaders vary from Adolph Hitler to Mahatma Ghandi. In the current United States society, there are, or have been, examples of leaders who have gained a following because of their charismatic qualities. Martin Luther King, through his actions and words, was able to popularize the cause of civil rights and sensitize large segments of the population to the humiliation and unreasonableness of legalized discrimination. Ralph Nader has popularized the concept of consumerism, and he now "leads" a loosely knit group of consumer-oriented organizations throughout the country. Even though Nader may not be directly involved with many of these organizations, they look to him as their example and follow the tactics that he popularized in his numerous consumer studies. In the same way, Gloria Steinem became the "spokeswoman" for a large segment of the women's liberation movement. Why the particular individual became the leader is only partially clear, but it is obvious in each case that there were charismatic features about the individual that led people to identify with him or her and the particular cause that was being espoused.

---

[3] Max Weber, *The Theory of Social and Economic Organization,* trans. and eds., A. M. Henderson and Talcott Parsons, Oxford University, New York, 1947.

The second type of leader gains authority from *tradition*, whereby authority is granted to the leader by his followers because of the history and tradition of the society or organization. This was the primary basis of authority that royalty used to establish and to pass on their authority during the Middle Ages. Tradition is a major source of power for the pope. Likewise, J. Edgar Hoover moved to develop a sense of tradition within the Federal Bureau of Investigation, and his success both inside the organization and with the public greatly increased the prestige of the FBI and Hoover's personal power.

Weber's third type of leader is the *bureaucratic* official whose authority is based on the written rules of the organization. It is with this particular type of leader that the ensuing discussion is primarily involved, for our society is run in a bureaucratic manner. (This statement is not meant as a normative comment about how well or poorly society is run; it is meant as a statement of fact. Almost all the major organizations influencing our lives—public, private, political, social, religious, or economic—are operated under the bureaucratic structure.) Therefore, it is most important to comprehend the strengths and weaknesses of bureaucratic leadership. While most modern organizations are bureaucratic in structure, it is possible to point out prototypical bureaucratic organizations, thus leading to a better understanding of the concept through example. The organizations that most nearly approximate the bureaucratic form in the United States are the military services and the uniformed police departments (which are often described as paramilitary). In these cases, the leaders of the organizations have someone outside the bureaucracy to whom they are responsible (the appropriate elected officials—president, governor, mayor, etc). The ultimate power of the leader is based on the laws, rules, and regulations pertaining to the authority of specific officers. All the laws have been established by the groups or individuals outside the organization who have that authority; the rules and regulations are established as the laws are interpreted by public administrators during the ongoing operation of the organization. All the laws, rules, and regulations are written and codified in a manner that allows appeal to them whenever necessary.

## LEADERSHIP TRAITS

Close your eyes and try to picture in your mind the ideal president of the United States. What physical characteristics does your ideal president possess? Consider also such characteristics as personality, educational background, experience, and intellectual and moral integrity. Can you identify in your mind a set of characteristics that make up the image of your ideal president? Now, try the same exercise, but his time focus on a chief of police for a large metropolitan community. Once again, try to picture an ideal university president and a president for the United Mine Workers. Undoubtedly, your images for each of these positions vary in some details. However, if you examine your images, you will find that some characteristics are common to all the leaders, even though they are placed in quite different roles. These commonalities have fascinated many students of organization, and from this interest have come numerous attempts to find out if there really is a set of traits that all leaders possess. Just as Weber posited the bureaucratic model of organization as typical, numerous researchers have sought the typical leader. From this research, a great deal of valuable information has been developed that can be used to help one learn about leadership. A brief survey seems to be in order.

Literally hundreds of studies have been completed during the last seventy years in an attempt to decide which traits are common to leaders. Ralph Stogdill has put together a comprehensive survey of most of the theories and research on leadership.[4] Stogdill reviewed the various trait studies in 1948, and he completed another review in 1973 with well over 200 studies included in the two reviews. After combining the factors in the 1948 study, Stogdill classified the results under the general headings of:

1. Capacity (intelligence, alertness, verbal facility, originality, judgement).
2. Achievement (scholarship, knowledge, athletic accomplishments).
3. Responsibility (dependability, initiative, persistence, aggressiveness, self-confidence, desire to excel).
4. Participation (activity, sociability, cooperation, adaptability, humor).
5. Status (socioeconomic position, popularity).
6. Situation (mental level, status, skills needs and interests of followers, objectives to be achieved, etc).[5]

These appeared to be the traits most commonly mentioned as being essential to anyone in a leadership position. After finishing the second review in 1973, Stogdill summarized the results of all the work by saying,

The leader is characterized by a strong drive for responsibility and task completion, vigor and persistence in pursuit of goals, venturesomeness and originality in problem solving, drive to exercise initiative in social situations, self-confidence and a sense of personal identity, willingness to tolerate frustration and delay, ability to influence other persons' behavior, and capacity to structure social interaction systems to the purpose at hand.[6]

[4] Ralph M. Stogdill, *Handbook of Leadership: A Survey of Theory and Research,* Free Press, New York, 1974.

[5] *Ibid.,* p. 63.

[6] *Ibid.,* p. 81.

When one pauses to contemplate the skills and personality characteristics of prominent public officials and public administrators, it is apparent that these individuals have many of the characteristics that have just been listed.

The ideal combination of these characteristics may create a "charismatic" leader. It is possible to use this type of individual in the public bureaucracy. When social (or charismatic) and formal (or legitimate) authority are combined in a single individual, an especially potent leader exists. Examples of such types of leaders may be drawn from a variety of areas in society, and around each there develops a mystique that the members of the organization accept and magnify. Vince Lombardi was an individual who combined these qualities in sports. Arturo Toscanini possessed this mystique in the world of music. Robert E. Lee was such a leader during the Civil War. Franklin Roosevelt illustrated this strength during his first two terms as president. The reason for such potent leadership capabilities lies in the fact that the individual is able to call on so many of the power sources that were mentioned earlier. Any such bureaucratic leader has legitimate power; however, referent power is also his to use as he sees fit. Thus, a much wider variety of reward power and coercive power can be used, for not only are all formal rewards and reprimands effective but so are the often more potent psychological motivators. Followers of such a leader not only know that the order is legitimate but also want to carry out the order in the most effective way possible because they believe in the leader. The two forces combined create the strongest type of motivation possible for proper performance in the organization.

## Situational Interpretation of Leadership

As one looks at the results of the various studies as Stogdill has done, it becomes obvious that there is very little agreement among the researchers as to what are the essential traits for leaders. While examining 124 documents of research, Stogdill found only five characteristics mentioned in fifteen or more studies with an additional ten characteristics mentioned in ten or more studies; thus, fifteen characteristics were common to ten or more of the 124 studies. This is not a very high "batting average" even if there are methodological excuses for some of the failure to reach common results. Such results do not invalidate the consideration of leadership traits, for such factors must be considered; however, the results of the research raise the question of whether or not other factors are more important in studying leadership. This question has led to the situational interpretation of leadership. It is an increasingly accepted idea that leadership is situational; in many cases, a person becomes the leader because of the particular situation. Certainly, the individual must have the proper combination of traits needed to be a leader, but the combination varies according to the individual; unless the particular situation arises where that combination is the one needed, he or she will not become the leader. An individual will also remain a leader only as long as he or she can change as the situation changes. Leadership also varies with the values of the group being led and with the conditions of the environment surrounding the group.

The United States and Great Britain share a common language, similar values, and many political institutions, but their views regarding public bureaucratic leadership vary widely. An individual who is a political or administrative leader in our country might very well fail to achieve a similar position in Great Britain. In the United States, professional expertise is of primary importance in moving into a position of leadership. Most of the leaders at the top of the United States governmental bureaucracy have risen to those positions from specialized fields— even though the top leadership positions require generalist qualities. Leadership also seems to be associated with aggressive and emotional characteristics.[7]

In Great Britain, on the other hand, political and administrative leaders are trained in the famous public schools, such as Eton and Harrow, with the major part of their training being within the areas of the classics and humanities. Inculcated into these leaders is a disdain for applied science, a belief in the superiority of the amateur, an authoritative style of speech, and a poise in mannerisms. The general populace expects this type of background and this type of behavior from its leaders.[8] Two equally talented individuals, one from each country, would not necessarily achieve equal levels of success in the public bureaucracy of either nation, because the values of the bureaucrats and the general population vary dramatically in the two countries.

The surrounding environment is also an important factor in deciding who will be the leader; the leader's ability in dealing with that environment will determine her success. Historians have often debated "whether great men make the times or the times make great men." In other words, do leaders become great because they force events to develop in the direction that is best for the country? Or does the situation force leaders to act in a way that causes them to be seen as great even though they would not be considered outstanding under any other circumstances? Undoubtedly, both interpretations are partially right, because the most memorable leaders have had the ability to unify and to motivate people to achieve important goals; it is also true that one of the reasons these leaders are remembered is that they operated during critical moments in the history of their organizations. Winston Churchill was considered somewhat of a misfit by his fellow members of Parliament before World War II; when the war started, Churchill's skills were dreadfully vital in rallying the British people, uniting them in their resolve to withstand the German blitz, and coordinating

[7]W. Lloyd Warner, et al., *The American Federal Executive: A Study of the Social and Personal Characteristics of the Civilian and Military Leaders of the United States Federal Government,* Yale University, New Haven, 1963. For a similar study of business leaders done at the same time, see: W. Lloyd Warner and James C. Abegglen, *Big Business Leaders in America,* Harper and Brothers, New York, 1955.

[8]John M. Pfiffner and Robert Presthus, *Public Administration,* Fifth Edition, Ronald, New York, 1967, p. 89.

the vast and complex machinery of a modern nation in total war. Once the war was over, Churchill soon relinquished his position of leadership, because he could not or did not wish to cope with the dissolution of the British Empire.

Charles DeGaulle, on the other hand, not only was the leader of Free France during World War II but he also returned to a position of leadership, serving as the prime creator of the Fifth Republic when the Fourth Republic was tottering on the brink of chaos and collapse. Was DeGaulle able to change his leadership style and tools to meet the new crisis, or did the new crisis demand the use of the same skills in a new application? This question raises the issue of the leader's ability to change tactics as the pressures of the environment change. A leader may function very well in one situation, but he or she may not be able to change if the situation changes. For example, a personnel director, who does an excellent job of creating the personnel department in a growing community, may cease to function well once that office has become large, specialized, and bureaucratized. Once again, one of the never-to-be-resolved debates of historians is whether or not Abraham Lincoln would have maintained his great reputation if he had lived to complete his second term as president. As Clinton Rossiter has remarked, "through the boldness of his initiative, through an unprecedented plea of necessity, and through a unique interpretation of executive power, Lincoln raised the Presidency to a position of constitutional and moral ascendancy."[9] Many students of the presidency have argued that the primary reason Lincoln retained his image as a great leader was because he was assassinated just at the end of the Civil War. The abilities that made Lincoln a great wartime president would not necessarily have served him well in the ensuing battle with the Radical Republicans in Congress over the policies of reconstruction. He might have suffered some of the same difficulties faced by Andrew Johnson, and these battles might have sullied Lincoln's image. Of course, others argue that his skills, along with his strong position as the "president that saved the Union," would have given him the victory over the Radical Republicans. Since he died before the end of his term as president, the argument can go on interminably, but the argument points out the importance of the situation and the centrality of the problem of environmental change in the determination of leadership style and leadership success.

## LEADERSHIP STYLE

"Leadership style" is inextricably bound up in the leader's ultimate success or failure; therefore, this term holds a position of importance in any discussion of leadership. Leadership style is defined as the consistent behavior patterns of a leader as perceived by those around him.[10] Every leader develops a pattern in

[9] Clinton Rossiter, *The American Presidency,* Harcourt, Brace and World, New York, 1956, p. 101.

[10] Paul Hersey and Kenneth H. Blanchard, *Management of Organizational Behavior: Utilizing Human Resources,* Prentice-Hall, Englewood Cliffs, N.J., 1969, p. 95.

the way he handles the people who work for the organization and the various situations and crises that arise in the organization. The important thing to remember when talking about style, and the most difficult thing for many leaders to understand, is that style does not refer to the way a leader thinks he behaves but how those around him perceive his behavior. This is true because

if a leader's followers think he is a hard-nosed task-oriented leader . . . it makes little difference whether he thinks he is a relationships-oriented, democratic leader, because his followers will behave according to how they perceive his behavior.[11]

In order to determine the style of a public manager, it is only necessary to mingle with the employees who have access to the leader and to observe their actions and listen to their comments as different problems arise. Comments such as "The old man doesn't want to hear about the reasons why it can't be done; he just wants to know how it can be done," "It sure is hard to get her to listen," or "He doesn't seem to mind questions and he always has the right answer," give the observer quick insights into the leader's style. These styles can vary dramatically; indeed, they *must* vary! President Eisenhower delegated responsibility and authority to such an extent that some critics claimed that his subordinates, especially Sherman Adams, had more power than was maintained by Ike himself. Franklin Roosevelt deliberately duplicated lines of responsibility so that the ensuing conflicts allowed him additional information about, and power over, the activities of his administration. In examining the leadership style of local administrators, such as city managers, almost every conceivable style of leadership can be found. Nor is there any exclusive style that is always right; the style that is best suited for one circumstance is not the best style for another situation. A leader (who can also be referred to as a manager or administrator in a bureaucratic organization) may even find that the style of management must change from individual to individual, for some people seem to prefer strong, close supervision, while others operate best when given the greatest possible latitude in their actions.

Even though a great variety of management styles is required, and any style may be successful when applied at the right time and place, over the years there have developed both a categorization of the styles and a limited agreement as to the most appropriate styles for the efficiently operating, healthy organization. Basically, the various styles of management can be combined into two major categories, with some cases being hard to place in one category or the other. These two categories are somewhat idealistic, with few managers falling completely at one end of the spectrum or the other; nonetheless, the groupings are valuable and must be discussed at length.

[11]*Ibid.*

The most common and the longest accepted differentiation is between authoritarian and democratic leadership styles. The dichotomy between the two types of leadership in bureaucracy is pictured by Berelson and Steiner as follows:[12]

| DEMOCRATIC | AS AGAINST | AUTHORITARIAN |
|---|---|---|
| Employee-oriented | | Production-oriented |
| Participatory | | Autocratic |
| Considerate | | Initiatory |
| Loose | | Close |
| Integrative | | Dominative |
| Persuasive | | Arbitrary |
| Self-defined as group leader | | Not so defined |

Democratic leaders are interested in the employees and recognize their individuality; they take into account occasional aberrations that appear to limit or curtail immediate or short-range achievement of maximum production (although this *only* applies in the short run). Democratic leaders accept employee participation in decision making and tactic selection, and they are quite willing to consider ideas that are presented by the members of the group. While they are aware of the necessity of keeping the various members and divisions of the organization aimed toward a common goal, and of maintaining an adequate level of efficiency, these leaders do not practice close supervision; they allow the maximum independence and flexibility possible. Instead of handing down mandates, democratic leaders are willing to explain why decisions have been made and to use their persuasive powers (the use of a little charisma) to gain compliance to orders. Since the democratic leader is self-defined as a part of the group, he or she is interested in creating a cohesive group—a group that accepts the leader as an integral part; therefore the group feels a common bond with the leader.

Authoritarian leaders, on the other hand, do not self-identify as a part of the group. Instead, the group is seen as separate, usually beneath the leaders, with the leaders dominating the group and its actions. Integration of the group, or of the leaders with the group, is not important. The most important part of the job, according to authoritarian leaders, is to attain maximum production; whatever must be done to achieve maximum production is justifiable. In most cases, these leaders hand down mandates that they expect to be followed without question; ideas are not welcome from other members. The only way to get the authoritarian leaders to accept an idea is to convince them that the idea is their own. Authoritarian leaders do not wish to share ideas in the other direction either;

[12] Bernard Berelson and Gary A. Steiner, *Human Behavior: An Inventory of Scientific Findings,* Harcourt, Brace and World, New York, 1964, p. 374.

they give no explanation for the decisions they make or the orders they give. Finally, supervision is quite close, because authoritarian leaders feel that employees are not capable of, or willing to, obey orders.

## McGregor's Theory X and Theory Y

Douglas McGregor was interested in management and motivation and the way the two intertwine. After considerable reflection, he became convinced that the traditional organization with its centralized decision-making, superior-subordinate pyramid, and external control of work is based on a set of assumptions about human nature and human motivation. These assumptions he calls "theory X," and they include the following:

1. Work is inherently distasteful to most people.
2. Most people are not ambitious, have little desire for responsibility, and prefer to be directed.
3. Most people have little capacity for creativity in solving organizational problems.
4. Motivation occurs only at the physiological and security levels.[13]

Because of a belief in these characteristics, a specific style of management is required:

1. Management is responsible for organizing the elements of productive enterprise—money, materials, equipment, people—in the interest of economic ends.
2. With respect to people, this is a process of directing their efforts, motivating them, controlling their actions, modifying their behavior to fit the needs of the organization.
3. Without this active intervention by management, people would be passive—even resistent—to organizational needs. They must therefore be persuaded, rewarded, punished, controlled—their activities must be directed.[14]

Under these assumptions, it is obvious that an authoritarian style of leadership is bound to develop. McGregor feels that this type of management is likely to fail because it attempts to motivate employees in the wrong way; the major reason that motivational attempts are misguided is because theory X assumptions about human nature are generally inaccurate.

---

[13] This list is taken from: Hersey and Blanchard, p. 41.

[14] Douglas McGregor, "The Human Side of Enterprise," in *Adventures in Thought and Action,* Proceedings of the Fifth Anniversary Convocation of the School of Industrial Management, Massachusetts Institute of Technology, 1957, pp. 23-30.

The key to better leadership is a new and more accurate understanding of human nature and of the things that motivate a person to work. This new perception of the worker McGregor calls theory Y. McGregor's view of work and workers includes the following:

1. Work is as natural as play, if the conditions are favorable.
2. Self-control is often indispensable in achieving organizational goals.
3. The capacity for creativity in solving organizational problems is widely distributed in the population.
4. Motivation occurs at the affiliation, esteem, and self-actualization levels, as well as physiological and security levels.
5. People can be self-directed and creative at work if properly motivated.[15]

With this view of workers, a new picture of management emerges. Management is still responsible for organizing the elements of productive enterprise, just as this is enunciated in the description of management style under theory X, but the other steps in the process are dramatically different under theory Y. According to McGregor,

1. The motivation, the potential for development, the capacity for assuming responsibility, the readiness to direct behavior toward organization goals are all present in people. *Management does not put them there.* It is a responsibility of management to make it possible for people to recognize and develop these human characteristics for themselves.
2. The essential task of management is to arrange organizational conditions and methods of operation so that people can achieve their own goals best by directing their own efforts toward organizational objectives. This is a process primarily of creating opportunities, releasing potential, removing obstacles, encouraging growth, providing guidance.[16]

*Creating opportunities* for employees and *releasing their potential* are at the opposite end of the spectrum from what many managers see as their traditional role. McGregor and the other disciples of the human relations school (the same group discussed in the prior chapter on motivation) argue that this factor has led to the differing definitions of management and leadership. The followers of McGregor believe that management, if it is successful in our modern society, must move from the position of a negative, control-oriented operation to a position where the manager serves as a *leader* precisely because of management's capabilities in helping the public employees to meet the goals of the organiza-

[15] Hersey and Blanchard, p. 41.

[16] McGregor, pp. 23-30. Numbering was changed to fit the context. Emphasis added.

tion, and at the same time, to meet their own goals. Furthermore, this idea appears to be supported by some current research. For example, in their study on *Work in America*, the task force established by the Secretary of Health, Education, and Welfare discussed the attitudes of young workers in an attempt to predict some of the directions in which work may move in the future.

The members of the commission came to the conclusion that, in opposition to the view held by decision makers in business, labor, and government, young workers do not "have a lower commitment to work than their elders."[17] The commission found that

the young worker is in revolt not against work but against the authoritarian system developed by industrial engineers. . . . Yet, many in industry continue to support a system of motivation that was created in an era when people were willing to be motivated by the stick. As an alternative to this approach, many . . . managers have offered the carrot as a motivator, only to find that young people also fail to respond to this approach.

From our reading of what youth wants, it appears that under current policies, *employers may not be able to motivate young workers at all. Instead, employers must create conditions in which the worker can motivate himself.* This concept is not as strange as it seems. From biographies of artists, athletes, and successful businessmen, one finds invariably that these people set goals for themselves. The most rewarding race is probably one that one runs against oneself. Young people seem to realize this. They talk less positively than do their elders about competition with others. But they do talk about self-actualization and other "private" values.[18]

Therefore, the commission report tends to agree with Maslow that leaders do not motivate employees but help employees to fulfill their own drives toward success and excellence.

Those who accept the rationalist approach to organization and motivation argue that the "theory X and theory Y" dichotomy is useful, as far as it goes, in explaining the dynamics of leadership; however, McGregor's theory Y only deals with one dimension of leadership, while the problem of leadership must be dealt with from a systems approach. When discussing a single variable, it is impossible to account for the impact of the other important variables that are operating contiguously to the one being considered. In reality, these variables are all acting on the organization and on management at the same time. It is important to consider all the various parts of a particular situation, and this includes some factors outside of the main topic of investigation as long as these factors influence, or are influenced by, the main subject. Thus, when we

---

[17]Task Force to the Secretary of Health, Education, and Welfare, *Work in America,* Massachusetts Institute of Technology, Cambridge, 1973, p. 49. Emphasis added.

[18]*Ibid.,* p. 50.

speak of leadership systems, we are dealing not only with the leaders and their actions but also with many other factors, such as the technology of the organization, the type of employees in the organization, and the political environment in which the organization operates. This last variable ultimately may be the most vital aspect in the environment of all public bureaucracies, because it is the part of the environment that has the most pervasive and lasting impact on the organization.

Studies have generally shown that organizations are more effective when they are operating under democratic leadership. For example, Argyle, Gardner, and Cioffi found that pressure for production was generally unrelated, or even negatively related to output; such factors as general supervision (as opposed to close supervision), democratic supervision, and employee-centered supervision all correlated with higher output.[19] However, one particular aspect of these findings should be emphasized. A democratic supervisor must have the power to allow the aspirations created among the employees to be satisfied, or the ultimate reaction will be extremely negative because of frustrated expectations. These results point out the aspect of leadership that the rationalists feel must be stressed; the leader is responsible for the position and the power of the organization, and the power of the organization may be the essential ingredient in gaining employee cooperation. It may be more important to maximize the total amount of power in the agency than to try to equalize it. If this is true, the nonpersonal decisions about such factors as the demand for services, technology, competition, or organizational structure, appear to have far more consequence for the effectiveness of leadership than decisions as to how to lead people.[20] Therefore, leadership must consider not only motivation but also the other functions of management (decision making, planning, controlling, and communicating); when all these factors are added to the consideration of the employees, the leader is more likely to be successful.

This dual approach to leadership has been presented in a model developed by Robert Blake and Jane Mouton and known as the "Managerial Grid" (see Figure 8). In the Grid, two variables (organizational needs for production and human needs for mature and healthy relationships) are interrelated with the purpose being to examine how these two characteristics change a manager's style of leadership as the emphasis shifts from one variable to the other. The question is, How do the two concerns interact? Managers may emphasize neither factor (in which case they are simply trying to maintain enough stability and production to protect their jobs), one of the factors (which means that their management style, and organizational culture, may be out of balance), or both of the factors (the healthy management style and organizational culture). The

---

[19] Michael Argyle, Godfrey Gardner, and Frank Cioffi, "Supervisory Methods Related to Productivity, Absenteeism, and Labour Turnover," *Human Relations, XI,* 23-40 (1958).

[20] Charles Perrow, *Complex Organizations: A Critical Essay,* Scott, Foresman, Glenview, Ill., 1972, p. 109.

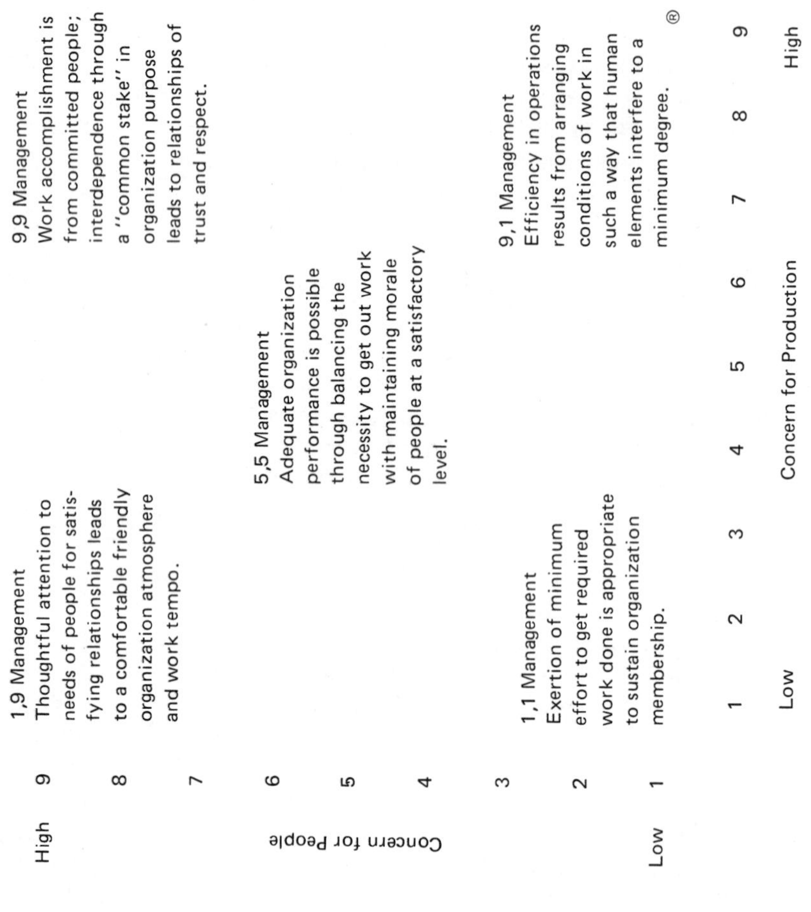

1,9 Management
Thoughtful attention to needs of people for satisfying relationships leads to a comfortable friendly organization atmosphere and work tempo.

9,9 Management
Work accomplishment is from committed people; interdependence through a "common stake" in organization purpose leads to relationships of trust and respect.

5,5 Management
Adequate organization performance is possible through balancing the necessity to get out work with maintaining morale of people at a satisfactory level.

1,1 Management
Exertion of minimum effort to get required work done is appropriate to sustain organization membership.

9,1 Management
Efficiency in operations results from arranging conditions of work in such a way that human elements interfere to a minimum degree.

Concern for People
High 9
8
7
6
5
4
3
2
Low 1

1  2  3  4  5  6  7  8  9
Low        Concern for Production        High

**Figure 8. The Managerial Grid®.** (*Source. R. R. Blake and J. S. Mouton, The Managerial Grid. Houston: Gulf Publishing Company, © 1964, p. 10. Reproduced by permission.*)

theories that explain the results at the various prominent intersection points on the Grid are, according to Blake and Mouton, the

. . . theories that every manager uses when he thinks about how to get results through people, *whether he realizes it or not.* They also can be used to analyze the patterns of interactions among managers which comprise the (organizational) culture.[21]

The Grid is used as the basis for an intensive management, interpersonal relations, and organizational development course; however, the principle interest that it has for our present study is its expository value. Here, two variables from the total system are examined together, and it becomes apparent that their combined forces have a dramatic impact on leadership style. More insight into the actions of managers can be gained by examining these two factors together than by looking at them separately. As can be seen from the Grid diagram, each combination creates a unique management style. The 1,9 manager, in the top, left corner of the Grid, puts the major emphasis on people; this style of management is sometimes referred to as country club management. As has been pointed out in the last chapter, however, happy civil servants may not be productive civil servants; an emphasis on human relations alone does not guarantee a healthy organization. On the other hand, just as the carrot alone does not work, neither is the stick alone guaranteed to succeed. The 9,1 manager forgets the human part of the job and becomes preoccupied with production. This creates difficulties because such a management style causes human relations problems; while contented workers do not necessarily produce more, unhappy employees do produce less.

The 5,5 manager is what is referred to as the "organization man," whose general attitude is to "Get results, but don't make waves." This position is the easiest one to take; therefore, it is probably also the most common in public bureaucracies. If people do their jobs, do not create any negative feelings, and wait the appropriate length of time, promotions up the ladder will automatically come. Of course, this is a better situation than that of the 1,1 manager, who is described by Blake and Mouton as follows:

It may not seem that any manager could have almost no concern for either people or production, yet people managing in this manner have been found in many businesses, going through the motions of being part of the firm but not really contributing to it. They are not doers, but freeloaders. They have not quit their jobs, but they walked out mentally, perhaps many years ago.[22]

[21] Robert R. Blake and Jane S. Mouton, *Building a Dynamic Corporation Through Grid Organization Development,* Addison-Wesley, Reading, Mass., 1969, pp. 60-61.

[22] *Ibid.,* p. 61.

Finally, there is the manager who is sensitive to the necessity of production while emphasizing human relations. The manager deals with employees in a way that exploits their strengths and strengthens or supports their weaknesses. Although she recognizes and respects individuals, the manager also emphasizes the goal of delivering the most of a service or product that can be produced while maintaining proper quality. This manager stresses threshing out problems in an open and aboveboard way; this creates among the people involved a feeling of a "common stake in the outcome of their endeavors."[23]

## LEADERSHIP, PUBLIC BUREAUCRACY, AND THE DEMOCRATIC POLITICAL SYSTEM

The problem faced by the public manager is bounded by the two forces of human relations (participatory leadership) and productivity (giving the taxpayers their money's worth). It is imperative that a good relationship be maintained with and between employees. At the same time, the legislature, higher administrators, and interested public are constantly pressing for greater effectiveness from the programs supported by the taxpayers. The public bureaucracy is often considered to be inefficient; therefore, the manager must guard against any semblance of inadequacy. In order to deal with these forces, two questions must be faced: first, which form of leadership should be used, and, second, which form of organization best allows that style of leadership?

Throughout recent (the last twenty years) literature on motivation and leadership, there is a recurring suggestion that increased participation by all organization members will solve many bureaucratic ills. This demand has gained acceptance among many of the scholars and practitioners in the field of public administration. Numerous federal and state agencies, along with many city bureaucracies, are attempting to go through special training or are applying new management techniques to their organizations, in the hope that greater "democracy," otherwise referred to as participation, will improve the overall performance of their establishments. One of the greatest problems in responding to this demand is in defining "participation." What is meant by that term is not specified, "and there is not necessarily agreement among all proponents of the concept as to its meaning."[24] As Marvin Meade reports,

Basically, the theory, in its contemporary form, proposes that organizational effectiveness is enhanced by increasing the participation of organizational members, including those at the lowest levels, in decisions affecting their work. Such participation has "involving," motivating effects which improve worker performance. Participation also increases the quality of organizational decisions by decentralizing them to those points in the organization where the real expertise and best information are located. . . . Members at the lowest levels

---

[23] *Ibid.,* p. 62.

[24] Marvin Meade, "Participative Administration—Emerging Reality or Wishful Thinking," in Dwight Waldo, ed., *Public Administration in a Time of Turbulence,* Chandler, Scranton, Penn., 1971, p. 169.

of the organization possess resources of creativity and capabilities for making worthwhile contributions to the management of the organization. Moreover, as mature (or potentially mature) personalities, these individuals desire to enlarge their scope, to realize their full potential: and therefore they seek and will respond to the opportunity for meaningful participation.[25]

Such an amount of participation requires leaders to give up many of the rights and privileges that have been considered essential to "good government" in the past. As Dwight Waldo has pointed out, orthodox public administration ideology has held tenaciously to a value orientation that conceives of democracy as a political principle that is external to the professional field of administration and alien to the administrative process.[26] The founders of public administration emphasized the bureaucratic hierarchy, centralization of decision making, and the concept of discipline, because they were especially interested in the maintenance of responsibility and accountability within the government's administrative branch. Added to the emphasis on accountability are the norms of efficiency and economy and the public's negative perception of the governmental bureaucracy on these issues. With the public complaining about the cost of government and the high tax rates, there is a constraint on administrative freedom to experiment with management processes which might prove less efficient or less responsive to society's democratic ethic. For a city manager or a governmental department head to take such a chance requires a degree of courage— some would call it recklessness—because such an action also goes against the old political argument that

. . . public employees, as servants of the people, have no legal or moral claim to assert a voice in the management of the state's administrative organizations, especially where to do so might be seen as subordinating the interests of the masters (the sovereign public) to those of the servants (the public employee).[27]

To those who cry for participation in the management of public agencies, Charles Perrow responds with his own warning "against the tendency to call for the transformation of men into committed polities in organizations where centralized power and unobtrusive means of manipulation and control are necessities."[28] Therefore, the answer to the first question (Which form of leadership should be used?) is the unsatisfactory response that some balance of the two styles is best, and that the balance must be decided by a combination of factors that make up the "situation" of the organization and that include (1) the goal, or purpose, of the organization, (2) the composition of the membership,

---

[25] *Ibid.,* pp. 170-171.

[26] Dwight Waldo, "Development of the Theory of Democratic Administration," *American Political Science Review,* XLVI, 81-103 (March 1952).

[27] Meade, p. 176.

[28] Perrow, p. 204.

(3) the characteristics of the leaders, (4) the desires of the public, and (5) the requirements necessary to protect the democratic political system.

The answer to the second question (Which form of organization best allows that style of leadership?) can be more specific; however, in order to answer this question, it is necessary to return briefly to the discussion of the types of power that are used by leaders, because the success of leaders depends on the power base that is available to them and how they use it. All leaders can use reward and coercive power whether they are charismatic, traditional, or bureaucratic, but their ability to use them is limited by the unique characteristics of their other powers. Rewards can only be drawn from the resources and conditions under the control of the leader, as are the potential punishments that can be meted out. All leaders can use financial rewards or affiliation and esteem, notably through recognition by the leader, but charismatic leaders may look upon self-actualization (among followers) as a threat to their bases of power, unless the achievement of self-actualization among followers is the goal of such leaders. The type of leader who can most comfortably accept participation and employee growth and development among subordinates is the bureaucratic leader; his position is prescribed by law, or by the rules and regulations of the system. At the same time, the system also gives the leader the power to reward or punish employees, as is necessary, in order to make sure the organization is headed toward its goal and working within its legally defined means. Only within the bureaucratic system can both control *and* personal freedom be guaranteed. While many writers currently bemoan the growth of bureaucracy and pray for its demise,[29] they are really complaining about the dysfunctions of the system and

---

[29] Warren Bennis epitomizes the critics of bureaucracy when he says,

I have recently cataloged the criticisms of bureaucracy, and they outnumber and outdo the Ninety-five Theses tacked on the church door at Wittenberg in attacking another bureaucracy. For example

1. Bureaucracy does not adequately allow for personal growth and the development of mature personalities.
2. It develops conformity and "group-think."
3. It does not take into account the "informal organization" and the emergent and unanticipated problems.
4. Its systems of control and authority are hopelessly outdated.
5. It has no adequate juridical process.
6. It does not possess adequate means for resolving differences and conflicts among ranks and, most particularly, among functional groups.
7. Communication (and innovative ideas) are thwarted or distorted because of hierarchical divisions.
8. The full human resources of bureaucracy are not being utilized because of mistrust, fear of reprisals, etc.
9. It cannot assimilate the influx of new technology or scientists entering the organization.
10. It will modify the personality structure such that man will become and reflect the dull, gray, conditioned "organization man." ...

Bureaucracy, with its "surplus repression," was a monumental discovery for harnessing muscle power via guilt and instinctual renunciation. In today's world, it is a prosthetic device, no longer useful. ...

Bennis, *Changing Organizations: Essays on the Development and Evolution of Human Organization,* McGraw-Hill, New York, 1966, pp. 6-14.

attempting to get bureaucracy to operate as it would if it was operating in its ideal form.

## A CASE STUDY

Any public executive, who has experienced the misfortune of official and citizen reaction to past bureaucratic slipups, may be expected to hesitate when asked to give up a system that has been designed to protect against errors through multiple levels of review and clearance and to install a leadership style instead that will allow employees greater freedom to make decisions or to participate in decision making. It is even more discouraging to discover that some public organizations may not be ready for such changes; preliminary steps may need to be implemented before any thought about organizational change can be seriously considered, but such is the case. Until the employees have reached a minimal level of both technical expertise and professionalism, and unless the political climate is amenable to an attempt at system change, any movement toward changing the leadership style will probably fail. Even when all of these factors are ideal, there is no guarantee that they will remain in that state while the effort at change is taking place; it must be remembered that any dramatic change in the organization will take a protracted period of time to complete. Finally, maintaining the system once it is established also requires strenuous effort, even though such a system tends to be self-renewing. Perhaps the complexity of this process can be best understood by looking at an example of the difficulties experienced by one city manager as he led his city from a typical authoritarian, hierarchical bureaucracy to a style of public management based on openness and participation.

The city of Delong was famous, or infamous, as the community with the highest property tax rate in the state. At the same time, the level of services was not sufficient to meet the needs of the community. The city manager decided that it was time to attack some of the more pressing problems; in order to do so, he thought that it would be appropriate to change the organizational system by moving from a system where he had to initiate policies and actions to an arrangement where ideas could be developed and presented by his staff and the city's employees; hence, the employees would have a greater role in deciding how goals would be accomplished. In order to establish this new system, the manager had to go through a multiple-year program. The first year was spent in a two-pronged attack on the problem. The manager and his immediate staff spent a great deal of time learning about the various methods that could be used internally to change the city bureaucracy; at the same time, the council, which had agreed to the manager's challenge, established a series of community forums to examine the nature of the problems being faced by the city and to measure citizen recognition of, and willingness to attack, the problems.

The result of this first year's work was twofold. First, the management team agreed to try the application of two major system changes: management by objectives (MBO) and program budgeting (PPBS), both of which are designed to increase the participation of employees in the operation of the organization. Second, the council found that the problems were of vital concern to the citizens, but that two additional governmental bodies needed to be involved in the deliberations. The major capital improvement needed by the city was a new sewage treatment plant (a problem that everyone passing the community on the highway was made aware of through their olfactory senses). The sewage treatment problem was in the hands of a separate board, as there was a special sewer district. The other group that had to be included was the school board, for the schools were inadequate; yet, it was the school property tax rate that created the greatest part of the total tax bill. Thus, the city manager found that he had started a process that had expanded to include three overlapping governmental jurisdictions rather than just the city government. Therefore, "participation" in the resolution of the major problems of the community included not only his staff, the city employees, the council, and the citizens but also the governing bodies and staffs of two other jurisdictions, each of which had its own particular ties to the citizens of the city.

Such an arrangement would usually discourage the authoritarian leader from continuing in the present direction, because there is too much danger of losing control. In this case, the manager decided to continue because he had committed himself to the open leadership style and because he could see no better way to solve the difficulties that had to be faced at some point in the near future. Therefore, the second year of the program was carried out with a two-pronged attack. City employees and management were given special training in both MBO and PPBS, with the initial steps in the implementation process commencing. At the same time, the city forums resulted in the development of a set of objectives for the total community. It was decided that these goals should include the input of all three governmental jurisdictions and be accepted, where relevant, by those units. All three units created self-study committees charged with consideration of alternative ways to meet the goals established by the community.

During the third year, dramatic results began to occur. After protracted negotiations, the Commission for the Sanitary District concluded that the most economical alternative for solving the problem of capital improvements for the disposal plant was to connect the entire system into the new plant being completed by a larger city next to them and to annex the district into the neighboring system. This meant that the commission had voted itself out of existence—a rather uncommon occurrence among elected officials. The school board and administration worked out an arrangement with the city council whereby a moratorium on building was declared; no residential building permits were to be issued until the school tax rate had decreased to a certain level. This meant that an adjustment had to be made in the plans of the city's government, with new projections for capital improvements being prepared.

Of primary interest, however, was the activity internal to city organization. The new leadership style adopted by the manager was welcomed by most of the employees, but a few individuals, including some members of the management team, were unhappy and uncomfortable, even to the point of leaving the organization. Everyone found that the new style of leadership required retraining and rethinking on the part of each member of the bureaucracy. The hard work appeared to be rewarding, however, and solutions to problems and more efficient ways of handling duties were discovered in surprising places. After a great deal of conflict, the fire and police departments agreed that a "department of public safety," combining the manpower of the two agencies, would best serve the city. Another example of the solutions developed was in the planning and building of recreational facilities in the city. Instead of hiring costly professional consulting firms to plan parks and facilities, the planners, recreational specialists, and public works employees pooled their talents in creating some of the most unique and functional recreational facilities in the region.

The establishment of community objectives, organizational objectives, and the program budget had led to several reorganizations in the structure of the bureaucracy, and the managerial staff had been reduced by 20 percent. The total program seemed to be successful, but every step required a special effort on the part of the manager, for he was still responsible to the council if anything went awry. In these situations, some problems always cropped up, and the manager had to resolve the issues before they created unanswerable questions. The ultimate problem arose during the third year of the program when three new council members were elected to the council (which was composed of five members.) These newly elected officials were not antagonistic to the activities that they saw taking place in city hall, but neither were they supportive; they were somewhat upset with the "imposition," as they saw it, of program budgeting. They were especially wary because they were not experts in governmental operation; therefore, they were afraid that the program budget was being used by the "experts" on the management team to control the ends of the city government and that decisions were being made by the civil servants.

In addition to his other activities, the manager had to attempt to educate the new council members about the managerial systems that were being used. In order to educate the council, a series of weekend retreats and special sessions were established. The manager had two purposes in mind for these retreats. First, he felt that it was necessary to convince the new council members that, in the words of Marvin Meade,

Participative management represents . . . a reordering of the organization's internal governmental structure and processes in the interest of achieving the same goals . . . more efficiently.[30]

However, the educational program was important for a second reason that was closely allied to the first. The best way to remove the distrust among the council members was to familiarize them with the system, because ignorance breeds fear and because the council members, once they knew how the system worked, were aware of its strengths and weaknesses and how they could use them to their advantage. After the extended meetings, the council was solidly behind the program of the manager, and the city moved on to the issues that they were

[30] Meade, p. 171.

facing. Of course, the next election, or some other factor in the environment that could appear at any moment, could require further effort to maintain the system.

Was it worth it? Did the change in leadership style pay off? The manager, the employees, the council, and the citizens who were aware of the efforts of the city manager generally agreed that the benefits far outweighed the costs; however, everyone was aware of the costs, and no one thought that the change had come about easily. This is the judgment of most people who have examined the problem of democratic leadership of the public bureaucracy in a democratic system. Nevertheless, in order to use the knowledge that has been collected about human motivation, it is necessary to inaugurate change in leadership styles. These two factors that are so central to the management of a bureaucracy cannot be separated. In the end, the bureaucracy is made up of people; therefore, public organizations will never function better than do the people in them; how well the people do their jobs depends on how well they are motivated and led.

## SUMMARY

Leadership (the ability to influence the behavior of others in a group, to set goals for a group, to formulate paths to the goals, and to create some social norms in the group) is central to the success of any public agency. Five types of power (reward, coercive, legitimate, referent, and expert) can be used by the leader whether he or she is a charismatic, traditional, or bureaucratic leader. Many scholars have attempted to ascertain whether or not those leaders who are most successful have characteristics in common. The most commonly noted personal traits, as classified by Stogdill, are capacity, achievement, responsibility, participation, status, and situation. However, there is little agreement on any of these characteristics. The most important factors that influence the accomplishment of a leader may very well be the situation into which a leader is thrust and the style of leadership that he or she applies to those being led.

Although a wide variety of leadership styles exists, and any style may be successful when applied at the right time and place, over the years a categorization of styles has developed. The oldest differentiation is between authoritarian and democratic leadership. Closely allied to this differentiation is McGregor's theory X and theory Y, which uses a behavioral perception of followers as the explanation for why leaders act as they do. Theory X (authoritarian) leadership takes a relatively negative view of human nature; therefore, the authoritarian leader closely directs and controls employees. On the other hand, theory Y (democratic) leadership takes a positive view of human nature; therefore, democratic leaders allow a great deal of freedom and flexibility to their employees.

Equally as important as the leader's view of the employees is the ability of the leader to maintain the position and power of the organization. Therefore, leadership must consider not only motivation but also the other functions of management (decision making, planning, controlling, and communicating). The Managerial Grid shows the interaction between the requirements for productivity and satisfaction; a successful leader needs to have both high productivity *and* employees who are satisfied with their role in the organization. In a democratic state, the public administrator should strive for a leadership style that will take into account (1) the goal of the organization, (2) the composition of the membership, (3) the desires of the public, and (4) the requirements of the political system while always recognizing the administrator's own personality. In spite of all the arguments demeaning the bureaucratic system, it still appears to be the system most suited to achieving the appropriate situation for constructive and dynamic leadership while protecting democratic principles.

# BIBLIOGRAPHY

Barnard, Chester, *The Functions of the Executive*, Harvard University, Cambridge, Mass., 1938.

Berelson, Bernard, and Gary A. Steiner, *Human Behavior: An Inventory of Scientific Findings,* Harcourt, Brace and World, New York, 1964.

Blau, Peter M. "The Hierarchy of Authority in Organization," *American Journal of Sociology, XXXV,* 201-218 (April 1970).

Dubin, Robert, et al., *Leadership and Productivity*, Chandler, Scranton, Penn., 1965.

Fiedler, Fred E., *A Theory of Leadership Effectiveness*, McGraw-Hill, New York, 1967.

Hersey, Paul, and Kenneth H. Blanchard, *Management of Organizational Behavior: Utilizing Human Resources*, Prentice-Hall, Englewood Cliffs, N. J.,1969.

Jacobs, T. O., *Leadership and Exchange in Formal Organizations*, Human Relations Research Organization, Alexandria, Va., 1971.

Katz, Daniel, and Robert L. Kahn, *The Social Psychology of Organizations*, Wiley, New York, 1966.

Levinson, Harry, *The Exceptional Executive: A Psychological Conception*, Harvard University, Cambridge, Mass., 1968.

Likert, Rensis, *New Patterns of Management*, McGraw-Hill, New York, 1961.

Likert, Rensis, *The Human Organization*, McGraw-Hill, New York, 1967.

Luthans, Fred, *Organizational Behavior: A Modern Behavioral Approach to Management*, McGraw-Hill, New York, 1973.

March, James G., ed., *Handbook of Organizations*, Rand McNally, Chicago, 1965.

Marrow, Alfred J., David G. Bowers, and Stanley E. Seashore, *Management by Participation*, Harper and Row, New York, 1967.

Maslow, Abraham H., *Eupsychian Management*, Richard D. Irwin, Homewood, Ill., 1965.

McGregor, Douglas, *The Human Side of Enterprise*, McGraw-Hill, New York, 1960.

Mechanic, David, "Sources of Power of Lower Participants in Complex Organizations," *Administrative Science Quarterly, VII*, 349-364 (December 1962).

Meyer, Marshall, "Two Authority Structures of Bureaucratic Organizations," *Administrative Science Quarterly, XIII*, 211-228 (September 1968).

Myers, M. Scott, *Every Employee a Manager: More Meaningful Work Through Job Enrichment*, McGraw-Hill, New York, 1970.

Peabody, Robert L., *Organizational Authority*, Atherton, New York, 1964.

Perrow, Charles, *Complex Organizations: A Critical Essay*, Scott, Foresman, Glenview, Ill., 1972.

Porter, Lyman W., and Edward E. Lawler, III, *Managerial Attitudes and Performance*, Richard D. Irwin, Homewood, Ill., 1968.

Selznick, Philip, *Leadership in Administration*, Row, Peterson, Evanston, Ill., 1957.

Stogdill, R. M., and A. E. Coons, eds., *Leader Behavior: Its Description and Measurement*, Bureau of Business Research, Ohio State University, Columbus, 1957.

Vroom, Victor H., *Work and Motivation*, Wiley, New York, 1964.

Vroom, Victor H., and Edward L. Deci, eds., *Management and Motivation*, Penguin Books, Baltimore, 1970.

Weber, Max, *The Theory of Social and Economic Organization*, trans. and eds., A. M. Henderson and Talcott Parsons, Oxford University, New York, 1947.

# PUBLIC PERSONNEL ADMINISTRATION

*Accommodating to changing forces while maintaining an ethical public service is certainly a major challenge to our bureaucracy.*

*N. Joseph Cayer*

The ultimate objective of a democratic government is to serve the general public. Toward this end, the political system establishes a variety of policies, but the implementation of these policies is left to the civil servants under the supervision of the elected or appointed executive. Legislators measure the success of government by comparing policy implementation to the original intent of the law. On the other hand, citizens measure the success of government primarily through their feelings. While they may observe the overall efficiency and effectiveness of agencies and programs, the factor that most favorably impresses the average citizen is the speed and courtesy with which their problems and com-

# CHAPTER 13

plaints are handled when they come into contact with the governmental bureau-cracy. Unless major forces are affecting the lives of large segments of society in a way that is obvious to most citizens—such forces as war, inflation, and recession —the "success" of government is wrapped up in the semitangible interaction of the public and their "servants." Therefore, the success of government cannot be separated from the quality of its employees.

The personnel system becomes increasingly important as one moves from the federal to lower levels in government, because personnel costs become a larger segment of operating expenditures. The national government spends a very small portion of its budget on salaries and fringe benefits for employees; how-ever, 80 percent or more of a city's operating budget is tied up in such costs. For a city manager, a mayor, or city council member, the personnel system and the way that it functions and changes are of vital importance. This means that every public administrator should be familiar with the way the personnel system operates. It also infers that one of the more important positions within the governmental bureaucracy is that of the personnel specialist. In fact, the field of public personnel administration is so important that one or more courses specifically dealing with the field appear in most college curricula dealing with public affairs and public administration. This chapter offers an overview of public personnel administration and notes the historical antecedents that led to the contemporary stage of development in the system (affirmative action and the movement toward unionization). After looking at these general areas of the personnel system, a case study is presented to show how all these factors interact and how a public manager must combine and use all these factors when adminis-tering a personnel program in a public organization.

## THE PUBLIC PERSONNEL SYSTEM

Our present public personnel system, the one used by most units of government, is established to concern itself with the human resources of the organization. All the functions pertaining to personnel that can be centralized and handled best by specialists are combined and placed under the auspices of a staff department. Therefore, personnel administration is composed of a variety of functions, and it is difficult to define the system in a brief statement other than in general terms such as those in the first sentence of this paragraph. There are many similarities between the personnel functions in the private and public areas, but the differ-ences that exist are extremely important; if they are not taken into account, one may fail to comprehend the unique characteristics of public personnel adminis-tration.

Most modern public personnel systems are based on the principle of merit, or "a personnel system in which comparative merit or achievement governs each individual's selection and progress in the service and in which the conditions and rewards of performance contribute to the competency and continuity of the service."[1] This is a principle that is shared with private industry; however, the concept of merit takes on special significance because of the omnipresence of politics, which is often partisan, throughout the environment of the public employee. The merit system accepts as one of its basic tenets the idea that politics has no direct input into the appointment, promotion, and retention process. For public employees, this is a critical matter. Patronage systems still exist in some state and local governments; therefore, where a merit system exists, the employees still are eternally vigilant in protecting themselves from the reinstitution of any vestiges of patronage. The fact that a merit system exists, however, does not mean that politics is not an important factor influencing the personnel system. Public personnel systems have always been affected by the political system to a much greater extent than have private corporations— although with the advent of Affirmative Action and the Equal Employment Opportunity Commission, private industries are experiencing an increased governmental involvement in their personnel activities.

The successful public administrator must be aware of the political forces operating around the personnel department. Both the formal political entities and the numerous informal political groups are constantly attempting to influence the decisions that are made and the actions that are taken. After all, the personnel function gains its authority to act from other agencies of government. The department is created and given its authority by the legislative branch of the government; its powers are enumerated, defined, and rearranged by the chief executive; and the courts are becoming increasingly active in reviewing the actions of personnel departments and forcing corrections wherever the judges deem such action necessary.

The national civil service system is a good example of the interaction of political forces on a "nonpolitical" system. Each department's personnel section is guided by the policies of the U. S. Civil Service Commission. At one time, the commission kept direct control over much of the personnel activity within the departments, but during the last decade, the functions have become more decentralized, with the commission serving primarily as a policymaking and reviewing agency. At the same time, personnel policies are reviewed by a wide variety of agencies, so there is a good deal of policy input from around the national government. The Office of Management and Budget (OMB) watches developments in the personnel area very closely; OMB is the chief budgetary agency of the government, and it is interested in how personnel policies will affect budget policies; OMB is also the president's special representative in the area of management analysis and administrative reform, so this gives the agency a second justification for becoming involved in personnel matters. The president and the Senate are directly involved, since the president appoints the members

[1] O. Glenn Stahl, *Public Personnel Administration,* Sixth Edition, Harper and Row, New York, 1971, p. 31.

of the Civil Service Commission with the advice and consent of the Senate. When making these appointments, both the president and the senators are especially interested in the experience, the political persuasion, and the personnel philosophy of the appointees, for this is the point at which the politicians may have a major impact upon the policies established by the commission.[2]

In addition to these influences, the personnel system must take into account policies that are established by executive agencies such as the Department of Labor and the Department of Health, Education and Welfare. Meanwhile, congressional sentiment must be considered because Congress is the originator of the statutory provisions for the civil service system and regularly passes new laws that have an impact on that system. In fact, the House Committee on Post Office and Civil Service is a permanent committee established to oversee the total personnel system of the national government and to suggest any new legislation that may be needed. Congress also has final authority over the pay scale that is established, so the elected representatives of the people have numerous chances to make their wishes known on personnel matters.

As was noted earlier, the president appoints the commissioners to the Civil Service Commission. Donald Harvey suggests that the commission actually is becoming the personnel arm of the president much in the same way that OMB is the budgeting arm of the president.[3] While the president cannot directly influence many of the bureaucracy's actions, he does have the power to order reductions in force and other similar major actions, and these orders must be carried out by the personnel officers.

Finally, the courts have become increasingly involved in the personnel function; one of the major causes for this involvement is the growth of unions among public employees. Unions demand contracts, or written agreements, with government agencies; once an agreement is in written form, disputes are more likely to be resolved in court. Unions represent groups of people also, and an issue takes on added significance when it deals with many people; this leads to greater pressure for satisfactory resolutions to problems in interpretation of contract clauses pertaining to employee and management rights or obligations. Unions have greater resources; therefore, they can afford to fight battles in courts that individuals will not pursue for lack of money. The increased activity of the courts cannot be attributed solely to the unions, however, for the courts would be interjected into the personnel system anyway. The national government has become increasingly interested in issues such as equal employment opportunity; it is a common occurrence now for an agency of the national government to bring suit in court against a state or local government by demanding that the court force compliance with federal guidelines for personnel transactions. A third factor, the general trend throughout the United States for people to turn

---

[2] For a discussion of who influences the Civil Service Commission see: Donald R. Harvey, *The Civil Service Commission*, Praeger, New York, 1970.

[3] *Ibid.*, pp. 10-31.

to the courts to resolve issues that were settled out of court in prior years, must be included when considering the involvement of the courts in the personnel process. This is very important because courts do not solicit cases. The court is a passive branch of government in that it must wait for someone to bring an issue to it. The courts are receiving more issues than has ever before been true in our history.

In addition to the formal political institutions, there are numerous informal political groups, similar to unions, that must be considered by the successful public administrator. Public employee unions usually have close ties with the other unions in the area, and they can work together whenever they consider it advantageous to do so. Public employees, if they act as a unified group, can have a major political impact. For instance, there is a concentration of civil servants in the congressional districts directly contiguous to the District of Columbia; this guarantees that congressmen from these districts will pay a great deal of attention to the interests of federal civil servants. Similar types of political power with differing levels of potency exist for state and local civil servants, and personnel administrators must take these powers into consideration when deciding on particular policies or actions.

At various times in our history, other interest groups have become quite interested in the personnel system; their interest usually continues once they get involved in this area of government policy. For over a century, reform groups have been attempting to change the personnel system and to protect the reforms once they have been accomplished. Such groups as the National Civil Service League maintain a constant vigil in the area of personnel policies. In addition to these older organizations, new groups are taking an interest in personnel systems. Especially active are groups representing the minority citizens, for they are now demanding that government personnel systems not exclude minorities from equal opportunities.

Numerous other groups could be mentioned that have a regular impact on the personnel system of government, but special attention must be given to one force that has tremendous influence on the system even though it is not an organized political entity. Public personnel systems are constantly in competition with the private sector for the best employees. In many cases, the government operates at a slight disadvantage, for it often takes longer to go through the testing and selection process of the government, and in most cases the starting salaries in government positions are slightly below those in private industry. Governments must make constant adjustments in an attempt to remain competitive, and they have been relatively successful in accomplishing this goal; however, the effort is more difficult in many cases because salary levels are set by legislative action, and changes in other policies must be achieved through actions by civil service commissions or other similar bodies. Therefore, the reaction time of public personnel systems to changes in their environment tends to be slow; nevertheless, government has been relatively successful in attracting and keeping talented and dedicated employees.

# THE PENDULUM OF MERIT AND PATRONAGE

The method by which public servants have been chosen from among the avail-able pool of citizens desiring to work for the government has shifted throughout our history, and each shift in personnel policy has marked a concurrent muta-tion in the dominant political groups. By noting the phases of development, it is possible to understand better the forces that have shaped the current political system and to realize the dynamism of the system as it is functioning; even now, new forces are attempting to reshape the system. Although the changes may not be dramatic, they will have a permanent impact. As one looks at the history of the public personnel system, there seems to be a movement similar to that of a pendulum, with a slow swing back and forth between increased emphasis on merit and increased emphasis on personal factors. The swinging pendulum can be observed as one looks· at the major phases in personnel system development.

### 1789-1829: Government by Gentlemen

President Washington was placed in a unique position that has been shared by no other president because he had the opportunity, or burden, of founding the national government's bureaucracy. Washington had to balance two major forces as he set about his work: first, there was no deep-seated faith in, and support for, the new government, so it was important to have a bureaucracy that would deliver the services demanded by the people in a way that was absolutely above reproach; second, there was a philosophy of egalitarianism that required the rejection of elitism, but the egalitarianism was not as broadly defined or ac-cepted as it is today. Therefore, the president had to base his choice on what Frederick Mosher calls the "special construction of 'merit'."

"Fitness of character" could best be measured by family background, educational attainment, honor and esteem, and, of course, loyalty to the new government—all tempered by a sagacious regard for geographic representation.[4]

The early public service consisted of two broad categories of personnel very similar to the present system. First, there was a high-ranking group of offices composed of political executives. This group included cabinet members and their immediate assistants, territorial governors, bureau chiefs, chief accountants, and registers of land offices. These positions were usually filled by persons classified by the current society as aristocrats, and it was accepted practice for these positions to be filled anew by each president. The second group of employees comprised the "workers" rather than the "policymakers," and they were drawn largely from the middle and upper-middle classes of society. At this level of the civil service, the merit system, such as it was, worked relatively well, for the work of the government employees

---

[4] Frederick Mosher, *Democracy and the Public Service,* Oxford University, New York, 1968, p. 57.

. . . generally required that they have a minimum of elementary education—at least the "three R's." A few had had training or apprenticeship in a profession, such as law or medicine, and some others had specialized backgrounds in accounting or other crafts. Although in the main the members of this group were accorded no statutory or other legal job protection, it seems to have been taken for granted from the very beginning that their tenure was for life or for the duration of their effective service. . . . Even under Jefferson and his successor Republican presidents, the practice of "rotation in office" did not take hold for the bulk of the civil service. For this group, the mores and the practice of job security do not appear to have differed substantially from the legally protected security enjoyed by the present-day classified service.[5]

Within these general guidelines, President Washington allowed flexibility in appointments and he listened attentively to the wishes of the members of Congress when they had particular people whom they wanted appointed, as long as those people met the required standards. However, a sense of merit was created around the civil service, and that period was remarkably free of nepotism, patronage, and corruption.

## 1829-1883: The First "Reform"

With the election of President Jackson, a turning point occurred in the government of the United States. Egalitarianism, which had been used as a tenet of the new government, became a reality. Jackson was elected by the western states, those between the Appalachian Mountains and the Mississippi River, rather than the original colonies, and he was elected on the basis of free elections that included the masses as well as the property owners. The idea of having government employees from the middle and upper classes, who held Federalist or Jeffersonian views, was unacceptable to the politicians who were swept into office by this new constituency. Instead, these politicians wanted civil servants to be dependent upon the elected officials; if the administrators and employees were chosen by the elected officials, there would be a common bond of political ideology and personal loyalty that would increase the responsiveness of the administration to the mandates of the public. Finally, the idea of rotation in office was acceptable to this group because, as President Jackson stated in his first annual message to Congress,

The duties of all public offices are, or at least admit of being made, so plain and simple that men of intelligence may readily qualify themselves for their performance; and I can not but believe that more is lost by the long continuance of men in office than is generally to be gained by their experience.[6]

---

[5] *Ibid.,* p. 59.

[6] James D. Richardson, *Messages and Papers of the Presidents,* Volume II, Bureau of National Literature and Art, New York, 1903, p. 438.

What Jackson practiced in moderation, other politicians used with abandon. Senator William L. Marcy of New York argued that politicians could "see nothing wrong in the rule, that to the victor belong the spoils of the enemy"[7]; from this statement came the term, *the spoils system*, which is still used today to describe the patronage system. The tenets of the spoils system were consistent with the egalitarian ideology that was dominant, and the spoils system may have been essential to the times and circumstances that surrounded the government. But before long, the spoils system began to lead to periodic chaos when administrations changed, incompetence in office because officials were chosen for personal loyalty rather than technical competence, development of political machines in state and local governments, and unbelievable demands by job seekers on the elected officials. All these aberrations undercut the original intent of the "reform," because

the egalitarian drive which spurred and rationalized the spoils system proved decreasingly effective as a guarantor of popular direction and control of administration. Jackson and his successors reduced the influence of the old aristocracy and opened the gates of public service to the common people. But the new criteria for appointment produced administrations little more representative of the whole people than before, and they made more effectively possible than before decision-making behind the scenes—"invisible government" as it was called. Our public administration at the close of the nineteenth century was little more *responsible*, in the sense of being answerable to the whole people, than it had been at the close of the eighteenth century. Nor was it more *responsive* to popular needs and interests. We had effectively though not completely transferred governmental power from one group (the gentry) to another (the politicians); in the process, we suffered a considerable degradation of public office and widespread corruption. We also planted the seeds for a kind of civil service reform quite different from that instituted by Andrew Jackson.[8]

## 1883-1964: Development of a Merit System

By 1860, the spoils system was creating such degradation and degeneration of public service that a movement began which demanded the reform of the civil service. Abraham Lincoln's election represented both the high point of the spoils system and the beginning of its decline. Faced with a rebellion, Lincoln used the patronage system to assure the loyalty of public officials and to consolidate the Republican party which he had to unite behind his policies. He made wholesale changes, but, at the same time, he acted primarily to save the Union; he refused to make the same number of changes at the beginning of his

---

[7] Quoted in Leonard D. White, *The Jacksonians*, MacMillan, New York, 1954, p. 320.

[8] Mosher, p. 63.

second term. Of course, Lincoln's successor, Andrew Johnson, was impeached and nearly removed from office over the question of the role Congress played in the removal of officials who had been appointed by the president *with the advice and consent of the Senate.* The battle between Johnson and the Congress marked the beginning of increased congressional interest in and control over presidential appointments, patronage, and the civil service system as a whole.

Surprisingly enough, President Grant was a supporter of civil service reform; he proposed and supported a civil service reform bill and accepted the Civil Service Act of 1871. In this act, the president was given the power to establish rules and regulations for public employees; even more importantly, he was given the power to appoint advisers to help him draw up and administer the rules. The seven men appointed by Grant made up the first civil service commission, and they helped the president to develop and issue a set of executive orders which established a limited use of merit principles. Congress quickly put an end to this upstart body by refusing to fund the system after 1873; in spite of its short life, the recommendations of that body form much of the system under which the national government now functions.

Although the reformers suffered a temporary setback, they continued their efforts, and they were able to succeed over the long run with the aid of the political changes that were occurring throughout the country. N. Joseph Cayer presents a series of factors that led to reform, and he notes three significant events, all occurring between 1880 and 1882, which led to the Pendleton Civil Service Act of 1883. The first event, and the most spectacular, was the assassination of President Garfield by an unsuccessful seeker of patronage employment. Second, the Supreme Court upheld the guilty verdict of Newton Carter in *Ex Parte Curtis.* Mr. Carter, a Treasury Department employee and treasurer of the New York Republican party, was guilty of forcing federal employees to make party contributions, which was in direct violation of the law. The third major factor was the election of 1882, for the Republican Party slipped badly in the election; if the trend continued they realized that they might lose the presidential election of 1884, and along with the presidency would go the power to appoint public servants. "Wanting to insure against large-scale purges of Republican officeholders, congressional Republicans saw wisdom in supporting reform."[9] Under the Pendleton Act, only 10 percent of the employees in the national government were covered by the merit principles, but as time passed, more and more civil servants were covered by the system. With each ensuing presidential election, the number of employees under the jurisdiction of the Civil Service Commission increased, because most of the presidents extended the coverage to protect a portion of their appointees, while only a few presidents exercised their power to roll back the coverage. Today, approximately 90 percent of federal government civilian employees are under some type of merit system.

[9] N. Joseph Cayer, *Public Personnel Administration in the United States,* St. Martins, New York, 1975, p. 25.

There were other factors beside elections and protection for politically appointed employees that led to the increased dominance of the merit system. One major factor was the ability of the civil service reformers to capture the moral argument, thereby equating the merit system with all that was good about the political system while identifying patronage with all that was displeasing. Although no such simple division existed when talking about the merit versus the spoils systems, such a publicity campaign, and its general acceptance by the public, was a coup for the reformers since it made the choices available to Congress very limited—"right versus evil." A second factor that heightened the movement toward the merit system was the election of Theodore Roosevelt as president, for he was an avowed reformer and an ex-commissioner of civil service. As Cayer notes, "Roosevelt did much to improve the service's image and to increase its coverage. From that day on, with minor exception, the commission's position has been a strong one."[10] The commission's position was further enhanced by the increased emphasis on personnel policy, especially the problems of employee welfare, benefits, and rights. This was an issue that became more important as unions gained in strength during the early part of this century. Demands from organized employees required centralized policymaking and a uniform system of positions, pay, and privileges for employees throughout the entire government; the only way to achieve such uniformity was by increasing the authority of the commission. Finally, the greatest pressure to increase the scope of the merit system may have been created by totally impersonal forces inherent in the Industrial Revolution, because

in 1883, the jobs of public servants were still primarily clerkships, but the Industrial Revolution had changed technology, and the post-Civil War era brought on a period of intensified development in the economy. Technological advances and their consequences generated new demands on the political system and resulted in an ever larger public service. In addition, specialization of function created new demands on the personnel system. Jobs became more specialized, and with this development came the need for yet another specialty—the personnel administrator.[11]

It should be noted that the state and local governments went through the same cycle as that experienced by the national government, except that the subnational governments originated the patronage system since they accepted the concept prior to the ascendancy of Andrew Jackson to the presidency. Patronage also lasted longer in the state and local governments. Today, some state and local governments still retain large patronage systems, with merit principles being accepted only so far as necessary in order to qualify for federal

[10] *Ibid.*, p. 28.

[11] *Ibid.*

funds. However, most of the state and local governments have imitated the national government's personnel system; in many cases, the legal base of the state and local commissions has given them more independence and autonomy than that of the national commission.[12]

With all the development and expansion of the merit system, it was inevitable that changes in the way employees were chosen, retained, and promoted would, in turn, have a major impact on the total political system. As a result of the merit system, the country went through two phases within the public service described by Frederick Mosher as "Government by the Efficient" (1906-1937) and "Government by Administrators" (1937-1955). The first era emphasized the morality of efficiency and used the techniques of management science to achieve its goal. The second era, while not dismissing the goals of the efficiency experts, placed its emphasis on the public servant as an initiator of programs or a coequal participant in the policymaking process.

## 1964-    : Redefining Merit

The merit system was so basic in the thought of most citizens, politicians, and academicians during the period from 1940 to 1960, that the only question considered by these groups was that of how to strengthen its protection, broaden its coverage, and therefore share its blessings with everyone. During the turbulence of the 1960s, however, some aspects of the merit system that had been unassailable were suddenly placed under furious attack and careful, often hostile, scrutiny. The reason for the attack was directly traceable to the tenets that had been so successfully espoused during the prior generation. One of the major claims of the proponents of the merit system was that the resulting body of employees was representative of the population that they served, or that there was no better way to assure that the bureaucracy was representative. The openness of the civil service, the ability of citizens in the lower echelons of society to use the civil service as a means of social mobility, while at the same time representing their social constituents, was one of the blessings of the merit system according to its proponents.

When the system was examined, it was discovered that the claims were not wholly true. The merit system, as it had come to be practiced, was vulnerable to the charge that its procedures had systematically excluded people from some segments of society. Whether such a result was deliberate, an unanticipated consequence of administrative negligence, or the natural result of screening out groups of people who were inadequately prepared to do competent work within the government, a demand arose among the excluded groups that corrective action be taken so that the civil service would become truly representative. From this pressure came the movement toward equal employment opportunity and affirmative action.

[12] Mosher, p. 70.

During the same period a second factor became important in deciding the future of the merit system. This factor was the increasing role of unions, or public employee organizations, in the making of policy about and for the public service. The scope and impact of the merit system of the future may very well be decided by the way in which these two major issues are determined. Before continuing this discussion, however, it is necessary to describe how a personnel system is constructed and how its various parts function.

## PERSONNEL SYSTEM ACTIVITIES

The modern personnel office in any middle-sized or large governmental organization is a beehive of activity, with specialists in a wide variety of fields practicing their arts. The increasing complexity of our society has had a similar effect on government personnel; in order to carry out the numerous duties of government, people with every type of expertise are needed. Personnel people for the federal civil service regularly comment that every imaginable career category falling within the legal sphere of society is required and hired in the civil service; since the Watergate hearings and the excitement over the activities of the intelligence agencies, more than a few "civil service wags" have suggested that perhaps their statement was too limited. Whatever the facts might be in this particular case, it is true that a relatively complex system is required to keep up with all the duties and obligations of the personnel office. In order to understand this system, let us examine the various functions individually, keeping in mind how they fit together. Even though the numerous systems that exist at the national, state, and local level vary widely in detail, all of them must deal with the following general processes: classification; compensation; recruitment; testing and selection; evaluation; and promotion, transfer, termination of employment, and discipline.

### Classification

Public personnel systems in the United States are founded on the concept of position classification. All of the other activities of the personnel department are based on the results of the classification procedure. As defined by Stahl:

Position classification is the organizing of all jobs in an enterprise into groups or classes on the basis of their duties, responsibilities, and qualification requirements. In other words, the subject is work performed or to be performed, the process is analysis and evaluation, and the result is classification or arranging of work units into classes.[13]

[13] Stahl, p. 61.

Not all nations use position classification in their public services to the extent that it is used in the United States, but then the concept was conceived in this country as a tool for implementing the merit system; the merit system created a necessity for information about what duties were included in various groups of positions and what qualifications were required. The reformers argued vehemently that there should be "equal pay for equal work," and only through classification could this slogan become reality. Finally, classification was seen as a means to the end of greater economy and efficiency in government, for

> . . . if the organization setup was to be rationalized, if lines of authority in the administrative hierarchy were to be clarified, if more direct control was to be exercised over the flow of work, it became necessary first of all to study the duties of the various positions involved and to discover the lines of authority and the relationships existing among them. Moreover, the new principles of centralized financial control also demanded classification if their full possibilities were to be realized. Uniform accounting required a uniform job terminology in place of a hodgepodge of nondescript and conflicting titles.[14]

The idea of classification is based on the idea of "position," as was noted in Stahl's definition, for the concept assumes that the position can be filled by numerous individuals who have the required skills. In other words, emphasis is placed on the duties, responsibilities, and qualifications rather than on the person who does the job. The individual in the position being classified gives a narrative description of the various tasks that compose the job, including percentage figures on the time spent in each task; in addition, a questionnaire, which covers approximately the same information, may be completed. The individual's immediate supervisor is then asked to review the statement and to comment on the completeness and correctness of the responses. Higher administrators may review the responses if such action is deemed necessary. In some cases, it may be necessary to go through still another step in order to collect the necessary data. Where disparities in job descriptions exist, or where the information still demands clarification after it has been reviewed by the appropriate supervisors, it may be necessary to interview the employee or to perform a "work audit" where a monitor observes the worker functioning on the job and attempts to verify or clarify the description of the job so that it fits reality.

Once all the data have been collected, the positions are distributed among the appropriate classes. A class is a group of positions sufficiently alike in their duties and responsibilities to justify common treatment in the various employment processes.[15] Placing all the jobs of a government into classes

[14] *Ibid.,* p. 63.

[15] *Ibid.,* p. 69.

requires discrimination and judgment, for there are many positions that cannot be easily placed in any single category or that lack similarity to any other current job. The goal in classifying jobs is to strive for simplicity by having *the lowest number of positions possible while recognizing every unique job classification that must be included.* Since many people have multiple roles, it becomes quite difficult to know which role is the most important or how much weight should be given to each role. In order to help deal with this problem, the decisions of the classification specialists are publicly announced prior to final acceptance; this allows individuals to appeal decisions if their placement is unsatisfactory. Publicly posting the classification scheme also has the effect of removing any fear of "deals" that might have been made behind the scenes; in addition, it helps to stop rumors and misinformation that often spread through an organization. After all appeals have been heard and settled, the system can be established and used as the basis for operating the personnel system from that point on.

As new positions are established, a job description must be prepared; from this description, the position is classified and placed within the personnel system. This is the first step required before any other personnel functions can be performed, and it is the basis from which all further actions proceed. Closely associated with the classification concept, and springing directly from it, is the new emphasis on job design and enrichment. Now there is a concerted attempt in many organizations to increase employee discretion and to diversify activities so that employees can realize greater challenge and involvement in their work. Such a job enrichment system allows an employee to use his full range of skills, and it also creates the possibility for employees, through experience and training, to move toward promotion and fulfillment of career goals. Of course, personnel evaluations and promotions, as well as counseling and training programs, are based on the classification system.

Since position classification is so central to the personnel system, it has been a source of endless debate and regular attempts at improvement of the process. Other people argue, however, that position classification as a whole is so rigid that governments would be well advised to discontinue its use. They argue that the classification system has led to overspecialization and narrow job descriptions that have served to limit the availability of candidates rather than helping to recruit qualified individuals. Other detractors have complained that the classification system has led to a rigidity in thinking about positions and structure; this creates organizational inflexibility at a time when the government is faced with the necessity of being able to shift employees between task groups in order to maximize the use of individual skills in solving complex but temporary public problems.[16] Whether or not the detractors are right, the classification

[16] For discussions of the problems in the position classification system, see the following: Merrill J. Collett, "Rethinking Position Classification and Management," *Public Personnel Review, XXXII,* 171-176 (July 1971); Frederick C. Mosher, "The Public Service in the Temporary Society," *Public Administration Review, XXXI,* 46-62 (January-February, 1971); see also E. S. Savas and Sigmund G. Ginsberg, "The Civil Service: A Meritless System," *The Public Interest, XXXII,* 70-85 (Summer 1973).

system will probably remain at the foundation of the personnel system throughout the foreseeable future.

## Compensation

Closely allied to the classification system is the compensation scale. Salaries are attached to the classes instead of taking into consideration the individuals who fill the positions. By combining these two structures, the personnel system attempts to see that the goal of the reformers is achieved; in other words, this is the combination of factors that leads to "equal pay for equal work." Under such an arrangement, all administrative assistants, or clerk-typists, receive equal wages, whether they work for the mayor or the public works department at the local level or for the Director of the Office of Management and Budget or the Department of Defense at the national level. At the same time, it is important that the pay scale take into consideration the differences in responsibilities, duties, and skills that are always present in any organization. It may be impossible to compensate individuals fully for their contribution to the organization, and it may not be necessary if recent studies of motivation are correct; however, inequities in pay must be held to a minimum or else serious morale problems may be generated.

Compensation in the private sphere of employment has usually been greater than that in the public sphere, but Congress has attempted to correct the most conspicuous of these inequities. In 1962, Congress passed the Salary Reform Act through which an attempt was made to achieve a greater comparability between public and private salary schedules; the act also led to a correction of many of the internal inequities of the public pay scale. The public organization has two problems in setting salaries that the private business or industry does not face. First, governments must arrive at a satisfactory pay agreement with workers who fall into the "trades" category. These employees are normally represented by unions; however, they have not been allowed to strike in the past. Second, governments have some categories of employees for which no comparable group exists in the rest of society. In both of these cases, special arrangements have been established to take care of the problems that such situations create.

For skilled blue-collar workers, the problem of establishing comparability in pay is solved with relative ease. As early as the 1860s, Congress provided that the pay of workers in the Navy shipyards should be set by making it equal to the pay of workers in the private shipyards. This concept has spread throughout all levels of government, until now most salaries for skilled workers are established by wage boards which collect information about prevailing wages in the private sector and establish an equivalent pay scale for workers in government. The problem of establishing a fair wage rate for those workers in uniquely governmental jobs is much more difficult. If the government hires carpenters, plumbers, or computer programmers, it is possible to compare wages in the public and private sectors of the society; but with what groups in the private sector can police officers, fire fighters, and military personnel be compared? There are no exact counterparts for these people in the private sector, so salaries cannot be set by accepting those established in the competitive marketplace. The general solution to this problem has been that local governments, which are those most often faced with the problem, have turned to maintaining comparability between each other. Local governments keep statistics on salaries paid in similar jurisdictions, and they try to maintain competitive salaries. In this way the employees are guaranteed a salary close to that of their compatriots (see Figure 9).

State and local government salaries tend to lag behind those paid at the national level. Still, with the fringe benefits that are included, governments are able to attract many talented and dedicated individuals into government work. Many other factors beside pay must be considered when the attractiveness of public employment is being discussed, but pay is and will remain an important factor in recruiting quality public employees. At the same time that governments are experiencing limitations on taxing powers, taxpayers' revolts, and difficulty in balancing budgets, public employees are becoming more militant in their demands for higher and more equitable pay. Therefore, compensation will undoubtedly remain at center stage during the next few years as legislators, public administrators, and increasingly organized public employees try to achieve the will-o-the-wisp solution that "pleases everyone."

## Recruitment

Public employment has been the fastest growing sector of the labor market for the last decade, and it is projected to continue so during the next ten to fifteen years. This means that the governments must carry on an active and effective program of recruitment in order to attract an adequate supply of qualified individuals to fill the new positions being generated by the growth. In addition, there is the necessity of replenishing the existing civil service because of retirement and resignations. The government has historically had a problem in luring qualified individuals into the public sphere; however, the tables have turned during the early 1970s, for now there are more competent individuals in society than there are positions available. At the same time, governmental pay has improved as has the prestige of public employment; now the problem of many governmental jurisdictions has reversed, with public agencies having to deal with policies established to guarantee that recruitment is carried out *in an appropriate fashion*, even though most positions could be filled by simply sitting and waiting for applicants to come to the personnel office.

Governmental personnel agencies must maintain contacts with a variety of educational institutions, training programs, and parts of society so that potential recruits will know about job opportunities. Of course, included in this process is

. . . a great deal of planning regarding the needs of public agencies as well as analysis of manpower policies and availability. With information on the needs

**National Average Monthly Salary Offers by All Types of Employers.**

### BACHELOR'S DEGREE CANDIDATES

| BY TYPE OF EMPLOYER | NON-TECHNICAL CURRICULA | | | | TECHNICAL CURRICULA | | | |
|---|---|---|---|---|---|---|---|---|
| | NO. OFFERS 1974-75 TOTAL | AVERAGE $ OFFERS | | | NO. OFFERS 1974-75 TOTAL | AVERAGE $ OFFERS | | |
| | | 1974-75 TOTAL | 1973-74 TOTAL | 1972-73[a] TOTAL | | 1974-75 TOTAL | 1973-74 TOTAL | 1972-73[a] TOTAL |
| Business | 5,491 | $ 901 | $ 846 | $ 796 | 387 | $ 860 | $ 829 | $ 776 |
| Manufacturing/Industrial | 2,729 | 912 | 852 | 801 | 13,001 | 1,109 | 993 | 921 |
| Government — Federal | 328 | 812 | 782 | 734 | 1,064 | 951 | 871 | 781 |
| Government — Local & State | 381 | 769 | 753 | 693 | 491 | 940 | 869 | 825 |
| Non-Profit & Educ. Organization | 281 | 692 | 651 | 636 | 298 | 784 | 721 | 709 |
| | 9,210 | | | | 15,241 | | | |

[a]1972-73 data taken from special tabulation combining men's and women's offers plus study data on additional curricula, positions, and types of employers not previously reported.

**Figure 9.** (Source. The College Placement Council Salary Survey: Final Report, July 1975.)

of government for particular types of personnel and on availability of such personnel, recruitment becomes meaningful.[17]

Thus, recruitment is based on an analysis of future trends, as well as current needs, and current needs are expressed as positions that have been spelled out just as described when discussing position classification. The chain of interconnected activities within the personnel function begins to lengthen.

## Testing and Selection

If recruitment has been successful, a governmental jurisdiction should have more applicants than available positions. This gives the organization a chance to choose the individuals best suited for the agency and for the job. The problem is one of finding the most appropriate way to measure the abilities and attitudes of the applicants so that everyone can be sure that the best candidates have been selected. The cornerstone of the public merit system is the competitive examination, which allows everyone meeting the minimum qualifications to apply for the open position and to take the same tests, thereby objectively measuring the skills of each individual and comparing his or her results to those of all the other applicants.[18] A single *examination* for a position may include several *tests,* written, oral, and applied. Once the testing procedure is completed, the new employee is chosen from among those who scored highest on the examination. In this way, it is believed that personal factors that are irrelevant to one's ability to do the job—factors such as political persuasion, religious belief, sex, age, or race—are not included within the selection process.

Before testing begins, several issues must be considered by the personnel office. First, it must be determined if the test is for a particular position, occupation, program, or career group. Should the exam measure the practical tools needed for doing a specific job or should it emphasize the selection of individuals who possess a "capacity for growth and development"? Second, since at least some emphasis must be given to the position for which the test is being given, those who are preparing the test must use the position classification (sometimes referred to as "minimum qualifications" or "job specifications") to make sure that the test actually measures the skills and knowledge that are required to perform adequately on the job. In this way, the groundwork that has been done during the prior steps of the personnel procedure is vital to the testing process.

Tests are considered to be effective only if they achieve the three criteria of objectivity, validity, and reliability. *Objectivity* refers to the idea mentioned above, which states that no extraneous factors—such as race, creed, or national

---

[17] Cayer, p. 73.

[18] The standard, and most comprehensive, work on recruitment and testing for governments is: J. J. Donovan, ed., *Recruitment and Selection in the Public Service,* International Personnel Management Association, Chicago, 1968.

origin—are considered in the selection process. Objectivity is sought in terms of identifying those characteristics of mind and skill necessary, and only those necessary, to the given purpose, whether it is to fill a particular position or to begin a career.[19] A test is *valid* if it actually measures what it purports to measure. This sounds relatively simple, but how does one decide if a test is really measuring the criteria that have been established for efficiency and effectiveness in police officers or social workers; it is almost unbelievable that a commonly accepted definition of efficiency and effectiveness has been achieved in the first place. Finally, a test may be both objective and valid, but it is still not an effective test unless it is reliable. A test is *reliable* when it is consistent. In other words, if a person takes the test at two different times, he or she should make the same score each time. However, it is highly unlikely that any individual who takes the same test twice will receive an identical score both times, if for no other reason than that the test taker should score better on the second attempt because of familiarity with the exam and "learning" that occurs during the process of taking the exam. Therefore, a better way of stating the concept of reliability is to say that *over a period of time* the test continues to measure the same variables in the same way with the same results.

Few systems of selection are so rigid that the supervising manager has no choice in the final decision as to whom among the applicants gets the job. In almost every case, the department head has the right to choose from at least the top three names on the eligible list developed through the examination process. Thus, the ultimate selection, within relatively strict limits, still rests with the individual who will be the new employee's superior. The limitation of choice to the "rule of three," as it has come to be known, once again guarantees a certain minimum of objectivity in the selection process; while some choice is left to the hiring official, it is impossible to reach further down the list to hire unless a justification can be made for such an action. Selective certification, as the process is called when an individual is moved from a lower place on the list to the top of the list, can only be carried out after the justification for the action has been stated in writing and approved by those in charge of the personnel system.

## Evaluation

Once an employee is hired into a public organization, the personnel office's interaction with the employee changes in its focus. At this point, the personnel office usually becomes a monitoring agency and a personnel policymaking body. Central records are kept on all personnel-related activities, and all employees come back into contact with the personnel office when they seek promotions or transfers, win awards for excellence, get disciplined for malfeasance, or terminate their employment for any reason. Thus, the personnel office is constantly hovering in the background as public employees go about their

[19] Stahl, p. 117.

normal tasks, and at many of the important junctures in their careers, the personnel office plays a vital role in the resolution of decisions and actions.

Most public organizations make use of an evaluation system for their employees. Under such a system, all employees are rated as to the quality of their performance on the job, with the ratings occurring at regular intervals. The goal of the evaluation system is to improve the performance of employees—and therefore the organization—by guaranteeing that there will be meaningful communication between supervisors and employees about working conditions and the quality of work. These evaluations start while the employees are still on probation (most merit systems have a probationary period during which the employees can be dismissed very easily); once they are past the probationary period, the evaluations continue to build a history about the employees' work records which follow them throughout their careers.

Performance ratings, as the evaluations are often called, have come under sharp attack during recent years; in fact, some jurisdictions have discontinued their use. However, evaluations play a central role in a merit system; therefore, criticism leads to attempts at improving the tools rather than doing away with them. The problem when creating evaluation tools is that they need to have the same criteria for effectiveness as those discussed for examinations: objectivity, validity, and reliability. This means that some way must be found to force supervisors into an objective frame of reference when they are rating their employees. An employee's personality should be considered only to the extent that it directly has an impact on that employee's ability to do his job properly. Far too often, employees are rated on their ability to get along with the supervisor; on the other hand, it is relatively common for a supervisor to rate every employee as superior, because the supervisor either refuses to be put on the spot or wishes to "make all of his or her subordinates happy." Such ratings are a waste of time, and the reason for giving ratings is sabotaged.

Validity and reliability are also problems with evaluations. Since everyone is evaluated, there is pressure to develop a rating tool that can be used throughout the organization for purposes of comparison, yet it is difficult to develop a single instrument that is meaningful when considering the wide variety of skills and knowledge that must be evaluated. When a single rating tool is used throughout an entire governmental organization, comparability of response may be maintained; however, there may be serious questions about the validity of that tool when it is recognized that clerks, engineers, maintenance workers, and budget analysts have all been evaluated by the same tool. Yet, how many different rating forms can be used while maintaining some usefulness to the overall system? It is equally important to be sure that similar terms have the same definition, and the same weight is given to comparable factors, when ratings occur at relatively infrequent intervals.

In spite of all these problems, the evaluation system still plays an important role in the careers of most public employees. The performance ratings may affect merit pay increases, promotion opportunities, and disciplinary actions or attempts at removal from the civil service. For these reasons, the personnel office must wrestle with the problems of evaluation and attempt to find a satisfactory method for achieving the goal.

## Promotion, Transfer, Termination of Employment, and Discipline

Public agencies are usually referred to as bureaucracies since they exhibit most, if not all, of the characteristics mentioned by Max Weber in his masterpiece describing the form of modern organizations.[20] As noted earlier, the personnel system is organized in terms of positions, giving only a minimum of consideration to the individuals who fill them. It is also taken for granted that individuals will follow a career pattern within the bureaucracy by entering the public service at an "entry level" position (or as a specialist) and moving up through the ranks at appropriate intervals. Promotions within the public service often come through an examination process that closely resembles the entry examination. Before anyone can take a promotional exam, however, it is necessary to meet the minimum qualifications; these qualifications often include a stipulation that applicants must have a certain number of years of experience in jobs with particular types of responsibilities and skills before they are eligible for the position being advertised. Everyone meeting the advertised qualifications may then take the exam and compete for the position.

One of the most serious questions faced by public organizations when they are contemplating how to handle promotional opportunities, including all positions above the entry level, is the decision as to whether or not promotion to the position should be "open" or "closed." An *open* examination for a supervisorial or managerial position allows anyone to apply for the job, whether or not they currently work within the organization. A *closed* examination is limited to those who already work in the organization. Arguments can be presented for both types of promotional systems. The open system is more competitive, and it more closely represents the merit concept. It also allows "fresh blood" to enter an organization, while the closed promotional system may lead to managers who are thoroughly socialized in the system and who cannot break out of the thought patterns they developed "on their way up through the bureaucracy." On the other hand, the closed system guarantees that managers will be thoroughly grounded in the policies and processes of the organization when they move into positions of power; it also guarantees that bright, faithful employees will be rewarded.

Closely allied to the issue of promotion is that of transfers. Personnel systems and their rules decide whether or not individuals can transfer and when they can afford to transfer. The promotion rules within an organization may limit the ability to transfer between agencies or governments, but more often the

[20] Max Weber, *The Theory of Social and Economic Organization*, trans. and eds., A. M. Henderson and Talcott Parsons, Oxford University, New York, 1947.

limitations on lateral movement are based on problems in transferring accrued retirement benefits or other fringe benefits. For those jurisdictions that genuinely wish to practice open merit principles, a way has to be found around such problems. One way to overcome the problem of retirement benefits, for instance, would be to establish a statewide, or even nationwide, system for all members of a particular profession or trade. For example, firefighters or police officers could then move to new positions and take their accrued benefits with them, thus greatly increasing their mobility. Other problems of a similar nature could be worked out so that transfers could be managed, if they were to everyone's advantage.

Throughout an organization, there is a constant turnover of people. As each employee quits or in a few cases is terminated, the personnel office becomes the final contact point between the employee and the particular jurisdiction. Many personnel offices have a policy of carrying out a "separation interview" with employees leaving the organization, so that the employee's attitudes and ideas about the organization can be examined. From such interviews, the personnel office can develop a perception of the employee's views about the system. This is one more bit of information that can be added to the data about employee satisfaction and employee motivation; it is the task of the personnel office to maintain and use the information in a way that will improve overall employee performance.

In any public organization, there are going to be a limited number of cases where employees are disciplined or terminated and where the employee appeals the action as unfair or discriminatory. The personnel office must usually investigate such cases and present the findings to the appropriate adjudicatory bodies, such as a civil service commission or hearing officer inside the organization, or a court of law if the case is appealed outside of the organization. In this way it becomes apparent that the involvement of the personnel office with the public employee begins prior to entry into the governmental system and ends only after the employee has left. With such an intense and continuous involvement from beginning to end, it is obvious that the personnel office and the personnel officers have a tremendous impact on the success or failure of any governmental jurisdiction or organization. The actions of the personnel officer help to decide the quality of employees in the organization and have a major influence on the motivation of the employees as they go about their daily work.

## NEW EXTERNAL FORCES
## AFFECTING THE PERSONNEL SYSTEM

The public administrator always faces a dynamic environment, so change is neither unusual nor unexpected; however, sometimes the rate of change is faster than expected, and in these cases, the public administrator begins to feel like he is on a merry-go-round, with the political environment spinning so fast that it is hard to focus on any point in the surroundings in order to maintain an equilibrium and a realistic perspective of the world. Public personnel administration has been on the merry-go-round since 1960, and it shows no signs of slowing down. Numerous policy changes, court orders, and public pressures have contributed to this phenomenon, but two special forces have had the greatest impact on the public personnel system—the growth of public unions and the introduction of affirmative action. These two topics have influenced government policies toward employees so much that it is essential to consider both subjects.

## The Growth of Public Employee Organizations

Unionism within the United States dates back to the last century; however, most of the activity in the area of employee organizations has existed in the private sphere. While unions in the private sphere were gaining in size and strength, public employees were often prohibited from organizing, and when they did organize, it was considered unthinkable for them to use the ultimate weapon of all unions—the strike. As public employment grew in significance because of new programs and increasing technological demands, the organization of government employees also grew. Today there are 14 million public workers; more than 7.6 million of these employees work for state and local government. Of the 3.2 million federal workers, 1,369,000 are union members; at the state and local level, 1,091,000 belong to the American Federation of State, County and Municipal Employees, the Teamsters Union, The American Federation of Teachers, and a wide variety of independent unions.[21] Much of the growth in unionization is occurring at the state and local levels. This may be caused by the fact that merit systems are less developed at the lower levels of government, or it may be due to the balking of state legislatures in passing collective bargaining bills. State and local governments may be the most fertile area simply because the national government has moved to recognize unions at an earlier date.

The Lloyd-LaFollette Act of 1912 recognized the right of federal employees to organize, but they had no bargaining rights. Even so, federal unions were influential in such actions as the passage of the Retirement Act of 1920 and the Classification Act of 1923, as well as other measures designed to strengthen the merit system and to increase pay. In 1962, as partial repayment for strong labor support in the presidential election, John Kennedy guaranteed public employee unions recognition and bargaining rights.[22] All federal agencies were required by the order to institute policies for informal, formal, and exclusive recognition of bargaining agents. President Nixon centralized the administration

---

[21] U.S. Department of Labor, Bureau of Labor Statistics, *Handbook of Labor Statistics, 1974,* U.S. Government Printing Office, Washington, D.C., 1974, p. 363.

[22] Executive Order 10988, January, 1962.

of the process and modified recognition procedures, which limited recognition to "consultative rights" and "exclusive recognition."[23] According to Cayer,

Consultation means that a labor organization representing a "substantial" number of employees may discuss issues with the agency on their behalf. Exclusive recognition exists where a majority of employees vote secretly for representation by a union organization and bargaining by any other agents is precluded.[24]

State and local government laws relating to unions vary from denial of the right to collective bargaining to legislation permitting both collective bargaining and the right to strike.[25] Many states that have not recognized unionization in the past are now beginning to pass legislation that allows representation for employees and mandates on public officials the requirement to "meet and confer" with the employee organizations whether or not an agreement is reached between management and labor.

Central to the "unionization of public employees question" is the specter of the public employees' strike. As stated by Theodore Kheel,

The basic question—and the great challange—is how to prevent strikes that imperil the public interest while still providing millions of public employees with the opportunity to participate in the process of determining the conditions of their work, an opportunity not only guaranteed employees in the private sector but also accepted as socially beneficial.[26]

The original approach to this question was to prohibit all strikes and to fine and/or imprison any public employee who violated these prohibitions. This meant that employees could bargain through union negotiations, but they were forced ultimately to accept whatever the legislative or executive body established as final terms. These laws have regularly failed. Most citizens are familiar with public employee strikes, either through firsthand experience or through observations in the various news media. No final solution has been found for this puzzle, but various combinations of voluntary agreement, mediation, and arbitration are required by the different laws; nevertheless, the best solution ultimately depends on voluntary agreement between the negotiating parties.

[23] Executive Order 11491, October, 1969.

[24] Cayer, p. 119.

[25] For a review of the scope of state laws and why they vary, see: William D. Torrence, "Collective Bargaining and Labor Relations Training of State-Level Management," *Public Personnel Management, II,* 156-160 (July-August, 1973).

[26] Theodore H. Kheel, "Strikes and Public Employment," *Michigan Law Review, LXVII,* 932 (March 1969).

The growth of unionization will have both short-term and long-term effects on the civil service system. Over the short term, it might be concluded that agencies and governments with strong merit systems can expect them to be supported by employee unions, and those areas where merit systems are weak or nonexistent can expect militant union agitation to begin and strengthen the merit principle. However, public managers must realize that the central purpose behind union positions and activities is always the protection and enhancement of the working and living conditions of the members. Therefore, over a longer time frame there are some trends which, if carried to their ultimate extremes, could lead to serious challenges to the merit system. One can presume that affiliated unions (unions belonging to the AFL-CIO or the Teamsters Union) will gradually assume primacy as they have in private industry. As they do, they may be expected to follow certain trends toward the principles of collective bargaining which are parallel to those in private industry. The principles of collective bargaining and of the merit system often come into conflict.

At the present "state of the art" in public personnel administration, it is difficult to make collective bargaining and the merit system compatible. Under a merit system, for example, selection is made through open competitive examination. The traditional bargaining approach by unions might lead to an attempt to require union membership or an occupational or professional license as a prerequisite to selection. While merit systems emphasize competitiveness, with seniority as only one factor in the promotional scheme, the typical union approach to promotion considers seniority as the major, if not the only, relevant factor. Again, unions would prefer classification to be negotiable, while under the merit system it is based on objective analysis related to the required skills and the level of responsibility inherent in the position. Through it all, however, pay and incentives will probably continue to receive a major share of union attention.

The powers and weapons of public unions are different from those in the private sector. Public unions use primarily political rather than economic weapons. As union membership grows, it will become a more forceful influence with legislatures. In the end, public opinion will be the major check to attempts by public unions to press their collective bargaining demands to excessive or unreasonable levels.

In summary, it would seem reasonable to expect a progression to occur in three phases over the years. During phase I, public employee union membership will continue to increase rapidly. Unions can be expected to profess support for merit systems during this period, and they will be increasingly militant toward those systems not operating on merit principles. Phase II will bring out the conflicts between collective bargaining and merit systems. The compromises that will be worked out will involve basic concessions by governments on the concept of sovereignty (the doctrine which holds that, as the sovereign employer, the government cannot be compelled to accept any obligation it shuns or to continue to respect a commitment if it later decides it cannot or should not)[27] and some modification of the ideal of individualism in the merit system. These adjustments will result in the strengthening of the individual's relationship with her employer, and they will allow the individual to act in a group, thus acquiring more power and control over her condition. With these benefits will come some disadvantages, for with unionism comes a tendency toward conformity and mediocrity. The public will probably find that the compromises tend to increase the cost of public services. Hopefully, however, phase III will find an evolutionary process that will lead to a condition where both the individual needs of the employee and the needs of the merit system will be met. The employee will have the power necessary for dignity *and* participation, while the personnel system will be furnishing effective and responsive government through more realistic, and therefore, strengthened merit processes. Governments that already have merit systems may experience a movement directly into the second phase, and it is probable that the first and second phases will overlap for nonmerit governments; however, the phases will still be discernible in most situations.[28]

### Equal Employment Opportunity and Affirmative Action

A second force has entered the sphere of public personnel during the last five years, and with it has come a flurry of activity and anxiety just as momentous as that created by the growth of public employee unions. This new force is affirmative action.

The initial steps in the development of affirmative action began in 1964. Prior to that year there was no agency of the government that was responsible for assuring that all citizens had an equal opportunity for positions in the labor market. The national government began to intervene in this area as Congress passed the Civil Rights Act of 1964;[29] under title VII of the act, the Equal Employment Opportunity Commission (EEOC) was established as an independent executive agency to administer the law; specifically banned was job discrimination because of sex, race, religion, or national origin. In 1972, the coverage of the law was expanded to include *public* employers of fifteen or more persons, and the power of the EEOC was expanded not only to seek remedy for discriminatory practices through conciliation and mediation but also to sue on behalf of complainants when conciliation failed.[30] Thus, the

[27] Felix A. Nigro, *Management-Employee Relations in the Public Service,* International Personnel Management Association, Chicago, 1969, p. 26. "Sovereign" means that the government is the *supreme authority*. As Nigro comments, "The origins of this view of government's rights are in the English common law doctrines that the king could do no wrong and that no individual could sue the state without its consent."

[28] For an example of how the two phases become intermeshed when recognition of employee organizations and the development of a merit system coincide, see Nigro, pp. 42-46, where the Delaware experience is related.

[29] Public Law, No. 352, 88th Congress, 2nd Session, July 2, 1964.

[30] Public Law, No. 261, 92nd Congress, 2nd Session, March 24, 1972.

national, state, and local governments were brought under the jurisdiction of the EEOC, and the commission was given additional powers to force compliance with the law.

Since the vast majority of these public jurisdictions were already operating under a merit system, logically it would not appear that their inclusion under a law insisting on what they claimed to be already doing would cause consternation; however, that is exactly what occurred, because the guidelines established by the EEOC assaulted and challenged several practices that had become traditional throughout public personnel systems. Practices that had become pseudo-sacred because of their longevity, and therefore had gone on for years without being reexamined even though the sociopolitical environment had been going through a steady transition, were suddenly forced into the center of attention by the new rules and regulations.

Public organizations generally wait for potential candidates to come to the personnel office. The national government has a recruitment operation that actively seeks out potential employees on college campuses, and it gives examinations to graduating students during their last year of college study.[31] The national government is often criticized for its failure to compete adequately for employees, but the state and local governments have a record that is much less impressive than that of their big brother. In fact, when considering college graduates, most cities will not even go as far as the national government. In the past, if a job required a college degree, not only would cities not go on campus to recruit potential candidates for the job, but also they generally would not allow an individual to start the testing procedure for the position until the degree was completed. Thus, if a college student was interested in working for the city and went to the city's personnel office, he or she was further discouraged from carrying on the attempt because it was necessary to go through the time-consuming testing and selection process which often took months *after* graduation. This meant that one had to go through a process that did not guarantee success. In contrast, jobs offered by private sector employers, where employment was often more rewarding materially and where there was no waiting for the testing and selection process to reach its ultimate end, often became acceptable by necessity, even if those jobs were not the individuals' first choice.

The recruiting system suffered from another more serious problem. A system of recruitment that waited for potential employees to come to city hall to find out about jobs automatically excluded many parts of the minority community, because these people refused to go to city hall for a variety of reasons; they did not feel welcome because city hall had been a place of difficulty for them during other visits. Therefore, important segments of the population, primarily minorities, were not being reached, informed about jobs, and attracted into the pool of recruits for public jobs. The affirmative action program forced govern-

---

[31] The PACE (Professional and Administrative Career Examination) is used for a wide variety of liberal arts and business students and more specialized exams for students or professionals in special fields.

ment personnel offices to make direct efforts to reach all segments of society during the recruitment phase of the personnel cycle.

The testing process has also come under sharp attack. Specifically, many standardized tests that are used by personnel offices have higher failure rates for minorities than for nonminorities; yet little evidence can be presented to show that the differential in test achievement is related to differences in job performance. Even though the tests are applied neutrally and without an intent to discriminate, the result often leads to a disparate effect, and such a result is unconstitutional unless the employer can prove the test procedures are job related. This rule is firmly stated in the U. S. Supreme Court decision in *Griggs* v. *Duke Power Co.* The decision says,

The Act (Section 703 of Title VII of the Civil Rights Act of 1964) proscribes not only overt discrimination, but also practices that are fair in form, but discriminatory in operation. The touchstone is business necessity. If an employment practice which operates to exclude Negroes cannot be shown to be related to job performance, the practice is prohibited.[32]

Therefore, the EEOC has established a set of guidelines by which tests used in selecting employees must be validated. Tests must be directly related to the qualifications and skills needed in the job for which the test is being given, and any irrelevant material or testing methods must be expunged from the testing process. Especially questionable are aptitude tests (that often tend to be culturally biased), oral examinations (which may be subjective and cannot be easily validated because it is impossible to check the interviewers' mental processes), and exams that include supervisory ratings as part of the total score or ranking of candidates (which face the danger of introducing subjective and irrelevant issues). The introduction of affirmative action has led to a revolution in the testing process, with every aspect of testing being itself tested, inspected, evaluated, and challenged in court.

Similiar affirmative action was mandated to correct prior injustices in the areas of compensation and promotion. When minority or female employees managed to gain employment, their salaries were lower than that of their white male counterparts. The problem of pay comparability for women and men is a good example of the issue. When the salaries of men and women were compared within occupation groups for 1970 (see Table 1), the differentials varied from 42.8 percent to 66.7 percent, with the median earnings of women in 1970 being 59.4 percent of those earned by men, a drop from 63.9 percent in 1955.[33] Within particular occupations, men usually received better pay. For example,

---

[32] *Griggs v. Duke Power Co.,* 401, U.S. 424, 1971.

[33] "Fact Sheet on the Earnings Gap," U.S. Department of Labor, Employment Standards Administration, Women's Bureau, December, 1971. This report was based on data from: *Current Population Reports,* P-61. U.S. Department of Commerce, Bureau of the Census.

Table 1.

**Median Wage or Salary Income of Full-Time Year-Round Workers, by Sex and Selected Major Occupation Group, 1970**

| Major Occupation Group | Median Wage or Salary Income | | Women's Median Wage or Salary Income as Percent of Men's |
|---|---|---|---|
| | Women | Men | |
| Professional and technical workers | $7,878 | $11,806 | 66.7 |
| Nonfarm managers, officials, and proprietors | 6,834 | 12,117 | 56.4 |
| Clerical workers | 5,551 | 8,617 | 64.4 |
| Sales workers | 4,188 | 9,790 | 42.8 |
| Operatives | 4,510 | 7,623 | 59.2 |
| Service workers (except private household) | 3,953 | 6,955 | 56.8 |

*Source.* U.S. Department of Commerce, Bureau of the Census: *Current Population Reports*, P-60, No. 80.

Table 2.

**Median Salary of Full-Time Employed Civilian Scientists, by Sex and Field, 1970**

| Field | Median Salary | | Women's Median Salary as Percent of Men's |
|---|---|---|---|
| | Women | Men | |
| All fields | $11,600 | $15,200 | 76.3 |
| Chemistry | 10,500 | 15,600 | 67.3 |
| Earth and marine sciences | 10,500 | 15,000 | 70.0 |
| Atmospheric and space sciences | 13,000 | 15,200 | 85.5 |
| Physics | 12,000 | 16,000 | 75.0 |
| Mathematics | 10,000 | 15,000 | 66.7 |
| Computer sciences | 13,200 | 16,900 | 78.1 |
| Agricultural sciences | 9,400 | 12,800 | 73.4 |
| Biological sciences | 11,000 | 15,500 | 71.0 |
| Psychology | 13,000 | 15,500 | 83.9 |
| Statistics | 14,000 | 17,100 | 81.9 |
| Economics | 13,400 | 16,500 | 81.2 |
| Sociology | 11,000 | 13,500 | 81.5 |
| Anthropology | 12,300 | 15,000 | 82.0 |
| Political science | 11,000 | 13,500 | 81.5 |
| Linguistics | 11,300 | 13,000 | 86.9 |

*Source.* National Science Foundation: "National Register of Scientific and Technical Personnel," 1970.

when the salaries of full-time employed civilian scientists were compared by field and sex, the disparity continued although the difference was smaller (see Table 2). However, the figures did not indicate only that women were receiving unequal pay for equal work. Exacerbating the problem was the fact that few women had risen to management positions, as was pointed out in referring to positions held by women in the public elemenatary and secondary schools:

In public elementary and secondary schools, women were less than 20 percent of the principals; superintendents; deputy, associate, and assistant superintendents; and other central office administrators in 1970–71.

Among professional and technical workers in business, women are concentrated in the class B and class C computer programmer positions, while men are more frequently employed in the higher paying class A positions. Similarly, women are usually in the lowest category of draftsmen and engineering technicians.

Among managers and proprietors, women frequently operate small retail establishments, while men may manage manufacturing plants or wholesale outlets.

In the manufacturing of men's and boys' suits and coats, women are likely to be employed as hand finishers, thread trimmers and basting pullers, and sewing machine operators—jobs where their average hourly earnings are less than $2.70—while men are likely to be employed as finish pressers (hand or machine), underpressers, cutters, and markers—with average hourly earnings of $3.50 to $4.25.

In the service occupations, women are likely to be cooks, nurses' aides, and waitresses, while men are likely to be employed in higher paying jobs as bartenders, guards, custodians, firemen, policemen, and detectives.[34]

The problems of minority citizens were, and are, similar to those described for women. When the public employment systems were examined, it was found that a discrepancy in salaries existed; the differential was associated directly with the facts that women and minorities held lower jobs in the public hierarchy and that they had not received promotions. Thus, there were fewer women and minority employees in public agencies, except in particular jobs that were deemed "appropriate" for these people; since they were primarily in lower skilled and lower paying jobs, there was a differential in the remuneration received by these employees.

The attempts of the Equal Employment Opportunity Commission to correct these inequities through the Affirmative Action Program have created a flurry of activity and controversy. The governmental units had enjoyed immunity from EEOC action until 1972, when the amendment placed all governmental units hiring fifteen or more employees under the jurisdiction of the EEOC. Suddenly

[34] "Fact Sheet on the Earnings Gap."

the governments had to face the reality of finding a solution to the past inequities while maintaining the essence of the merit system.

Regardless of the actions taken in attempting to overcome the predicament, some group of individuals is either inconvenienced or else feels that the new rules and procedures discriminate against them. Furious debate rages as to whether or not the regulations promote "true equal opportunity" or actually lead to a form of "reverse discrimination" in an attempt to correct previous discriminatory practices. Few people attack the concept of equal employment opportunity, (even though a few people probably do *not* accept the thesis); the arguments are over the procedures that are being used and the definition of equal opportunity. The results, however, have been to delay the accomplishment of the goals established by the EEOC and the growth of the litigation in the courts over a variety of grievances—both those of the minority members who are trying to gain what they believe is justice and those of the majority population who believe that the new rules are simply a fresh brand of discrimination that compounds old evils.

The goal of affirmative action is the establishment of a completely representative bureaucracy. If the bureaucracy is a reflection of the general population, it is believed that the government will be better able to understand and to respond to the desires and demands of the citizenry. This philosophy goes back to the time of Andrew Jackson; it has been especially well stated by Paul P. Van Riper, who says that,

a representative bureaucracy is one in which there is a minimal distinction between the bureaucrats as a group and their administrative behavior and practices on the one hand, and the community or societal membership and its administrative behavior, practices, and expectations on the other. Or, to put it another way, the term representative bureaucracy is meant to suggest a body of officials which is broadly representative of the society in which it functions, and which in social ideals is as close as possible to the grass roots of the nation.[35]

The Affirmative Action Program is the last in a series of movements that have had just such an end in view. The reason that there has been a series of movements is that the general definition of "citizen" has been expanded at several key times in our history, and with each expansion of the term, a new group has become eligible for employment in the government. At first, the definition of "citizen" usually included only male property-owners. Soon universal manhood suffrage included all males; therefore, the public service opened to a much wider segment of the population. During this period, there was no explicit exclusion of women from public bureaucracies; on the other hand, women did not play a major role among bureaucrats. With the granting of female suffrage, the women were able to claim a full role in government, including positions in the civil service. Of course, the Thirteenth, Fourteenth, and Fifteenth Amend-

[35] Paul P. Van Riper, *History of the United States Civil Service,* Row, Peterson, Evanston, Ill., 1958, p. 552.

ments had already guaranteed that blacks and other minorities would share in the rights of citizenship; however, the full impact of the constitutional mandates have been felt only in the last two decades. The public personnel system, and therefore the public personnel administrator, is faced with a new set of pressures that must be successfully coped with while maintaining those parts of the merit system that are worthwhile. Or rather, perhaps a new and broadened definition of merit must be developed so that

... instead of treating merit as a static concept which judges an individual by rigid standards of education and experience, there is now an opportunity to develop a dynamic concept of merit in which motivation and dependability and the intangible quality of potential create a more flexible and more humane standard of judgement.[36]

The success or failure of the personnel administrator may have a vital role in deciding how well the people accept the efforts of the government to serve all the citizens, both those of the majority and the numerous minorities. Being placed in such a position may be uncomfortable for the public personnel administrator, but it also makes the position challenging and exciting. Very seldom does any position offer challenge without some risk.

## A CASE STUDY

In July of 1971, the United States Congress sent to President Nixon a piece of legislation entitled the Public Employment Act of 1971.[37] The United States was suffering from an economic lull; the bill was passed with the hope that it would act as a temporary spur to the economy, as an aid to the people who were displaced by the recession, and as a means of helping those who had consistent records of underemployment. President Nixon signed the bill into law and the Department of Labor set in motion the administrative machinery that it had developed in anticipation of final passage.

While Congress was considering the legislation, the city of San Jose was notified by its "Washington lobbyist"[38] that there was a strong likelihood that federal money would become available for the hiring of temporary employees. The city was understaffed as a result of 200 position reductions that had occurred during the prior year, so the city council was pleased to be able to replenish the staffs of the various departments. Therefore, when the money

---

[36] Earl J. Reeves, "Making Equality of Opportunity a Reality in the Federal Service," *Public Administration Review, XXX,* 43-49 (January-February, 1970).

[37] Public Law, No. 54, 92nd Congress, 1st Session, July 12, 1971.

[38] Many of the larger cities in the United States hire individuals to represent them in both the state and national capitals. These people serve as a liaison with politicians and public officials, and they are expected to inform cities of new programs or legislation that directly affects the welfare or interest of local government.

became available, the city was prepared to move, and within a few weeks, the city had signed an agreement with the Department of Labor. However, the agreement was signed without a great amount of attention being paid to the contractual commitments contained in the grant. One particular commitment stated that the city would accept as a goal the placement of 50 percent of its *temporary* employees in *permanent* positions, either public or private, by the end of the program which was to extend over a two-year period. Before the end of the second year, this part of the agreement was to bring about some drastic rethinking of personnel practices and philosophies.

The agreement gave the city over 3 million dollars with which it was possible to hire 399 employees, 317 of whom were hired directly by the city, while 82 were hired by other local jurisdictions, such as the schools, through sub-contracts with the city. All of these positions were filled within two weeks, and the program settled down to a steady routine. The permanent employees of the city were thankful for the help of the temporary employees, but little serious thought was given to the problem of placing these employees in per-manent positions or of deciding how the work they were doing would be ac-complished if they had to leave the city at the end of the program.

As the first year of the program came to a close, the dual problems of meet-ing grant commitments and of carrying out the various city programs were brought home rather forcefully when a review of the program was completed by members of the city manager's staff, the personnel department, and the U. S. Department of Labor. Halfway through the expected life of the program, only 4 of the 317 employees hired under the Emergency Employment Act had been transferred into the city's regular civil service system. With this rev-elation, the city manager suddenly realized that it was going to be quite dif-ficult to meet the goal of placing half of the temporary employees in permanent jobs, because most of the people were going to have to be placed in the city's civil service. At the same time, it became apparent to the supervisors and department managers that they were threatened with the loss of numerous employees on whom the departments had come to depend and toward whom most of the immediate supervisors had developed very positive attitudes. The psychological impact of realizing that half of the time had passed during which these people would be available suddenly spurred interest among those in charge of services and programs; the supervisors felt that the employees had functioned well in their positions and that the positions were essential to the effective and efficient completion of the city's work.

In an attempt to remedy this predicament, the city manager appointed a personnel specialist, Mr. Robert Farnquist, to run the Emergency Employment Act (EEA) Program; Mr. Farnquist was given almost complete control over the program so that he could work toward resolving the problems that were pre-eminent in everyone's mind. Control over the EEA Program was just a beginning, however, because no such program operates in a vacuum; this is especially true when considering personnel programs that affect every other operating system. Mr. Farnquist's task was to develop a strategy that would allow the city to meet its commitment on placements in permanent jobs by moving a large number of the temporary public employees into permanent civil service jobs. In order to meet this objective, it was necessary to gain the acceptance or support of widely divergent groups, including the departments in the city, the city council, the Civil Service Commission, the unions, and numerous citizens' groups within the community.

Immediately after taking the position as director of the EEA Program, Mr. Farnquist set aside five days during which he thoroughly examined the grant agreement between the city and the Department of Labor, the legislation as it was passed by Congress, and the policies and practices of the overall program. Participating in this study was a variety of people concerned with the program. From this analysis came an understanding of the commitment made by the city, the powers and limitations granted through the federal law, and the stumbling blocks that existed in gaining the cooperation and support of the various groups involved at the local level.

After completing the study, it became apparent that a three-pronged plan would have to be implemented in order to accomplish the program's objectives. First, all the tactics were prepared with the understanding that the actions had to fit into the general framework of the merit system, but it was also realized that the basic concepts of merit allowed a rather wide latitude of interpretation without sabotaging their intent. Therefore, the major thrust of the attack was aimed at a reinterpretation and reshaping of the rules governing entry into the city's civil service. This would require the active participation of the Civil Service Commission, for the commissioners had to accept the new rules that were to be proposed. The second part of the strategy was to educate the city's managerial and supervisorial staff, the employees already in the civil service, the public-employee unions, and the city council that the new rules were beneficial to everyone concerned. Third, the rule changes had to be explained to the employees who had been hired through EEA, and these employees had to be prepared for the steps that they would need to take in order to be accepted into the civil service as permanent city employees.

The basic proposal that would alleviate the problem of placing the EEA employees in permanent jobs was a complicated regulation dealing with both the city's testing procedures and selection system. The major problems with meeting the city's commitments existed in two areas: First, when the personnel department reviewed its records, it was discovered that very few examinations had been given during the time that the EEA employees had been working with the city. Tests usually were given at two-year intervals or as the eligible list was depleted—whichever came first. Therefore, most of the temporary employees had not been given the opportunity for a permanent position through the normal channels. Second, in those cases where the temporary employees had been able to take tests, they had either failed to pass the exam or had been unable to score among the top three; the city had a strict "rule of three" procedure whereby appointments had to be made from the top three names on the list *as ranked by the examining process.* Therefore, employees not only had to be able to *take* the test, but they had to *pass* the test, and the rule of three had to be circumvented without, at the same time, destroying the principle of objectivity and impersonality that is the basis for the rule.

In order to deal with these problems, it was proposed that the Civil Service Commission make two changes in the procedures for testing and selection. The first suggestion was that as positions became open within the city's civil service, new tests be given in all cases where the current list of eligibles was more than one year old. Under such a ruling, almost all the current lists of eligibles would be invalidated and new tests would have to be given. This would give all the temporary employees a chance to take the tests for the jobs they were currently holding.

The second suggestion was more sensitive, for it proposed that a system of "selective certification" be available for use when an EEA employee was on the eligible list from which an appointment was to be made. As previously noted, selective certification is a process whereby a name can be moved to the top position on a list of eligibles because of special qualifications, even though the individual does not score the highest on the tests. Since this appeared to be a·step away from the merit principle, selective certification raised misgivings on several fronts. The Civil Service Commission felt that it was conceivable to give the tests sooner than usual, but the idea of breaking with the "rule of three" seemed to be an unacceptable dilution of the concept of ability. The unions were equally hesitant in this area because they feared that the use of selective certification could set a precedent that would be prejudicial to the regular city employees when promotional tests were given. The supervisors of the temporary employees also suffered from mixed emotions when the idea of selective certification was presented to them, even though the work of the EEA employees had been very satisfactory. Most of the supervisors had expressed their desire to keep the employees; however, the supervisors were constantly defensive about their powers, and they were afraid that their acceptance of the selective certification clause would lead to an erosion of their power because an outsider might be able to order them to hire an employee over their own objections.

In order to overcome these doubts, the use of selective certification was carefully circumscribed, and the rule was established only after serious consultation with all of the interested parties, including the EEA employees. The ultimate set of rules that was established included the following stipulations, so that the bona fide interests of everyone would be protected while allowing selective certification to be utilized. First selective certification could be used *only* in appointing temporary city employees to the job they presently held, and it could not be used in any promotional exams. Second, the employee was required to pass the standard entry test—in other words to meet the minimum requirements of the regular merit system by being somewhere on the list of eligibles—before selective certification could be applied. Third, before selective certification could be invoked in appointing a temporary employee to a permanent civil service position, that individual had to have held the position to which he or she was being appointed for at least one year; furthermore, his or her performance evaluations had to have been satisfactory throughout that period. Fourth, in no case could selective certification be requested by anyone but the supervisor under whom the temporary employee had been and would be working.

After considerable discussion, the various parties were satisfied that their interests were not only protected but actively supported by the use of selective certification. For instance, the unions saw a chance to gain additional members, and once the current members no longer saw selective certification as a direct, personal threat, they were willing to have the union spokesmen strongly support the proposal. As a whole, the supervisors were quite satisfied because their personal prerogative was protected, and, as was noted above, the majority of the supervisors wanted to hire these employees permanently because their work records had been quite satisfactory. The Civil Service Commission felt that the merit principles were protected, and the EEA employees were grateful for an opportunity to prove themselves.

The achievement of agreement among all of these groups had taken several weeks of tough negotiations, because prior to this time these groups "could hardly agree on a room to meet in, much less get together on substantive issues."[39] Now the package of proposals was ready to present to the city council. It had been deemed inappropriate to approach the council before the several groups involved had united behind a single plan; however, the council members had been furnished with a steady flow of information about the EEA Program, its problems, and its prospects. Now that agreement had been reached, the proposed program was formally accepted by the Civil Service Commission and sent to the city council for its approval. Two additional occurrences added considerable strength to the plan and put pressure on the council to accept the proposal. First, the U. S. Department of Labor had been following the developments very carefully, and full approval was given to the program that had developed. The EEA Program managers had worked diligently to keep the Department of Labor representatives informed of everything that was happening; the department responded by wholeheartedly supporting the program once the questions of maintaining the merit principle were clarified. Second, the issue of affirmative action had just arrived on the scene, and the resolution of the EEA question was going to have a major impact on the "good faith" of the city in establishing its Affirmative Action Program. Among the EEA employees were minorities in large numbers (the EEA contingent included 35 percent Chicanos and 15 percent blacks in a city where they made up 18 percent and 2 percent, respectively, of the population). These figures meant

[39] Barry S. Bader, "San Jose, California: A Study in Successful Civil Service Reform," *Advance, II,* 4 (Summer 1974). *Advance* is a journal dealing with studies in public manpower modernization published by the National Civil Service League's Center for Public Personnel Management.

that acceptance of the selective certification proposal would be a major sign of commitment to the concept of affirmative action, since all of these minority employees would be given a chance to become part of the city's permanent work force. Likewise, the failure of the council to accept the program would signal a lack of good faith to both the Equal Employment Opportunity Commission and the minority community in the city.

Both of the above factors, added to the united voice of the various city organizations and pressure groups, led to a formal acceptance of the program by the city council; nevertheless, agreement came only after one final amendment was attached to the ordinance. The city of San Jose was faced with the same problem, a financial squeeze, that plagued most other local governments. The EEA employees were being paid from federal funds, and the city lost those funds as each of the employees went on the city's payroll. Therefore, in order to maintain the flow of EEA money into the city, it was decided that all of the employees would remain on the EEA payroll for the duration of the program with the understanding that, upon completion of the EEA Program, all of those who had been properly certified and appointed by the city would automatically be transferred to the general fund payroll. In this way, the city was assured that the maximum amount of federal money would be received, while the employees would be guaranteed permanent jobs.

As the negotiations with the other groups had been progressing, Mr. Farnquist and his staff had prepared an attack on the third aspect of the program. After the first year of the program, the EEA employees were suffering from low morale. Only four of the employees had been able to make it into the permanent civil service. In addition, there seemed to be a psychological differential between the permanent and temporary employees, with the temporary employees holding an inferior position. The low morale led to the normal problems; many of the EEA employees felt bitter because they believed their contributions were not appreciated, and there was a constant undertone of worry about what would happen as the program came to an end, which distracted individuals as they tried to do their work. Furthermore, many of the employees realized that although they were performing satisfactorily on the job, they could not pass the tests required for the appointments, or even if they passed, they could not hope to be among the top three candidates. The diagnosis of the morale problem led to a prescription that focused on a concentrated training and education effort.

The federal guidelines to the Public Employment Program allowed an ample amount of the budget to be used for training. Until this time, the city had done very little for its employees in the way of supporting their education and training. Outside of the usual on-the-job training offered to all the new employees and an occasional workshop or training session dealing with special problems, the city had done little to improve the skills and knowledge of its employees. This deemphasis of training was unintentional, and it had occurred primarily because the city, like many other civil service organizations, had generally recruited and hired individuals who already had the minimum qualifications for the jobs being offered. In addition, these individuals had generally come from a white, Anglo-Saxon background that had prepared them for the written and oral examinations used by the city; therefore, the problem of intensive training or upgrading of employees had not occurred before this time. The staff in charge of the EEA program was able to use this new concept—training—as an instrument for increasing morale. For the first time, city employees were able to receive substantial aid in the form of tuition and released time to attend local educational institutions and external training programs. A special effort was made to point out the special benefits that this made available to EEA employees; *these were not available to the civil service employees.* The publicity campaign was so successful that the regular employees began to lobby through the unions for similar benefits.

A second aspect of the training program included special instruction and preparation for the exams that had to be passed by the EEA employees. These training sessions were open to other city employees if they wished to participate, thus avoiding any questions of discrimination or favoritism; nonetheless, the main group using this training was the members of the EEA Program. Although the actual examination was not available prior to the test date, the job descriptions were known, and from this information it was possible to construct sample questions. Some publishing companies had also prepared manuals on how to take written examinations and had included sample tests that could be used in the instruction sessions. The major problem of the potential examinees was not a lack of knowledge, for they were already filling the positions satisfactorily. The problem was teaching these individuals how to read and respond to questions. It was also necessary to remove the fear of civil service exams, which proved to be the major obstacle for most of the trainees.

Added to these training efforts, the EEA personnel staff began publishing a monthly newsletter which was mailed to every concerned employee. These newsletters included the latest and most complete information about funds for the program, training that was available, tests that were approaching, and rights and privileges of EEA employees. Special features, such as letters from the city manager, union leaders, or fellow employees, were also included. The newsletter was especially successful in minimizing the effect of rumors and maximizing the sense of identity among the EEA employees, both of which helped to improve the morale and motivation of the concerned workers.

A final part of the "educational program" was aimed at the total city staff, but with a particular goal in mind. The goal of this informational system was to emphasize the value of the EEA employees to the city as a whole. A steady flow of information was released about the roles fulfilled by EEA employees, both as individuals and as a group. This "propaganda" also helped to increase the morale of the EEA employees through recognition on their own part of their importance within the city and through the recognition and admission of their significance by their co-workers, the permanent employees.

All of these carefully calculated tactics led to a dramatic increase in the morale of the EEA employees and to a significant improvement in the placement of temporary employees in permanent positions. At the end of the two-year time limit, the program was extended for a third year by the federal government. The strategy developed during the intensive negotiations at the beginning of Mr. Farnquist's directorship was continued during the extension. When the program came to a close at the end of the third year, the city was able to report that its commitment had been more than fulfilled; over 90 percent of the employees hired under the auspices of the Public Employment Program had been placed in permanent positions with the city, other governmental units, or private industry. In addition, many of these employees had appreciably improved their skills and knowledge, and they had obtained increases in their income levels. The success of the program was directly attributable to the effective utilization of management principles, the understanding of the principles of public personnel administration, and the proper diagnosis of the political environment. All these skills are essential to competently fulfill the role of the public personnel administrator.

## SUMMARY

The ultimate success of government depends on the quality of the civil servants who are carrying out the programs established by the political process. Most modern public personnel systems are based on the concept of merit (a personnel system in which ability and achievement govern each individual's selection and progress in the service and in which the conditions and rewards of performance contribute to the competency and continuity of the service), although some local government systems still operate under patronage (a personnel system in which personal factors, especially party affiliation or loyalty to a political official, are considered to be important elements in appointment and promotion). No personnel system can be removed totally from politics, but the involvement of individual employees in partisan electoral politics can be made voluntary and external to the job. Even so, astute public personnel administrators are aware of the fact that they must pay close attention to the ideas and actions of interest groups, political parties, legislators, chief executives, and judges.

The pendulum of personnel policy has swung between merit and patronage throughout the history of our country. President George Washington and the Federalists accepted a limited type of merit principle in filling government positions. With the election of President Andrew Jackson, patronage came into ascendancy and remained there until the beginning of the twentieth century. With the establishment of the Pendleton Civil Service Act of 1883, the pendulum began to move back toward the merit principle. The merit principle is still widely accepted, but some redefinition of the term is occurring at the present time due to the development of affirmative action concepts and public employee unions.

The public personnel system is composed of several subsystems: classification; compensation; recruitment; testing and selection; evaluation; and promotion, transfer, termination of employment, and discipline. Each subsystem of the system interacts, and no personnel system can be more effective than its weakest part. The new forces of public employee unions and equal employment opportunity (affirmative action) are requiring careful reevaluation and restructuring of all parts of this system.

# BIBLIOGRAPHY

Bakke, E. Wight, *The Mission of Manpower Policy,* The W. E. Upjohn Institute for Employment Research, Kalamazzo, Michigan, 1969.

Byers, Kenneth T., ed., *Employee Training and Development in the Public Service,* Public Personnel Association, Chicago, 1970.

Case, Harry L., *Personnel Policy in a Public Agency: The TVA Experience,* Harper and Row, New York, 1955.

Cayer, N. Joseph, *Public Personnel Administration in the United States,* St. Martins, New York, 1975.

Commission on Organization of the Executive Branch of the Government, *Personnel and Civil Service,* U.S. Government Printing Office, Washington, D.C., 1955.

Donovan, J. J. ed., *Recruitment and Selection in the Public Service,* Public Personnel Association, Chicago, 1968.

Fish, Carl Russell, *The Civil Service and the Patronage,* Harvard University, Cambridge, Mass., 1904.

Harvey, Donald R., *The Civil Service Commission,* Praeger, New York, 1970.

Heisel, W. Donald, *State-Local Employee Relations,* Council of State Governments, Lexington, Ky., 1970.

Jones, Charles O., "Reevaluating the Hatch Act: A Report on the Commission on Political Activity of Government Personnel," *Public Administration Review, XXIX,* 249-254 (May-June, 1969).

Kator, Irving, "The Federal Merit System and Equal Employment Opportunity," *Good Government, XXXIX,* 4-8 (Spring 1972).

Kilpatrick, Franklin P., Milton C. Cummings, Jr., and M. Kent Jennings, *The Image of the Federal Service,* Brookings Institution, Washington, D. C., 1964.

Kranz, Harry, "How Representative Is the Public Service?" *Public Personnel Management, II,* 242-255 (July-August, 1973).

Lieberman, Jethro K., *The Tyranny of the Experts: How Professionals Are Closing the Open Society,* Walker, New York, 1970.

Loewenberg, J. Joseph, and Michael H. Moskow, eds., *Collective Bargaining in Government, Readings and Cases,* Prentice-Hall, Englewood Cliffs, N. J., 1972.

Lopez, Felix M., Jr., *Evaluating Employee Performance,* Public Personnel Association, Chicago, 1968.

Macy, John W., Jr., *Public Service: The Human Side of Government,* Harper and Row, New York, 1971.

Markoff, Helene S., "The Federal Women's Program," *Public Administration Review, XXXII,* 144-151 (March-April, 1972).

Martin, Phillip L., "The Hatch Act in Court: Some Recent Developments," *Public Administration Review, XXXIII,* 443-447 (September-October, 1973).

Mosher, Frederick C., *Democracy and the Public Service,* Oxford University, New York, 1968.

Municipal Manpower Commission, *Governmental Manpower for Tomorrow's Cities,* McGraw-Hill, New York, 1962.

Nigro, Felix A., *Management-Employee Relations in the Public Service,* Public Personnel Association, Chicago, 1969.

Reynolds, Lloyd G., *Labor Economics and Labor Relations,* Sixth Edition, Prentice-Hall, Englewood Cliffs, N. J., 1974.

Shafritz, Jay M., *Position Classification: A Behavioral Analysis for the Public Service,* Praeger, New York, 1973.

Shafritz, Jay M., *A New World: Readings on Modern Public Personnel Management,* International Personnel Management Association, Chicago, 1975.

Stahl, O. Glenn, *The Personnel Job of Government Managers,* Public Personnel Association, Chicago, 1971.

Stahl, O. Glenn, *Public Personnel Administration,* Sixth Edition, Harper and Row, New York, 1971.

Stanley, David T., *The Higher Civil Service: An Evaluation of Federal Personnel Practices,* Brookings Institution, Washington, D. C., 1968.

Stanley, David T., *Managing Local Government Under Union Pressure,* Brookings Institution, Washington, D. C., 1972.

U.S. Commission on Civil Rights, *For All the People . . . By All the People: A Report on Equal Opportunity in State and Local Government Employment,* U.S. Government Printing Office, Washington, D.C., 1969.

Van Riper, Paul P., *History of the United States Civil Service,* Harper and Row, New York, 1958.

Warner, W. Lloyd, et al., *The American Federal Executive,* Yale University, New Haven, Conn., 1963.

White, Leonard D., *The Prestige Value of Public Employment in Chicago,* University of Chicago, Chicago, 1929.

White, Leonard D., *Further Contributions to the Prestige Value of Public Employment,* University of Chicago, Chicago, 1932.

Zagovia, Sam, ed., *Public Workers and Public Unions,* Prentice-Hall, Englewood Cliffs, N. J., 1972.

# PUBLIC FINANCIAL ADMINISTRATION

*A budget system is synonymous with a clarification of responsibility in government, whether the range of governmental programs is broad or narrow.*

*Jesse Burkhead*

It was once accepted procedure to speak of the budget, the plan for expenditures during the fiscal year, as a document separate and distinct unto itself; now, almost everyone has recognized the budget as a segment of a larger process of governmental management known as public financial management. Financial administration must consider both revenues and expenditures in order to maintain the proper financial base for the jurisdiction, and the "proper" base varies for each level and each type of government. At the national level, the president and his advisors must consider several factors such as international trade and monetary policy as they try to manage the national economy; at the local level, the primary problem of the mayor or manager is to make the outflow match the income.

# CHAPTER 14

In this chapter, we deal with two aspects of financial administration—revenues and budgets. It is impossible to ignore the issue of revenues because the revenue-generating capabilities of the different levels of government, and of the various public organizations and special districts, lead to distinctive problems for each group of policymakers. The central topic of the chapter, however, is the budgetary process, for this is the process by which much of the planning and control takes place in public management. The first section of the chapter contains a history of the development of government financial administration; second, revenues and their impact on budgetary decisions are considered; third, there is an in-depth discussion of the budgetary process; fourth, the attempts at budgetary reform are reviewed; and, fifth, a case study of a nonprofit health agency is presented in order to show how the financial administration process works in a practical, ongoing situation.

## A BRIEF HISTORY OF GOVERNMENT FINANCE

For centuries, indeed, for as long as history can be examined, pharaohs, emperors, kings, and popes have developed budgets and levied taxes; however, the roots of our current budgetary system are directly traceable to the British government and to the control over the king's taxing power that was established in 1217 with the Magna Charta. The emergence of parliamentary control over the monarchy is a historical development which has had an immense impact on our budgetary process. It is interesting to note that "the barons at Runnymede were apparently not concerned with King John's expenditures, but they were very much concerned with the levies that he imposed on them."[1] For this reason Article 12 of the Magna Charta stated,

No scutage or aid shall be imposed in the Kingdom unless by the common council of the realm, except for the purpose of ransoming the King's person, making his first-born son a knight, and marrying his eldest daughter once, and the aids for this purpose shall be reasonable in amount.

Throughout the long struggle between Parliament and the Crown, the center of the controversy was control over taxation and protection of the taxpayer; this power was permanently placed under the aegis of Parliament with the Revolution of 1688 and the establishment of the Bill of Rights in the next year, because the Bill of Rights included a provision that, "henceforth shall no man be compelled to make any gift, loan, or benevolence, or tax, without common consent by Act of Parliament." At the same time, Parliament established unto itself the right to authorize all expenditures made by the Crown, and "the House of Commons asserted its supremacy over the House of Lords in the initiation of supply bills—the acts to authorize expenditure."[2]

---

[1] Jesse Burkhead, *Government Budgeting,* Wiley, New York, 1956, p. 3. Much of the history presented in this section is drawn from Burkhead's book.

[2] *Ibid.*

The American Revolution had taken place and the upstart thirteen colonies had won their independence before Parliament established a consolidated fund (1787) which received all revenue and which paid all expenditures; it was thirty-five years later when the chancellor of the exchequer presented a complete statement of finances to Parliament for its guidance and action. Finally, beginning with the Gladstone era (1868), the budget—dealing with both revenues and expenditures—became the major expression of the government's program. Gladstone's recognition of the central importance of the budget was best expressed in his statement that

budgets are not merely matters of arithmetic, but in a thousand ways go to the root of prosperity of individuals, and relation of classes, and the strength of kingdoms.[3]

## The United States

One of the quarrels that led to the American Revolution was that of "taxation without representation," so it appeared that the colonists were continuing the battle that had begun between Parliament and the Crown several hundred years earlier. In spite of the fact that the American colonies had just won their independence from Great Britain, the background of most of the leaders in the colonies was British; therefore, the British traditions were strongly represented in the institutions established by the new government. The budget system of Great Britain was not fully developed when the Revolution occurred, so there was no set of practices that could be copied. Under the Articles of Confederation, the national government was given no power of taxation; instead, all revenue-generating powers were given to the states, and the national government had to request funds from the states in order to meet the costs of operation. Of course, the powers of the national government found it difficult to solicit sufficient funds to remain solvent; therefore, the financial crisis that ensued was one of the factors that led to the creation of the new federal government.

The Constitution says little about financial matters, and requires only that:

No money shall be drawn from the treasury, but in consequence of appropriations made by law; and a regular statement and account of the receipts and expenditures of all public money shall be published from time to time. (Article I, Section 9)

In addition, the Constitution requires that all revenue legislation must originate in the House of Representatives. All the laws concerning our current budget process have developed from these very meager beginnings. Originally, cabinet officials maintained direct contact with Congress, and the House of Representa-

---

[3] David H. MacGregor, *Public Aspects of Finance,* Clarendon, Oxford, 1939, p. 45.

tives operated as a committee of the whole; soon the Committee on Ways and Means was established to take care of both revenue and expenditure matters. Although cabinet officials soon ceased their practice of direct relationships with Congress, the departments continued to present and defend their budgets before the legislature; this practice was standard until the Executive Budget was established in 1921.

During this time, the government did not face the problem of a shortage of funds. Alexander Hamilton, as secretary of the treasury under President Washington, performed what many considered to be a minor miracle by paying off the accumulated state debts for the Revolutionary War;[4] from that point on until the 1890s, the national treasury usually was relatively solvent, although an occasional war created temporary problems. Indeed, during the 1880s and early 1890s, the federal government actually faced the interesting problem of trying to dispose of its embarrassing riches. On December 6, 1887, President Cleveland protested to Congress:

You are confronted at the threshhold of your legislative duties with a condition of the national finances which imperatively demands immediate and careful consideration.

The amount of money annually exacted, through the operation of the present laws, from the industries and necessities of the people largely exceeds the sum necessary to meet the expenses of the Government. . . . The public treasury . . . becomes a hoarding place for money needlessly withdrawn from trade and the people's use, thus crippling our national energies . . . and inviting schemes of public plunder.[5]

Needless to say, this was not a period of close control over expenditures, but, surprisingly, neither was this a time of high taxes. The primary source of revenue was from tariffs on imported goods and a variety of consumption taxes. The government simply was not large enough to require substantial sums of money.

As long as there was no financial crisis, the government could afford to be somewhat careless; the graft and corruption that had been the hallmark of the latter half of the nineteenth century, while not condoned by most people, had not caused serious difficulties. But with the beginning of the twentieth century, the surpluses disappeared as the government took on an increasing role in society and as expenditures expanded accordingly. The surpluses became deficits, and with the new, uncomfortable revenue-expenditure gap, known as deficit spending, came an increasing clamor for efficiency and economy in government opera-

---

[4] One of the bargaining points for accepting the new Constitution was that the national government would assume and pay off the debts still remaining from the Revolutionary War. These debts were causing financial misfortune for several states.

[5] *Journal of the Senate of the United States,* 50th Congress, 1st Session, December 6, 1887, p. 8.

tions. Even the "discovery" of a new source of revenue, the income tax,[6] did not remove the need for improved efficiency and better budgeting; therefore, the inevitable movement toward budgetary reform continued.

Much of the impetus for budget reform at the national level came about because of the successes that the reformers had experienced at the state and municipal levels. The National Municipal League, the New York Bureau of Municipal Research, and other similar organizations sprang up in major metropolitan areas, and they worked diligently at applying "business principles" to government operations. The advocates of budget reform were ardent apostles of "good government"; good government meant efficiency, efficiency meant the application of the scientific method to government, and business had led the way in applying scientific management to the human enterprise. Close to the idea of efficiency was the principle of responsibility: the only way to assure efficiency was to centralize, or focus, responsibility for the functions of the bureaucracy on the chief executive. However, the added responsibility required added power, and the best way to achieve the added power was through the establishment of an *executive budget,* in which all the departments of the government presented their budgets to the legislative body in a single document that was under the control of the chief executive, who had the final authority over the figures presented by the departments to the legislature. The chief executive was also the ultimate authority on the way the budgeted funds were expended.

The reformers were successful in establishing the executive budget as one of the early steps toward good government. Although the budget reform movement began about 1900, by the mid-1920s most major American municipalities

. . . had undergone a more or less thorough reform in municipal financial practices and had established some sort of a budget system. In the 1920's the pace of adoption was accelerated by the financial stringency which followed the passage of the 18th Amendment and the corresponding loss of municipal revenue from the sale of alcoholic beverages. It was also accelerated by demands for increased municipal programs, such as paved streets to accomodate the automobile and new school buildings to accomodate the increase in school population.

In appraising the forces which accounted for this rather rapid adoption of the budget system in American cities, it should be noted that while the reformers were important, the zeal for good government significant, and the need for increased municipal outlays evident, these alone would not have been enough. The crucial element of support which led to the adoption of the budget system was pressure from the business community. The slogan "more business in government" probably did more for budgetary reform than the agitation of the reformers against "invisible government." Budget reform came to be identified, realistically or not, with retrenchment in government, with a reduction in expen-

---

[6] Sixteenth Amendment, United States Constitution.

ditures with a view to reduced taxes; not, as the reformers intended, with the strengthening of government for the more efficient conduct of programs of social welfare.[7]

When the Budget and Accounting Act was finally passed on June 10, 1921, the forces that led to its acceptance were approximately the same as those that led to municipal reform. The major themes of the act's supporters were the introduction of business principles to the federal government and the need to pinch pennies. Midway through the first year under the new budgetary system, the "members of the government's business organization," as President Harding referred to them, met to hear an interim report on the progress to date. The philosophy behind this new system was clearly, if not eloquently, stated by General Charles G. Dawes, the first director of the Bureau of the Budget, when he referred to "the members of the Cabinet as nothing but the administrative vice-presidents of this organization"; he continued by suggesting that they should realize that

there is no reason why, because the government of the United States does the largest business in the world, it should be the worst conducted. What I want to do is to listen to a discussion of simple business principles in a simple way, just as if we were members of a smaller corporation.[8]

In addition to preaching the "gospel of business," Dawes was able to report that the executive departments were able to reduce the national budget for the year from 4,550,000,000 dollars to 3,974,000,000 dollars, a savings of 576 million dollars, or more than 10 percent of the total budget. It would seem, therefore, that retrenchment, or economy, was an important value to the originators of the Bureau of the Budget.

Wherever the new executive budget was established, there was a third purpose behind the action. The country was emerging from an era where graft and corruption had been a way of life, an era when Boss Plunkit could proudly proclaim that he saw his opportunities and he took them. The city and state bosses had strangleholds on the political machinery, and they and their followers used the political machinery to make personal fortunes. It was intended that the budget reform would help to stamp out the misuse of public funds by placing all of those funds in a single place and making the chief executive accountable for the way the money was spent. Thus, another major reason for budget reform was to establish better accountability of public funds. With this purpose in mind, the Budget and Accounting Act established a General Accounting Office (GAO)

---

[7] Burkhead, pp. 14-15.

[8] Charles G. Dawes, *The First Year of the Budget of the United States,* Harper and Row, New York, 1923, p. 172.

that was independent from the president. There was a comptroller general heading the office, who was appointed by, but who could not be removed by, the president. The office reported its auditing results directly to Congress. The addition of GAO was the answer of Congress to the problem of accountability in the executive departments.

Since the initial establishment of the budget systems at the several levels of government, there have been some dramatic changes in the philosophy of budgeting. The philosophical changes have been the result of, or have led to, equally momentous alterations in management ideology; however, before considering these issues, let us examine the impact of revenues on the total financial system of governmental jurisdictions.

# REVENUES AND THEIR
# IMPACT ON BUDGETS

It is impossible to accomplish much in a modern, technological society without money. This is one of the factors that sharply limits the ability of most voluntary organizations to accomplish complex tasks. The leaders of an organization that depends on volunteer workers must usually expend funds on materials and capital, and workers must be enticed to serve for intangible rewards. In this case, the leaders are faced with two problems: First, the organization is confined to setting goals that can be reached with the amount of work attainable from the volunteers; thus, the leaders lose some control over the quantity of goods or services delivered. Second, it is impossible to do anything that in any way disenchants the workers, because disenchantment will lead to almost instantaneous withdrawal from service. Since most complex tasks require that some distasteful work be done, as well as the more agreeable tasks for which there are often surplus volunteers, the leaders also lose some control over the quality of organizational goals. Because of the limitations just mentioned, most complex organizations in our society are utilitarian organizations (organizations that pay individuals to participate in the delivery of specified services or products as efficiently and effectively as possible). Governments cannot operate through volunteerism. Many of the functions are distasteful, many more functions play a unique role in society, and all functions depend on management (and political) control of employees. In addition, of course, there is the problem of obtaining all of the other resources required for the regular functioning of the government—materials that now range from atomic bombs to automobiles; therefore, one of the most important limitations on the number and quality of services delivered by any government is the amount of money available to that jurisdiction. Politicians and public administrators are vitally interested in the "revenue picture" for their organizations, and such an interest should be expected because the prospects for funding contrast as sharply as do the different jurisdictions. When discussing budgeting, therefore, it is essential to recognize the impact of the revenue picture on the budget process.

## Federal Government Revenues

The national government uses a variety of taxes, but the primary source of revenue is the *individual income tax*. In recent years, nearly half of the federal revenues have come from this source. There are good arguments for depending on the income tax. Joseph Pechman notes that

the automatic flexibility of the tax promotes economic stability, and the progressive rates reduce excessive concentration of economic power and control. Some believe that the income tax is needed also to moderate the growth of private savings of high income people, which is likely to hold down private demand for goods and services. Others believe that a high income tax impairs work and investment incentives and, therefore, reduces the nation's economic growth. . . . Nonetheless, it is correct to say that the modern individual income tax, if carefully designed and well administered, is a powerful and essential economic instrument for a modern industrial economy.[9]

Careful consideration of this statement clarifies a fact about the revenue picture that points out the unique position of the federal government. Raising revenue is only part of the use to which taxes are put at the national level.[10] Admittedly, the national government has the best revenue producer and takes the largest share of the overall tax dollar, but revenue is part of an overall political and economic policy that also includes monetary policy, international trade, and general rules for the distribution and redistribution of wealth within the society. Because of their role in the overall economic policy, the revenue value of taxes is only a part of the consideration when types and levels of taxes are established by Congress. Other issues, such as economic growth or recession, full employment, and price stability, are also considered by the financial and budgetary experts.

## State and Local Revenues

State and local governments have less desirable taxes as the foundation of their revenue systems. Although many states are levying an individual income tax, the rates that are used are much lower than those of the national government. The primary tax at the state level is the sales tax, and at the local level, it is the property tax; both levels of government raise additional revenues through a variety of license fees, user taxes, and other minor sources. Although it is true that the need for revenue has not been as great as at the national level because of lower levels of service, the problem of revenues has become an increasingly

---

[9] Joseph A. Pechman, *Federal Tax Policy,* Revised Edition, W.W. Norton, New York, 1971, pp. 53-54.

[10] For a discussion of the basic functions of budget policy, see: Richard A. Musgrave, *The Theory of Public Finance,* McGraw-Hill, New York, 1959.

vital issue, because the growth in public demand for services has tended to outstrip the ability of the state and local governments to collect the necessary revenues. It must be remembered, also, that most state and local governments must prepare balanced budgets; they cannot go into debt. Therefore, the search for additional revenue is constant, and it influences every budgetary decision made by both politicians and administrators.

The problem of balancing the budget, or "closing the revenue-expenditure gap" as it is often referred to, is a constant problem at both the state and local level; the point can be illustrated in a dramatic fashion by examining the situation of the city of Oakland, California, which Arnold Meltsner describes in his book, *The Politics of Local Revenue.* The interesting factor that he points out is not that a fiscal crisis occurs, because such crises are a part of the persistent plague of the city; what is of interest are the attitudes and practices that Meltsner claims the crisis engenders in the city manager, the council, and the department heads.

The city manager has superior tax knowledge, so he is a somewhat pessimistic "fiscal realist." He is constantly looking for revenue sources while at the same time he is striving for efficiency. He also fulfills the role of fiscal conscience by constantly informing the council and the department heads of the financial situation of the city.

Being efficient and searching for alternative sources of revenue are functional equivalents to cutting the (property) tax rate. No one directly pressures the manager to do these things. He looks for efficiencies, tries to cut costs and find money, because this is the way he defines his administrative role. The norms of his profession are such that good managers do these things.[11]

The city council of Oakland is influenced by the actions of the manager; the members are aware of the problems of raising sufficient revenue and holding down the property tax rate while carrying out the essential city services. Meltsner states that "the fiscal imperative of the council is: hold the line, or, if possible, cut the property tax rate."[12] Every item of expenditure is thought of as an addition of pennies to the tax rate, and the goal is to show a tax cut, or at least a low tax rate, because a low tax rate is a sign of efficient government. At the same time, the council is always looking for new sources of revenue. The problem with developing new revenue sources is that any widespread or dramatic increase in taxes, fees, or any other charges to the citizens will almost certainly raise a howl of protest from the community, and it could very well be political suicide for a politician. During the last decade, there has been an increasing incidence of taxpayer revolts in which citizens have refused to ap-

[11] Arnold Meltsner, *The Politics of City Revenues,* University of California, Berkeley, 1971, p. 52.

[12] *Ibid.,* p. 64.

prove new bond issues, have voted out politicans who raised taxes, and have supported special laws placing ceilings on local governments' property tax rates. In order to avoid these types of reactions, the Oakland city council seeks new taxes that have been tested and accepted in other cities, indirect taxes (such as the transient occupancy tax, cigarette tax, and utilities consumption tax), or taxes that affect only a small portion of the general public.[13] Thus, small increments of additional revenue are established by the council, and equally small increments of change are usually allowed in the budget.

Department heads constantly receive from both the manager and the council a constant stream of orders saying: "Do not ask for more money"; "Tighten your belt"; "Do not ask for a new program unless you have a way to finance it"; and "Find ways to generate more revenue within your department." The department heads generally ignore the advice or commands. In the area of generating revenue, the departments maintain the status quo, for there is a common philosophy among the departments that it is unfair, or "not quite kosher," to charge for the services. Departments are also fearful that increased fees will be offset by reductions in general tax support. On the other side of the coin, the department heads regularly ask for more money and suggest additional programs. The general attitude is that "since everyone else will ask for more money and programs, I have to protect my department by doing likewise, and, anyway, it never hurts to ask." The department heads also see themselves as professionals in their respective fields, and they consider themselves as negligent in their jobs if they do not express their attitudes as to what is necessary to do the job properly. Does the approach of the department heads lead to increased budgets; more specifically, if department heads ask for greatly increased budgets, are they successful in getting more money? Meltsner is unable to give a definitive answer; however, he does say that

in a fiscally deprived situation, asking for more probably has some minor short run payoffs, but in the long run it does not make much difference in the expenditure level of a department. . . .For example, in examining budget request and expenditure patterns since 1960, I found that the Police Department was consistently lower in its requests than the other major departments. On the average, the police chief asked for a 3.4 percent increase (over the previous appropriation), while the recreation superintendent asked for a 32.7 percent increase. . . . But the average increase in expenditures for both departments was about the same: the low-asking Police Departments' expenditures increased 8 percent per year while the high-asking Recreation Department expenditures increased 6.9 percent per year.[14]

---

[13]*Ibid.,* p. 98. Meltsner argues that the search for revenue at the local level is fragmented and superficial because, "given the limited resources which the subsystem can devote to revenue search, city officials are satisfied to find a few revenue sources which can be added to the tax structure.

[14]*Ibid.,* pp. 169-170.

Nevertheless, the administrators recognize the financial position of the city and learn to live with the frustration of fiscal frugality.

Local governments have had to compensate for the lack of revenue; in addition, they have faced another limitation in the face of the revenue problem—local governments generally must operate within a stringent debt limitation. Although they are expected to deliver a variety of services that require mammoth capital expenditures, cities and counties in most states are not allowed to have a debt larger than a specific percentage of their assessed value. Many combined impacts of limited revenues and restrictions on indebtedness have led to a trio of responses on the part of local governments: (1) local governments have become increasingly dependent on transfer payments from the states and, especially, from the national government; (2) special districts have proliferated at the local government level; and (3) local governments have turned to contractual arrangements with private organizations when the cost of public delivery of services became too high.

Tax rates are limited (in several states they are frozen), new sources of revenue are not available, and local governments have stringent rules concerning debt. In order to continue operating, state and local governments have looked to the federal government for aid. In 1950, a total of 2.3 billion dollars was given to state and local governments, while in 1971, that figure rose to 29.3 billion—an increase of 1174 percent.[15] Even with this aid, the proliferation of special districts has continued. When tax rates reach either their political or legal limits and when it is impossible to increase indebtedness although citizens still demand additional services, the only way to meet the demand may be to establish a special district which has taxing and bonding powers to carry out the function. For example, as a small community grows, there is a point in time when the community must establish a sewer system. If the town government cannot afford this capital expenditure because of the debt limitation, the only way to meet this need may be through the establishment of a special sewer district. In like manner, when a service becomes extremely costly, a city may not be able to afford to deliver that service. If the service is necessary, however, the city may establish an ordinance that allows a private corporation to carry out the service and charge the users a fee. Then the city may receive bids and award a contract to the lowest bidder. For example, if garbage collection has become expensive, and the city wants out from under the cost of delivering the service, the city may contract out the garbage collection to a private scavenger company. Under the terms of such a contract, the scavenger company has exclusive service rights within the community for a given length of time, after which the company must once again bid for the next contract. Rates charged for the service may be cleared with the council so that some control will be maintained over the cost of the service to the citizens. This relieves the city of the cost for delivering the service and, at the same time, guarantees that the service is available.

---

[15] Otto Eckstein, *Public Finance*, Third Edition, Prentice-Hall, Englewood Cliffs, N.J., 1973, p. 36.

Problems of finance have serious repercussions on the budgetary process. Most federal money has "strings" attached which tell state and local governments where the funds can and cannot be spent. Services that are contracted, or are delivered by a special district, are nominally beyond the control of the city. When money is not available, necessary services may not be delivered or may be curtailed. All of these factors, which are directly aligned with the problems of revenue, work as limitations on the discretion of the legislators, the chief executive, and the budget administrators, leading to the spending of an inordinate amount of time by these policymakers on the problems of revenue; therefore, a lesser amount of time is spent on the expenditure side of the financial administration system.

## THE BUDGETARY PROCESS

The budget process naturally falls into a cycle with four major phases: (1) revenue forecasting and budget preparation; (2) budget submission and approval by the legislature; (3) budget execution; and (4) audit, or review by an outside body (see Figure 10). While this may be the easiest way to remember the phases of the budget cycle, it may oversimplify the process because the budget phases overlap and run together. Various members of the Office of Management and Budget (at the national level) are simultaneously working on different phases of several budgets. Forecasts are being prepared by the Treasury Department and the Office of Management and Budget at the same time appropriations hearings are going on in the House and Senate. Meanwhile departments and agencies are operating under the current fiscal year's budget, and the departments are being audited by the General Accounting Office in relation to their expenditures, contracts, and programs for the previous year.

Throughout the entire budgetary cycle there are two competing processes—one political and one administrative—in operation, and each process is based on a different perspective of the use of the budget. Politicians and citizens perceive the budget as a reflection of alliances among competing interests; to these participants in the budgetary process the final document shows who won and who lost, who was able to form appropriate coalitions and work out satisfactory compromises, and who was not able to accomplish these political feats. According to this perception of the budget, it is a political tool that shows which policies are currently in ascendancy, with much less attention given to the processes by which these policies are achieved or administered. However, department heads, budget officials, and operating public managers perceive the budget as a managerial tool which has as one of its major functions the presentation of a plan for government operation. These participants in the budgetary process are primarily interested in developing a document that presents a meaningful plan showing both ends and means so that it can also be used as a control device. Between these two groups stands the chief executive, who must attempt to use the budget both ways. The two perceptions of budget cannot be separated; therefore, both perceptions will appear throughout the following discussion. Public administrators must recognize the validity

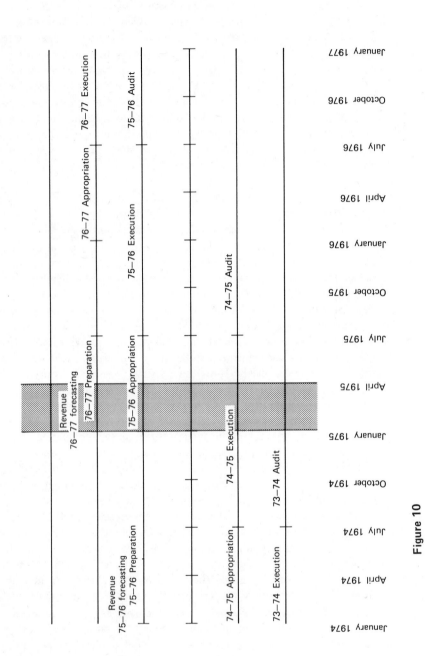

**Figure 10**

Overlap in the federal budget cycle. Examine any quarter of the budget cycle and you will find all of the process steps occurring simultaneously.

of both perspectives if they are to understand fully the uniqueness and importance of the budgetary process, because they must understand whether or not each important decision should be made based on a political or administrative perspective—or based on a combination of the two perspectives.

Revenue forecasting and budget preparation must be intimately combined. At the national level, this combination is essential because of the interest in fiscal policy; in other words, the president and his advisors attempt to influence economic policy by creating a budget deficit or surplus. At state and local levels, the revenue forecast is important because deficit budgets are not allowed. In any case and at any level of government, it is impossible to prepare a meaningful budget without a reasonable idea as to the amount of money that can be spent.

Therefore, the first document in the budget preparation process is a letter from the chief executive to the department heads that requests the preparation of a budget within a specified set of limitations. Initial budgets are prepared by each department, with these documents being forwarded to the appropriate official. As pointed out by Robert Lee, Jr., and Ronald Johnson, the interesting aspect of this procedure is that

budgeting begins, then, not at the presidential, gubernatorial, or mayoral levels, not in the limelight of public attention, but rather in all segments of the executive bureaucracy. The process involves innumerable calculations made by administrators regarding such questions as how to handle the bureau's or office's responsibilities, how many and what kinds of resources will be needed, and, of equal importance, how to persuade one's superiors that the requests for resources are warranted.[16]

No administrator expects to get all the funds that are requested. In order to obtain the best possible result, however, a continuous process of bargaining is carried out in which a balance between desires and absolute needs is reached. Most budget requests go through multiple review before they appear as final figures in appropriation requests. This means that if the budget has been properly viewed as a tool of managment planning and control, the figures that are finally released in the form of "the budget" are the result of much planning, analysis, priority examination, and discernment of fiscal, political, and technological reality. For this reason, and because there has all too often been a failure in exactly this area of budgeting, continuous efforts at reform have focused on the preparation phase of the cycle. The attempted reforms will be discussed later in this chapter.

The appropriation phase of the budget has been studied in depth by numerous scholars. The budget is approved by a legislative body, whether it be the Con-

---

[16] Robert D. Lee, Jr., and Ronald W. Johnson, *Public Budgeting Systems,* University Park, Baltimore, 1973, p. 84.

gress or a school board. Once again, the budget is usually broken down and considered in several segments. In Congress, a series of subcommittees of the Appropriations Committee considers the budget for each department. Even at the county, city, and special district level, it is common to break down the budget, with individual members or committees serving as watchdog over, and liaison with, different segments of the executive organization.

It is at the appropriations level that the public administrators who serve as department heads, budget officials, and chief executives must display their political prowess. The chief executive and budget administrators have established what they believe to be an optimum budget that considers fiscal and political realities. These officials are always cognizant of the fact that it is impossible to give everybody—whether in the bureaucracy, the legislature, or the public—everything that they want. If, after the budget has been prepared by the chief executive, major changes are made in the appropriations to any agency, the changes are likely to trigger a series of related alterations that may completely upset the plans of the chief executive. Therefore, the mayor, city manager, governor, or school superintendent will attempt to maintain the budget in a form as similar as possible to that which was originally presented to the legislature.

At the same time the chief executive is fighting to maintain the proposed budget, the heads of the various departments and programs are attempting to convince the legislature that changes need to be made. Some people may feel that the department heads are being disloyal or immoral when they contradict and oppose the chief executive, but it must be remembered that several factors lead to this opposition as a natural phenomenon. First, the chief executive establishes priorities from a different point of view than does a department head. The mayor must consider the needs of all departments in the city, whereas the administrator of the city hospital or the director of the public works department is primarily interested in only one department. The difference in overview is bound to cause different perceptions about the necessary allocation of resources. Second, the two administrators serve different constituencies. The governor must think of the needs of all the people in the state, but the head of the Department of Corrections is concerned with the needs of a very select group of people who may be generally forgotten, or looked down on, by a majority of the citizens in the state. Third, the two administrators are leaders of, and therefore responsive to, different segments of the bureaucracy. The president must play the role of chief executive to all the federal civil service, while the director of the National Park Service is the chief executive of a group of civil servants who are vociferously interested in a particular program of the national government. Finally, and closely related to the third element, department and program heads are most likely to come from professions that are closely related to that program. Professional orientation regularly biases the perspective of the individual within that group, and this factor reinforces all of the other reasons for differences of opinion between the chief executive and the public administrators at the next level of the bureaucracy. For all these reasons, in addition to other psychological, organizational, and political factors, it is to be expected that department administrators will carry out their own campaigns to get their budgets increased.

Aaron Wildavsky notes two types of strategies that are universally used by good budgetary politicians. The first type, ubiquitous strategies, is designed to gain confidence and clientele. These strategies are called ubiquitous because "they are found everywhere and at all times in the budgetary system."[17] Every public administrator works diligently at finding and cultivating a clientele, for contented clients can become ardent and vociferous supporters if they can be mustered against legislative threats. Before they can be used in such a way, however, they must feel that they have received competent service and have nowhere else to turn for the same service. Perhaps the epitome of this situation was illustrated in the Army Corps of Engineers during the first half of the 1900s. The corps had assiduously courted the favor of Congress; in fact, the corps was considered to be the direct arm of Congress and to be out of the purview of the president. The Army Corps of Engineers was in charge of many of the "pork barrel" programs that Congress pushed through each year; these programs widened rivers, built flood control levees and dams, constructed canals and locks, and carried out other assorted projects. These projects were carefully allotted, so that every congressman and senator got a portion of the goodies for his or her constituents. Both Congress and the constituents back home were pleased with their relationship with the corps; therefore, whenever a battle loomed between the corps and any other federal agency over control of a project, smart people put their money on the corps—if anyone could be found to take the wager.[18] This combination remained virtually unbeatable until the competency of the corps was challenged sufficiently to remove some of the confidence in the minds of both congressional and public supporters. The crisis of confidence led to a weakening of the corps' position; even so, it has been able to use its close ties to Congress, as well as its generally positive public image, to weather the storm and to remain a formidable foe in the scramble for federal funds.

Other organizations, such as the Veterans Administration, have used these strategies quite successfully, while a few, most typically the Agency for International Development, have suffered from an inability to use clientele in the budgetary process. Many local administrators have also become aware of the power of an organized clientele. With budgetary restrictions becoming more confining every year, some local agencies, such as police departments, that have previously been able to depend on their positive public image and their intra-organizational cohesion for success in gaining appropriations, have now actively turned to recruiting and organizing a clientele. A new development in

---

[17] Aaron Wildavsky, *The Politics of the Budgetary Process,* Second Edition, Little, Brown, Boston, 1974, p. 65.

[18] For a good example of how these battles took place and an analysis of why the corps managed to win, see: Arthur A. Maass, "The Kings River Project," in Harold Stein, ed., *Public Administration and Policy Development: A Case Book,* Harcourt, Brace and World, New York, 1948, pp. 533-572.

police department politicking is the local Fraternal Order of Police Auxiliary, which encompasses the entire spectrum of those in the community who are able to influence the city council; this includes businessmen, professional careerists, ministers of local churches, and others of similar rank in the community.

The second group of strategies mentioned by Wildavsky is called "contingent" strategies because they deal with particular situations, and administrators try to use these unique opportunities to the agency's advantage. The National Aeronautics and Space Administration (NASA) was an agency that was able to utilize the popularity of space exploration, President Kennedy's wholehearted support, and popular fear that the Soviet Union was gaining the upper hand in space exploration as arguments for larger appropriations. There were also some "raised eyebrows" when NASA space center headquarters was established in Texas, the home of President Lyndon Johnson (who had been Vice President Johnson and, before that, Senate Majority Leader Johnson). This site selection may have been established for the best of all possible reasons, but critics of the NASA program saw it as a blatant use of contingent strategies meant to guarantee full funding of programs important to NASA. Most programs do not get started in such a highly publicized way, or else the administrator is head of a program that has been in existence for some time. In these cases, department heads must work constantly to guard against cuts in old programs, to attempt to edge ahead, and to add new programs whenever possible.

As the chief executive and the department spokesmen compete for budget programs before the legislative body and the general public, some type of compromise is established and the legislature passes either a single budget document at the local level or a series of appropriations bills at the national level. The result of this process may produce a logical and well-thought-out budget document, or it may be a hodgepodge of individually considered and ill-mated documents that do little toward establishing priorities for the government. Whichever is the case, the chief executive, if an elected official, usually has the ability to sign or veto the bill or bills.

The type of veto power available to the chief executive may have a dramatic effect on the appropriations process. The president must veto a complete bill even if he is unhappy with only a small segment of the total legislation; therefore, Congress can force through some appropriations at a higher level than that desired by the president as long as a majority of the dollar amounts are within the president's range of acceptability. At the other levels of government, several governors and mayors have greater power because they can use the item veto, whereby they can veto specific portions of the bill but still sign it. In no case can the executive augment parts of the budget beyond the amount appropriated by the legislature.[19] Where the item veto power exists, the mayor or governor can maintain greater control over expenditure bills, because it is more difficult to

---

[19] Forty-three governors have some form of item veto power. (In Maryland, the governor has the item veto over supplementary appropriation bills only.) *Book of the States, 1972-1973,* The Council of State Governments, Lexington, Ky., 1973, pp. 162-165.

develop a coalition large enough to override the veto (which usually takes a two-thirds vote) when single issues are involved than when multiple issues are present in complete appropriations bills.

The execution phase of the budget runs during the fiscal year, which may vary but usually covers a period from July 1 to June 30 of the following year. The appropriated funds are allotted to the various departments, which usually have to prepare an operating budget (broken down by quarters) so that plans can be monitored during the year. The budget office, or the chief executive if the organization is too small to have a budget office, makes the quarterly apportionments. Special reserves may be established, reapportionments may be made, or money may be "frozen" at the discretion of the chief executive so that the programs of the government can be carried out. A standardized accounting and reporting procedure helps to maintain the appropriate review and control system throughout the entire year.

Finally, the audit phase of the budget cycle begins while the execution phase is still in progress. Two major types of audits are conducted: the accounting or bookkeeping audit, which is meant to guarantee that the expenditures have followed all the rules and that there is no waste; and the program audit, which encompasses studies of whether or not governmental programs achieve desired results. Most states have an elected auditor who examines all expenditures for legality and a state board of accounts that audits departmental records. The national government has the General Accounting Office, which is headed by the comptroller general. At the local level, some cities elect auditors, or auditors are appointed by the council, while in other situations certified public accountants or accounting firms are contracted to audit financial records. Whichever procedure is used, the most important factor within the auditing function is the measure of independence held by the auditor. President Wilson vetoed the first legislation to establish a federal budget system, because he argued that the head of the GAO should be responsible to the president, while the legislation made the comptroller general answerable to Congress. Congress was adamant, however, and its view was accepted by President Harding. Although the argument as to whom the auditor should be responsible to still continues at all levels of government, the proponents of independent auditors have generally carried the most weight.

## BUDGETARY REFORM

The focus of the reformers, who pushed for the executive budget at the beginning of this century, was on two concepts: efficiency was expected to allow lower tax rates through increased service per dollar; by the same token, accountability was expected to lead to greater efficiency because, once a single individual was given authority over the budget, he or she could be expected to monitor and control expenditures for inefficiency and dishonesty. The original type of budget that was used—and is still used by many governments—was especially geared toward these two goals. The line-item budget, as this form of budget is named, focuses on a recording of every item or service purchased by the expend-ing departments. In a state highway patrol budget, for example, there is a line for salaries, purchase of automobiles, maintenance of autos, purchase of gas and oil, purchase of weapons and supplies, and the purchase of office equipment— the list of lines continues at some length depending on the detail demanded by the particular state. The document that goes to the budget office usually will list every trooper by name and give his salary; it will also note the number of autos, uniforms, and other supplies needed in great detail.

Such a budget allows a great amount of control over expenditures; it also guarantees that an audit can be speedily and accurately completed. Legislators like this type of budget because it gives them a sense of control over expendi-tures and programs; it is possible for legislators to increase or cut expenditures for particular items, and legislators love to feel that they have "cut the fat out of the budget." Budget officers and chief executives can also observe detailed expenditure plans for a department and shift money or cut expenditures as they see fit. There are some serious drawbacks to this type of budget, however. First, it presents a fragmentary and incomplete picture of department programs. Instead of portraying the programs and discussing what the department is trying to accomplish, the budget talks about items of expenditure in no particular context. Second, it allows legislators and budget officials to bargain and strike compromises about dollars and items of expenditure without seriously consider-ing the effect of those budgetary changes on program goals, content, and output. Finally, this type of budgeting encourages an "incremental" approach to policy-making, whereby the programs already in existence are unquestioned and unchallenged; only minor changes are contemplated as the budget is prepared.[20] Advocates of different budget systems argue that the budget can be made into a more powerful policymaking tool if performance and programs are debated, rather than focusing on the inanimate objects that are used to carry out the policies. These reformers want the budget to be used in a positive way to make policy decisions, rather than in a negative way where the major emphasis is on accountability for expenditures.

### Performance Budgeting

The initial movement toward changing the focus of budgeting brought about the "performance budget." According to Jesse Burkhead,

> At a broad definitional level, performance budgeting can be most appro-priately associated with a budget classification that emphasizes the things which government does, rather than the things which government buys.

---

[20]Incrementalism is ardently defended by Aaron Wildavsky in *The Politics of the Budgetary Process,* and by Charles E. Lindblom, "The Science of 'Muddling Through,' " *Public Administration Review, XIX,* 79-88 (Spring 1959).

Performance budgeting shifts the emphasis from the means of accomplishment to the accomplishment itself.[21]

Performance budgeting breaks down the functions of government based on end products produced, and these are then measured in units such as.miles of street swept, gallons of sewage treated, or the number of physical examinations completed. After work units have been established, the budget is prepared by showing: (1) the number of units of work included for the year; (2) total costs for that work; (3) the "unit" costs (total costs divided by the number of units delivered); and (4) a distribution of outlays by objects of expenditure (similar to line-item budgets) for each of the work units.

This type of budget began to make the transition toward the consideration of programs, but it stopped short of the modern program budget. Performance budgeting was tried and dropped by many governments; later the concept was reintroduced in a different context when the Planning, Programming, Budgeting System (PPBS) was inaugurated.

### Planning, Programming, Budgeting Systems

The Planning, Programming, Budgeting System is the next step beyond performance budgeting; it has its historical antecedents in private industry, where it was practiced by General Motors as early as 1924;[22] it has its philosophical underpinnings in a modern interpretation of scientific management; it has its rationale in the use of systems theory. Planning, Programming, Budgeting (PPB) first appeared in the Defense Department in 1961, and by 1965, President Johnson directed all major departments and agencies to adopt this form of budget. The official sanctioning of PPB was withdrawn after the Nixon Administration came into office in 1968, and by the early 1970s, the term PPB was no longer used in the federal government.[23] (However, the concepts and analytical tools of the system still exist and are used.) Also, in one of those quirks of public policy, PPB—or many of its principles—was being mandated on state and local governments in connection with federal transfer payments even as the federal government was moving away from the system.

At the base of PPB is the concept of *sytems analysis*. A system includes the particular object or function being studied and *all other objects or functions*

---

[21] Burkhead, p. 133.

[22] David Novick, "Origin and History of Program Budgeting," Rand Corporation, Paper P-3427, October, 1966, reproduced in *Planning Programming Budgeting Inquiry of the Subcommittee on National Security and International Operations,* Government Printing Office, U.S. Senate, Washington, D.C., 1970, pp. 592-595.

[23] PPB's official demise is usually dated to coincide with Circular No. A-11, Revised June 21, 1971, Executive Office of the President, Office of Management and Budget. In this circular, OMB eliminated the requirement for the PPB documents to be included in budget submissions.

*being influenced by, or influencing,* the unit being studied. Systems analysis examines all the related elements as a whole and presents decision makers with a systematic and comprehensive comparison of the costs and benefits of alternative approaches to a policy goal. Perhaps Charles Schultze, then director of the Bureau of the Budget, best explained the nature of PPBS in his testimony before the Senate Subcommittee on National Security and International Operations in 1967. Mr. Schultze said,

As the *first* step PPB calls for a careful specification and analysis of basic program objectives in each major area of governmental activity. . . . The objective of our inter-city highway program for example, is *not* to build highways. Highways are useful only as they serve a higher objective, namely transporting people and goods effectively and efficiently and safely. Once this is accepted as an objective, it then becomes possible to analyze aviation, railroads and highways to determine the most effective network of transportation. . . .

At the same time, while we want to view our objectives broadly we are not helped at all by stating them too broadly. . . . In the case of highways, we want a specification of objectives broader than "laying concrete" but narrower than "improving our national life."

The *second* step under the PPB system is to analyze insofar as possible, the *output* of a given program in terms of the objectives initially specified in the first step. Again, for example, in the case of highways, we must ask not primarily how many miles of concrete are laid, but more fundamentally what the program produces in terms of swifter, safer, less-congested travel— how many hours of travel time are eliminated, how many accidents are prevented.

The *third* step is to measure the *total costs* of the program, not just for one year, but over at least several years ahead. . . . In deciding to build an expressway through a downtown area we must take into account not only the cost of the expressway, but also the cost of relocating the displaced residents and, in a qualitative sense, the effects of the freeway on the area through which it is to run. . . .

The *fourth* and crucial step is to analyze *alternatives,* seeking those which have the greatest effectiveness in achieving the basic objectives specified in the first step or which achieve those objectives at the least cost. In the highway case, for example, we should be comparing the effectiveness of additions or improvements to highways with that of additions or improvements to aviation and railroads as a means of providing safe and efficient transportation. This does not mean that we pick only one. Of course, we should not. But we do need to decide, at least roughly, which combination of alternatives is the preferred one.[24]

---

[24] From the testimony of Charles L. Schultze before the Senate Subcommittee on Government Operations Hearings, *Planning-Programming-Budgeting,* 90th Congress, 1st Session, August 23, 1967, pp. 19-21.

From this process should come: (1) a *plan* that defines the goals of the public organization, along with the methods, means, or processes that will be used to achieve the goals; (2) a *program* that schedules for implementation the particular projects designed to meet the goals; (3) a *budget* that estimates the cost of achieving each goal, program, and project; and (4) a *system review* that considers the effects of the program—both on the primary population toward which the program is oriented and on the secondary populations that are peripherally affected—and the alternatives that are reasonably available to the organization.

PPB does not move completely away from traditional budgeting methods; it is still necessary at some point to break down the program budget into figures for materials, services, and manpower. Therefore, a "crosswalk" is prepared at some point wherein the program budget is matched with the traditional items of expenditure such as personnel, office supplies, travel expenses, and equipment. PPB does not eliminate the necessity for having a line-item budget; it simply adds a new layer of budget to the old with a crosswalk between the two in the organization's budget office. Then why bother to add the extra work? Because program budgeting adds, or emphasizes, new or different tools in the budget process that should lead to more knowledgeable and incisive policy development if those tools are used properly. It is precisely these tools that are still being used in spite of the official demise of PPB.

The most pervasive of the new tools, as far as usage is concerned, is the concept of *cost-benefit analysis*, also referred to as cost-effectiveness analysis. Cost-benefit analysis measures program outcomes in monetary form; this allows the development of ratios of cost versus benefits. When the ratio of benefits to costs equals 1.0, then a program breaks even monetarily. If benefits are greater than costs, a program will actually repay dividends. (The fact that a program pays for itself, or pays dividends, may not make it a politically acceptable program.) Cost effectiveness measures outcomes that are quantitative but nonmonetary. For instance, it is impossible to quantify usage of a city or national park; it may be possible to measure the "amount of fun" or recreation that people receive from the park, but it is probably impossible to establish monetary values on the use of the park.

*Zero-base budgeting* is the other major concept that must be considered as essential to PPB. In a zero-base situation, the public official is supposed to start the fiscal year by erasing all prior arrangements from his or her mind. Instead, the official should begin by spelling out the objectives of the department and then asking, "What would be the best possible way to meet the objectives of this department, and how should the department be organized?" From an analysis of this type should come ideas as to what needs to be increased, changed, or replaced within the department. Zero-base budgeting produces a dispassionate and logical analysis of all aspects of a department in a programmatic way, with efficiency and effectiveness being the measuring stick.

If both of these tools of PPB are properly used, the result should be the generation of alternative approaches to policy implementation and an increase in knowledgeable debate about public policies. However, there has been a long and heated debate as to whether or not this has been the result. Several arguments have been raised by proponents and opponents of PPB. Those who were opposed to the system have argued that political issues were too complex to be handled in a systematic way and that the most important factors in any political issue were nonquantifiable; therefore, quantification and cost-benefit analysis led to oversimplification, an emphasis on quantifiable factors at the expense of the more important, but nonquantifiable factors, and an emphasis on efficiency rather than effectiveness. These complaints have been answered by proponents of PPB who have stressed the need to measure everything possible so that those measurable issues could be clarified and settled, after which there would be more time left for debating the other parts of the policies.

A second argument was presented which claimed PPB led to overcentralization. For example, Aaron Wildavsky asserted that PPB enabled former Secretary of Defense Robert McNamara to impose his will on the Department of Defense.[25] This contention was simply rebutted by scoffing at any such charge. If McNamara accomplished such a task, proponents of PPB argued, it was quite an accomplishment; he was the first secretary of defense to gain such control over the service heads. However, in a more serious vein, they argued that some centralization might be good, because it would make the "accountable" heads of departments stronger and less subject to "end runs" by subordinate units and officials. At the same time PPB *formalized* the involvement of a wide variety of administrators and employees, who heretofore were not guaranteed participation in the budgetary process, because initial program specification and evaluation were assigned to lower levels of the bureaucracy.

Closely related to the pressure for centralization was the fact that program budgeting might force reorganization because programs tended to cross traditional departmental boundaries. According to the opponents of PPB, the pressure for reorganization would lead to resistance by the departments and to a struggle that would dissipate energies better used to carry out department tasks. The proponents of PPB retorted by noting that little reorganization was needed; in fact, when programs crossed department lines, they helped to promote coordination and cooperation. However, in a few cases, reorganization might be the logical culmination of PPB, but in those cases the program structure would have pointed out situations where reorganization was essential to effective and efficient service. If this was true, reorganization seemed to be a small price to pay; public organizations had to be reminded that they *served the public* rather than the opposite, and, if reorganization improved service, it should take place even if it created some discomfort for the bureaucracy.

Finally, the opponents of PPB were fearful of the kinds of decisions that came from the process. This fear was rationalized in two ways: (1) the opponents of PPB argued that the system allowed technocrats—many new and inexperienced—to make decisions, or have major influence on decisions, by *selecting and preparing* the *information* from which the decisions were made; and (2) it

---

[25] Aaron Wildavsky, "The Political Economy of Efficiency," *Public Administration Review, XXVII*, 292-310 (December 1966).

allowed the justification of "bad" programs by making them impressive through the use—or misuse—of statistics and other figures. Proponents responded to these arguments by noting that the first charge was not true and by pointing out that this argument directly contradicted their claim that PPB gave the department head too much authority. As to the second point, proponents simply noted that any tool of decision making could be misused. Using a favorite metaphor of the politicians—who are constantly "cutting programs to the bare bones"—a sharp knife and the use of it are different; the method and the use of the method are two different things.

The argument was furious and continued for most of a decade; in fact, the impact of the program on the government was not as dramatic as was the argument. In early 1971, Allen Schick observed that "overall . . . the view in Washington is that PPB has not had much impact, that program decisions continue to be made in the pre-PPB fashion, and that there are few traces of planning and systems analysis in the annual budget process."[26] The basic attitude toward PPB at the federal level was one of indifference. At the state level, the results appeared to be the same; Schick surveyed state governments and reported that by mid-1970, "PPB was not yet operative in a single state. . . . Budgeting in the states operated as it had for more than half a century."[27] At the state and local level, however, some progress was made. The Ford Foundation helped five cities, five counties, and five states to implement PPB. Selma Mushkin, the director of this program, stated that a beginning was made in these jurisdictions in the areas of analytical problem solving, cost-effectiveness, and the training of staff. Numerous other cities and counties were also asking for aid in developing program structures and techniques.

One of the major reasons for the interest at the county and city level was that, while the federal government failed to make PPB work, many grant programs to local jurisdictions demanded the use of program structures and techniques in applying for money and in ensuing reports and evaluations that had to be given to the granting agencies. At the same time, the professional managers at the local level were able to see, without the same level of political reservations experienced at the state and national level, the value of the program as a management tool.

The battle over the Planning, Programming, Budgeting System as a method of budgeting further accentuates the central role of budgeting as a bridge between policy formulation and policy implementation. No other single process or document approaches the importance of the budget, because it is the direct link between the desires of the legislature and the actions of the executive branch. Administrators, or politicians, who know the budget procedure and how to use

[26] Allen Schick, "From Analysis to Evaluation in Social Science and the Federal Government," *The Annals of the American Academy of Political and Social Science, CCCXCIV,* 67 (March 1971).

[27] Allen Schick, *Budget Innovation in the States,* The Brookings Institute, Washington, D.C., 1971, pp. 1-2.

it to their advantage can have a powerful influence on public policy. Congress has realized the importance of the budget and inserted itself more forcefully into the budgetary process. According to the new legislation, Congress will specify expenditure levels as well as required revenues and expected deficits or surpluses in much the same way that the president makes these projections. Such a procedure will give Congress a more equal role with the president as the budget is passed.[28] The battle, and the maneuvering, will never end; nor should it, because the budget is the ultimate expression of public policy priorities.

## A CASE STUDY

In 1964, the Planned Parenthood Association of Northwest Indiana, Inc. came into existence by borrowing 12,000 dollars with which a program was started in Lake County. By 1975, the association was operating in the seven northwestern counties of Indiana and offering nine different services to the public, with a total budget of 700,000 dollars for the year. The explosive growth of the program had caused some intense growing pains; it had especially led to difficulty in budgetary planning and control; therefore, the director turned to program budgeting as a means of improving the entire operation of the association. The national association, Planned Parenthood/World Population, also developed guidelines for program budgeting that were helpful to the local organization. During the period of time when Planned Parenthood was attempting to develop program budgeting, one of its funding sources, the local community fund-raising organization, introduced the nationally mandated functional budgeting system that was to be implemented by every affiliate of the national organization.

The movement from the normal line-item budget to a functional budget, as the individuals at Planned Parenthood referred to the program budget, required a five-year transition period. During this period, all the employees were trained in the preparation of objectives and in the use of those objectives as management tools. Surprisingly, the employees who had the hardest time in making the switch in budgetary and management thinking were the employees closest to the financial process. Actually, such a finding should not come as a surprise, because those employees who had developed a tradition, or a set of habits and thought patterns, as they worked with the budget over a period of years had to "unlearn" the traditional method of handling the budget before the newer ideas and procedures could be applied to the process. During the process of changeover, two employees who were involved with budget preparation left the organization, either because they felt uncomfortable with the new system or because they refused to make the adjustment necessary to help prepare the budget according to the new process.

Why does an organization such as the Planned Parenthood Association commit itself to the effort of budgetary reform? The only rational answer must be that the benefits of the new system outweigh the costs of establishing it. The

[28] Budget Reform Bill. Public Law, 93-344, 93rd Congress, 2nd Session, August 12, 1974.

director of the Planned Parenthood Association of Northwest Indiana, who is responsible for the change in budgetary planning for the association, is very quick to point out the strengths and weaknesses of the functional budget; she is also very quick to note that the benefits far surpass the cost of the system.

The strengths of the program budget, as they apply to the Planned Parenthood Association, can be grouped under three general statements: the process strengthens internal understanding and motivation among employees and board members; the program and objective breakdown helps in fund-raising; and the breakdown aids in managerial control and in external reporting on the use of grant moneys. The program budget process creates a situation that requires a great deal of interaction among the employees, volunteers, the board of directors, and the medical advisory board. There is no preconceived idea of what the final budget figure will be for any year; obviously, most of the people are familiar with the experience of the previous year, but any program may be deleted, added, or changed in any way. No discussion of money is included in the initial debate over programs, objectives, and priorities; instead, the deliberations center on the objectives of the organization and what it should be accomplishing given the needs of the surrounding community. Every member of the group is encouraged to suggest new programs or goals for the organization and to present them to the total group.

Once all the goals and objectives are before the group, a priority ballot is presented to each member; on this ballot all the objectives are placed under one of seven functional headings, and the individual is asked to set priorities for the different objectives by ranking them from one (for most important) to ten (for least important). The scores of the voters are then combined and announced at the beginning of the meeting where the final list of priorities is developed by a series of negotiations. By the time the list is completely set, everyone has had a chance to discuss all the objectives, to argue for differing priority listings, and to develop an understanding of why the ultimate priorities were established.

After the priority list of objectives is finalized (including the number of units to be served), the process of attaching dollar figures to the objectives begins. At this point, prior unit cost figures become very important; by applying unit costs to the quantified objectives, it is possible to arrive at dollar figures for major segments of the program; then dollar amounts can be attached to the remaining objectives that are new or nonquantifiable. Once this has been accomplished a total budget figure is established, and the management of the association can assay the possibility of raising that amount of money.

In the meantime, the impact of the process on the commitment and motivation of the employees is tremendous. Every board member or employee has the right to challenge any objective and to demand an explanation of its importance. Since disagreement is natural in such a situation, there are vigorous debates regarding such issues as the precise meaning or definition of the programs and objectives; the way in which numerical goals are established; the procedures by which goals are expected to be achieved; the reasons behind the particular priority listing; and the way that the various objectives and programs combine to make up the annual and multiyear plan for the association. Complete understanding helps to create commitment and motivation, because the people know how their efforts fit into the overall functioning of the organization. They also know that they have had some part in deciding what these functions are, even if they do not agree totally with the final results; therefore, they feel a "pride of ownership" or "authorship" in the goals that have been set for the organization. In fact, commitment is so great that when cutbacks have to be made because of a lack of funds, the employees and volunteers occasionally work extra time or increase their personal effort in order to achieve goals to which they feel a close affinity.

The program budget also helps in other ways when cutbacks have to be made because of a lack of funds. If for any reason the association fails to raise sufficient money to cover all of its goals for the year, it is possible to work through the priorities in reverse order as goals are deleted or revised. In other words, budgetary cutbacks can be made on the basis of particular goals rather than making across-the-board slashes in all programs, deleting programs haphazardly, or running at full operational levels for part of the year and reduced levels for the remainder of the year once the money has been depleted. The director has the authority to go over those priorities that are lowest under each general heading. At this time, she can decide which goals should be deleted and which of the numerical service levels should be reduced in order to meet the new budget figure. Those programs that receive the lowest priority ratings are the first to go; and the process can be continued, with programs being chopped in reverse order to their priority listing, as long as is necessary. In this way, decisions on reductions in service can be made in a much more logical manner, and when reductions are made, those who supported the reduced or deleted programs know why those particular cuts are chosen. Once again, knowledge helps to squelch rumors and hard feelings; those who see their projects cut are involved in the process, so charges of favoritism, politics, or "shady deals" are minimized and therefore help to hold down strife, dissension, and destructive conflict.

Fund raising is the second major area where the program budget has helped. Most private foundations and government departments that control grant money have certain categories of programs to which grants are made. Directories that inform agencies about existing foundations and other funding sources usually spell out these interests (e.g., The Nelly Smith Foundation, established to aid in research dealing with children who have psychological problems created by the traumatic loss of a parent, donates 1,255,720 dollars per year). The members of agencies such as the Planned Parenthood Association pore through directories looking for potential funding sources for part of their program or for new projects that they wish to start. Grantsmanship (the ability to find grant sources, to develop proposals that are tailored to the demands of the granting agencies, and to court the grantor in such a way that the application has a high probability of success) is an art that is highly valued by all voluntary organizations (as well as state and local governments). The natural breakdown of the agency's activities in a program budget is a delight for grantsmen because it is relatively easy to lift out specific objectives and goals of the agency and to combine them into a package that is geared toward the interests of the specific foundation or federal bureau. Through this procedure, the Planned Parenthood Association developed various proposals that brought in 475,000 dollars during the 1974–1975 fiscal year (this figure does not include the allotment of 47,000 dollars from the local fund-raising agency.) From these figures, it is possible to see how successful the association is in using program objectives in writing grant proposals.

Appeals to the local fund-raising organization are also strengthened by the use of the program budget. Each year this organization parcels out several million dollars to social, educational, and health-oriented organizations in the area. Under the new guidelines that have been established by the fund-raising organization, all agencies must present requests for funds that break down proposed expenditures into several of sixty specific functions. In 1973, the fund-raising organization surveyed the community to establish the priorities for sixty-nine human services offered in the Lake County area. The findings showed that the largest segment of funds had been going to organizations that were primarily involved in delivering services that were ranked at the bottom of the priority list. At the same time, the Planned Parenthood Association was able to request funds within the category of "community health education," which was ranked fifth on the priority list. This allowed the association to use the community fund-raising organization's own information as a major argument for increased allocations. Once again, the Planned Parenthood Association was able to guarantee a specific contributor that contributions would be used in a way that satisfied the highest priorities of the donor. Not surprisingly, the allocation to the association has grown at a higher than average rate, and the increased support has been used as matching funds for other grant programs.

The third area in which the program budget is helpful to the Planned Parenthood Association involves problems of control and reporting. The control problems are internal, while the reporting problems are primarily external. Two of the major difficulties of any administrator in a multiproject organization are those of keeping track of where funds have been expended and of knowing which program to charge expenditures against. The problem becomes acute when decisions have to be made regarding the way in which general expenditures, such as administrative costs, are to be divided among the various objectives.

In order to deal with these problems, the budget is prepared with a crosswalk that breaks down the amount of personnel costs that are charged to each project. For instance, a part of the director's salary is assigned to each function in the budget, with the amount being determined by the time that it is expected she will give to that project or function during the year. The same process is carried out for all the other employees, as well as for all the supplies, equipment, and other materials used by the association. In this way every penny of the association's budget is accounted for by function and also by the line-item method, which is important for accounting purposes. This type of dual budget preparation allows a more precise allocation of costs; it also helps in control during the year, because administrators can check the actual time, material, equipment, and money expenditures against the projected figures to see if projects are proceeding as planned. When variances appear, the managers and employees can use the figures to make the necessary adjustments so that programs fall back within their cost guidelines or to make the numerical objectives more closely resemble probability given the new cost figures.

All federal grants and most grants from private foundations now ask for funding proposals to be prepared according to their particular type of program budget. Just as the Planned Parenthood Association finds their budget useful in preparing these proposals, the budget also helps when it is time to report back to the funding sources. These sources almost always ask for quarterly or semiannual reports in addition to an annual review (and, perhaps, an annual audit); the reports must include the initial numerical goals that were presented in the funding proposal, with an up-to-date figure showing the success of the agency in reaching its established goals. The preparation of these external reports is greatly simplified by the budgeting and accounting system of the association, because the various projects can be easily broken down into the necessary figures for the reports.

Two major problems exist in dealing with the program budget. The first problem concerns the amount of effort that should be expended in using the budget as a control device for small projects. When projects are very small, the utility of the program format becomes questionable. For instance, when the association has a project that only involves 10,000 dollars (out of a total budget of 700,000 dollars), it becomes quite difficult to cut that project *in size*; about the only choice available is either to carry the project at its current size or to do away with it completely. Likewise, when controlling expenditures, it is almost impossible to make sure that the amount of resources stated is all that is applied to a small project. In other words, the usefulness of the program budget process disappears when dealing with small amounts of money, because it costs more to apply the process than can possibly be saved.

However, the second problem is the more difficult issue; the reason for the difficulty is because of the inclusion of outside organizations that cannot be controlled by the Planned Parenthood Association. The problem is one of agreeing on a common definition as to what comprises a "unit of service." This is not necessarily a problem when the association is dealing with an outside funding source in a one-on-one situation, because the two organizations can work out a mutually understandable and acceptable definition; the problem of a clear definition of a unit of service is critical when the association is dealing with an organization that allocates funds to several community organizations. The local fund-raising organization allocates money to a wide variety of organizations, yet it insists that all of the organizations involved in health care report a unit cost for patient services. Therefore, when requesting funds, all of the community organizations report a unit cost to the fund-raising organization; however, there is no way to use these reported figures when allocation decisions are made, because there is no single definition as to what constitutes a unit of service. Some organizations count every individual who walks through the door as a client served, even if the individual is only given information about another agency that can better serve his needs. Other organizations work with individual clients in a counseling mode over a lengthy period of time; therefore, they have low client totals at high unit costs.

Even within a single organization like the Planned Parenthood Association, there are wide divergencies in cost per unit of service delivered (see Table 3). The association expects to serve 7000 contraceptive patients during a year; of this number, 4000 are continuing patients and 3000 are new patients. Old patients receive continuing medical care and materials; on the other hand, new patients are interviewed, receive initial medical exams, and then are given any additional counseling or medical care that the initial screening indicates is necessary. Therefore, a difference in cost must be included, depending on the number of new patients contained in any annual budget. In other activities of the association, the cost per unit varies more widely. For example, the Planned Parenthood Association carries on an outreach program through which people will be informed of the services available in case they, or others they know, have need of the services; this program expects to reach 12,000 new people at a cost of 80 cents per contact. At the other extreme, the association performs about 24 sterilizations per year at an average cost of 300 dollars. The question faced by the Planned Parenthood Association is, How can all of these services be grouped into a single patient service cost figure for the funding request? Of course, the answer is that no single figure is meaningful—it cannot be done. The presentation of a "cost per patient" figure is meaningless. Interestingly enough, the evaluations and auditing reports required by the fund-raising organization are based on the old line-item concept of budgeting; therefore, even though it uses program concepts in its budget request forms, no follow-up on the program data is ever completed.

The problem, in this case, appears to be that an organization contributing funds to the Planned Parenthood Association is using program budget concepts

Table 3

**Unit Costs per Type of Patient Service**

| | |
|---|---:|
| Contraceptive patients | |
|     Initial medical and processing | $62.85[a] |
|     Annual medical and processing | 37.87 |
| Medical exams only | 18.96 |
| Supply receipt only | 1.78 |
| Counseling[b] | 27.44 |
| Pregnancy test | 5.00 |

[a]Supplies not included. This is a cost for personnel services only.

[b]Various kinds of crisis counseling—including problem pregnancies.

without understanding the meaning of those terms or knowing how they should be applied. Since the national administration of the fund-raising organization says that program concepts are to be used, and since all of the forms and processes are spelled out, the local fund-raising organization applies the new budget system, but it does so without adequate training in or commitment to the process. Consequently, the program budget process is dutifully applied, but it has no impact on the actual decisions; in fact, the misapplication of the program budget process could have a deleterious effect, because the information about unit costs and functions could be selectively used to justify political decisions. This is the major fear of the Planned Parenthood Association.

It can be seen from this discussion that a program budget brings with it both positive and negative ingredients. The program budget allows more participation by all concerned people in the budget preparation, it allows more flexibility in administration of the agency, and it serves as a useful tool in fund raising. Some problems in control do exist, but the greatest problem occurs when the agency has to deal with other parts of its environment that do not understand or use properly program budget concepts and processes.

## SUMMARY

Public financial administration must always include at least the factors of revenues, expenditures, and borrowing possibilities; at the national level, such additional factors as international trade and monetary policy must also be included. Historically, however, the primary interest, which led to the beginning of what became our current financial system, was the limitation of the government's taxing powers. In order to limit taxation, more and more power over expenditures was given to the legislative body. When the Constitution was written, the British budgetary process was not yet fully developed; thus it was 1921 before the executive budget was fully developed in the United States.

The modern society is dependent on money (the common medium of exchange) if it is to accomplish most of its goals; therefore, the amount of revenue, and the source of that revenue, are major limitations on the programs operated by each level of government. The national government uses the income tax as its primary source of revenue. This tax is especially appropriate for the national government because of the emphasis on overall fiscal policy at the national level; this tax is most useful when working with issues of economic growth or recession, full employment, and price stability. At the same time, the income tax is the most prolific revenue producer, so the national government has returned some of the revenue as intergovernmental transfers of funds.

State governments depend primarily on sales taxes, while local governments raise their revenue through property taxes. These taxes are not as productive as the income tax; at the same time, most state and local governments must operate under debt limitations. Therefore, state and local governments operate under greater overall financial restrictions than does the national government. State and local governments have felt the dissatisfaction of taxpayers as new bonds and taxes have been defeated at the polls. The limitations have led to the development of numerous special districts in order to deliver all the services demanded by the public.

The budget process falls into a cycle with four major phases: revenue forecasting and budget preparation; budget submission and legislative approval; budget execution; and audit. Most of the attempts to improve the budgetary system have focused on the preparation and approval stages. The major political maneuvering occurs at the approval stage as department heads attempt to maximize their appropriation from the legislature. Both ubiquitous and contingent strategies are applied in order to gain political advantage.

Budget reform has centered around the shift from line-item appropriations to planning, programming, budgeting systems. The line-item budget is an effective control document, but it allows a fragmentary, incremental approach to governmental programs. Program budgeting attempts to consider the budget as a tool for systematic planning and control, because it allows greater specification, analysis, and comparison of alternatives as the budget is prepared. Through cost-benefit analysis and zero-base budgeting, a greater amount of meaningful policy debate is expected to take place. Arguments for incrementalism and programming are still being presented, and the final outcome has not been decided.

# BIBLIOGRAPHY

Anderson, William H., *Financing Modern Government: The Political Economy of the Public Sector*, Houghton, Mifflin, Boston, 1973.

Burkhead, Jesse, *Government Budgeting*, Wiley, New York, 1956.

Caputo, David A., ed., "Symposium on General Revenue Sharing," *Public Administration Review, XXXV*, 130-157 (March-April, 1975).

Cleland, David I., and William R. King, *Systems Analysis and Project Management*, McGraw-Hill, New York, 1968.

David, James W., Jr., ed., *Politics, Programs and Budgets*, Prentice-Hall, Englewood Cliffs, N.J., 1969.

DeWoolfson, Bruce H., Jr., "Public Sector MBO and PPB: Cross Fertilization in Management Systems," *Public Administration Review, XXXV*, 387-395 (July-August, 1975).

Dunbar, Roger L. M., "Budgeting for Control," *Administrative Science Quarterly, XXVI*, 88-96 (March 1971).

Forbes, Russell, *Purchasing for Small Cities*, Public Administration Service, Chicago, 1951.

Lee, Robert D., Jr., and Ronald W. Johnson, *Public Budgeting Systems*, University Park Press, Baltimore, 1973.

Maxwell, James A., *Financing State and Local Governments*, Revised Edition, Brookings Institution, Washington, D. C.; 1969.

Meltsner, Arnold J., *The Politics of City Revenue*, University of California, Berkeley, 1971.

Mowitz, Robert J., *The Design and Implementation of Pennsylvania's Planning, Programming, Budgeting System*, Institute of Public Administration, Pennsylvania State University, University Park, 1970.

*Municipal Finance Administration*, International City Manager's Association, Chicago, 1962.

Normanton, E. L., *The Accountability and Audit of Governments*, Praeger, New York, 1966.

Novick, David, ed., *Current Practice in Program Budgeting (PPBS): Analysis and Case Studies Covering Government and Business*, Crane, Russak, New York, 1973.

Oldman, Oliver, and Ferdinand P. Schoettle, *State and Local Taxes and Finance: Text, Problems and Cases*, Foundation Press, Mineola, N.Y., 1974.

Pechman, Joseph A., *Federal Tax Policy*, Revised Edition, W. W. Norton, New York, 1971.

Pyhrr, Peter A., *Zero-Base Budgeting: A Practical Management Tool for Evaluating Expenses*, Wiley, New York, 1973.

Rovetch, Warren, and John J. Gaskie, *Program Budgeting for Planners: A Case Study of Appalachia with Projections Through 1985*, Praeger, New York, 1974.

Schick, Allen, *Budget Innovation in the States*, Brookings Institution, Washington, D.C., 1971.

Sharkansky, Ira., *The Politics of Taxing and Spending*, Bobbs-Merrill, Indianapolis, 1969.

Waldo, Dwight, ed., "Planning-Programming-Budgeting System: A Symposium," *Public Administration Review, XXVI*, 243-310 (December 1966).

Waldo, Dwight, ed., "Planning-Programming-Budgeting System Reexamined: Development, Analysis, and Criticism: A Symposium," *Public Administration Review, XXIX*, 111-202 (March-April, 1969).

Wildavsky, Aaron, *The Politics of the Budgetary Process*, Second Edition, Little Brown, Boston, 1974.

# INDEX